Education in Southern Africa

Education

in

Southern Africa

BRIAN ROSE
General Editor

COLLIER-MACMILLAN
SOUTH AFRICA (PTY.) LTD
JOHANNESBURG
COLLIER-MACMILLAN LIMITED, LONDON
THE MACMILLAN COMPANY

Collier-Macmillan Limited
10 South Audley Street, London W 1

The Macmillan Company
Collier-Macmillan Canada Ltd, Toronto

Copyright © Collier-Macmillan Limited, 1970

Library of Congress Catalogue Card Number: 68–10128

First printing 1970

Printed in Great Britain
by Western Printing Services Ltd, Bristol

Introduction

Dr E. G. Malherbe's study of education in South Africa was in its day a major work. Completely out of date now, it has nevertheless deservedly become a classic which no subsequent educationist has effectively surpassed. Indeed, it may be questioned whether specifically national studies, removed from their more meaningful regional settings, are as pertinent today as they were a quarter of a century ago.

The post-war period has seen changes in the Southern African region which may be portentous for the future. The brief experiment of the Rhodesian Federation soon broke under political stress, creating in its dissolution three separate states, Zambia, Rhodesia and Malawi. To the south, Britain speeded up the independence of her former High Commission Territories, which became Lesotho, Botswana, and Swaziland (the only one to retain its former name). Flanking this associated complex of states are the Portuguese territories of Angola and Mozambique. Commanding the southern tip of the continent is the Republic of South Africa.

Setting aside the still slightly ambiguous South West Africa for a moment, we have then nine countries, whose geographical and historical association cannot be denied. If they are divergent politically, they have much in common, not only in terms of economic and capital development, but in the still more basic problems of education and basic resources. Africa is a country in which natural and human resources are distributed unevenly. Scarce resources, such as water and power, occupy planners not only in Botswana, but in South Africa and Zambia. The concept of unilateral action in major planning is becoming increasingly unpractical. Lesotho, for instance, is destitute of most of the gifts of nature except its hardy and proud people, and water. But in order to make use of its water economically, it must sell it – and the only buyer available is the Republic of South Africa. Any attempt to plan other than co-operatively would be futile, for one has to have a market in mind when one plans a sales campaign. When one considers transport costs and market facilities, it is clear that for countries neighbouring on South Africa – most of which are moving from a subsistence economy to a cash-crop economy – the Republic will continue to be their best market for the foreseeable future. And furthermore, these countries have an economic stake in the stability of the Republic despite occasional public postures to the contrary.

The Cabora Bassa hydro-electric scheme on the Zambezi exemplifies South Africa's function as a regional catalyst in a multi-national endeavour that will ultimately benefit the whole region of Southern Africa. Its completion will mean that a region that had no major source of power for economic development now has access to a supply which no single state could possibly have contemplated unilaterally. South Africa's advanced industrial know-how, her capital resources, the strength of her financial position in the western world all had much to do with the lifting of a blue-print from the drawing boards. Even her capacity as a market for much of the initial power output was essential until such time as her neighbours would be sufficiently advanced to absorb greater increments of supply.

To a large extent South Africa is integrated into the partnership of the western world. One of the most industrialized countries in Africa today, she faces the problem of markets. While her trade with Britain and the continent of Europe is lucrative and extensive, its profitability is reduced by high transport costs. The obvious policy would be to develop local markets in Southern Africa. But economically a 'market' is not only a 'need' that can be met – it is a capacity to pay for the goods supplied. Southern Africa is full of potential markets, the people who would like to buy if they had the money.

The problem of the induction of Africa into the twentieth-century urban-industrial society with its technological controls is vast. At present, according to the United Nations, South Africa is the only country on the African continent that can be classified as a 'developed country'. Its industrial extension is already considerable, and its potential still greater. With 6 per cent of the continental population, South Africa generates 20 per cent of the continental income. Something like 50 per cent of the continental electrical power and the railway rolling stock is located in South Africa.

Eighty per cent of all young South African Bantu are literate. In most other countries of Africa, 80 per cent are illiterate. Twelve thousand Bantu own their own businesses, and some bank close on $3,000 a day. Three Bantu are reputed to be millionaires. The purchasing power of the South African Bantu is over $1·5 billion a year. *Per capita*, the national income of South Africa is three times that of Ghana and five times that of Nigeria.

Trade with the rest of Africa is increasing. South African exports to the rest of Africa jumped by 25 million dollars in the two-year period,

1963–5. 'We have,' said the South African Prime Minister, Mr John Vorster, 'a wealth of experience and of technological and managerial talent, as compared with other countries of Africa. We are willing and anxious to assist other African states in coping with the tremendous problems of economic and social development that confront them. All we ask is that such states in seeking and accepting such assistance, should do so on the basis of mutual recognition of the right of all states themselves to decide what should be the pattern of their economic and social development.

'We recognize, against this background, that in many ways we have, with respect to much of Africa south of the Sahara, a responsibility for assisting in development. Although we do not publicize it, we are in fact doing quite a lot in this field.'

The problem of giving effect to a mutually acceptable strategy of Good Neighbourliness is initially an economic one that involves (probably for another generation) the planned improvement of agriculture around which can be built not only a cash market, but those essential concomitants such as roads and other communications, together with the technical manpower support required to service and maintain them. African states, in other words, have to move into a cash-crop economy as an escape from their present subsistence economy as the first step in the generation of savings, with which they can then promote capital investment and further development.

This apparently simple concept involves what is in fact a major social revolution for most Africans since it implies the concept of some form of landownership (whether individual or in some corporate sense like the kibbutz). It involves the concept of 'overproduction' (in the sense of producing more than is necessary for the needs of oneself and one's family) in order to have goods for sale; it involves the concept of the technical improvement of agricultural and other skills so as to command a better price in a competitive market – and this involves a revolution in the village school. It is at this point that educational planning becomes significant.

It is part of the 'expectation of Uhuru' that African rulers must continue to aim at universal literacy to be achieved through the elementary schools. But whilst they are obviously obligated to such a policy for political reasons at present, it is doubtful whether the deployment of very limited funds entirely into one educational area is sound policy. Many African states are realizing that the neglect (not always either intentional or realized) of secondary education is costing them dearly. Unable to fill top state positions by primary school 'graduates', and unable to supply adequately trained people from their own educational system, they pay dearly for expatriate manpower, professional or otherwise.

African rulers are involved in the very problematic exercise of estimating future manpower needs in order to plan education in such a way that a pyramid of skills and abilities is created which can meet national needs – for it is on such a basis that educational blueprinting can proceed. This may be one of the many levels in which interstate co-operation between South Africa and her neighbours would be profitable.

Any educational policy that is not merely drifting needs to be integrated into the economic potential of the land. There seems to be little or no good sense, for instance, in developing an educational basis for mining management skills in Lesotho – which has, unfortunately, no mineral resources worth recording. On the other hand, a technology for the maintenance of motor vehicles, tractors, farm equipment is a basic necessity in most African communities. It would seem, therefore, that apart from providing for legal, administrative and teaching staff, the problem facing most African countries is that of using education as the essential foundation on which to build a modern agricultural economy which can extend slowly into secondary service industries. At that point of development the stage may be reached where mineral and other natural resources that have not been developed can be capitalized from savings. The great risk of attempting to rush an illiterate and poor country into hasty industrialization would seem to be an inevitable economic neo-colonialism.

In being able to assist her neighbours to draw up long-term developmental strategies which are closely related not only to educational planning, but to syllabus structure and subject methodology in the classroom, South Africa has much to offer. Such exchanges do in fact take place – without much publicity, as the Prime Minister has noted. The creation of a South African Co-operative Educational Agency to which neighbouring states could apply for help, and to which South Africans could volunteer their services, might well provide a useful boost to the Good Neighbour Policy.

The publication of *Education in Southern Africa* marks an initial attempt to assemble descriptions of educational systems and educational needs in the Southern Africa region. We have tried as far as possible to set the educational system against a broad background of social, historical and economic development, even though the limitations of space often militated against all but the briefest notice. And while we recognized the right of every contributor to his private political views, we tried, as a contributing team, to present our material as factually and unemotionally as possible.

Descriptions of educational progress in South Africa are reasonably easy to find, and there is growing literature on the other countries of the Southern Africa region, most of which is inaccessible to the ordinary student or reader. We have aimed at bringing together a topical survey, not as a definitive description, but as an introduction to an area that needs so much further study and goodwill.

The incorporation of material by Senor Eugenio Lisboa concerning the Portuguese African Provinces of Angola and Mozambique represents one of the few educational contributions *in English* and one of still fewer available in book form. Senor Lisboa has made available facts and statistics not easily accessible to those who lack connection with metropolitan Portugal.

Every book should have an audience in mind. This one was planned not only for the student of education in Southern Africa, but for students from other countries who are interested in the study of African problems. If this book proves seminal for further endeavour, it will have achieved its purpose.

ABOUT THE CONTRIBUTORS

Brian Rose: Born in London, educated in Eastbourne and Dublin (Trinity College) and University of the Witwatersrand and the University of South Africa. He became Senior Lecturer in Educational Psychology at Johannesburg College of Education. He had a two-year residence in Swaziland and a short teaching assignment in Botswana. He was most recently visiting professor at Mount Holyoke College, Massachusetts, U.S.A.

R. G. Macmillan: Professor of Education at the University of Natal. He belongs to that small band of educationists on the Southern African scene who have had experience in teaching at almost every level. Few contemporary educators would be better equipped to delineate White education in South Africa.

Robert C. Jones: Associate Dean and Associate Professor of Education, School of Education, College of William and Mary, Williamsburg, Virginia, U.S.A. He has published several articles on the education of the Bantu in Africa. He obtained his Ph.D. at the University of Oklahoma in 1966 and has made the education of the Bantu one of his special interests.

Raymond Tunmer: Born and educated in South Africa, he is at present Senior Lecturer in the Department of Education at the University of the Witwatersrand. He read Education at the University of Cambridge, England. Since his return to South Africa he has directed his research towards the educational problems in non-White fields.

James S. Robertson: Secretary of the Council of the Church Colleges of Education, London. He served in Zambia 1945–1965. His early experience in the management of schools in remote rural areas prepared him for later work in teacher training at Chalimbana Training College, Lusaka, where he became Principal in 1958. This college pioneered the first training of secondary school teachers in Zambia, under the aegis of the Institute of Education, University College, Salisbury. From 1965 to 1968 he was head of the Education Department, Bede College, Durham.

Franklin Parker: Born and educated in U.S.A., he is now Professor of Education at West Virginia University, Morgantown, West

Virginia, U.S.A. Professor Parker has travelled, lectured and conducted research covering wide areas of comparative education. He is a recognized expert on education in Rhodesia and has written several books and articles on the subject.

L. W. Lanham: Born and educated in South Africa, he obtained his Ph.D. at the University of the Witwatersrand. He is at present Professor and Head of Department of Phonetics and Linguistics. He is also Director of the University Speech and Hearing Clinic, and English-Language adviser to the South African Broadcasting Corporation.

Eugenio A. Lisboa: Born and educated in Portugal, he qualified as an engineer in 1955. His interests, however, lie much more with literature and education. Senor Lisboa's contribution constitutes a first general description in English of the educational systems in the Portuguese territories of Angola and Mozambique.

Contents

Education in Southern Africa

1· Economic Problems in African Education

BRIAN ROSE

For the underdeveloped countries the relationship between education and economic expansion is one of special interest. Dr E. F. Denison has shown that in America between 1929 and 1957 there had been an increase of 80 per cent in the average amount of schooling, which had raised the quality of labour by 30 per cent.[1] Professor Strumilin of Moscow has said that 70 per cent of the Russian people were illiterate at the beginning of the Soviet era,[2] a point underlined by Professor Jamin of Moscow University, who states that whilst some 10·6 million people were receiving tuition in 1915/16, by 1961/62 the number had risen to 56 million (a figure that included inservice industrial courses).[3] The history of the economic development of Russia is contingent on the emerging countries of Africa and Asia, and it may be worth examining some of the salient facts.

Years of schooling for unskilled worker	Earnings per lifetime in roubles (1924)	Difference from previous year
0	10,434	—
1	11,999	1565
2	13,199	1200
3	13,981	782
4	14,555	574
5	15,025	470
6	15,390	365
7	15,598	208

[1] Denison, E. F., 'Measuring the Contribution of Education to Economic Growth', in Robinson, E. A. G. and Vaizey, J. E. (eds.), *The Economics of Education*, Macmillan, 1966.
[2] Strumilin, S. G., 'The Economic Significance of National Education', in Robinson, E. A. G. and Vaizey, J. E. (eds.), *The Economics of Education*, Macmillan, 1966, pp. 276–323.
[3] Jamin, V., 'The Economic Effects of Populace Education in the U.S.S.R.', in Robinson, E. A. G. and Vaizey, J. E. (eds.), *The Economics of Education*, Macmillan, 1966.

Strumilin conjectures that education may be expected to double the national revenue. His figures show that profits from more productive labour are 27·6 times greater than state expenditure in schools, and he concludes that capital expenditure on education is redeemed with interest within the first one-and-a-half years of adult work. With an estimated 37 years for a full worker's lifetime, using the Marshaelevsky formula, 35·5 years are pure profit to the state.

Russian education (like that of so many African countries) is concerned with the farm worker, who (to use Strumilin's phrase) is 'using the most primitive methods and machinery'.[4] The introduction of compulsory primary education increased the educational bill by 43 times. But, says Strumilin, the profitability of the expenditure will exceed 125 per cent in the following three decades, whilst the financial burden of these reforms will only be felt by the country for the first five to six years. Although he accepts the law of diminishing returns as applying throughout formal education, the additional worker productivity is recovered in national productivity at the rate of 430 per cent, and the annual pure profit for the country over 30 years is greater than 14 per cent. If the unskilled worker's life of 37 years is used as a base, a student who has been involved in education for 13 years raises his productivity to 148 years, which is 11 times more in value than the expenditure on his education.

Unlike Dr John Vaizey and most American and European educationists, Dr Okigbo of Nigeria[5] believes that it is possible to develop a measure by which the state could rank educational investment along with any other investment. He proposes to do this by using Vaizey's[6] 'benefit-cost' approach in which costs (not only school fees but income foregone) are compared with benefits estimated in terms of increased earnings over those who have not had a similar education – a device not dissimilar to that used in Soviet Russia. The weakness of this approach is its neglect of innate individual differences, since it seems to hold constant such factors as intelligence, aptitude and temperament.

In Nigeria (at least until the Civil War) one third of the recurrent budgets were spent on education at the primary level. The Ashby Commission[7] stressed the need to develop the higher and intermediate levels of manpower in the 1960–80 period in order to maintain a 4 per

[4] *Ibid.*
[5] Okigbo, P. N. C., 'Criteria for Public Expenditure on Education', in Robinson, E. A. G. and Vaizey, J. E. (eds.), *The Economics of Education*, Macmillan, 1966, pp. 479–96.
[6] Vaizey, J., *The Economics of Education*, Faber, 1962.
[7] *Investment in Education*, Lagos, Federal Ministry of Education, 1960.

cent rate of growth. It is estimated that 16 out of every 1,000 children aged 12 should go on to the intermediate and higher manpower category. The probability that a child aged 12 would enter a secondary school was put at 0·07, that a child at secondary school should graduate at 0·9 and that he would proceed to further training at 0·4. In order to achieve an intake of 8,000 technicians, as Harbison predicted from a careful analysis of the Ashby statistics, some 500,000 children aged 12 should be in the primary school, with a total primary enrolment of 1·7 million. Thus would be formed the base of a pyramid that would ensure that some 30–35 thousand children entered the secondary school annually. Archer[8] has translated these implications into educational dynamics. In 1958 the Nigerian primary system had 0·8 in excess of the Harbison figure. But the wastage rate of 42 per cent in the 5th year made the existing school system so inefficient that the Harbison proposals would actually have been cheaper.

If it is agreed that there is some definite but as yet undetermined relationship between the economy of a country and its educational system, a group of problems remain unsolved for the African administrator: the assessment of manpower needs, the funding of education and overcoming wastage within the educational system.

I. ASSESSMENT OF MANPOWER NEEDS

The Ashby Commission in Nigeria seems to have proceeded from an analysis of essential leadership needs and then to have worked downwards through a supporting educational pyramid. It may well be that the Nigerian figures (*supra*) provide at least a rough guide for other African territories. Frost has maintained that 25 to 33 per cent of a population will be economically engaged at any one time – and in view of the active participation of women in African agriculture, the upper limit may well be more appropriate. With certain exceptions, about 90 per cent of the population of most African states is engaged in subsistence farming. With an educational system built around late-Victorian literacy, there is little connection between the schools and the economic employment of the majority of Africans except the facility acquired to use English as a tool – a factor that is not without importance in higher education. Although diversification of employment (as a facet of a more general diversification of the economy) is important, agriculture is likely to remain the key industry for most

[8] Archer, J. N., *Educational Development in Nigeria 1961–1970*, Lagos, Government Printer, 1961.

African states during the foreseeable future. In Kenya and Tanzania subjects such as woodwork, accountancy, farming and secretarial skills have found their way into the curriculum. English is no longer obligatory for university, and Swahili is compulsory in the schools. Coming close to some of the Eiselen recommendations in South Africa, the educational 'New Look' in East Africa represents an attempt to integrate educational planning into economic realities. It is estimated that Tanzania, which is the poorest of the East African territories, has an illiteracy level of 90 per cent, and that of the school leaving population, 90 per cent will remain on the land. Hence its educational system needs a complete regearing. Planning for agricultural improvement and for industrial expansion raises further problems. The rationalization of agriculture in most African countries will not come about without a major break with the traditional system of land tenure. Land is held by the tribe in community, and the chief allocates its use to individuals during their life-time. This system supports group cohesion and militates very strongly against individualism. No African from a traditional community would consider planting a tree or fencing an area of his land. Not only does he not consider the land as belonging to him (he has *usu fructu*, not ownership), but any attempt at alienation of the land from the community by fencing or by a similar permanent development would represent an aggressive individualism for which he would be made to pay dearly. African agrarian reform involves a social reform not unlike that experienced in Britain during the collapse of the manorial system. Economically there is a need to change to a market economy. The manpower needs in this situation are the immediate problem of staffing agricultural services and agricultural training colleges, and the provision of field officers and market advisers. The break-up of the extended family (or kinship group), which to a considerable extent makes possible a subsistence economy, will aid the introduction of a money economy. Secondary school education is usually associated with areas of population density when boarding accommodation is provided. Not only does the situation tend to separate the educational élite from their rural matrix, but from an economic point-of-view a new class alienated from the subsistence economy is being created. From such people future leadership may be drawn. But there will be acute problems during transition. In Botswana, for instance, the primary school system creates in the successful pupil 'job expectations' far removed from the dull routine of his rural family – expectations that are most unlikely to be fulfilled unless he proceeds through the secondary system. So, whilst thoroughly discontented with his traditional place in the extended family, he discovers that he has not those skills that ensure him his place in the 'new nation', and he very easily becomes an out-of-work lounging around whatever town takes his fancy.

It would seem, therefore, that African educational planning cannot, for perhaps several generations, be permissive. Another consideration in regard to assessing future manpower-needs arises in planning industrial expansion. Each government tends to push ahead with its own regional development scheme – largely because this diversifies employment as well as provides the government with a source of income. Generally speaking this has meant that neighbouring territories have each become involved in the easiest developmental areas, and have flooded the market because of this non-co-operative policy. This is what is happening, according to K. G. V. Krishna[9] in East Africa. As he says: 'One consequence of unco-ordinated development is the saturation of the East African market with products that are easiest to manufacture'. As Krishna also foresees, the displacement of limited resources from agriculture to industry might interrupt the general tendency from subsistence agriculture to cash-cropping. That this would be lamentable is underlined by World Bank Missions in East Africa which have in each country emphasised the need to raise the earnings of the agricultural sector as prerequisite for industrial expansion. Hence preliminary attempts at industrialization should not be for export but to meet the needs of a growing local market created by agriculture. African countries, therefore, would be well advised to treat educational policy as pivotal in their national economic strategy. The immediate needs should be estimated and the schools geared not only in terms of *per capita* output but also in terms of educational input. African countries can as little afford haphazard education as they can afford irrational economic development.

II. THE FUNDING OF EDUCATION

All talk of improved education is futile unless plans can be actualized by funds. Education thus becomes part of the overall economic strategy of a nation. In a community that has hitherto existed largely at a level of subsistence economy the concept of saving is alien. The subsistence economy of most African communities, by its very nature, does not necessitate the use of money, and hence savings (where they exist at all) tend to be in kind and of a short-term nature. The intro-

[9] Krishna, K. G. V., 'Resources and Problems of Economic Development', in Diamond, S. and Burke, F. G. (eds.), *The Transformation of East Africa*, Basic Books, 1966.

duction of money into African economics, whilst it is essential for the generation of savings and the build-up of capital, is socially traumatic, if for no other reason than it introduces that very individualism which is traditionally seen as threatening group security. It is perhaps for this reason that a move from subsistence agriculture to a cash-crop economy represents a transitional stage through which most African states may have to pass. Whether their destination is to be the highly developed capitalistic individualism of America or a form of communal capitalism peculiar to the African tradition and not dissimilar to that attempted in certain areas of Yugoslavian agriculture in which labour was involved in profit-sharing, remains to be seen. The communal tradition in the economic life of Africa seems (paradoxically enough) to preclude any real likelihood of the invasion of political Communism.

The generation of capital as a function of savings is the major problem facing every African government. But capital is not only savings. It is represented in specialized labour skills and in plant – much of which inevitably has to be imported. Apart from gifts, importations are paid for by exports. Zambia provides an example of a country whose exports of copper help to fund its educational establishments. In Swaziland the export of iron ore to Japan has also provided a boost to the economy, although even the exploitation of these minerals has necessitated the import of skills and developmental capital.

The problem of creating savings in African countries can be solved not only by building up trade, but by substituting for previously imported goods, goods now produced locally – a procedure in keeping with the recommendations of the World Bank (*supra*). Whilst all primary producers are subject to the vagaries of world market prices, there are occasions of windfall, and it is at such times that the Government should draw off part of the windfall into national savings.

If education is seen as a key factor in economic planning, the need for regional co-operation is crucial. Industrial development depends not only on mineral resources, but on the availability of power, of communications in the form of roads and railways, of labour and of markets. From this point of view a regional planning organization for the Southern Africa Region would seem to be long overdue, and it might well become a prototype for the rest of Africa. At present The South African Industrial Development Corporation largely serves that purpose. Its Chairman, Dr van Eck, speaking in London in 1966, outlined the development of the Caborra Bassa dam on the Zambezi, which had a power potential of 17,000 million kilowatt hours per annum. Whilst this power would be a tremendous stimulus to industrialization in northern Mozambique, Rhodesia and Zambia, it would be far in excess of their immediate requirements. Dr van Eck suggested that the Republic of South Africa would be able to absorb 15,000 million kilowatt hours by 1975. Tenders have already been accepted and work started on this scheme. In a similar way, with international co-operation, the recently discovered mineral resources in Botswana may accelerate interest in the harnessing of Okavango for hydro-electric purposes, a plan put forward by Professor Midgeley of the University of the Witwatersrand that would bring into production large areas at present covered by swamps. With co-operation from South Africa, Zambia and Rhodesia, power and water resources thus created could be shared with great advantage. Education is intimately concerned in economic planning of this nature, because increased national earnings can be ploughed back into better educational services, and because national earnings depend on manpower, which is an educational product.

III. OVERCOMING WASTAGE WITHIN THE EDUCATIONAL SYSTEM

In many African educational systems the wastage is excessive. It is generally accepted that unless a child remains in the educational system for at least four years, his cost to the school system is not offset, because he has not achieved even a basic literacy. With this fact in mind it will be appreciated that 'drop-out' accounts for much of unproductive educational expenditure. But this drop-out is more of a symptom than a cause and is merely a label rather than an explanation. The causes are manifold. There is the custom of using boys as herdsmen, the demands of the initiation schools – both of which involve traditional attitudes often inimical to modern education. But there is also the matter of low expectations which are confirmed by lack of employment opportunity and overcrowding (the teacher : pupil relationship is all too frequently on the basis of 1 : 60). African educational planners go even further than conservative planners in White communities in regarding the child as a manipulable variable in a *system* that is *non-variable*. The result is that a system of education imported (frequently from Victorian Britain and sometimes from other European countries) is proving less and less satisfactory for modern Africa. The high drop-out level of the system may indicate not so much the low calibre of present pupil intake, as the fundamental inadequacy of the system itself. This view would certainly receive support from scores of recent studies in cultural deprivation, both in

Britain and America. There is nothing sacred about an educational format; it serves a teleological process in society that demands constant re-assessment and adjustment – a process long overdue in most African countries. Probably the key to the refurbishing of educational policy and the resultant reduction of wastage (human and financial) lies in teacher training. The introduction of new methods of second language teaching, of new concepts of science teaching, of new maths (to mention but some of the more important areas of change in education today) might provide a useful basis for a Co-operative Educational Conference in which the Republic of South Africa could act usefully as a catalyst and a major resource – a function well within the Government's Good Neighbour Policy. The key both to educational and economic planning in Africa, would seem therefore to lie in rural productivity. Increased agricultural productivity can be induced by sociological reforms, such as the kibbutz-type community or by co-operative farming schemes, to replace the frequently economically stultifying effects of traditional tribal organization with its reactionary conservatism. Although Soviet evidence in regard to adult education shows it to be less efficient than formal schooling, it may (at initial stages of community change) be essential. Lewis conjectures that in most West African states there would be economic dislocation if more than 50 per cent of the child population entered school. But since it is generally estimated that only 25 per cent of all children are actually at school between the ages of 6 and 14 in most African territories, there is a long way to go before dislocation is reached.

Population growth does not make matters any easier for African countries. The over-all growth of the African continental population between 1960 and 1980 is expected to be in the region of 109 million, varying from country to country at the rate of 2 per cent to 3 per cent. Callaway[10] points out that in similar stages of economic development European countries seldom exceeded one per cent yearly increases. Capital accumulation during the nineteenth century took place over several decades during low population increase rates and at a time when public funds were not demanded for social services. African states, he points out, are attempting to increase capital formation during a period of high population growth and heavy public expenditure on social services. Today 35 per cent to 40 per cent of the African population is under the age of 15.

African faith in education is often breathtaking, to the extent for instance, that the Eastern Region of Nigeria (prior to the Civil War)

[10] Callaway, A., 'Unemployment among African school leavers', *Journal of Modern African Studies 1*, No. 3, 1963, pp. 351–71.

was setting aside 45 per cent of its budget for educational purposes, with a 1964 projection of 60 per cent. Uganda's 1968 educational budget was 27 per cent of its national expenditure. Whilst school education should be 'liberal' in the sense that it is *not* vocational, it urgently needs blueprinting. Recalling the position in India in the 1930s, W. Arthur Lewis reminds us of the position in which the over-supply of university graduates matched the oversupply of primary school graduates in some West African states. When there is *shortage of supply*, as Mr Lewis has pointed out, the graduate, instead of starting at a salary equivalent to that of a miner, starts at a salary five times as great. So that, in relation to national income, higher administrative and supervisory services are unduly expensive in poor countries.[11] The same problem operates in regard to educational costs. Teachers in the U.S.A. receive $1\frac{1}{2}$ times the *per capita* national income, five times in Ghana and seven times in Nigeria, so that (at 1961 prices) eight years of primary education for every child would cost (U.S.A.) 0·8 per cent of the national income; Ghana, 2·8 per cent; and Nigeria, 4 per cent.

When Dr R. K. A. Gardiner, the eminent Ashanti economist, spoke in Addis Ababa in October 1967, he listed African problems as follows: very low *per capita* income, high mortality rate, low levels of school enrolment, lack of industrial development, and low level of agricultural production. The whole continent had an income approximately to that of Italy, he said. He saw the main hope for the future in the training of manpower. It is at this point, *the training of manpower*, that educational and economic planning should overlap.

Do they?

[11] Lewis, W. Arthur, 'Education and Economic Development' in *Social and Economic Studies*, University College of the West Indies, Jamaica, X, No. 2 (June 1961), pp. 94–101.

2· The Education of Whites in South Africa

R. G. MACMILLAN

I. SOME BACKGROUND

South Africa lies outside the tropics, the climate, with its variations, being an important factor in its development. The coastal belt, which is about fifty miles wide in the east, is largely sub-tropical. In the cooler south, this belt is some 150 miles wide, rising in a series of mountain-edged steps which enclose the semi-desert Karoo, to the plateau which averages 4,000 feet in altitude. There is a high rim of mountains on the east and south, sloping gently to the interior and west. This inland high veld or temperate grassland, like the rest of the country (except for the winter rain area of the south-west), has summer rain, a long hot summer and a relatively mild winter.

White South Africans come from the original Dutch settlers with later infusions of English, Scottish and German stock, mainly middle-class farmers, artisans, miners, missionaries, professional men, civil servants and traders. The energy, initiative, technical skill and financial enterprise of the contributory groups have laid the foundation of much of the later commercial and industrial development in South Africa.

Conflict between White and Black resulted in White conquest of the interior; conflict between the Boer Republic and Britain culminated in the war of 1899–1902 which resulted in a defeat for the Boers and a divided White population. Many years of dour, bitter political struggle followed, but the development, in spite of ups and downs, has been towards a sovereign independent state which was fully achieved in 1961 when South Africa became a republic outside the Common-wealth of Nations.

The economy of the country, until the discovery of gold and dia-monds in the last quarter of the nineteenth century, was based almost entirely upon the soil. The later discovery of iron, coal, silver, coffee, tin, manganese, platinum, chrome and asbestos deposits has resulted in rapid developments in the fields of primary industry. Agricultural production of maize, sugar, tobacco, sub-tropical deciduous and citrus fruits, wines and brandies has grown steadily and is of basic importance to the country.

The White population consisted, in 1962, of an estimated 3,185,000 persons representing roughly 19·1 per cent of the total population. Immigration, almost entirely of West European peoples, has made good progress in the last few years. By 1985, it is estimated that there will be 4½ million Whites in a total of approximately 27¾ million people. Some 37·1 per cent of the Whites use English as the home language and 58·1 per cent Afrikaans, a small but increasing proportion using both languages. The great majority of Afrikaans-speaking South Africans are Protestants who are strongly Calvinistic in outlook and practice. The rest of the White population is also mainly Protestant with a firm belief in education. There is, and always has been, an acceptance of the important role of the state in the provision and control of education. A section of the English-speaking group prefers the single-sex, private boarding school of the English public-school variety. By and large class distinctions are not strong, however, amongst Whites. Religious instruction of a non-dogmatic type has been, and is, an integral part of the educational practice of the country.

The early Dutch settlers spoke Hollands but they were isolated and cut off, to an extent, from the sources of their culture. During the nineteenth and early twentieth centuries, there was a danger that, as a result of conquest, apathy and the policies of anglicization which were followed, the Dutch language would disappear. During this period, however, a new modern language, Afrikaans, originally a patois of Hollands, began to emerge and, with it, the firing of a developing national consciousness. Eventually Afrikaans was recognized by the provinces in 1914 and later became a medium of instruction in schools. A two-stream policy in education was followed; this meant that two streams of schools developed, those based upon instruction through the medium of Afrikaans to pupils whose home language is Afrikaans and those based upon instruction through the medium of English to those pupils whose home language is English. In all schools, the second language (Afrikaans or English, as the case may be) is taught as a subject.

It has often been argued that lingually separate schools emphasize differences and tend to maintain traditional groupings and attitudes and that the parallel-medium school, in which the two separate streams may operate under one headmaster, would build national unity more effectively. To the English-speaking group, functioning as they do on 'exterior' lines from a recognized, growing world language and culture, there has been little real fear of loss of identity, language and culture. To the Afrikaner, however, in the past, this has not been the case. The Afrikaans language became the symbol of the struggle for identity and a place in the sun, of the growing personality and national consciousness of a people. The focal point of the developing culture became the school, where the unity of cultural development could be preserved and fostered, religion, home and school being seen as integrated parts of the mosaic of Afrikanerdom. The support, therefore, of the Afrikaans-medium school by Afrikaners has been consistently strong.

To a greater or lesser degree, White South Africans have always had segregation based upon colour. The victory of the Nationalist group at the polls in 1948 began the development of a philosophy of separate development, which was to be implemented in all fields of human activity in South Africa. Each racial or ethnic group was to develop as a separate group with eventual full responsibility for the development of that ethnic section by the constituent members themselves who must be educated and made ready to serve their own people. Whatever the ultimate pattern of this theory may be, e.g. geographic partition or the separate handling of each group's needs within industrialized complexes, it has had a profound effect upon the education of all groups. In the field of educational control, for example, there are some ten separate departments of education today doing the work of the original five (prior to 1954). The vertical division is on the basis of racial groupings, each department, or group of provincial departments, being under the control of a central government Minister of State. (A more detailed explanation of the pattern is given later in this chapter.)

Supporters of this segmentation of educational control say that it is a moral and educationally effective solution to difficult social and economic problems, resulting in fair opportunity for all, and providing the necessary challenge within each group. Opponents of separate development in education argue that education is indivisible; that a serious fragmentation of education has taken place; that the solution is political and not educational; and that a caste system of education may develop.

Ideology therefore has had, and will continue to have, considerable impact upon educational principles and practice.

In the economic field, primary industry, with gold as the mainstay, has served the country well, but it is in the field of secondary industry that the most recent and significant developments have taken place. Over the period of the last 35 years, the rate of economic growth (allowing for certain adjustments) has been a steady average of $4\frac{1}{2}$ per cent per annum. The Government's Economic Development Programme for 1964–9 however, considered that a target of $5\frac{1}{2}$ per cent per annum is possible.[1] The Gross National Product for the period 1962–4 showed an increase of as high as 8½ per cent. Economists foresee no reversal in the industrialization process or slowing down of the growth rate, the main bottleneck being 'a dearth of skilled labour'. Industrialization has brought about mechanization and a rapid urbanization so far as Whites are concerned, of the basically rural Afrikaans-speaking group. The following figures are most revealing:

URBAN DISTRIBUTION OF POPULATION – REPUBLIC (%)

	European	Bantu	Asiatic	Coloured
1911	51·6	12·7	Unknown	Unknown
1936	65·2	17·3	66·3	53·9
1960	83·8	31·8	83·2	68·6

It is clear that a higher proportion of non-Whites are entering, and will continue to enter, occupations requiring a higher degree of education and vocational skill. Whites will continue to provide managerial, supervisory and professional skills, there being scope for vertical movement within each such sphere. Within each non-White group, however, such skills will increasingly be provided by non-Whites themselves.

The structure of the labour force is changing, too. There is a significant increase, for instance, in the proportion of white-collar workers (including professional, technical, administrative and clerical); secondly, there is a rapid drop in the proportion of the population engaged in agriculture; and thirdly, a rise in the proportion of skilled labour and a fall in the proportion of unskilled labour. The great majority of economically active Whites are skilled workers and the very areas of the labour market where demands for their services are increasing, are those which require more and better education. Amongst Whites (in 1960) 36·9 per cent were economically active compared with 37·2 per cent in 1951, the decrease being due to the higher proportion of Whites whose education is becoming longer and more intensive than in the past.

The proportion of Whites engaged within certain skilled occupations will tend to fall considerably, e.g. 76·6 per cent of all white-collar workers in 1960 were White whereas the estimate for 1980 is 56·0 per cent. Similarly, in the case of carpenters, bricklayers and plasterers, the figures are 58·1 per cent and 35·8 per cent and for mechanics 92 per cent and 80 per cent respectively.[2]

[1] Republic of South Africa, Department of Planning, *Economic Development for the Republic of South Africa – 1964–69*, Pretoria, Government Printer.
[2] The 1961 Education Panel – Second Report, *Education and the South Economy*, Johannesburg, Witwatersrand University Press, 1966.

In such a rapidly expanding economy shortages exist and will continue to do so, there being great need to handle present manpower resources as efficiently as possible. In the expansion which is taking place, the non-White is assuming a more important place and the shifting of boundaries between what is considered to be White and non-White work is already taking place, with consequent economic, social and political change.

The quantity and quality of education are key factors in this whole process. Compulsory primary education has been in operation for many years, White primary schools (seven-year schools) having reached optimum density. No quantitative expansion is necessary at this level other than that required to cope with the natural increase of population through birth or immigration. Education for White children up to and including Standard VIII (i.e. 10 years of schooling) or 16 years of age is compulsory. The maximum practical enrolment of pupils in Standard VIII is in sight; the 1961 Education Panel estimating, in its Second Report, that the proportion reaching Standard X will reach 50 per cent of an age-group by 1980.[3]

It is fairly clear that White primary and secondary school education has nearly reached saturation point and that further developments must be in the qualitative field of more effective differentiation and better preparation for academic and technological study. There is great need for flexibility in the educational system because of the technological, social and political changes which are continually and progressively taking place.

Amongst Whites, the percentage of the population between the ages of 18 and 21 attending universities (not including the University of South Africa) was 5·1 in 1930, 17·0 in 1961, and an estimated 37·0 by 1980. If this latter figure is to be realized, then great changes will need to come about in the expansion and organization of tertiary level institutions, the differential entrance qualifications to such institutions and the teaching methods used, because numbers will be greater and lower levels of academic capacity accepted. It is essential that the standards of university level study must be maintained and improved.

There must be, at late secondary and tertiary levels, the elimination of wastage of human resources. This will depend to some extent on the expenditure on education of considerably more than the 3 per cent of the Gross National Product which is currently spent on all education. In particular, more money will have to be spent on the universities, technological education, educational research and planning and levelling up the per capita expenditure on the various ethnic groups.

[3] *Op. cit.*

Much more will depend, however, upon the supply and quality of the teachers, of whom there is a very serious shortage, contributed to in no small measure by the general economic expansion, with resultant competition on all sides for the educated and qualified section of the White community.

South Africa is a country of many cultures and one in which both a highly developed White civilization is to be found alongside those of less developed peoples. The leadership given by the Whites in many directions has resulted in a fast-developing industrial economy in which all sections of the population are being absorbed with consequent rapid change for all, economically, socially and politically.

II. THE ORGANIZATION AND ADMINISTRATION OF WHITE EDUCATION

A. Structure

The Cape, Orange Free State, Transvaal and Natal, which formed the Union (not federation) of South Africa in 1910 comprised the erstwhile British colonies and northern republics. They brought to the conference table fairly well-developed systems of education based upon a pattern of state-controlled education which had begun to emerge in the Cape as early as the 1830s, the policy in the establishing of schools being based upon state aid for local educational enterprises. Local bodies, representative of parents, were usually given certain powers.

These ideas spread north and east. Natal, however, favoured centralized control with no real representation of parents whilst the two northern republics, the Orange Free State and the Transvaal, preferred centralized control, with a fairly strong say being given to school boards and school committees.

The Act of Union stated that the provincial councils (the legislative bodies administering the constituent states) were to be given control of 'Education other than higher, for a period of five years and thereafter until Parliament otherwise provides'. Later, in 1961, the Republic of South Africa Constitution Act re-stated the situation in almost the same words, but included Bantu Education, as follows: 'Education, other than higher education and Bantu education, until Parliament otherwise provides'.

This horizontal division has been the cause of constant controversy because the definition of higher education varied, coming to include, for instance, special education and all vocational education. The latter forms of education came to resort, after some years, under the Union Department of Education, the central state department set up to look after higher education. Various definitions, too, of vocational education have been given but none have been really satisfactory. The position of teacher-training also became anomalous, because the provinces assumed control of this service which, through the years, has become post-secondary (or 'higher') in practice. The passage of the National Education Policy and the Educational Services Acts during 1967 has had the effect of bringing about reform in the areas of secondary education and teacher-training both of which have functioned for many decades under divided control. Legislation in 1969 completed the process. Prior to 1953, the Union Department of Education was in charge of university, technical, vocational and special education. The provinces controlled primary and general secondary education for all sections of the community, the children of each group attending separate, racially segregated schools.

Under the policy of separate development each main racial group is controlled as a total separate entity under a central government Minister of State, education being handled as a part of this total group concept and within the particular group. The passage of the Bantu Education Act (No. 47 of 1953) with the creation of a central state Department of Bantu Education under a Minister, was the first step taken in the vertical segmentation of education. The next step was the transfer of Coloured education to the Department of Coloured Affairs in 1963 and that of Indian (or Asiatic) education to the Department of Indian Affairs in 1965.

White education found itself in the anomalous position of being under decentralized provincial control in respect of the general education of the vast majority of the pupils, and under centralized governmental control in respect of vocational and specialized education. In 1962, a National Advisory Education Council was established with the aim of advising the Minister of Education, Arts and Science on all matters affecting White education. Then in 1967, the two Education Acts referred to above were passed, placing the control of policy in respect of the education of Whites in the hands of the Minister but leaving the administration of education in the hands of the provinces.

These developments are consistent with the policy of the ruling party, but they raise many questions in the minds of students of education. For example, where the racial composition of a people is heterogeneous, to what extent can educational philosophy be effectively formulated and controlled at a national level? To what extent can segmentation of this nature (which has had some advantage to the non-White groups, in particular, and which is an effort to simplify the complexities of multi-racial problems) with its high degree of centralization and tendency towards isolation, be effective in the handling of the vast educational and administrative problems being encountered? Are there not too many education departments (ten in number) making administration top-heavy and causing a great strain on the White leadership in education because, as yet, the top officials are White in all departments? Outside of the Cabinet, there is, at present, no educational body providing an overall view of the national educational pattern. As a result of rapid commercial and industrial development alone, such oversight would appear to be essential.

There are clearly many sound arguments, mainly financial, for increased centralized control of education, but the need for decentralization in terms of homogeneous regions in a country which is becoming industrialized at a great rate, is very necessary. The ultimate solution in this matter will probably be found in centralization in respect of a few selected factors e.g. finance but with decentralization of the interna of education. The major difficulty, however, is that South Africa is tending to centralize in terms of educational philosophy and to decentralize administration.

B. Educational Agencies Conducting White Education

1. *Central Government*

The Department of Education, Arts and Science is responsible for:

(i) Specialist schools which it actually conducts. These are technical colleges, technical, commercial and housecraft high schools, industrial schools, special schools and teacher-training establishments which are wholly supported by the state. A number of institutions like the universities, some special schools and vocational institutions are state-supported.

(ii) Auxiliary educational services such as liaison services with other countries, etc.; the National Bureau of Educational and Social Research which undertakes and sponsors research; a number of libraries specializing mainly in education; an examinations division which conducts a wide range of examinations, both within and beyond the borders of the Republic; and as co-ordinator for a large number of national committees.

Other state departments, like the Department of Defence, the Department of Mines, the South African Railways and Harbours, the Department of Police, etc., run training institutions for their own staffs.

2. *Provincial systems*

The four provinces provide roads, hospitals, education and parks and fisheries within their respective boundaries. They are responsible for primary, general and vocational secondary education.

The Minister of Education, Arts and Science, in consultation with the National Advisory Education Council and the provincial administrations lays down the policy as outlined in the National Education Policy Act.

The direction and control of provincial education is vested in the Administrator (a state appointment), an Executive Committee and the Provincial Council. In charge of the Education Department is a Director or Superintendent-General of Education whose function it is to exercise powers and perform such duties as are conferred or imposed upon him by law. The educational policy is laid down by the National Education Policy Act and the individual provincial ordinances, which cover matters like the legal right to establish schools, compulsory and free education, medium of instruction, religious instruction, the conditions of service of teachers, etc.

Most of the provincial departments of education are organized in two main wings:

(i) Professional, which includes school inspection, medical, psychological and vocational guidance services, syllabuses, examinations, the training of teachers and so on.

(ii) Administrative, which includes staffing (appointment, leave, resignations, retirement, etc. of teachers and administrative staff), local government in education, planning (buildings, hostels, etc.) and accounts.

The Transvaal has had an Education Advisory Council for a number of years and, more recently, an Advisory Committee on the training of teachers. All the various departments of education in South Africa are introducing planning patterns.

Provincial education is financed through central government subsidies amounting to approximately 50 per cent of the previous year's expenditure, the remainder coming from direct taxation.

3. *Private schools*

More than 90 per cent of South African children attend state schools, the numbers in private schools being numerically small. All such schools, which may be either independent or state-aided, must be registered as approved schools by the provincial education department concerned. The great majority of the schools are non-denominational or Roman Catholic, the rest being Anglican, Methodist and Presbyterian in that order. In 1963, there were 312 private schools (independent and aided) with 66,000 pupils in attendance. Natal provides subsidies to those schools wishing to apply; the Cape limited subsidies to certain schools and the Transvaal subsidizes only those private schools established before 1953 and which desire financial assistance.

Private schools are supported, in the main, by the English-speaking group, the Afrikaans-speaking section favouring state education, as a rule.

C. LOCAL CONTROL OF EDUCATION

Local government in education is fairly well developed in the Cape, Orange Free State and Transvaal provincial systems. In Natal there are no school boards or school committees, the only link between parents and the authorities being through advisory committees. After 1905 the school boards in the Cape paid approximately 50 per cent of the cost of the local schools raised, as a rule, by means of school fees and a school tax, the province finding the rest. With the Act of Union, however, the financial responsibility of the school boards was taken over by the provincial councils and the school board without power to tax became a feature of education in South Africa. At present, in the Cape, there are over one hundred school boards; the Orange Free State has twenty-five and the Transvaal, twenty.

Generally speaking, a school board consists of nine or twelve members, one-third of whom are appointed by the Administrator or other body and the remainder elected in varying ways (through registered parliamentary voters, electoral unit systems or through school committee delegations) for periods of three years. Members in the Transvaal, for instance, must be White South African citizens resident in the particular province, of sound mind, not having been convicted of certain offences or be unrehabilitated insolvents. Employees of Departments of Education or those who have financial interest in private schools are disqualified.[4]

The function of such boards is to exercise supervision over local provincial educational institutions; advise the Director of Education on many matters, including the provision of sites and buildings; receive money for the maintenance of school buildings, school furniture, transport and bursary schemes; be responsible for the enforcement of compulsory school attendance and make recommendations in respect of the appointment and promotion of teachers.

Generally speaking, the functions of these school boards are too

[4] Transvaal Education Department, *Education Ordinance, 1953*, Pretoria, Government Printer.

limited to make them educational institutions of real value. It is likely that they will undergo considerable reform in the years to come.

School committees are found in the Cape Province, the Orange Free State and the Transvaal, but not in Natal. They comprise five to seven members who are, as a rule (but not always) parents of pupils attending a local state school. In the Transvaal, the Education Ordinance of 1953 lays down that committees 'shall be established for every primary . . . school' thus making them obligatory.[5]

The powers and duties of such committees are, in the main, to exercise general supervision over a school and to advise the board in matters affecting its welfare. They are legally provided for in the Education Ordinances of the provinces and so have a good deal of power; they recommend appointments of teachers, principals and vice-principals. The dangers of influences and factors other than those educational entering into such a situation are very real. In Natal, appointments of teachers and principals of schools are carried out by the Department; in the Transvaal, a professional Selection Board for this purpose was set up in 1963, its function being to screen and adjudge applicants for promotion posts, a selected panel of applicants being referred to the school committee and school board concerned. In this way, the teaching profession is being judged on more professional grounds.

It is clear that a statutory school committee, dedicated to the service of the school, can be of great value, serving, as it does, as a link between parents and school and between school and school board or department. There is need, however, to define its functions very clearly in terms of what such a body of laymen is really capable of doing adequately. Otherwise, such committees do not necessarily foster co-operative relationships between school and community.

Parent-teacher associations which are voluntary organizations are fairly well developed throughout the country.

D. LANGUAGE

In South Africa there are two official languages, Afrikaans and English, the schools being organized on this basis. There are thus two streams of schools – Afrikaans-medium schools in which the medium of instruction is Afrikaans and English-medium schools in which the medium of instruction is English. These are usually separate schools, but in the rural areas particularly, the two media are organized under one roof and one principal, such schools being known as parallel-

[5] *Op. cit.*

medium schools. Dual medium schools, in which both languages are used, have become rare.

The decision as to which language is to be the child's medium of instruction (variously known as the 'native' tongue, mother-tongue or home-language) has had a long history, many factors entering into the crystallization of the present practice.

All the provinces, with the exception of Natal, lay down that the medium of instruction in schools shall be the home language of the pupil. This is defined as the language better known by the pupil. The Education Ordinance of the Cape Province Section 182 (i) reads as follows:

> The medium of instruction of every pupil in all standards in a school up to and including the eighth standard shall be either Afrikaans or English according to which of these languages he knows the better; provided that, if a pupil knows both the said languages equally well, the medium of instruction of such pupil in the said standards shall be either Afrikaans or English as the parent may elect or, if the parent fails to exercise such right of election, as the principal teacher may decide; and provided further that, on admission of a pupil to the sixth standard, the parent of such pupil may claim to have the medium of instruction of such pupil changed if he produces a certificate by the principal teacher of the school at which such pupil passed the fifth standard, countersigned by an inspector of schools to the effect that such pupil knows both languages sufficiently well to be able to receive instruction through either medium.[6]

The Ordinances of the Transvaal and the Orange Free State are much the same. It will be noted that the principal of the school must decide as to which language the child knows better.

In Natal, up to the present, the medium of instruction of the pupils in government schools is that of the official language selected by the parent.

In 1963, 62·4 per cent of all White pupils were receiving their education through the medium of instruction of Afrikaans and 37·2 per cent through the medium of English, those being taught through the media of both languages standing at 0·3 per cent. In general, where there is a small minority (fifteen pupils, as a rule) of the other home language group, then parallel-medium classes may be established. Such schools are regarded in a province like the Transvaal, as more administratively advantageous than educationally effective, the policy being the establishment of single-medium schools. Such schools have many advantages in their unilingual homogeneity but, in a rapidly industrializing and urbanizing country with the historically rural,

[6] Province of the Cape of Good Hope, *Education Ordinance, 1956* (No. 20 of 1956).

agricultural Afrikaans-speaking group becoming an integral part of the urban, industrial complexes, the whole policy needs close objective examination and re-moulding in the light of the needs of the country as a whole. Experimentation with parallel-medium classes where this may be desirable in terms of the balance of the two sections in the local population and with dual medium education in which both languages are used, could well be considered.

E. INSPECTION

An important part of the control and supervision of education in South Africa is that of inspection. The pattern is much the same in all the provinces where experienced principals of schools are appointed as inspectors, functioning in their own provinces and exercising jurisdiction over *all* schools in his circuit or district. Specialist inspectors are not used, but panels of inspectors visit high schools so as to provide adequate coverage of specialist subjects. The Department of Education, Arts and Science employs inspectors on a national and specialized basis.

The work of the inspector has tended to become more and more that of the educational consultant, the problem being that the increasing load of administration which each inspector has to carry makes the fuller realization of consultation very difficult indeed.

SOME STATISTICS (1963): PROVINCIAL, AIDED AND
PRIVATE SCHOOLS (WHITE)

	Cape	Natal	Transvaal	Orange Free State	Total
Number of schools (provincial and aided)	1,132	239	873	300	2,544
Number of pupils (provincial and aided)	207,826	71,839	336,611	65,387	681,663
Number of private schools (independent only)	97	20	86	6	209
Number of pupils in private schools (independent only)	18,275	3,776	25,076	1,557	46,884
Number of teachers (state and aided)	9,428	3,530	12,629	3,409	28,996
Number of private schools (independent only)	1,112	207	1,211	71	2,601

III. ORGANIZATION OF EDUCATIONAL INSTITUTIONS

A. Nursery Schools

The development of nursery school education has been slow, the main reason being the fact that the education of children of pre-school age has never been considered an integral part of the whole system of education, an attitude, however, which is undergoing steady change.

The need for nursery schools showed itself amongst the poorer sections of the community nearly forty years ago, the first institutions being established and supported by some municipalities, welfare organizations and private sources. A number of commissions on education gave qualified support to the movement and the provinces, with the support of the central government, gradually accepted increasing responsibility for the support of nursery schools. In the Orange Free State, the salaries of qualified nursery school teachers are paid by the Department of Education; in the other provinces a per capita grant is made irrespective of the fees which parents pay. In Natal the fees paid vary to some extent with the parents' means.

Subsidy is paid to registered schools which conform to the standards of accommodation, etc., laid down by the Nursery School Association of South Africa. Much support still comes, however, from municipalities and private sources. The central government has established its own schools for handicapped children and institutions attached to nursery school teacher-training centres.

B. Primary Schools

Primary schools are free and compulsory – in Natal and the Transvaal, books and other requisites are also provided free.

Compulsory education developed fairly early in South Africa, the Orange Free State taking the lead in 1895 when a restricted form of school attendance was made compulsory; the Transvaal and the Cape followed suit in 1905 and Natal in 1910, the ages of compulsory attendance being set at between 7 and 14 years of age.

The present position is that seven years of age remains the legal age for school attendance, the onus being upon parents to see that their children attend a state or registered private school, unless exemption is obtained. In all the provinces the parent may be prosecuted for failure to obey the school attendance law. Provisions vary, but the development in recent years has been towards extending the lower limit of attendance downwards by legally permitting children to attend school in the year in which they turn six. The majority of White South African children actually go to school when they are five years of age.

The upper limit of compulsory attendance, is, with small exceptions, the end of the year in which the pupil turns sixteen years of age. As a rule if Standard VIII is completed before reaching the compulsory age, the pupil is legally entitled to leave school.

The distribution of pupils according to the medium of instruction has been given earlier. Many primary schools in rural areas are of the parallel-medium type. Throughout the country, the policy is for provincial primary schools to be co-educational, except where sex-segregated schools have been in existence for a long time. Private schools are generally of a single-sex structure.

The primary schools are usually seven-year schools consisting of two grades or sub-standards and five standards. Except for a number of all-range schools in some parts of the country, they are self-contained. In many populous areas junior schools, accepting children for the first three years, are fairly common.

A policy of centralization has concentrated the traditional one- and two-teacher schools of the rural areas into larger groups. Well-developed transport schemes and good boarding facilities make it possible for children in sparsely-populated areas to benefit fully from the educational facilities provided.

In urban areas, the rapidly increasing population and the difficulties of obtaining school sites has made it almost impossible to keep the maximum enrolment to the 450 mark widely recommended by South African educationalists. The general policy at present is that schools should not be bigger than 600–800 pupils, but many are larger.

Pupil-teacher ratios have not improved in the last decades, the figures ranging from 1 : 25·9 to 1 : 31·0. In urban areas, classes of 35 are common and many much higher, rural areas being more fortunate, on the whole. The overall pupil-teacher ratio in White schools is as follows:

PUPIL-TEACHER RATIOS

	Cape	Natal	Transvaal	Orange Free State	South Africa
1945	22.6:1	17.5:1	25.9:1	21.05:1	23.2:1
1962	22.1:1	20.6:1	26.5:1	20.9:1	23.2:1

The allocations of time to each subject vary with the different provinces, but for a twelve-year old child, the pattern is broadly as follows:

	Hours per week
Religious Education (including Assembly)	$1\frac{1}{2}$–$2\frac{1}{2}$
First Language	5
Second Language	4
Arithmetic	$3\frac{1}{2}$–4
History, Geography and Nature Study	3–4
Health Education (including Hygiene)	2
Music	1
Handcraft	1–2
Art	1

In addition there are periods for library, films, writing, general knowledge, gardening and so on, depending on the school.

As a result of the improvement in the qualifications of teachers and of progress in inspection methods, it has been possible to rid the primary school of the formal external examination, thus making it a more autonomous institution with less rigid and prescriptive syllabuses. Promotions from class to class are now usually carried out by the principal and staff who set their own standards and make their own assessments.

The lock-step system of year by year promotion based on the standard of the average is now under severe fire. Promotion is still largely based upon scholastic achievement, but chronological age, physical and social development are being given increasing weight.

The even progress made by White pupils is made clear by the following figures for the Republic:

NUMBER OF WHITE PUPILS IN PRIMARY CLASSES (1963)

Sub A and B	Std. I	Std. II	Std. III	Std. IV	Std. V
148,875	72,142	69,319	67,635	63,755	60,166

MEDIAN AGE OF PUPILS (IN YEARS)

	Boys	Girls
Sub A	6·5	6·5
Sub B	7·5	7·5
Std. I	8·6	8·5
Std. II	9·6	9·5
Std. III	10·6	10·5
Std. IV	11·6	11·5
Std. V	12·6	12·5

C. SECONDARY SCHOOLS

A number of colleges or high schools of a private or state-aided nature were established in the Cape Colony from 1829 on. They later prepared pupils for the examinations of the University of the Cape of Good Hope. After 1890, with the increasing demand, a number of high schools were set up and secondary 'tops' added to many primary schools, mainly in rural areas. Natal established two high schools as early as 1863; later in the urban areas, high schools were set up with intermediate schools growing up in the rural areas. Developments in the Transvaal and the Orange Free State were along broadly similar lines.

Many education commissions made recommendations in connection with the education of the adolescent. It was clear that the old academic concepts did not succeed in reconciling the claims of the few and those of the many. *The Report of the Commission on Technical and Vocational Education, 1948* (the de Villiers Commission Report) recommended a national scheme of education in which the primary schools would be seven years in length instead of the then eight-year pattern. Thereafter all pupils would be admitted to a junior high school (12+ – 15+ years of age). Thereafter, in turn, there would be two kinds of high school.

(i) Senior academic high schools.

(ii) Vocational high schools.

This report had considerable impact on educational thought in South Africa. In 1950, the Cape Province, following these recommendations, introduced a new primary course based upon a seven-year school with a junior secondary course to follow. Full account was to be taken of individual differences and the secondary course was to be a continuation of the general education of the primary school thus indicating the resistance to overmuch specialization. The present position in the Cape is that a compulsory core of subjects which includes the two official languages, general science and non-examination subjects such as physical education, religious instruction and music and three optional subjects, provides a sound general education with 'clear avoidance of the pre-vocational type of technical, commercial course'.

In Natal, a system of streaming was introduced in 1962, two streams rather than three being favoured because of 'the relatively small number of pupils'. The 'Advanced' Stream, which includes approximately two-thirds of the pupils follows the Senior Certificate courses and the 'Ordinary' Stream takes the rest. Special syllabuses were drawn up for this latter group which now proceeds to Standard X and writes its own examination, the Senior Certificate (Ordinary Grade). It is clear that the names applied to the courses are not really suitable and that the 'Advanced' group is too heterogeneous and could well form two groups. Otherwise, this pattern of differentiation has met with fair success and should lend itself to subject 'setting' which has not, as yet, been adequately tried.

For some fifteen years, up to 1950, the Transvaal experimented with the separate junior high school, a non-selective three-year school, but it failed, for similar reasons to those experienced by Scotland. By 1951, all secondary schools in the Transvaal became full-range five-year schools, so that all pupils had the opportunity of going as far as they were able. It was clear that the separate type of secondary school, other than the vocational type, was not supported in South Africa and that a comprehensive type was favoured, a number of committees recommending this principle. In the Transvaal, however, the Oversea Mission of 1956 made full recommendations for its implementation which were carried into effect in 1958.

The present practice in the Transvaal is as follows:

(i) There are semi-comprehensive high schools which are geographically zoned and supplied by 'feeder' primary schools. The transfer of pre-Standard X vocational education to the provinces under the 1967 National Education Policy Act should have the effect of gradually bringing about a more fully comprehensive high school.

(ii) The schools are non-selective, all pupils being transferred from the primary school without external assessment.

(iii) The aim is homogeneous grouping based upon the child's total scholastic achievement. The following factors, however, are taken into consideration in allocating children to groups after a preliminary period in Standard VI: level of intelligence, scholastic attainment, aptitude and interest.

The homogeneous groups are as follows: Group A (or the University Entrance Course), with I.Q.s of 110+; Group B (or Standard X Course), with I.Q.s of 100–110 and Group C (or Standard VIII Course), with I.Q.s of 80–100 and Group D with I.Q.s of 80 or less.

These groups constitute approximately 20 per cent, 30 per cent, 43 per cent and 7 per cent respectively of the pupils.

Opportunity is given for any pupil to change his/her course 'at any stage of the entire secondary school career'.

In practice it has been found that the two upper groups comprise nearer 80 per cent of the total instead of 50 per cent and that Group C comprises about 20 per cent instead of 43 per cent. This is probably due to the pressure of public opinion which has always resisted the stigma of the 'inferior' pupils being grouped separately.

(iv) The curricula for the groups are differentiated to offer 'a broad general training which will serve as the foundation for vocational or specialized education at a later stage'. There is a compulsory core of subjects with a gradual increase in the number of optional subjects as the pupils move up the school. The core includes religious instruction, home and second languages, history, general science, general mathematics, industrial arts or domestic science, physical education, school music, guidance and race studies. Geography becomes an option after Standard VI; a third language is optional from the beginning and a wide range of options (third and fourth languages, mathematics, bookkeeping, typing, shorthand, etc.) is offered.

Guidance services are an integral part of the pattern.

(v) There are differentiated syllabuses in each subject, differentiated methods, measurement and testing and certification to suit the needs of the different groups.

The Oversea Mission recommended schools of 750 pupils with a maximum of 1,000 but the present accepted policy is for schools of 1,200 pupils, the argument being that it is thus possible to provide fuller differentiation. At the same time efforts are being made to create forms of internal school organization which will ensure that the institution functions in the best interests of each pupil.

The number of secondary pupils has increased nearly two-fold in the last fifteen years and the schools are showing stronger retentive ability, over 40 per cent of pupils in 1963 staying on for the full five-year course compared with 16 per cent in 1932. It is clear that a wide range of ability and capacity has to be educated. Throughout the country, the comprehensive concept is favoured with a compulsory core of subjects and differentiation of subjects to suit homogeneous groups in terms of content, examination and certification. As yet there is little attempt at differentiation in terms of tempo and 'setting' of subjects. There is concern about the size of some of the Transvaal schools in terms of South African tradition of high schools of 600–750 pupils. The average pupil-teacher ratio is approximately 1 : 19·1 with the Transvaal figure at 1 : 21·4. The median ages of boys are as follows: Standard VI, 13·7 years; Standard VII, 14·7; Standard VIII, 15·7; Standard IX, 16·6; Standard X, 17·6 (Girls are generally about 0·1 of a year younger throughout).

These figures (cf. the primary school figures) show clearly that the pupils are progressing through the schools in a smooth, regular manner.

The drop-out figures for 1947-on and 1959-on (in percentages) are as follows:

	Std. VI	Std. VII	Std. VIII	Std. IX	Std. X
1947	100				
		79·2			
			57·9		
				35·8	
					31·4
1959	100				
		93·2			
			77·5		
				59·6	
					44·9

The rapid improvements in little more than a decade are obvious.

D. Examinations

External examinations, except for the Standard X School Leaving Certificate, have steadily disappeared from the educational scene in South Africa. The Joint Matriculation Board (a statutory body established by Act of Parliament in 1916) includes representatives of the universities, provincial and central departments of education and the private schools and lays down the matriculation exemption standards for admission to South African universities. Under the control of the Board however, the various departments of education conduct their own examinations. These are grouped-subject examinations in which pupils are required to pass (40 per cent) in each subject of a group of four (main language, second official or another language, a science subject or mathematics and a third language or mathematics (if not already included) or history or geography). A fifth subject must be taken, $33\frac{1}{3}$ per cent only being required; sixth and seventh subjects may be taken, the choice being wider. An aggregate of 45 per cent must be obtained. A fairly representative grouping for university admission is English or Afrikaans (Higher Grade), Afrikaans or English (Lower Grade), a third language, mathematics, a science and history.

A lower standard of $33\frac{1}{3}$ per cent in individual subjects with an aggregate of 40 per cent is accepted for School Leaving Certificate purposes.

Developments in secondary education, the changing composition of the school population and the demands made by the universities have brought about a need for reform of the matriculation pattern. An 'accreditation' scheme involving twenty Transvaal high schools came into full operation at the end of 1967 making internal assessment and not external examination serve as admission to certain universities in the Transvaal from selected schools. Further suggestions for improvement include an eleventh more specialized year at school, a smaller number of subjects at the present Standard X level and possibly higher and lower grades of subjects. It is certain that the present dual function of the examination as a university entrance examination and as a school-leaving certificate must be reformed. The Transvaal has already done this to good effect by instituting a university entrance group. Such a development should result in improved admission levels to the universities and a better educated school-leaver.

E. Technical and Vocational Education

The Dutch Reformed Church established the first industrial school in South Africa at Uitenhage in 1895. Such education had its roots in economic distress, the children of indigent parents receiving some instruction in general subjects and also training in cabinet-making, wagon-building, etc. From these simple beginnings, industrial education developed; it had, unfortunately, the stigma of delinquency added to that of poverty, the effect of which still lingers, although it is disappearing.

Technical education had different origins. After the discovery of gold, the need for trained personnel in industry, commerce, the mines and on the railways became urgent. Part-time classes were soon set up to train apprentices and commercial employees. In 1911, there were 500 such pupils: by 1955 the numbers had risen to 60,000.

Up to 1925, technical and industrial education fell under the provinces but was then transferred to central government control largely for financial reasons. The Vocational Education Act (No. 7 of 1955) placed all technical colleges under the Department of Education, Arts and Science and gave a clearer definition of vocational education as commercial, technical, domestic science vocational education but not including vocational education given to the provinces under the Special Schools Act of 1948 (for handicapped children of certain kinds). Provincial secondary schools were limited by law in the amount of time they could allocate to courses of a commercial nature.

Under the National Education Policy Act of 1967, the provinces took over vocational education of a secondary type from April, 1968.

Certain technical colleges (Witwatersrand, Pretoria, Durban, Cape Town) will develop as advanced colleges of technology.

There are thirteen technical colleges in South Africa, multilateral vocational institutions which, in addition to the functions stated, are in essence community centres providing much organized adult and further education as well, the latter under the co-ordinating authority of the National Advisory Council for Adult Education. Full and part-time technical and commercial courses can be taken leading to Standard X, including matriculation exemption; the theory and practice in a number of trades; continuation classes for apprentices; adult education courses and correspondence courses. For many decades these colleges were state-aided and fee-paying, but today they are state institutions, tuition being free.

The trend is towards the separation of technical and commercial high schools from the technical colleges. There are twenty-six technical high schools, fifteen commercial high schools, nine combined commercial and technical high schools, eight housecraft high schools spread over the whole country, care being taken that rural towns are adequately served. One of the big problems has been the maldistribution of pupils in secondary schools, much of it the result of the lack of co-operation in education between the central government department and the provinces. Technical and vocational education had been isolated from the whole range of general secondary education and yet it tended to give, more and more, as the years passed, a parallel type of education. The demarcation of pupils between the two authorities has been a bone of contention, many agreements having been made, varying from admission at ex-primary school level to ex-Standard VIII.

The placing of all secondary level education under *one* educational authority should have the effect of unifying both problems and solutions.

The development of a selected group of technical colleges as technological institutions which can concentrate upon post-secondary study of pharmacy, secretarial practice, chemical technology, engineering of all kinds, mining, building construction through National Diplomas, etc., is good. 'Sandwich' courses are popular, as are the 'block-release' programmes for apprentices at the lower level.

These institutions too, will, continue to develop teacher-training programmes through National Teachers' Diplomas in art, physical education, commerce, home economics, technology and nursery school education. These courses are from one year to three years in length.

F. Higher Education

Apart from the more advanced technological colleges, the teacher-training colleges and some courses in Agricultural Colleges, all post-secondary work (i.e. after twelve years of schooling) is conducted in the universities. There are eleven universities, semi-autonomous, degree-granting institutions subsidized by the central government. There are no private or denominational universities. Four of the universities use English as the medium of instruction, five Afrikaans. One, the University of Port Elizabeth, was opened in 1965 and is dual medium, one or other of the official languages being used, or both. The University of South Africa has always been an examining body, but is today a teaching university in the sense that it conducts tuition on a correspondence basis through either official language to a wide range of external students, both White and non-White. A full-time academic staff conducts the courses.

The proportion of Whites attending universities is high, the ratio for full and part-time students (but not including the University of South Africa) is less than 1 : 100. The increasing number of matriculants, economic prosperity, stability and a changing attitude towards university study have all helped to increase the proportion of those attending institutions of tertiary education. In less than three decades, the full-time student population has increased 600 per cent. The proportion of women students is low, being under 30 per cent of the total.

The universities are organized on a departmental and faculty basis, as a rule. The degree patterns are very similar. Bachelor degrees in arts, science and commerce take three years to complete, two major subjects usually being taken for three years each, plus three or four other courses. For an Honours degree, a further year of study is necessary in one of the major subjects. Engineering and agriculture take four years; dentistry, law and architecture, five years and medicine, six years.

There has been a rapid growth of both subjects and faculties, the tendency being for an increasing range of subjects to be offered in each university. The number of degrees conferred has grown very rapidly.

Research is conducted at the Masters', Doctoral and post-Doctoral levels.

Some of the problems facing the universities in South Africa are as follows:

(a) *Admission requirements*
A level of admission operates which is considered to be too low, resulting in a high failure-rate at first-year level. There is a need to reform the admission requirements, in particular the matriculation examination. The aggregate mark at the matriculation examination was raised from 40 per cent to 45 per cent in 1960 and much study is being made of the problem in order to improve the situation.

(b) *Finance. The financing of the institutions*
The Government pays subsidies to the universities to the tune of approximately 70 per cent of their total budgets, but the formula used puts a premium on numbers of students. The financing of research is a matter of concern, at present.

(c) *Staffing*
It is difficult to obtain and retain well-qualified staff.

G. Teacher Training

At the time of Union (1910) it was generally agreed that the provinces would train primary teachers in their own training colleges and that the universities would train secondary teachers. The shortage of secondary teachers, however, has obliged the provinces to train such teachers and the technical colleges to train vocational specialists, for much the same reasons.

Nine South African University Departments of Education train graduates through one-year post-graduate courses. Some departments concern themselves solely with the training of secondary teachers, but a number conduct non-graduate two- and three-year courses for primary school teaching as well as specialist courses e.g. physical education, hard-of-hearing courses, and so on. Sixteen provincial subsidized training colleges prepare the bulk of the teachers over two- or three-year courses, the trend being towards the gradual elimination of the former. The three-year courses involve a final year of specialization in one of infant school method, physical education, domestic science, art, music, senior primary or commercial subjects. Specialization in academic subjects for work at a junior secondary level has grown in popularity; the Transvaal has recently introduced a fourth year of study in this field.

In the Transvaal, over forty years ago, the step was taken of linking teacher-training with the local universities. The students live in provincial hostels, the professional work being done in the colleges. The students attend nearby universities where bachelor's degrees may be completed. The Teachers' College in Bloemfontein and the Faculty of Education in the University of the Orange Free State have co-operated for some twenty years.

Five technical colleges which are under central government control provide three-year specialist courses for teachers of art, music, commercial subjects and physical education. The state, in one form or another, controls all White teacher-training, there being only one denominational college. Most are co-educational and unilingual and fairly small, with the exception of the big Transvaal colleges of education, some of which are over 2,000 strong.

The National Advisory Council on Education has given close study to the problems of lack of co-ordination in teacher training, to the lack of real co-operation between the various institutions, to unnecessary overlapping, duplication and competition, and improvements are likely to result.

BIBLIOGRAPHY

Books

The 1961 Education Panel, First Report, *Education for South Africa*, Johannesburg, Witwatersrand University Press, 1963, p. 170.

The 1961 Education Panel, Second Report, *Education and the South African Economy*, Johannesburg, Witwatersrand University Press, 1966, p. 151.

Behr, A. L. and MacMillan, R. G., *Education in South Africa*, Pretoria, Van Schaik, 1967, p. 386.

Coetzee, J. Ch. (ed.), *Onderwys in Suid-Afrika (Afdeling E.)*, Pretoria, Van Schaik, 1958.

Malherbe, E. G., *Education in South Africa (1652–1922)*, Juta, 1925.

Pells, E. G., *The Story of Education in South Africa*, Juta, 1938.

MacMillan, R. G. (ed.), *et al*, *Education and Our Expanding Horizons*, University of Natal Press, 1962. (Address by Dr I. L. Kandel on Principles of Educational Administration.)

Malherbe, E. G., *The Bilingual School*, The Bilingual School Association, 1943.

Bot, A. K., *The Development of Education in the Transvaal, 1836–1951*, Pretoria, Transvaal Education Department, 1951.

Van Zyl, A. J., *Meer Begniese Onderwys*, Pretoria, Pretoriase Tegniese Kollege, 1965.

Government Reports

Commission on Technical and Vocational Education, (de Villiers), U.G. No. 65, 1948.

Report of Oversea Mission in Connection with Differentiated Secondary Education (Van Wyk), Transvaal Education Department, 1955.

The School Committee and its Significance, Transvaal Education Department, Government Printer, 1958.

Education in South Africa, Pretoria, Department of Education, Arts and Science, 1964.

Report on the Experiment Involving the Use of the Second Official Language as a Medium of Instruction, Cape of Good Hope, Department of Public Education, 1951.

The National Advisory Education Council Act, 1962 (Act No. 86, 1962).

The National Education Policy Act, 1967 (Act No. 47 of 1967).

The Educational Services Act, 1967 (Act No. 42 of 1967).

Annual Reports of the Directors of Education, Transvaal, Orange Free State, Natal.

Annual Reports of the Superintendent-General of Education, Department of Education, Cape of Good Hope.

Report of the Provincial Education Commission, Province of Transvaal, 1939 (Appointed under Administrator's Notice No. 124, dated March 3, 1937, T.P. No. 5–1939).

Report of the Provincial Education Committee, Province of Natal, 1946 (Appointed under Provincial Notice No. 59, dated February 10, 1944, N.P. 2, 1946).

Report of the Provincial Education Commission, Province of the Orange Free State, 1951 (Appointed under Administrator's Notice No. 62 of March 27, 1946).

Union Year Books

Union of South Africa: Union Statistics for Fifty Years, Bureau of Census and Statistics, Pretoria, 1960.

Statistical Year Book, 1964, Bureau of Statistics, 1964.

Bulletin of Educational Statistics in the Union of South Africa, 1947, Union Education Department.

Statistics of Schools, Report No. 285, Bureau of Statistics, Pretoria, 1965.

Report of the Commission of Enquiry on Separate Training Facilities for Non-Europeans at Universities, 1953–4, Government Printer, Pretoria.

Report of the Committee of Enquiry into Quinquennial Revision of University Subsidy Formulae, 1964–68, Government Printer, Pretoria.

Republic of South Africa, Department of Planning, *Economic Development Programme for the Republic of South Africa – 1964–9,* Pretoria, Government Printer, para. 281.

Miscellaneous

Transvaal Education Department, Education Bulletins.

3· The Education of the Bantu in South Africa

ROBERT C. JONES

The intent underlying this chapter is to provide the student of education in southern Africa with a general but clear overview of the historical background, policies, and structure of the state system of education for the Bantu-speaking Africans in the Republic of South Africa. The discussion will begin with a statement of historical background, an understanding of which is essential to the consideration of Bantu education policy which will follow. With an understanding of the policy framework of the system, it then will be possible to examine the school and administrative structure which has been established, and to examine several of the most controversial issues which surround South African Bantu education.

I. HISTORICAL BACKGROUND

As is the case with all forms of social institutions, a reasonably clear perspective of Bantu education is contingent upon an understanding of the cultural developments, political, economic, and religious, which have shaped the country and the attitudes of its people. The complexity of the historical forces which have shaped South Africa and the fact that they are so poorly understood makes the need for an understanding of such background even greater than otherwise would be the case.

As an aim to be borne in view, it should be stated that historical developments have led to the firm control in South Africa of the Nationalist Party. This party traces its allegiances to the heritage of the Afrikaner and the rugged spirit of individualism and nationalism that characterizes the history of Afrikanerdom. Since 1954, Bantu education in South Africa has been controlled primarily by the Nationalist government and directed along the lines of *apartheid*, the Afrikaans term which designates the ethnic segregation policy of this government. It is claimed by the Nationalists that education should assist Bantu people in the development of their own semi-autonomous societies, such development beginning from the 'natural' basis of Bantu tribal tradition.

If Bantu education policy is to be understood, it is vitally important for the student to see clearly that *apartheid* is not a policy which the membership of the Nationalist Party has recently invented to protect its position of power from possible black takeover. Some opponents of Nationalist Bantu education policy claim that the government's primary objective is, in fact, to suppress the Bantu by providing educational opportunity that trains them to be nothing more than 'hewers of wood and drawers of water'. Historical evidence would indicate that, at best, this viewpoint is a gross over-generalization. Logical or illogical, feasible or unfeasible, politically and economically, *apartheid* as a basic element of South African political policy has its roots deep in the country's history, roots which pre-date by centuries the 'one man, one vote' wave which has swept the African continent since World War II. That it supports the wishes and well-being of the Nationalists is not to say that Bantu education policy was invented solely as an expediency in the face of the possibility of black political or economic domination.

From whence comes *apartheid* and what is the nature of the Bantu culture it proposes to preserve and keep separate?

To answer these questions it is essential to have an understanding of Afrikaner nationalism which has its beginnings in the middle of the seventeenth century. The Dutch East India Company had seen the need for a refreshment station for its ships travelling around the Cape, and in 1652, Jan van Riebeeck began the task of establishing such a station. To assist with the provision of foodstuffs, van Riebeeck brought in increasing numbers of immigrant farmers, as did his successor, Simon van der Stel. These settlers who came not only from the Netherlands, but also from Germany and France, provided the base stock from which has evolved the Afrikaner people whose language, Afrikaans, derives primarily from Dutch.

Despite a Company policy to the contrary, some colonists, who became known as *trekboere* (nomadic farmers), began to push further inland to occupy the free veld which was well suited to raising cattle. As a result of the geographic expansion, along with the slow rate of immigration, the small white population became dispersed. The frontiersmen thus led isolated lives that instilled in them conservative attitudes and a strong desire for total independence from 'outside' authority.

The firm sense of identity that the *trekboere* developed was also a result of his strongly Calvinistic religious beliefs, to which are related directly his attitudes toward non-Europeans. In his *The School in the Bush: A Critical Study of Native Education in Africa*, A. Victor Murray discusses the effect of Dutch Calvinistic theology on the Boer's racial philosophy:[1]

> A Calvinistic doctrine of election, and a verbal inspirationist view of the Scriptures which went along with it, characterized Dutch theology, and easily lent itself to a rigid division of classes and races. . . . To the Dutch Calvinist the coloured races were of the 'perishing progeny of Ham,' and the Old Testament religion of those days sanctioned a complete denial of the human rights of any races outside the pale of divine election.[2]

This religious interpretation of racial worth, along with paternalistic and self-sufficient Boer family life, provided the framework for the *trekboere's* social attitudes.

After some fifty years, the colonial government, through the organization of local administration in the outlying areas of the colony, caught up with the frontiersmen. By this time the attitudes of the *trekboere* toward government regulations and taxation had become increasingly hostile, and, as a result of this hostility, strong resentment grew over what they considered to be infringements on their natural liberties. In an effort to escape, they moved farther east until the last quarter of the eighteenth century, when they encountered Bantu-speaking African tribes which had been moving gradually south and west from the Natal and Transkeian areas. The line of Boer-African encounter was at the Great Fish River which extends southeast across the eastern part of the present boundaries of the Cape province. The vanguard of the Bantu migrants was the Xhosa tribe which was a formidable military opponent of the *trekboere*.

In 1795, about the time when the Fish River encounter was becoming most violent, the British occupied the Cape at the invitation of the Dutch king, who was more concerned with Napoleon's invasion than with governing the distant African colony. Although the Cape was returned to Dutch control in 1803 with the Treaty of Amiens, without invitation the British reoccupied the colony in 1806. In 1814, with the general European peace settlement, the colony formally became British. When the British took control for this second and last time, the Cape was an area of 80,000 square miles with the Fish River as its eastern boundary.

---

[1] 'Boer', the Dutch word meaning 'farmer', came to be used in English to refer specifically to the Dutch-descent South African farmer.

[2] Murray, Victor A., *The School in the Bush: A Critical Study of the Theory and Practice of Native Education in Africa*, Longmans, Green and Co., London, 1938, pp. 27-8.

The British government encouraged the emigration of English to their new colony, both to reduce unemployment at home and to provide a bulwark against the Bantu on the colony's eastern frontier. Thus, 168 years after the Dutch arrived, the first significant appearance of British settlers occurred with the arrival of 5,000 of them at the eastern part of the Cape.

The Boers had never liked being regulated by the Dutch, but they liked even less the new British colonial rule. In addition to imposing central government control, the British brought with them strong liberal ideas about racial equality and freeing slaves, ideas totally incomprehensible to the vast majority of the Boers. Murray has this to say about the conflicting philosophy of the British settlers concerning racial equality and slavery:

> The British had a different tradition . . . (from the Dutch) . . . the French Revolution had produced on the one hand a romantic humanitarianism which blended well with the doctrine of 'free grace' of the Evangelical Revival, and on the other hand, by reaction, a suspicion of the popular movements. The Industrial Revolution glorified the work of men's hands, and made industry a means by which a man might wrest the secrets of nature from her.[3]

British rule being intolerable to them, and the Bantu people to the east of the Fish River being a formidable barrier, the Boers began the Great Trek in the 1830s. Going north in order to avoid the Bantu, they trekked across the Orange River into what is now the Orange Free State. From there one group moved eastward and, after a violent encounter with the Zulu, established a new republic with Pietermaritzburg as the capital. The Zulu encounter, however, had spread Bantu unrest to the Cape borders and this, along with the fear of economic competition, resulted in the Cape Governor's persuading the British government to annex an area which included the new republic.

After annexation, some of the angry *trekkers* moved back across the Drakensburg mountains, then westward into the present Transvaal and Orange Free State areas. With little economic incentive to govern the territories involved, the British government formally withdrew all claims at the Sand River Convention of 1852, and the Bloemfontein Convention of 1854.[4] Hence, the two areas were established as independent Boer republics with constitutions that provided for the Boers to settle on vast tracts of land, often at the expense of the traditional

[3] *Ibid.*, p. 28.
[4] Marquard, Leo, *The Peoples and Policies of South Africa*, London, Oxford University Press, 1962, p. 12.

land rights of the Africans. For the moment, the Boer was able to live free of hated outside interference.

Several factors caused growing friction between the Boer and British interests:

(i) the discovery of diamonds at Kimberley in 1870,

(ii) the discovery of gold on the Witwatersrand,[5]

(iii) the imperialistic policies of Britain as epitomized by Cecil Rhodes,

(iv) the general *status quo* attitude of the agricultural, independent Boer republics.

The Cape Colony had been granted representative government in 1853, and full responsible government in 1872. Beginning in 1848, when the Cape was still under full British rule, the territory between the old Fish River boundary and the Natal boundary had been annexed, and European magistrates had been placed in charge of these Bantu areas. British missionaries had begun their work among the Bantu by establishing missions, schools, and hospitals.[6]

In 1895, the suspicion of the leaders in the Transvaal and Orange Free State Republics, resulting from this continual territorial expansion of the Cape, was confirmed. In that year, the Jameson Raid occurred, being no less than a devious military effort on the part of Rhodes, Prime Minister of the Cape, to seize political control of the Transvaal Republic. An immediate failure because of poor planning, the raid was nonetheless an important factor leading to the outbreak of the Anglo-Boer War in 1899.[7]

From the first, the outcome of this war was predictable – the two tiny Boer republics, joined in alliance, fighting against the British Empire. In 1902, after a relatively short but valiant fight, the Transvaal and the Orange Free State were made subject to the Empire. With the election of a Liberal government in Britain, however, the two former republics were granted responsible government in 1906 and 1907. Also, the Dutch language was recognized as being officially equal to English. The question of the African franchise was deferred.

In 1910, the Cape, Natal, the Transvaal, and the Orange Free State were joined together to form the Union of South Africa under a central form of government, with the administrative capital at Pretoria in the Transvaal and the legislative capital at Cape Town. Then in 1931, the

---

[5] The Witwatersrand is a 1,000 square-mile strip of land in the southern Transvaal near Johannesburg. The area is often referred to simply as the 'Rand'.

[6] Marquard, *op. cit.*, p. 16.

[7] Houghton, D. Hobart, *The South African Economy*, Oxford University Press, Cape Town, 1964, p. 5.

Union was recognized as a sovereign and independent member of the British Commonwealth by the Statute of Westminster. Thirty years later, on May 31, 1961, the Union became a republic and withdrew from the Commonwealth.[8]

As can be seen from the historical patterns of events already considered, no pervading social philosophy has arisen to create a generally common philosophical groundwork within the ruling white class. Political differences of opinion run deep into the society, yielding severe controversy on practically all social issues. An Act of Union, therefore, did little more than to establish a central form of government. Whereas the nationalism of the Afrikaner, beginning with the first clashes with the East India Company, had been geared towards independence and isolation, the Anglo-Boer War had proved it impossible for them to achieve independence. As has been pointed out, however, this realization that political independence could not be achieved by no means meant that the convictions of the Afrikaner nationalist had died. The Act of the Union, when considered in this light, had the single effect of pulling this struggle for national identity into the framework of a single parliamentary political system.

The political history of South Africa since 1910 has been a complex struggle between the conservative, nationalistic element which identifies strongly with Afrikaner heritage and attitudes, and the more moderate elements epitomized in the leadership of Jan Smuts. The latter were able for the most part to retain political control of the country until 1948. At that time, however, a coalition of two predominantly Afrikaner parties under the leadership of Malan and Havenga won the national election. Three years later the two parties, with Malan as leader, officially united to form the Nationalist Party, a party which has steadily increased its parliamentary majority in subsequent elections under the leadership, consecutively, of Strydom, Verwoerd, and presently Vorster.

It is clear at this point that South African society has developed in a peculiar and emotion-laden atmosphere. The prime elements of this atmosphere are not only the question of national identity, which is reflected in the friction within the ruling White class with the highly significant element of a nationalistic Afrikaner spirit, but also the question of the preservation of this ruling class' domination in the face of a rapidly growing non-White, particularly Bantu, population group.

It is this latter White versus non-White element, within the framework of Afrikaner nationalism, that contains the taproot of the policies

[8] *Ibid.*, p. 6.

of Bantu education that exist in the Republic today. In order to have a meaningful understanding of these (at times) seemingly illogical policies, it is necessary to shift consideration from general to more specific observations about the Bantu people themselves. It will be necessary first to consider the nature of their traditional culture and the social changes that have occurred during the period of contact with Western civilization. Within this context it then will be possible to look at the early education of the Bantu provided by the Whites and the subsequent establishment of the Nationalist government's centralized system of Bantu education based on the policy of *apartheid*.

II. THE BANTU PEOPLE AND BANTU EDUCATION UNDER THE MISSIONS

A. BANTU POPULATION AND CLASSIFICATION

According to estimates based on the last formal census taken in 1960, there were 10,927,922 Bantu in South Africa out of a total population of 16,002,797. The Bantu constituted 68·3 per cent of the population with the balance being: Whites, 19·3; Coloureds, 9·4; and Asians, 3·0 per cent.[9]

These nearly eleven million Bantu can be subdivided on the basis of three major categories of residence:

Urban areas	31.8 per cent
Farms owned by Whites	31.2 per cent
Bantu reserves	37.0 per cent[10]

Social anthropologists divide the Bantu people into four major ethnic groups with numerous tribal sub-groupings. Population percentage breakdowns for these groups include not only South Africa but also the Bantu population of the three former British High Commission Territories: Swaziland and Lesotho, which are both within the general borders of the Republic, and Botswana, which extends north from the north-central border of the Republic.

The largest ethnic grouping in the defined area is the Nguni, numbering about five million or nearly 60 per cent of the Bantu population of the Republic and former High Commission Territories.

[9] South African Institute of Race Relations, *A Survey of Race Relations in South Africa*, compiled by Muriel Horrell, assisted by Mary Draper, Johannesburg, Institute of Race Relations, 1963, p. 74.

[10] Estimated by Horrell through the combined use of the *National Census of 1960*, and the *Report on Agricultural and Pastoral Production for 1959-60, ibid.*, p. 75.

Nguni sub-groups are found in all four provinces of the Republic, but by far the two most important tribal groups are the Xhosa, in the eastern part of the Cape, and the Zulu with related tribal groups in Natal, the Orange Free State, and southern Transvaal. These two tribal groups constitute approximately 50 per cent of the Bantu in the area defined. The Swazi and Ndebele tribes are also in the Nguni group.

The second major ethnic grouping, the Sotho, number about three million and constitute about 36 per cent of the total southern Bantu population.[11] The sub-groups are:

(i) the Southern Sotho tribes of Lesotho, the Free State, and north-eastern Cape (16·7 per cent)

(ii) the Tswana of Botswana, northwest Cape, and western Transvaal (9·8 per cent)

(iii) the Northern Sotho of northern and northeastern Transvaal (9·3 per cent).

The two remaining major groupings are small relative to the Nguni and the Sotho. The Venda group numbers approximately 133,000 (1·6 per cent), and is found in an area east of Louis Trichardt, a northern Transvaal town located some 70 miles south of the Rhodesian border. The fourth group, the Tsonga, numbers about 340,000 (3 per cent), and is found chiefly in northeastern Transvaal.[12]

The basic unit in the social organization of traditional Bantu culture is the tribe having a nucleus made up of a group of families descended from common ancestors. According to the principle of inherited status, from this central group of families come the men of authority for the tribe, the most important of whom is the chief.

The household which is the local territorial unit, consists of a man, his wives, his sons and their wives and children, his unmarried daughters and other dependent kin. The social prestige of the household is measured to a large extent by the number of cattle in its possession, and marriages, closely regulated by tribal law, can only be entered into with the transfer of cattle from the family of the husband to the family of the wife. Cattle so used are generally referred to as 'lobola', but in recent years there has been some tendency to substitute other forms of wealth for cattle.[13] Often this substitute is money earned by the groom

---

[11] Sotho is pronounced Sŏŏ tŏŏ.
[12] Union of South Africa, *Report of the Commission on Native Education, 1949–51*, U.G. No. 53/1951, Pretoria, Government Printer, 1951, p. 12.
[13] Hoernle, A. W., and Hellmann, Ellen, 'An Analysis of Social Change and Its Bearing on Education', *Race Relations Journal*, Vol. 20, No. 4, 1953, p. 35.

at the mines and deposited with his father over a period of time.[14]

Within the social structure as a whole each individual has his special position, rights, duties and responsibilities. As the father is head of his own family, responsible for exercising control and authority over its members, so the chief is the 'father' of the entire tribe with reciprocal rights and duties in the economic, political and religious spheres knitting chief and tribesmen together.

The religious system of the Bantu is closely aligned with the kinship patterns which are based on seniority and hereditary status. These patterns are extended into the hereafter with dead ancestors believed to be leading the same sorts of existences as they did on earth. The ancestors are assumed to make certain demands, among them: they expect certain behaviour of their descendants in conformity with the tribal norms and they punish kinsmen for derelictions, and they demand regular offerings and sacrifices. The chief's ancestors are thought to exercise decisive influence not only over their immediate kinsmen, but, through them, over the entire tribe.[15]

The traditional Bantu economy is almost totally agricultural. Although cattle raising takes up a great deal of the time and resources of the tribe, it is primarily an uneconomic enterprise – cattle being valued more for their ritual than their economic uses. Most of the means for subsistence results from hoe cultivation of maize and kaffercorn by the women of the tribe. Although produced by most inefficient techniques, the tribe depends highly on these grains both for food and for beer, the latter having nutritional as well as ritual value.[16]

Before the coming of the European, education was an integral part of the Bantu social structure. If viewed only as the passing on of culture to new generations, the education of the Bantu child was efficient. The Eiselen Commission Report, which will be discussed later, devotes this one short summarizing paragraph to traditional education:

> Bantu traditional culture makes ample and sufficient provision for the education of its youth. Each social institution inculcated the attitudes, emotions, and values which were important to its continuance and preservation. The family developed character, religious attitudes and knowledge of technical and economic matters. The local and tribal organization developed a knowledge of and a care

[14] Interview with Xhosa initiates at Ncera in Middledrift District of Alice, Cape Province, August 12, 1964. Interpreter, Victor Gitywa, curator of the museum at Fort Hare University College.

[15] Hoernle and Hellmann, op. cit., p. 35.

[16] Union of South Africa, Summary of the Report of the Commission for Socio-Economic Development of the Bantu Areas Within the Union of South Africa, U.G. 61/1955, Pretoria, Government Printer, 1955, p. 3.

for matters on a wider scale. The numerous rites which marked the growth and development of the individual from birth to death not merely affirmed certain ideas and values but created them in the minds of the participants. There was thus a harmony between the values and patterns expressed in the life of tribal institutions and the lessons which the individual learnt in his progress upwards in the hierarchy of tribal life.[17]

Bantu traditional society and the character of Bantu education have been greatly changed by the influence of the European. The geographic expansion of the White population has resulted in the concentration of many Bantu into legally defined reserve areas where the traditional Bantu agricultural techniques have devastated much of the land. At the same time, attitudes of the Bantu under European influence are becoming more materialistic. This change has resulted, in part, from the development of a system of migratory labour, which has, at the same time, worked toward the destruction of the traditional social patterns of the Bantu.

B. Bantu Education Under the Missionaries

Despite increasing social and economic disruption, formal education for Bantu children was first established for the primary purpose of Christianizing him rather than for helping him adapt to his changing environment and his shifting social status. The general character of Bantu education under the missions was both paternalistic and sporadic in its growth – one of the greatest barriers to the expansion of mission education being the parsimonious attitude of subsidizing governmental agencies up until 1945.

The British colonial philosophy of guardianship included as a primary rule the conversion of the heathen to Christian convictions. At the same time, the Dutch Reformed Churches, while teaching racial inequality, nevertheless considered evangelization of the Bantu a basic social responsibility of the Afrikaner. Under these influences, the first school was established in the Cape in 1799; in Natal, in 1835; in the Transvaal, in 1842; and in the Free State in about 1833.[18]

The history of the Bantu mission schools is complex because of the number of administrative bodies involved. As a generalization, it can

---

[17] Union of South Africa, *Report of the Commission on Native Education, 1949–51*, pp. 12–13.
[18] *Ibid.*, p. 31.

be noted that there were few genuine attempts at systematically developing teacher-training facilities and school curricula or at financing programmes for the education of Bantu children. A limited number of outstanding mission schools are significant; particularly in the Cape where institutions such as Lovedale offered industrial-training and teacher-training as early as the 1840s.[19] Also, a few men and women had a vision of Bantu education that went beyond literacy levels sufficient for Bible reading. Sir George Grey, an early governor in the Cape, is an outstanding example of a person who had this vision.[20]

C. Some Origins and Developments until 1953

So far as academic standards are concerned, Horrell reports in *African Education*:

It would seem that in the mid-nineteenth century the standard of secular education provided at most of the mission schools then in existence was a very low one. In 1862 Dr. Langham Dale, the then Superintendent-General of Education in the Cape, found, as the result of a tour of inspection, that only five per cent of the African pupils in these schools had any useful knowledge of reading, writing, or arithmetic. Few of the teachers had passed even Standard IV. At outstations unqualified African assistants were in charge of so-called schools, with the nearest missionary some days' journey away. No school books were available in the African languages. There was sufficient school accommodation to admit only a very small fraction of the children of school-going age, and those who did attend came irregularly. Few of the pupils possessed any western clothes. Sir Thomas Muir, who succeeded Dr. Dale, found that 60 per cent of the African children at school were below Standard I. Mr Donald Ross, the then Inspector-General of the Schools in the Cape, reported that . . . [of the schools] . . . in the Colony that were attended exclusively or mainly by Africans, half could be closed without loss to educational advancement. Mr Ross submitted an excellent report on Lovedale, however, stating that it was 'probably the greatest educational establishment in South Africa'.[21]

While probably in all cases missionaries were personally convinced that their motives were unselfish in educating the Bantu, and while this unselfishness was most assuredly the case at times, denominational

---

[19] Horrell, Muriel (ed.), *African Education: Some Origins and Developments until 1953*, Johannesburg, South African Institute of Race Relations, 1963, p. 7.
[20] *Ibid.*, pp. 7–8.
[21] *Ibid.*, pp. 11–12.

rivalries and petty proselytizing were common. In 1906, the Superintendent-General of Education in the Cape deplored the denominational rivalry he observed among Bantu schools.[22] In a book published in 1917, C. T. Loram of the Native Affairs Commission wrote about the provinces in general:

> The jealousy and unedifying quarrels of missionaries of different denominations have brought their work into disrepute in many parts. Attempts at proselytizing are not unknown, and sometimes material advantages are offered to natives to induce them to join a particular church.[23]

Up until 1910, mission schools throughout South Africa were generally unco-ordinated, offering for the most part a European classical curriculum. Government financial assistance was universally poor.

After the Act of Union in 1910, Bantu education remained primarily a missionary undertaking. However, the Act declared the provinces responsible for the control and financing of Bantu education. In 1922, the Union government passed the Financial Relations Fourth Extension Act, which forbade the direct taxation of Bantu by the provinces. This taxation had been a primary source of the money used by the provinces for subsidizing the mission schools. To prevent the reduction of these subsidies, the Act provided central government grants to the provinces on the basis of the amounts that each province had spent for Bantu education in 1921–2. With a total of £340,000, the provincial breakdown was as follows: the Cape, £240,000; Natal, £49,000; Transvaal, £46,000; and Free State, £5,000. Although the 1922 Act did not prohibit provinces from spending additional money from general revenues, they now 'regarded the obligation to extend and develop native education as having been taken over by the Union Government'.[24]

That the Union Government was little more concerned about Bantu education than were the provinces is indicated by subsequent financial history. In 1925, the Union government passed an act establishing the Native Development Fund to provide for education, general advancement, and welfare of Africans. The Minister of Native Affairs was to decide how much of the money was to go to each province. The

[22] *Ibid.*, p. 14.
[23] Loram, C. T., *The Education of the South African Native*, 1917, p. 17 as quoted in *ibid.*, p. 15.
[24] Union of South Africa, *Report of the Interdepartmental Committee on Native Education, 1935–6*, U.G. 29/1936, Pretoria, Government Printer, 1936, para. 299.

£340,000 mentioned earlier was paid into this fund, along with one-fifth of the general tax paid by Africans – the other four-fifths remaining in the Consolidated Revenue Fund of the government.

The percentage of African tax paid into the Native Development Fund was gradually increased in the following sequence: seven-twentieths of the total tax in 1935; two-fifths in 1936; three-fifths in 1937; two-thirds in 1940; five-sixths in 1942; and finally the whole amount in 1943. In 1944, the total contribution of Bantu to the fund through their taxes was £1,459,831, while £340,000 continued to be the limit of the contribution from European taxes.[25]

The Native Education Commission of 1949–51, summarized the general deterioration under this financing scheme.

> The significance of these Acts of 1922 and 1925 was profound. The taxation of the Bantu had been changed from a provincial to a Union matter, and the provision of funds for Bantu education became entirely the responsibility of the Central Government. But the administration of education still remained with the provinces.
>
> Nevertheless, the most important change was the acceptance by implication of the principle that any development or extension of Bantu education beyond the standard reached in 1921–22 should be financed out of direct taxation paid by the Bantu.
>
> The period 1926–45 was marked by increasing financial difficulty due to the operation of a number of factors over which the Native Affairs Commission had no control. The Bantu population was increasing at the rate of 1·95 per cent per annum (compound interest), growing from 5,225,100 in 1925 to 7,686,000 in 1945. The years from 1927 to 1931 were marked by a sharp drop in the national income. The urbanization of the Bantu was taking place at a rapid pace; the number of Bantu classified as urban in 1921 was 587,000; by 1946 this figure had risen to 1,794,212. This urbanization was accompanied by all the usual maladjustments of people: overcrowding, shortage of housing, the breakdown of family control and the consequent cry for more schools in the urban areas to combat neglect of children and juvenile delinquency. In short, the desires for education by the Bantu and their needs for education grew far more rapidly than the funds available under Act No. 41 of 1925.[26]

During the years 1925 to 1935, the number of Bantu children in school increased by nearly 75 per cent, while during the same period of

[25] Horrell, op. cit., p. 31.
[26] Union of South Africa, Report of the Commission on Native Education, 1949–51, p. 37.

time expenditures on their education rose only 50 per cent.[27] As a result of this deterioration, the government appointed a committee in 1935 (Interdepartmental Committee on Native Education) to study the situation. In its report, the Committee recommended that the Union government finance Bantu education on the same basis as White education; that is, on the basis of 110 per cent of the children in attendance the previous year. A per capita annual grant of £3 12s 9d was recommended[28] – a 41·3 per cent immediate increase in expenditure.[29]

TABLE I   ANNUAL PER PUPIL EXPENDITURE ON EDUCATION IN SOUTH AFRICA FOR SELECTED YEARS DURING THE PERIOD 1930–45, BY RACIAL CLASSIFICATION

		Racial Classification	
Year	Whites	Coloureds and Asians	Bantu
1930	£22.12. 0	£4.12.3	£2. 2. 8
1935	£23.17. 2	£5. 4.1	£1.18. 6
1940	£25.14. 2	£5.15.6	£2. 4. 4
1945	£38. 5.10	£10.16.2	£3.17.10

Source: National Bureau of Educational and Social Research, *Bulletin of Educational Statistics for the Union of South Africa, 1947*, Pretoria, Government Printer, 1948.

In 1945, action was finally taken on the Committee's recommendation. An act was passed declaring that increased expenditure on Bantu education would no longer be limited by the amount of taxes taken from the Bantu. Each year the Parliament would determine the allocation which would then be taken entirely from the Consolidated Revenue Fund. Under the new system, £4,747,657 was voted for Bantu education in 1949 – under the old system the amount would have been only £1,540,000.[30] The expenditure continued to rise until it reached £7,856,194 in 1953–4.[31]

Since the passage of the Bantu Education Act of 1953 the Central Government, as will be discussed further at a later point, has reverted

[27] Woolheim, Oscar D., 'Crisis in Native Education: The Present Position', *Race Relations Journal*, Vol. 10, No. 2, 1943, p. 2.
[28] The corresponding grant for white children was £20 (Union of South Africa, *Report of the Interdepartmental Committee on Native Education*, 1935–6, paras. 304–5, p. 60).
[29] Union of South Africa, *Report of the Commission on Native Education*, 1949–51, p. 42.
[30] *Ibid.*, p. 38.
[31] Horrell, *op. cit.*, p. 33.

TABLE 2 ANNUAL PER CAPITA EXPENDITURE ON EDUCATION
IN SOUTH AFRICA FOR SELECTED YEARS DURING THE
PERIOD 1930–45, BY RACIAL CLASSIFICATION

		Racial Classification	
Year	Whites	Coloureds and Asians	Bantu
1930	£4.13.2	£0.10. 5	£0.2. 1
1935	£4.14.7	£0.16.10	£0.2. 0
1940	£4.19.5	£0.18.11	£0.2.11
1945	£7. 4.7	£1.19. 8	£0.6. 0

Source: National Bureau of Educational and Social Research, *Bulletin of Educational Statistics for the Union of South Africa, 1947*, Pretoria, Government Printer, 1948.

to the old principle of a fixed government expenditure for Bantu education.

D. APARTHEID AND THE PRESENT SYSTEM OF
BANTU EDUCATION

In preparation for an examination of Bantu education today, it is necessary to pull the historical developments which have been considered into focus on the current Bantu education policies of the Nationalist government. This can be done through the examination of three recent events:

(i) the formal development of the 'Christian-National Education' concepts of the leadership of the Afrikaner community

(ii) the report on Bantu education prepared by the Eiselen Commission at the request of the government, and

(iii) the stated Bantu education policy of the Nationalist government.

1. *Christian-National Education*

The *Christelik-Nasionale Onderwys Beleid* (Christian-National Education Policy) has its origin in a national conference in 1939 of the *Federasie van Afrikaanse Kultuurvereniginge* (F.A.F.), an influential Afrikaner social organization.[32] At the conference, the Institute of Christian-National Education (I.C.N.E.) was organized to insure 'the continual propaga-

[32] Translated: Federation of Afrikaans Cultural Societies (F.A.C.S.).

tion and furtherance of the historically-developed ideal of Christian and National education and for insuring that the general lines of policy laid down . . . [by the Institute] . . . should find acceptance in a systematic way.'[33]

Ten years after its establishment, the executive committee of the Institute published its policy statement. According to the preface of the publication, written by the Chairman of the F.A.C.S., the policy as presented had been endorsed by all Afrikaans organizations that are connected with education. Van Rooy writes as follows:

> Various drafts of this policy were considered by the full Institute, all the executive bodies of the F.A.C.S., and all the bodies and institutions represented in the I.C.N.E. and the F.A.C.S., and that *means all the Afrikaans bodies and institutions which are in some degree interested in education*. The document in its present form has therefore been approved of by the whole of Afrikanerdom in so far as it is represented in its organized ranks in the F.A.C.S.[34]

Perhaps more indicative of the totally Afrikaner-oriented nature of this educational policy is the dedication that was written by the Executive of the I.C.N.E. Appearing on the front page of the booklet is this dedication:

> . . . to all the men and women who work with love and devotion for the education of the youth of our people and who wish to be true to the ideal of handing over unspoilt to the younger generation all that is good and pure and noble in our people's past and of helping to build on the foundation of our people's history the future of the Boer nation.[35]

There is, of course, nothing historically surprising about this total devotion of preserving the Afrikaner 'nation'. It is fully consistent with the early development of bitterness between English-speaking and Afrikaans-speaking White South Africans and, at the same time, with the related struggle for the recognition of the Afrikaans language. However, the approach toward the effort to preserve the nationalism of the Afrikaner people as it is found in Christian-National Education was somewhat new and proved to have profound effects on Bantu education.

Part 1, Article 1 of the C.N.E. policy statement is a summary of the

[33] Federation of Afrikaans Cultural Societies, *Christian-National Education Policy*; drawn up and published by the Institute for Christian-National Education, Johannesburg, F.A.C.S., 1949, p. 2.
[34] *Ibid.* (Italics added.)
[35] *Ibid.*, p. 1.

premises upon which the total policy was formulated. While these premises are related directly to the education of Afrikaans-speaking children, it is quoted at length because the same premises are established for Bantu education later in the statement.

> . . . Afrikaans-speaking children . . . must be educated on the basis of the Christian-National view of life and the world of our nation. In this view of life and the world, the Christian and National principles are of fundamental significance, and their object is the propagation, protection and development of the Christian and National nature and character of our nation. The Christian foundation of this view of life and the world is *based on Holy Scripture and formulated in the Articles of Faith of our three Afrikaans churches*. By the National principle we mean *love for everything that is our own*, with special reference to our country, our language, our history and our culture. We believe that both these principles must be applied to the full in the education of our children, so that these two principles may be characteristics of the whole school as regards its spirit, aim, curriculum, method, discipline, staff, organization and all its activities. Corresponding to the basic structure of our Christian-National life and world view, the National principle must always be under the guidance of the Christian principle: the National must grow on the Christian foundation.[36]

The serious student of education in South Africa, Bantu or otherwise, should study in detail the I.C.N.E. policy statement. Limitations of space for this discussion, however, necessitate consideration only of the specific reference to Bantu education in Part II, Article 15. In order to avoid misinterpretation, this article is reproduced in its entirety.

> We believe that the calling and task of white South Africa with respect to the native is to christianise [*sic*] him and to assist him culturally, and that this calling and task has already found its clearly defined expression in the [three] principles of [:] guardianship, no levelling, and segregation. Therefore we believe that any system of education of the native should be based on these three principles. In accordance with these principles we believe that the education of the native should be based on the life and world view of the European, more particularly that of the Boer nation as the senior European guardian of the native, and that the native should be led to a *mutatis mutandis* but independent acceptance of the Christian and National principles in education, as these principles are more fully described in the foregoing articles 1, 2, and 3. We believe also

[36] *Ibid.*, p. 2.

that the mother-tongue is the basis of native education, but that the two official languages of the country should be learned as subjects because they are the official languages of the country and are for the native the key to that 'culture-adoption' which is necessary for his own cultural advancement. Because of the cultural immaturity of the native we believe that it is the right and duty of the State in co-operation with the Christian Protestant [sic] churches to provide for and control native education. We believe however, that the education of the native and the training of native teachers should be under-taken by the natives themselves as soon as possible, but under the control and guidance of the state; with this proviso, however, that the financing of native education be placed on such a basis that it does not take place at the cost of European education. We believe finally that native education should lead to the development of an independent self-supporting and self-providing native community on a Christian-National basis.[37]

Both the definition of 'Christian' in terms of Afrikaner concepts of Christianity and the definition of 'nation' purely in terms of the Boer nation appear to preclude the participation of the predominantly Anglican, English-speaking White. Afrikaner Calvinism, in turn teaching God-ordained racial inequality along with the concept of Afrikaner guardianship, logically led to the formulation of some type of separate educational programme for the Bantu.

Briefly summarizing C.N.E. policy as it applies to Bantu education, it should be emphasized that the primary element of Bantu education, according to C.N.E., is to be a *mutatis mutandis* form of 'Christianity' and of 'Nationalism'. Unlike the mission schools in 1949, where an official language replaced the mother-tongue after the first three or four years of a child's education, instruction must be in the vernacular throughout primary and secondary schools. Both Afrikaans and English are to be taught as subjects; and again this was contrary to the curriculum policies of most mission schools in 1949.

The state has the 'right and duty' to control Bantu education; whereas, in 1949 the provinces had control.[38] While the policy includes support for a more active participation of Bantu in the control of their children's education and in the education of the Bantu teachers, the state maintains general control and guidance. State finance of Bantu education is to be limited in that it must never be at the expense of 'European education'.

[37] *Ibid.*, pp. 14–15.
[38] *Ibid.*, p. 10. It might be argued that the use of the term 'state' implies inclusion of provinces. In Part 1, Article 7, however, the state and province are clearly con-sidered separate entities.

2. *The Eiselen Commission Report*

Shortly after the Nationalist government under the leadership of Malan took office in 1948, it became clear that 'Christian-National education' had official support. A commission was appointed by the Governor-General, G. B. van Zyl, to study the existing system of Bantu education from the standpoints of its value to the Bantu, the country as a whole, and the maintenance of desirable race relations.[39] The chairman of the Commission, W. W. M. Eiselen, had been Chief Inspector of Native Education for the Transvaal and was Professor of Social Anthropology at the University of Pretoria in 1949. He was later appointed Secretary for Native Affairs.[40] The remaining seven members of the Commission had had extensive experience in Bantu education.

After three years, the Commission presented its findings and recommendations to the government as a 233-page report. The Report is divided into three parts:

(i) 'The Bantu and the Present System of Education',

(ii) 'Critical Appraisal of the Present System of Bantu Education', and

(iii) 'Proposals and Recommendations'.[41]

In large part, the recommendations of the Eiselen Commission have become subsequently the blueprint for the government's system of Bantu education. For this reason, the Commission's report must be considered in some detail.

It was the conclusion of the Commission that the education of Bantu children in mission schools had, for the most part, proved totally inadequate. Bantu education had 'no organic unity' and it was 'split into a bewildering number of different agencies'.[42] Further, the Commission concluded that Bantu education was 'conducted without the active participation of the Bantu as a people, either locally or on a wider basis'; and financing was handled in such a way that it achieved 'a minimum of educational effect on the Bantu community'.[43] By this

---

[39] South African Bureau of Racial Affairs, *The Commission on Native Education (1949–51), Summary of Findings and Recommendations*, Stellenbosch, S.A.B.R.A., 1952, p. 2.

[40] Hartshorne, K. B., *Native Education in the Union of South Africa: A Summary of the Report of the Native Education in South Africa* – U.G. 54/1951, Eiselen, Johannesburg, South African Institute of Race Relations, 1953, p. 1.

[41] Union of South Africa, *Report of the Commission on Native Education, 1949–51*, pp. 3–5.

[42] *Ibid.*, para. 752.

[43] *Ibid.*

latter point the Commission meant that the Bantu had no sense of contributing financially to their own educational advancement.

The general conclusion of the Commission was that Bantu education needed statewide planning and control which would develop schools whose functions were closely related to an overall government programme for the social and economic development of the Bantu community in South Africa. The European-type schools which the churches had established for the Bantu, the Commission concluded, are schools 'which are concerned primarily, not with reinforcing or being reinforced by other social institutions of Bantu society, but more largely with the transmission of ideas, values, attitudes, and skills which have not been developed in Bantu society itself and are often not in harmony with its institutions'.[44]

In developing Bantu education the government should follow, according to the Commission, eleven 'guiding principles' which have been summarized as follows:

(i) Bantu education must be broadly conceived so that it can be organized to provide adequate schools 'with a definite Christian character', along with social institutions to harmonize with the schools.

(ii) Bantu education should be planned and administered by a government department 'to secure efficient and thorough co-ordination of planning . . .'.

(iii) '[Bantu] education must be co-ordinated with a definite and carefully planned policy for the development of Bantu societies', with special emphasis on economic development.

(iv) 'Increased emphasis must be placed on the education of the mass of the Bantu to enable them to co-operate in the evolution of new social patterns and institutions'.

(v) The Bantu languages must be developed to include both terminologies for expressing modern scientific concepts, and also to include more effective numerical systems.

(vi) The limited funds available for Bantu education must be 'spread . . . as far as is consistent with efficiency'.

(vii) '[Bantu] schools must be linked as closely as possible with existing Bantu social institutions, and a friendly though not necessarily uncritical attitude maintained between the school and these institutions'.

(viii) 'The mother-tongue should be used as the medium of instruction for at least the duration of the primary school'. As the languages are developed, 'they should in increasing measure be recognized as

[44] *Ibid.*, para. 759.

media of instruction'. The importance of this lies in the positive contribution which the schools can make in the development of the Bantu languages both for their own use and for other institutions of Bantu life, e.g., Bantu Courts and Councils'.

(ix) 'Bantu personnel should be used to the maximum to make the schools as Bantu in spirit as possible as well as to provide employment'.

(x) 'Bantu parents should as far as practicable have a share in the control and life of the schools'.

(xi) 'The schools should provide for the maximum development of the Bantu individual, mentally, morally and spiritually'.[45]

In line with these guiding principles, the Commission recommended that the central government establish a framework to administer Bantu education as well as Bantu development generally. The intent, however, was not to exclude the Bantu people from the administration or finance of their own education. Local authorities made up of the 'local chief (if any), and elected and nominated members', would collect Bantu taxes and use this revenue, along with a 'fixed scale' government subsidy, to administer all local services including primary education.[46] More broadly based Bantu Regional Authorities and Boards of Education would handle the 'conduct of secondary education in their particular region'.[47]

With strong emphasis being placed initially on the attainment of universal Bantu literacy, and, thus, on the primary schools, the Commission recommended a tri-level school system:

(i) a lower primary school to provide a minimum of literacy for all children;

(ii) a higher primary school which will serve not merely to continue the work of the lower primary school but will sort out the children most suited for further education and begin to guide them in appropriate directions;

(iii) a series of post-primary schools whose functions will vary but which will provide the types of educated Bantu necessary for the development of Bantu society.[48]

The proposed lower primary school would correspond with Substandards A and B, and Standards I and II, of the educational system being used when the Commission was writing.

These schools would concentrate on the tool subjects (three R's) and would to a large extent cover the work at present done in the Sub-

45 *Ibid.*, para. 766.
46 *Ibid.*, para. 789.
47 *Ibid.*, para. 822.
48 *Ibid.*, para. 847.

standards and in Standards I and II. Promotion would be automatic provided an adequate attendance by the pupil can be shown. . . . Admission would be limited in each class to a number of pupils with which the teacher could cope satisfactorily. It should be emphasized that the idea to be aimed at in these schools should be that every pupil admitted to Sub-standard A will remain in school until he or she has completed Standard II. Some means should therefore be devised by the authorities whereby while admissions will remain voluntary, attendance could be made compulsory.[49]

The Commission's purpose for proposing both automatic promotion and compulsory attendance for those admitted to the lower primary school was to accelerate the movement toward a high percentage of minimum literacy among the Bantu. According to the statistics for 1949, approximately two-thirds of the children who start school drop out by Standard II.

The curriculum for the lower primary school should include, in addition to the 'three R's' the teaching of one official language 'on a purely utilitarian basis, that is, as a medium of oral expression of thought to be used in contacts with the European section of the population'.[50] In addition, religious instruction, practical hygiene, handwork, and recreation should be included. 'An interest in the soil and in the observation of natural phenomena' should be stimulated.[51]

At the completion of Standard II, students 'should be tested in order to determine whether they have made sufficient progress to be able to benefit by the following course', that is, higher primary school.[52] In Standards III and IV, the Bantu child should continue with the subjects studied in the lower primary school. In addition to these subjects, history and geography should be studied along with 'gardening and agriculture'.[53] The instruction in the use of the official language begun in the lower primary school should be expanded to include the 'reading and writing of simple letters'.[54] In addition, a 'beginning might be made with the teaching of the second official language on a practical and oral basis'.[55]

The Commission believed that two educational tracks, one academic and one vocational, should be developed beginning with Standard V.

[49] *Ibid.*, para. 851.
[50] *Ibid.*, para. 853.
[51] *Ibid.*
[52] *Ibid.*, para. 852.
[53] *Ibid.*, para. 854.
[54] *Ibid.*
[55] *Ibid.*

. . . a careful study of the pupil's aptitudes should enable the teacher, in consultation with the Inspector of the Schools, to determine whether the pupil concerned would benefit by a continuation of the more academic education or whether his education for the following two years should have a more practical basis.

It should be clearly understood that manipulative skills and agriculture will still be taught in the academic classes and academic subjects in the classes with a vocational bias. . . . In practice it would probably mean that while the academic group would devote two-thirds of their time to academic and one-third to practical subjects, the position in the vocational group would be reversed to one-third for academic and two-thirds for vocational subjects.[56]

At the end of the higher primary school, two Standard VI examinations would be given, one with an academic, the other with a vocational bias.[57] Those students who pass the examinations will be given certificates which will qualify them, regardless of whether they have taken the vocational or the academic courses, 'to proceed to any of the post primary courses provided by the Department'. The natural assumption, however, 'would be that the pupil with the academic bias would enter high, polytechnic or [teacher] training schools, while the pupil with vocational bias would find his way into vocational schools'.[58]

Because of the conviction that the Reserves must provide the nucleus of Bantu development, agriculture and handwork are emphasized by the Commission throughout its report. It is believed that every possible attempt should be made to incorporate agricultural education effectively in the curricula of the various types of schools.

Your Commission is satisfied that some or other form of soil cultivation (gardening, agriculture or forestry) can make a valuable contribution to the education of the Bantu, not only because of its general educational value, but because of this knowledge in after-school life could exercise a tremendous influence on problems which affect the very economic existence of the Bantu. In this connection we think, e.g., of problems such as soil conservation, crop rotation, tree planting, over-grazing and the production of foodstuffs which will make it possible for the Bantu to eat a balanced diet. If the school can only get the child to absorb these lessons, the Bantu will within a generation or so devote attention to the matter not because of compulsion but of conviction.[59]

[56] *Ibid.*, paras. 855–6.
[57] *Ibid.*, para. 857.
[58] *Ibid.*, para. 858.
[59] *Ibid.*, para. 930.

The emphasis placed on handwork is with the hope that labour-intensive cottage industries will develop in Bantu areas. Instruction in handwork is suggested to develop the necessary skills and attitudes among the Bantu:

> ... handwork in the first four years of school should aim at the establishment of: (i) the habit of doing manual work; and (ii) the necessary correlation between the hand, the eye and the brain which leads to manual dexterity; ... thereafter more attention should gradually be paid to the practical use and economic value of the articles made by the pupils.[60]

Along with agriculture and handwork, very strong emphasis is placed on religious instruction.

Your Commission recommends—
(a) that religious instruction should be made a compulsory subject in all schools, including primary, secondary, and training schools; (b) that a definite time allotment be made for instruction in this subject apart from the time taken up by the opening exercises; (c) that inspectors and supervisors be expected to regard this subject as a compulsory school subject; to inspect the work done in this connection, to hear lessons and to report on the quality of the work being done; (d) that principals be expected to ensure that the subject is treated throughout the school on an equal footing with the other content subjects as an internal examination subject; (e) that, in consultation with religious bodies, a three-fold curriculum should be drawn up; (i) for the lower primary school; (ii) for the higher primary school and (iii) for post-primary education.[61]

The Commission suggests three types of qualifications for Bantu teachers:
(i) The Bantu Primary Lower Certificate
(ii) the Bantu Primary Higher Certificate, and
(iii) a post-matriculation diploma or a qualification connected with a [university] degree.[62]
The Bantu Primary Lower Certificate would require a three-year course, the entrance qualification being a Standard VI Certificate. Being geared toward the preparation of teachers for the lower primary school, after one year of academic study, candidates would be given two years of work with emphasis being 'placed on the principles and methods of teaching the "tool" subjects in their initial stages'.[63]

[60] *Ibid.*, para. 932.
[61] *Ibid.*, paras. 926–7.
[62] *Ibid.*, paras. 867–71.
[63] *Ibid.*, para. 868.

The Bantu Primary Higher Certificate would be a two-year course requiring a Junior Certificate for admission. Being geared toward the preparation of teachers for the higher primary school, the first year would be geared toward teaching 'the general principles and methods of education'.[64] In the second year, there would be some specialization in that 'females would . . . be trained specially for work in Standards III and IV while males would normally be trained for teaching the upper classes (V and VI)'.[65]

Little is said about the post-matriculation diploma other than that 'such courses might be conducted by existing universities and colleges, which cater specially for Bantu students, with a subsidy from the Department of Bantu Education'.[66] The Commission deals in a very general way with vocational schools, polytechnic schools, adult education programmes, special schools for physically handicapped children, and reformatories.[67] Two general conclusions are made about these schools: this area of education needs to be greatly expanded, and development in this area needs to be closely co-ordinated with a general socio-economic development plan and therefore should fall under the control of the proposed Division of Bantu Affairs.

All types of post-matriculation training, *even though this be undertaken by universities or university colleges,* should be planned in conjunction with the development plans. For this reason the subsidization of these institutions should be undertaken and controlled by the Department of Bantu Education, which will be responsible for the effective spending of public funds.[68]

Relative to the entire report of the Commission, very little is said about universities. The South African Native College,[69] located at the town of Fort Hare, which is in the eastern part of the Cape Province, was the only university-level Bantu institution at the time of the Eiselen study. External examinations were given to the students at the College under the auspices of the University of South Africa – a degree-granting correspondence institution. In addition, some of the White universities admitted a few Bantu students. The Commission recognized a need for increasing the number of Bantu who do university-level study.

[64] *Ibid.,* para. 869.
[65] *Ibid.*
[66] *Ibid.,* para. 871.
[67] *Ibid.,* paras. 872–87.
[68] *Ibid.,* para. 876. (Italics added.)
[69] Now called the University College of Fort Hare.

Bantu university education is still in its very early stages. The number of full-time Bantu students at the S.A. Native College, Fort Hare, in 1948 was 226. All told the number of full-time Bantu students at all university institutions was approximately 400, a very small number when compared with the Bantu population or even with the Bantu school population. There does not seem to be an over-production of university graduates. One of the chief avenues of employment for graduates is the teaching profession and there is a definite shortage of qualified graduate Bantu teachers in secondary, high and training schools. . . . The importance of university education for the Bantu cannot be over-emphasized, both to provide general education for leaders and to provide high grade technical men for their future economic and social development.[70]

Regarding the financing of Bantu education the Commission believed that the initial objective of the Bantu Education Department should be 'to provide by 1959 sufficient places in the first four classes of primary school to accommodate the estimated number of children in the Bantu population in the age group 8 to 11 years, inclusive'.[71] Fulfilling this objective would require:

(i) expansion in buildings and equipment for lower primary school

(ii) the training of increased numbers of Bantu teachers

(iii) the provision of facilities in the higher primary school 'for the increased number of children . . . [who] . . . will attend beyond the first four years', and

(iv) the provision of post-primary schools, i.e., academic high schools and vocational and polytechnic schools.[72]

Consideration of the means for financing even this initial step for increasing Bantu literacy brings the Commission to the question of the responsibility of the Bantu people for financing their own educational programme. More specifically, the question is: How shall the cost be apportioned between the Bantu local authority and the state?

In accordance with your Commission's recommendation that the Bantu local authorities should be set up and that a part of their responsibility should be the local administration and financing of schools under the regulations of the Bantu Education Department, it becomes necessary to examine the question of the proportions in which the State and the local authority should contribute to educational finance.[73]

[70] Ibid., paras. 708–9.
[71] Ibid., para. 1,031.
[72] Ibid.
[73] Ibid., para. 1,037.

The Commission points out that the direct contribution of Bantu taxes to the revenue of the central government has increased at a slower rate than Bantu population. Because of their low productivity levels, and therefore income, the Commission concludes that the Bantu are unable to shoulder a significant share of the cost of their own education.[74] This is considered an unhealthy situation because the Commission believes that the Bantu cannot fully appreciate an educational system that they themselves are not financing.

Bantu taxes, it is concluded, cannot be significantly increased until the development programme has increased Bantu incomes considerably. For this reason, in the early stages, the state will have to cover most of the cost for Bantu education as a 'pump-priming' measure.

> Your Commission does not hold the view that the Bantu should be solely responsible for the financing of their education but it does feel that the Bantu should play a direct part in the finding of a certain proportion of the funds used for that purpose.[75] . . . The contributions of each local authority should be clearly accounted for in the system of finance and the system should be designed to encourage local initiative and contributions.
>
> For a number of years, until the general development plan has had its effect, the contribution of the local authorities or communities will decline proportionately. . . . The extra contribution of the State will in effect constitute an investment or 'pump-priming'.[76]

The lengthy consideration of the Eiselen Commission Report has been necessary because the policies suggested in it, the vast majority of which have been adopted, clearly reflect the attitudes of the Nationalist government toward Bantu education.

3. The Tomlinson Commission and the Transkei

The appointment of the Commission for the Socio-Economic Development of the Bantu Areas within the Union of South Africa (the Tomlinson Commission) was a major step toward the implementation of the Eiselen recommendations. The Tomlinson Report, presented to the government in 1954, recommended that the Bantu reserves be developed so that territorial segregation might be increased to the

[74] *Ibid.*, para. 1,027.
[75] *Ibid.*
[76] *Ibid.*, para. 1,029.

limit set by the needs of industry in White areas for Bantu labour.[77] In essence, the Tomlinson Commission recommended the establishment of a South African federation of Black and White states. Having accepted in large part the Commission's plan, the government established the first *Bantustan*, or 'self-governing homeland', with the passage of the Transkei Constitution Act of 1963.

An area about the size of Denmark and located on the southeastern coast of the Republic, the Transkei is the home area of the Xhosa, as well as of smaller tribal groups.[78] The Transkei Constitution Act established a Legislative Assembly composed of sixty-four chiefs and forty-five members chosen by an electorate composed of all Bantu adults who fall in any one of three categories: (i) those who were born in the Transkei, (ii) those who have lived there for at least five years, (iii) those who, while living outside the Transkei, are members of tribes resident there.[79] The Assembly has been empowered to elect a cabinet consisting of a Chief Minister who also acts as Minister of Finance, plus Ministers of Justice, the Interior, Education, Agriculture and Forestry, and Roads and Works.

The Transkei is by no means politically autonomous. All acts passed by the Assembly must receive the assent of the State President of the Republic and the Republican Parliament retains complete control of matters concerning defence, external affairs, internal security, postal and related services, railways, immigration, currency, banking, customs, and excise, and the amending of the Transkeian constitution. Of especial importance, however, is the fact that education matters have been transferred to the Transkei Legislative Assembly. For an interim period the Transkei Constitution Act provided for a White Secretary for Education, 'seconded by the Republican government but responsible to the Transkei Minister of Education'.[80] The debate at the first session of the Assembly indicated that some significant changes in the areas of instruction-medium and syllabi might be expected.

[77] Union of South Africa, *Summary of the Report of the Commission for Socio-Economic Development of the Bantu Areas Within the Union of South Africa*, U.G. 61/1955, Pretoria, Government Printer, 1955, p. xviii.
[78] South African Department of Information, *The Transkei: Emancipation Without Chaos*, 1963, p. 2.
[79] Horrell, Muriel, *Legislation and Race Relations*, Johannesburg, South African Institute of Race Relations, 1963, p. 17.
It was reported that 880,425 people registered during the designated period from June 17 through August 17, 1963. Of these registrants who constituted some 90 per cent of those persons eligible, 270,000 resided outside the Transkei (Horrell, Muriel, 'The New Look in African Reserves', *A Survey of Race Relations in South Africa*, Johannesburg, Institute of Race Relations, 1963, p. 17).
[80] Horrell, Muriel, *A Decade of Bantu Education*, Johannesburg, South African Institute of Race Relations, 1964, p. 42.

4. *The Stated Bantu Education Policy of the Nationalist Government*

With the passage of the Bantu Education Act of 1953, the Nationalist government embarked on a course which has followed quite closely the one mapped out by the Eiselen Commission and further refined by the Tomlinson Commission.

Perhaps the clearest general statement of the nature of this course was made by H. F. Verwoerd before the Senate in 1954. As Minister of Native Affairs, Verwoerd had become, with the passage of the 1953 Act, head of the government department in control of Bantu education.

> It is the policy of my department that [Bantu] education should have its roots entirely in the Native areas and in the Native environment and Native community. There Bantu education must be able to give itself complete expression and there it will have to perform its real service. The Bantu must be guided to serve his own community in all respects. There is no place for him in the European community above the level of certain forms of labour. Within his own community, however, all doors are open. For that reason it is of no avail for him to receive a training which has as its aim absorption in the European community while he cannot and will not be absorbed there. Up till now he has been subjected to a school system which drew him away from his own community and practically misled him by showing him the green pastures of the European but still did not allow him to graze there. This attitude is not only uneconomic because money is spent on education which has no specific aim, but it is even dishonest to continue with it. The effect on the Bantu community we find in the much-discussed frustration of educated Natives who can find no employment which is acceptable to them. It is abundantly clear that unplanned education creates many problems, disrupts the communal life of the Bantu and endangers the communal life of the European.[81]

Several of the primary elements that have been discussed in connection with the development of South African society are clearly evident in this statement of policy. The Nationalist government not only views Bantu education within the context of the social segregation of Black and White but also views it as a means by which the Bantu child can be prepared for a life in a totally separate community – the community here being considered not only in the social but also in the geographic sense. At the same time, the reservation is made that 'certain forms of labour' are open to him in the European community – a reservation that is made because it is necessary for the continued prosperity of

[81] Union of South Africa, *Senate Debates*, Second Session, Eleventh Parliament, Fifth Senate, June 7 to June 11, 1954, cols. 2,595–622.

White industry. But essentially, the Bantu child is to be taught that he is a foreigner when he is in White South Africa.

Verwoerd's statement also makes it clear that he viewed the approach taken by the mission schools up to the time he was speaking as having been detrimental to Bantu interests. Earlier in his speech, Verwoerd had said that 'By simply blindly producing pupils who were trained in European ideas the idle hope was created that they [Bantu] could occupy positions in the European community in spite of the country's policy . . .' Previously the Bantu child had been taught 'European ideas'; now he was to be taught Bantu ideas.[82] Verwoerd saw this as consistent with the 'country's policy' of *apartheid*, a policy referred to with a revealing, but unstated, assumption that it is permanent in nature.

Clarifying even further the general policy of the Nationalist government concerning Bantu education, the then Secretary of Native Affairs and presently Minister of the Department of Bantu Education which was formed in 1958, made the following statement during the debate preceding the passage of the Bantu Education Act:

> . . . there are in South Africa today actually only two courses open. Actually there are only two possible trends of policy which can be followed in regard to the Native in general. One is the trend of liberalism which means uniform development. On the other hand, there is the trend adopted by the Nationalists which means development in their [the Bantu's] own sphere. On the one hand one has *liberalism* which *means nothing but intermingling*. On the other hand one has *nationalism which means segregation*. . . . The Nationalist Party's viewpoint is that the primary objective of education is not in the first place that the individual should be developed as an individual, but that the object of education should be to develop the individual as a member of society, so that he can take his rightful place within the society to which he belongs. Herein lies the fundamental difference between the liberalistic approach and the approach of nationalism. . . . *Native education is at present nothing less than an instrument in the hands of liberalism.* That is why, up to the present, *Native education has achieved nothing but the destruction of Bantu culture . . . nothing beyond succeeding in making the Native an imitation Westerner.*[83]

In August, 1953, the Bantu Education Bill had been presented to the House of Assembly of the Republic by the Minister of Native Affairs.[84] The Bill provided for the transfer of Bantu education, other

[82] *Ibid.*, col. 2,599.

[83] Union of South Africa, *House of Assembly Debates (Hansard)*, First Sitting, Eleventh Parliament. September 14 to September 18, 1953, cols. 3,611–12. (Italics added).

[84] Skinner, Joy, *Bantu Education: A Summary of Developments in the Field of Primary and Secondary Education and Teacher Training over a Ten-Year Period, 1949–59*, Durban. Institute of Race Relations, 1960, p. 1.

than higher education and education for handicapped children, from the provinces to the Union Department of Native Affairs.[85] In the Bill, it was proposed that there be three categories of Bantu schools:

(i) Bantu Community schools, established by local authorities, tribes, or communities and subsidized by the government where approved.

(ii) Government Bantu schools, established by the government or taken over from the provinces.

(iii) state-aided Bantu schools, including mission schools.[86]

It was specified that schools falling under the third category, state-aided Bantu schools, could not be granted subsidies by the Minister of Native Affairs unless he consulted with the local Bantu community concerned.[87] Furthermore, from a date to be set by the Minister, no school could continue to operate, or no new school could be established, unless it had made application for and had been granted 'registration' by the Minister.[88]

Under the twelfth clause, the Minister is granted the power to establish various types of Bantu and White advisory boards and councils on the national, regional, or local level.[89] As far as government schools were concerned, the Bill provided that the Minister might, if he wished, transfer control to a Local Authority.[90]

For all purposes, Clause 15 of the Bill grants the Minister total control of all aspects of Bantu education. This clause includes a long list of specific powers relative to government schools, for example, conditions for appointment of teachers, determination of the medium of instruction, conditions for the admission or expulsion of pupils. For the other two categories of schools – the Bantu Community and the state-aided Bantu – the Minister is granted the power to determine the conditions

---

[85] The definition of higher education in the Bantu Education Act is taken from the Financial Relations Consolidation and Amendment Act, 1955. Higher education is there defined to include 'education provided by Universities and the University College of Fort Hare; education provided by certain schools of art, mining, music, pharmacy, agriculture and nautical training; vocational education; education for persons who are not compelled to attend school; education for the training of secondary and nursery school teachers; any other education which is declared to be higher education' (Davis, Gordon, *Urban Native Law*, Acts and Regulations reproduced under Government Printer's Copyright Authority, Port Elizabeth, Grotius Publications, 1959, p. 293).

[86] Union of South Africa, *Bantu Education Act*, No. 47 of 1953, amended; as reproduced in Davis, Gordon, *Urban Native Law*, Acts and Regulations reproduced under Government Printer's Copyright Authority, Port Elizabeth, Grotius Publications, 1959, pp. 558–64.

[87] *Ibid.*, p. 560.

[88] *Ibid.*, pp. 560–1.

[89] *Ibid.*, p. 562.

[90] *Ibid.*

which must exist before subsidies will be granted by the government.[91] The intent of Clause 15 becomes doubly clear as far as government schools are concerned, with a final provision that reads as follows:

> The minister may from time to time make regulations . . . providing generally for *any other matter* relating to the establishment, maintenance, management and control of Government Bantu schools or which the Minister may deem necessary or expedient to prescribe for achieving the purposes of this Act, the generality of the powers conferred by this paragraph not being limited by the provisions of the preceding paragraphs.[92]

5. *The Administrative Structure of Bantu Education*

Following the passage of the Bantu Education Act, the control of Bantu education, on January 1, 1954, passed to the newly-formed Division of Bantu Education of the Department of Native Affairs.[93] Verwoerd appointed F. J. de Villiers, previously Chief Inspector of Native Education in the Cape, as Under-Secretary for Native Affairs in charge of the Division of Bantu Education. J. H. van Dyk was appointed to be de Villiers' assistant, and P. A. W. Cook, his professional adviser. Regional Directors were appointed for the Transkei,[94] the Ciskei,[95] and Western Cape, Natal, Transvaal, and Orange Free State.[96] The Department of Native Affairs proved to be too large for efficient operation, however, and was divided to form two separate Departments after the general election of 1958 – the Department of Bantu Administration and Development, and the Department of Bantu Education.[97]

As with other Ministers, there is a Secretary and a Deputy Secretary working under the Minister of Bantu Education.[98] In addition, there

---

[91] *Ibid.*, p. 560.

[92] *Ibid.*

[93] Department of Information, 'Education for the Bantu of South Africa', reprint from *Lantern* (n.d.), p. 7.

[94] The control of education in the Transkei subsequently has been transferred to the Transkei Legislative Assembly.

[95] A large reserve located in the eastern part of the Cape.

[96] Skinner, *op. cit.*, p. 2. Subsequent events have caused a redefinition of the regions as is indicated by the organization chart on p. 70

[97] Sneesby, G. W., 'Problems of Bantu Education', reprint from *Grocott's Daily Mail*, July 25, 1960, p. 1.

[98] Horrell, Muriel, *A Decade of Bantu Education*, Johannesburg, Institute of Race Relations, 1964, p. 42.

THE ADMINISTRATIVE STRUCTURE OF BANTU EDUCATION
Central Organization at Head Office

Minister
Secretary
Deputy Secretary

Chief: Planning and Control
Chief Education Planner
Sections:
General Planning
Bantu Language Planning
Psychological and Guidance Serv.
Special Education
Relieving Inspectors
Inspectors of Hostels
Inspector of Religious Education
Inspector and Inspectresses of Special Subjects

Under Secretary (Professional)
Sections:
Registration of Schools, Statistics and Services
Examinations

Under Secretary (Administrative)
Sections:
General Administration and Buildings
Staff Section

Chief Accountant
Sections:
Accounts
Stores

Personnel Manager

Decentralized Regional Organization

Northern Transvaal (Northern Sotho, Venda, Tsonga)
Director
Inspectors (11)
Bantu Asst. Inspectors
Organizers (Spec. Subjs.)
Bantu Supervisors
Supervisors

Southern Transvaal (Mainly Tswana)
Director
Inspectors (12)
Bantu Sub-Inspectors
Organizers (Spec. Subjs.)
Bantu Supervisors
Supervisors

Orange Free State (Southern Sotho and Tswana)
Director
Inspectors (7)
Bantu Sub-Inspectors
Organizers (Spec. Subjs.)
Bantu Supervisors
Supervisors

Natal (Zulu)
Director
Inspectors (12)
Bantu Sub-Inspectors
Organizers (Spec. Subjs.)
Bantu Supervisors
Supervisors

Ciskei (Xhosa)
Director
Inspectors (8)
Bantu Sub-Inspectors
Organizers (Spec. Subjs.)
Bantu Supervisors
Supervisors

Control Boards
Special Schools

Advisory Boards
Advisory Committees
Government Bantu Schools

School Boards
School Committees
Community Schools

Governing Bodies
Scheduled Schools

Managers
Farm, Mine, Factory and Hospital Schools
Non-subsidized schools, night schools and continuation classes

Source: Department of Bantu Education, *Annual Report for the Calendar Year 1965*, pp. 3-4.

are two Under-Secretaries, one dealing with the professional, the other with the administrative aspects of Bantu education.[99] The Professional Under-Secretary deals with general planning, language planning, psychological services, special subjects and schools (such schools for handicapped children were taken over in 1961), statistics, examinations and school registration. The Administrative Under-Secretary deals with staff, accounts, buildings, and organizations. The five Regional Directors have staffs of administrative and professional assistants, the latter including White inspectors and Bantu sub-inspectors and supervisors.[100]

An Advisory Board for Bantu Education was established in 1963, and is composed of fifteen Bantu members, seven of whom are appointed by the Minister to represent the main Bantu language groups. The other eight are appointed to represent the interests of university colleges, teacher training schools, farm schools, school boards, and churches.[101] The functions of the Board are to 'assist in determining the broad principles of sound education for the Bantu . . . [and to co-ordinate] . . . the educational policy generally with a view to adjusting the system to the character and needs of the Bantu, with due regard to the advisability of maintaining diversity which may be demanded by circumstances'.[102]

On the local and regional levels, school committees and school boards have been established for community schools and given certain responsibilities. The school committees are composed of parents, representatives of religious groups, and representatives of tribal authorities or of chiefs. Procedures for appointment to the committees vary, but all are subject to the approval of the Secretary of Bantu Education.[103] The responsibilities of the school committees include:

(i) establishment and control of school funds
(ii) maintenance of buildings and grounds
(iii) investigation of various types of complaints
(iv) expulsion of pupils
(v) the advisement of school boards concerning the performance of teachers.[104]

School boards are responsible for groups of community schools. Regional or district Bantu tribal authorities nominate six of the eight

[99] *Ibid.*
[100] *Ibid.*
[101] *Ibid.*, p. 43.
[102] *Government Notice R 895*, June 21, 1963, p. 42, quoted in *ibid.*
[103] *Ibid.*, p. 44.
[104] *Ibid.*

members of their board subject to Departmental approval, the remaining two members being appointed by the Secretary.[105] The appointment system for urban school boards varies somewhat, but all nominees must be approved by the Department.[106]

The school boards are the employers of the teachers in schools under their control. Again, however, all actions must be with the approval of the Department.[107]

Other duties of the school boards are to maintain and control school buildings, to plan and promote the erection of school buildings, to allocate and maintain equipment, to investigate complaints, and to supervise the finances of school committees.[108] Government schools still fall directly under the control of the Regional Directors of Bantu Education.

The importance of mission schools has been greatly diminished. Following the assumption of government control in 1955, the Secretary for Native Affairs announced that mission schools for Bantu would have three choices: to continue operating without state subsidies, to continue operating with a gradual reduction in subsidies, or to relinquish control of their schools to Bantu community organizations.[109] Similarly, three choices were given to missions operating Bantu teacher-training institutions: to rent or sell their schools and hostels to the Department, to rent or sell their schools, while retaining the hostels on a subsidized basis, or to close the teacher-training school and, instead, conduct a primary or secondary school.[110]

Considering the heavy reliance of missions on subsidies, the announced alternatives made it clear that there would no longer be a significant role for the missions in Bantu education. In 1953 there were over 5,000 state-aided Bantu mission schools; by 1965 there were 509 out of a total of 7,222 Bantu schools.[111]

It should be noted at this point that since 1954, the Vocational Education Act of 1955 effected the transfer of all existing technical schools, Bantu and White, to state control.[112] Then, in 1964, special schools for handicapped children were also placed under state control.[113]

[105] *Ibid.*, p. 45.
[106] *Ibid.*
[107] *Ibid.*
[108] *Ibid.*
[109] Letter from the Secretary of Bantu Education to missions operating teacher-training schools, August 2, 1954, as quoted in Horrell, *op. cit.*, pp. 20–1.
[110] *Ibid.*
[111] Department of Bantu Education, *Annual Report for the Calendar Year 1965*, Pretoria, Government Printer, 1966, p. 22.
[112] Horrell, *op. cit.*, pp. 108–9.
[113] Republic of South Africa, *Act, No. 24, 1964.*

6. The School System and Syllabuses

Following assumption of control, the government accepted the Eiselen Commission's recommendations on the organization of the school system. Primary schools have been divided into two parts, lower and higher, each providing a four-year course. Lower primary schools include pupils from Sub-Standard A through Standard II, and higher primary schools from Standard III to VI. With the completion of Standard VI, pupils write an examination, the results of which determine whether or not they will be permitted to enter a secondary school.

Secondary schools are organized on a Form I through V basis. If a student passes Form I, he proceeds to either an academic course leading toward the matriculation examination or to a commercial, vocational, or technical course. Students must pass an additional examination (Junior Certificate examination) at the completion of Form III prior to beginning the course leading to the Senior Certificate or Matriculation examination.

The syllabuses for all Bantu schools are determined by the Department. The syllabus for the lower primary school was first published in late 1954.[114] Since that time there have been several revisions, the latest having been done in 1963.[115] The primary characteristics of the current syllabus are these:

(i) Instruction is in the vernacular
(ii) an official language is introduced as a subject in Sub-Standard A, the second is introduced six months later
(iii) history, geography, and nature study are grouped into one course called 'environmental studies'
(iv) religious instruction, reading, writing, arithmetic, handicrafts, gardening, and singing are taught as subjects.[116]

The current syllabus for the higher primary school was also published in 1963.[117] With minor exceptions, the subjects studied in the lower primary school are also taught in the higher primary school but in

[114] Horrell, op. cit., p. 52.
[115] Department of Bantu Education, Syllabus for the Lower Primary School Course, rev. 1963, Pretoria, Government Printer, 1963.
[116] Ibid.
[117] Department of Bantu Education, Syllabus for the Higher Primary School Course, rev. 1963, Pretoria, Government Printer, 1963.

greater depth. When reading the syllabus, the general impression is that the subjects are closely geared to the Bantu child's environment. The complaint has been lodged that the courses in environmental studies and handicrafts are overly biased in favour of the rural child in a tribal environment.[118] This complaint would not appear to be justified for the social sciences.

The first part of the secondary school syllabus – a three-year course leading to the Junior Certificate – was published in 1958 and was revised in 1961.[119] Pupils must study in Form I three languages, that is, the vernacular, Afrikaans, and English. In addition, the pupils study arithmetic, general science, social studies, agriculture, arts and crafts, and homecraft or woodwork. Mathematics and Latin may be introduced if the principal of the school wishes to do so.[120]

For the academic course following Form I, students must study a Bantu language, Afrikaans, English, social sciences, and either general arithmetic or mathematics. In addition, each student in the academic programme must select two subjects from the following: Latin, mathematics, general science, physical science, biology, agriculture, arts and crafts, homecraft, or a commercial subject.[121]

Those students who follow the commercial course for the Junior Certificate are required to study a Bantu language, Afrikaans, English, social studies, and either commercial arithmetic or general arithmetic. In addition, they select any two of the following subjects: book-keeping, commerce, typewriting, shorthand, or a natural science.[122]

A variety of vocational courses are available, although few Bantu children have yet qualified to begin them.[123] The courses available cover such subjects as agriculture, textile production, the building skills, and mechanics.[124]

7. Schools and Enrolments

The Department of Bantu Education reported in its *Annual Report* for 1965 that there were 7,222 schools in the Republic, excluding the university colleges (discussed later), but including technical, vocational,

[118] Horrell, *op. cit.*, p. 52.
[119] *Ibid.*, p. 62.
[120] *Ibid.*
[121] *Ibid.*, pp. 62–3.
[122] *Ibid.*, p. 63.
[123] *Ibid.*, pp. 105–11.
[124] Department of Bantu Education, *op. cit.*, p. 31.

and teacher-training schools. Of this total, 6,709 were government or government-aided schools with the balance being unaided church-owned schools, 490 of which were Roman Catholic. Of the total of 7,222, primary schools constituted 6,940, with the balance of 282 including 175 junior secondary schools (Forms I through III), 34 secondary schools (Forms I through V), 5 teacher-training schools, 1 technical secondary school, and 13 vocational training schools. The remaining 54 schools offered courses of various combinations of primary, secondary, technical, vocational, and teacher-training.[125]

The total number of students enrolled in Bantu primary and secondary schools increased by over 240 per cent between 1949 and 1965. While enrolment increases have been substantial in all school-year levels, there remains a very small percentage of pupils surviving to the secondary school levels. In 1965, only 3·44 per cent of the total school population was enrolled in secondary schools which contrasted with 72 per cent in the lower primary schools and 25 per cent in the higher primary schools.[126] Only 0·14 per cent (2,307) were in vocational and technical schools and 0·22 per cent (3,668) in teacher-training schools in 1965[127] (see Table 3).

A key measure which resulted in the increase in enrolment was the instituting in 1955 of double-sessions in the Sub-Standards. Under this system the teacher handles two separate three-hour classes of pupils each day. In 1965, well over fifty per cent of the government and government-aided schools in the Republic had double sessions.[128]

Due to the double sessions and to increasing class sizes, the pupil-teacher ratio has risen until considerable hardships are worked on teacher and student alike, as the following data indicate:

1946—42·3 pupils per teacher
1959—54·1 pupils per teacher
1960—54·7 pupils per teacher
1965—61·9 pupils per teacher[129]

The problem becomes even more explanatory of the high drop-out rate when it is considered that these pupil-teacher ratios include secondary, vocational, and teacher-training courses. Thus, the above figures are underestimations of the severity of the situation in the primary schools.

[125] *Ibid.*, p. 14.
[126] *Ibid.*, p. 31.
[127] *Ibid.*
[128] *Ibid.*, p. 23.
[129] Rose, Brian, 'Bantu Education as a Facet of South African Policy', *Comparative Education Review*, Vol. 9, No. 2, June, 1965, p. 210; Department of Bantu Education, *Annual Report*, pp. 27, 31.

TABLE 3 COMPARISON OF BANTU ENROLMENT, 1949 AND 1965*

School Year	1949		1965		Percentage Change, 1949 to 1965	
	Enrolment	Percentage of Total	Enrolment	Percentage of Total	School Year	School Year as Percentage of Total for each year
Sub-standard A	251,181	33·1	428,181	25·9	168·6	− 7·2
Sub-standard B	127,412	16·8	306,206	18·5	240·3	1·7
Standard I	111,227	14·7	256,787	15·5	230·8	·8
Standard II	80,249	10·6	193,678	11·7	241·3	1·1
Standard III	64,580	8·5	148,409	9·0	229·8	·5
Standard IV	46,580	6·1	105,542	6·4	226·5	·3
Standard V	31,291	4·1	80,649	4·9	257·7	·8
Standard VI	26,413	3·5	73,066	4·4	276·6	·9
Standard VII—Forms I and II**	13,824	1·8	42,977	2·6	310·8	·8
Standard VIII—Form III	4,702	·6	10,362	·6	220·3	·0
Standard IX—Form IV	904	·1	2,420	·2	267·6	·1
Standard X—Form V	471	·06	1,183	·07	251·1	·01
Total	758,811	99·96	1,649,460	99·77		

Source: Union of South Africa, *Report of the Commission on Native Education, 1949-51*, p. 134; Department of Bantu Education, *Annual Report for the Calendar Year 1965*, p. 31.
* Excluding enrolment in vocational and technical courses.
** The system under the Department of Bantu Education includes an additional year (Form I) between the previous Standards VI and VII.

8. Teacher Training

A key barrier to quality education in the primary and secondary schools is the limited production of well-trained teachers. The policy of the Nationalist government has been to replace, as nearly and quickly as possible, the hardly significant numbers of White teaching personnel in the primary schools with Bantu – primarily Bantu women. Particularly in the lower primary schools, a large percentage of the teaching personnel is composed of Bantu women who have completed only Standard VI, plus an additional year of general education and two years of professional training (Lower Primary Teacher's Certificate). This situation has resulted from a government policy, first announced by Verwoerd in 1954, designed to increase rapidly the volume of teachers for the primary schools, and 'to save money in teacher training and salaries'.[130] In 1963, it was announced that since larger numbers of potential teachers were passing the Junior Certificate examination, it was possible to do away with the 'emergency measure' of the Lower Primary Teacher's Certificate course.[131] Schools began discontinuing the course in 1963, and by 1965, only 243 students wrote the L.P.T.C. examination, while 1,584 wrote the H.P.T.C. examination.[132] It goes without mention, however, that it will be many years before the new policy effectively raises the general level of teacher qualifications. In 1965, out of a total of 26,762 teachers in government and government-aided schools, 11,972, or 45 per cent, held only the L.P.T.C.[133]

The lack of well-qualified Bantu teachers is not limited to the lower primary schools. In order to be able to consider data on teacher qualifications, it is necessary to be familiar with the types of teacher training available to Bantu. These are summarized below:

(i) The Lower Primary Certificate – a three-year post-Standard VI course for women only. (Currently being phased out.)

(ii) The Higher Primary Certificate – a two-year post-Junior Certificate course for those planning to teach in higher primary schools (Standards II–VI).

(iii) South African Teachers' Diploma – a two-year post matriculation course including five post-secondary level courses in arts, four in sciences, and a programme of professional training.

---

[130] Horrell, *op. cit.*, p. 51.
[131] *Ibid.*, p. 94.
[132] Department of Bantu Education, *op. cit.*, pp. 42–3.
[133] *Ibid.*, p. 28.

(iv) Post-Graduate University Education Diploma – a one-year post-baccalaureate professional programme.

(v) University Education Diploma – a professional programme undertaken concurrently with a baccalaureate degree programme.

(vi) Special Courses – one-year courses in woodwork, homecraft, and arts and crafts for teachers qualified with at least the Higher Primary Certificate.

Little statistical analysis is needed to conclude that Bantu schools in South Africa are, for the most part, staffed with poorly qualified teachers. The data in Table 4 (p. 79) indicate the severity of the situation.

Each of the three Bantu university colleges which are discussed later, offers teacher training courses. With the low percentage of Bantu who matriculate, however, these institutions can have only a limited impact on the problem of improving the quality of Bantu teacher preparation. In 1965, there were 240 students studying at the university colleges to become teachers. A total of 225 of the 240 were pursuing diploma, not degree programmes.[134]

9. *Higher Education*

A significant development since 1954 concerns Bantu higher education. The extension of the control of the Department of Bantu Education to cover university-level institutions caused a great outcry of protest from many groups. Prior to 1960, Bantu students had been permitted to enrol at:

(i) the University of South Africa, a totally correspondence institution

(ii) the University of Natal in segregated classes

(iii) the non-White University College of Fort Hare, and

(iv) the 'open' Universities of Cape Town and Witwatersrand.[135]

The Afrikaans-medium Universities of Stellenbosch, Pretoria, and the Orange Free State, and Potchefstroom were closed to non-White students.[136]

As will be remembered, the Eiselen Commission had recommended that post-matriculation education should be planned in conjunction with the government programme for socio-economic development. This logically would place Bantu university-level education under the

[134] *Ibid.*, p. 35.
[135] Horrell, *op. cit.*, p. 121.
[136] *Ibid.*

control of the 'division of Bantu education', the formation of which was also proposed by the Commission.[137]

TABLE 4 QUALIFICATIONS OF BANTU TEACHERS IN GOVERNMENT AND GOVERNMENT-AIDED SCHOOLS 1965*

	Schools			
	Primary	Secondary**	Vocational	Total
L.P.T.C.	11,703	266	3	11,972
H.P.T.C.	7,899	646	2	8,547
South African Teachers' Diploma	14	200	—	214
Baccalaureate Degree	1	15	—	16
B. Degree plus prof. qualification	19	350	—	369
Neither Degree nor professional qualifications	4,706	111	13	4,830
L.P.T.C. or H.P.T.C. plus special course	317	107	1	425
Technical Qualification	32	8	19	59
Total	24,691	1,703	38	26,432

* Excludes white teachers in Bantu government and government-aided schools. In 1965 there were 330 such teachers of whom 287 taught in secondary, technical secondary, and teacher training schools and possessed university degrees in over fifty per cent of the cases.
** Includes technical secondary and teacher training schools.

The Nationalist moves toward gaining control of higher education began in 1953 with the appointment of the Holloway Commission, which was charged with the responsibility for investigating the practicability and financial implications of providing separate higher education facilities for non-Whites.[138] In the Commission's report, published in 1955, both the idea of establishing separate non-White universities and the idea of establishing separate non-White units adjacent to White universities were rejected on financial bases. Rather, the Commission suggested concentrating Bantu students at Fort Hare and at the already established non-White division of the University of Natal.[139]

Towards the end of 1965, despite the Holloway recommendations, the government appointed a committee to draw up a plan for the establishment of two Bantu university colleges in addition to Fort

[137] Union of South Africa, *Report of the Commission on Native Education, 1949–51*, U.G. No. 53/1951, para. 876.
[138] Horrell, *op. cit.*, p. 122.
[139] Union of South Africa, *op. cit.*, p. 123.

Hare: one in Zululand, and one in the northern part of Transvaal. The primary bases for the plan were not only racial but also tribal segregation. Fort Hare would be for Xhosa students, the Natal University College would be for Zulu, and the Transvaal University College would be for members of other tribal groups.[140] The report of this committee was published in 1957 and covered only the statistical aspects in the areas of potential enrolments, capital outlay, and operating expenses.[141]

Beginning in 1957, a series of parliamentary manoeuvres necessitated by some procedural controversies culminated in the Extension of University Education Act and the University College of Fort Hare Transfer Act, both passed in 1959.[142] The Extension of University Education Act provided for the establishment of segregated non-White university colleges, financed from the Bantu Education Account and controlled by the Minister of Bantu Education.[143] The Act specified that each university college is to be headed by a Rector appointed by the Minister. The members of the Administrative Council, along with those of the Advisory Council, are appointed by the State President.[144]

The Act also provides for a Senate and an Advisory Senate to deal with questions of professional policy. With the Council's consent, the Senate may delegate to the Advisory Senate powers to deal with matters relating to instruction, examination, and discipline.[145] Among other things the Minister appoints the members of the Senate, prescribes salary scales and conditions of employment (including rules relating to misconduct and inefficiency), and may deny any Bantu admission to a university college.[146]

The University College of Fort Hare Transfer Act of 1959 completed the legal framework for the government's plan.[147] The Minister was granted control of Fort Hare, including the hostels which were owned and controlled by the churches up to 1959, and the power to dismiss any members of the staff.[148] It has been reported by Horrell that on the basis of this power, the Rector was replaced; the Vice-Principal, a Bantu, resigned because his reappointment was made contingent on

[140] Horrell, *op. cit.*, p. 124.
[141] *Ibid.*
[142] Republic of South Africa, *Act No. 45, 1959*, and Union of South Africa, *Act No. 64, 1959*.
[143] Republic of South Africa, *Act No. 45, 1959*, p. 4.
[144] *Ibid.*, p. 6.
[145] *Ibid.*, p. 8.
[146] *Ibid.*, pp. 8, 10, 12.
[147] Union of South Africa, *Act No. 64, 1959*.
[148] *Ibid.*, p. 24.

his resignation from an African political organization; a professor and a senior lecturer were not reappointed; two professors, a senior lecturer, the registrar, and the librarian were dismissed by the Department on the grounds that they had retired on superannuation.[149] Considerable protest against the two university *apartheid* acts came from many groups. Mass meetings of students at the open universities were organized by the Student Representative Councils that received support from the administration of these universities.[150] The administration and faculty at Rhodes issued a statement in protest against the Fort Hare Act.[151] Protest marches of lecturers and students were held in Johannesburg, Cape Town, and Alice;[152] and organizations such as the Education League and the Institute of Race Relations published pamphlets protesting this extension of *apartheid*.[153] Notwithstanding all protests, university *apartheid* is a fact in South Africa today.

In March, 1960, the University College of the North at Turfloop and the University College of Zululand at Ngoya opened their doors, the first for Bantu of the Sotho, Tsonga, and Venda tribes and the latter for Zulu. The University College of Fort Hare in the Ciskei became the institution of higher education for Xhosa tribesmen. Programmes of instruction at these three institutions include arts, sciences, social sciences, languages, divinity, education, pharmacy, and administration. The total enrolment of the university colleges in 1965 was 939.[154]

The University of South Africa controls the syllabuses and examinations (for degree courses), and awards the degrees of the three Bantu university colleges. In addition, the University of South Africa enrols Bantu students in its correspondence courses – 1,480 in 1965.

10. *The Financing of Bantu Education*

One of the most controversial issues surrounding Bantu education has been the government's policies of finance. It will be recalled that the Native Education Finance Act of 1945 had introduced a revolutionary change in the financing of Bantu education in that all the funds to be

---

[149] Horrell, *op. cit.*, p. 137.
[150] *Ibid.*, p. 125.
[151] *Ibid.*
[152] *Ibid.*, p. 126.
[153] *Ibid.*, p. 127.
[154] Department of Bantu Education, *Annual Report for the Calendar Year 1965*, Pretoria, Government Printer, 1966, p. 7.

made available to the provinces were to be drawn directly from the general revenue of the Union. No longer were increases in expenditure dependent on the Bantu poll tax as had been the case since 1925.[155]

In March, 1954, the Minister of Finance announced in the Assembly that the total expenditure for Bantu education would be R17,000,000[156] in 1954–5.[157] He estimated that the Bantu contribution from their taxes was R4,000,000; the balance of R13,000,000 being paid by the general taxpayers. It was proposed that the general taxpayers' contribution should be 'pegged' at R13,000,000, that is, that future increases in expenditure would have to be financed by the Bantu themselves.[158]

Accordingly, the Exchequer and Audit Amendment Act of 1955 created a Bantu Education Account into which would be paid the following:

(i) A fixed amount of R13,000,000, a year from the General Revenue Account;

(ii) Four-fifths of the general tax paid by Bantu (increased to 100 per cent in 1963);

(iii) Such monies as Parliament might make available, in the form of recoverable advances, to meet any deficit in the Bantu Education Account;

(iv) Receipts arising from the maintenance, management and control of government Bantu schools, other than receipts arising from the sale of land or buildings;

(v) Any monies which might accrue to the Bantu Education Account from any other sources.[159]

During the debate preceding the second reading of the 1955 Act, Verwoerd said that with new organizational methods much greater educational activity would be achieved without increased funds.[160] Some of these 'new organizational methods' which have since been instituted or are in the process of being instituted, are outlined by the following summary of Verwoerd's policy statement:

(i) In urban locations the cost of erecting lower primary schools will

---

[155] *Ibid.*, pp. 197–8.

[156] At current rates, the South African rand exchanges for 1·4 U.S. dollars or 0·5 pounds sterling. South Africa has recently changed the name of its monetary unit from the 'pound' to the 'rand'. One rand is equal in value to ten shillings under the old system.

[157] Horrell, *op. cit.*, p. 13. *Assembly Hansard 8*, col. 2,629.

[158] *Ibid.*

[159] *The Exchequer and Audit Amendment Act, No. 7 of 1955*, as quoted in Horrell, *op. cit.*, pp. 14, 17.

[160] *Assembly Hansard*, January 31, 1955, as cited in Horrell, *op. cit.*, p. 14.

be recovered by the government through increased rental paid by Bantu living in the government-owned houses.[161]

(ii) Rural Bantu school boards will stand a 'better chance of success' if their applications for school facilities are 'accompanied by an undertaking to provide the necessary class-rooms . . .'.[162]

(iii) 'The daily cleaning of the school buildings and grounds will naturally be the work of the pupils under the supervision of the teacher's.[163]

(iv) Because four and one-half hours per day 'naturally overtakes the powers of absorption of . . . beginners, . . . school hours for pupils in Sub-Standards will everywhere be shortened to three hours per day'. This will make it possible for 'both teacher and the class-room . . . to serve two different groups of pupils every day'.[164]

(v) Since the Bantu teacher's salary should be established relative to the income of the Bantu community he serves and since 'Bantu teachers' posts are very much sought after' at the current salary rates, there can be 'no question of an increase' in Bantu teachers' salaries. Pay scales 'will be possibly less favourable' than they were previously.[165] (In actual fact, there have been two modest increases since 1955.)

(vi) Since women are 'by nature so much better fitted for handling young children', lower and, to a certain extent, higher primary school teacher posts will be filled with women teachers. Because 'male teachers receive not only a higher basic salary but also, in the case of married persons, a much higher cost of living allowance than female teachers' . . . 'This measure . . . will bring about a considerable savings of funds . . .'[166]

(vii) 'It will be the policy of the Department to do away entirely with the European teachers in Bantu primary schools'.[167] Ultimately, this policy will be extended to the higher educational levels. Since the White teacher's salary is higher than the Bantu, one result of this policy will be a lowering of cost.

Additional methods have been instituted to 'economize'. Bantu

[161] Verwoerd, H. F., *Bantu Education; Policy for the Immediate Future*, Statement by the Hon. Dr H. F. Verwoerd, Minister of Native Affairs in the Senate of the Parliament of the Union of South Africa, June 7, 1954, Pretoria, Information Service of the Department of Native Affairs, 1954, p. 22.
[162] *Ibid.*, p. 21.
[163] *Ibid.*, p. 4.
[164] Verwoerd, *op. cit.*, p. 15.
[165] *Ibid.*, p. 19.
[166] *Ibid.*, p. 20.
[167] *Ibid.*

community school funds have been established into which are deposited revenues from local money-making projects.[168] Further, school boards are permitted by the Department to levy annual fees on students attending secondary schools (up to 10 rand); and to ask for voluntary contributions from parents whose children attend primary schools.[169] The local funds are used to cover various types of school expenses.

Two other means for offsetting limited revenue have been increases in the fees charged for major examinations,[170] and the diversion of already greatly reduced school feeding funds to facilities expansion when requested by school boards.[171]

In spite of all efforts by the Department to economize and to increase income from non-tax sources, it soon became clear that the available funds for Bantu education were inadequate. In order to maintain the R13,000,000 ceiling on the contribution from the Consolidated Revenue Fund, Bantu tax rates were increased through the Natives Taxation and Development Act of 1958.[172] The poll tax was increased 75 per cent to R3·50 per year for every Bantu male eighteen years of

TABLE 5   INCOME TAX SCALES FOR BANTU AS ESTABLISHED
BY THE NATIVES TAXATION AND DEVELOPMENT ACT,
NO. 38, OF 1958

Taxable Income during previous year	General Tax Payable	
	Men	Women
Up to R360	R3.50	—
Over R360 to R480	R4	R2
Over R480 to R600	R5.50	R4
Over R600 to R720	R7	R6
Over R720 to R840	R8.50	R8
Over R840 to R960	R10.50	R10
Over R960	Add R2 for every R120 or portion thereof of taxable income	

Source: Horrell, Muriel, *A Decade of Bantu Education*, Johannesburg, South African Institute of Race Relations, 1964, p. 19.

[168] *Government Notice Number 251 of February 22, 1957*, as cited in Horrell, *op. cit.*, p. 16.
[169] *Ibid.*
[170] Horrell, *op. cit.*, p. 18.
[171] de Villiers, F. J., *Financing of Bantu Education*, Cape Town, South African Institute of Race Relations, January, 1961, p. 6.
[172] The Joint Matriculation Board charges 9 rand for the matriculation examination. This board, of course, is not controlled by the Department of Bantu Education (Horrell, *op. cit.*, p. 18).

age or older. In addition, those Bantu men or women earning over R360 per year became subject to a graduated income tax.

In 1954, per-student expenditure was estimated at R17·08; in 1957, at R15·68; in 1960, at R13·80; and in 1965, at R13·27.[173] Compounding the decline in real per-student expenditure, the South African economy has been experiencing a mild, but steady rate of inflation in recent years – 4·7 per cent from 1957 to 1962.[174]

E. Some Major Bantu Education Issues

Through investigation of the historical development of Afrikaner social attitudes it has been possible to achieve some perspective on the underlying rationale of South African Bantu education. In fact, an examination of the chain of historical events which has led South Africa to the present day has provided an amazingly clear picture of how, over time, the attitudes of a group of people can develop and be applied in an organized way to the modification of social institutions.

In summary, it can be said that the strong sense of nationalism of today's Afrikaner is the product of centuries of struggling for identity and recognition. From the earliest restrictions of the Dutch East India Company, through the challenges of English liberal thought and the ensuing war, to the present wave of Black African nationalism which has swept the continent, the Afrikaner nation has managed to preserve and strengthen its religious, racial, and political undergirdings. Christian-National Education Policy and, to a large extent, the recommendations of the Eiselen Commission are applications to education of the socio-political policy of *apartheid* which is the prime Afrikaner mechanism of defense against both Blacks and non-Afrikaner Whites. Within this context it can be understood why Verwoerd would have said that, for the well-being of the Bantu, their education should be based on traditional culture and should not develop desires in them to 'graze' in the 'green pastures of the European'.[175]

While the political objectives behind state systems of education must be identified and clarified before the systems themselves can be understood, the scope and objectives of the present discussion preclude a detailed philosophical analysis of *apartheid*. The interested student will find ample materials on this subject – unfortunately, often emotional

[173] de Villiers, *op. cit.*, p. 5. Department of Bantu Education, *Annual Report of the Calendar Year 1965*, pp. 17, 23.
[174] Houghton, *op. cit.*, p. 243.
[175] Union of South Africa, *Senate Debates*, Second Session, Eleventh Parliament, Fifth Senate, June 7, 1954, cols. 2,595–6222.

and highly subjective. Some questions, however, can be raised. The policy of *apartheid* being acknowledged as the over-arching issue, a brief examination can be made of a few sub-issues which centre around the Nationalist government's Bantu education policies.

The financing of Bantu education since 1953 is perhaps the major policy issue. While there can be little doubt that people tend to appreciate better that to which they have contributed financially, the issue is the extreme degree to which this principle has been applied. A concomitant question of principle relates to the obligation of a wealthier class to contribute to the education of less privileged classes so as to elevate the latter's intellectual and economic capacities to the benefit of all. To 'pull oneself up by the bootstraps' implies well-earned achievement, but the application of this concept to the extreme in the financing of Bantu education is as illogical as is the saying itself when viewed in relation to the law of gravity. This is, however, what is being done when increases in public expenditure for Bantu education are made contingent upon Bantu economic productivity and tax revenues, which are themselves directly dependent on the general level of Bantu educational achievement. The error of this policy is indicated by the extreme 'emergency' measures taken by the Nationalist government in order to 'economize'. The firm position of the government on this issue invites critics to conclude that the intention is to see Bantu educational development proceed slowly. It would appear to be to the benefit of the Afrikaner himself to see progress advance as rapidly as possible, *toward a well-educated Bantu population*, thus moving up the day when *apartheid* on social, economic, and territorial bases could be achieved to the fullest. What other conclusion can be reached if, as the government claims, the Bantustans are socially feasible, morally justified, and to the mutual benefit of all ethnic groups?

The South African Institute of Race Relations recommended in 1958 that Bantu education be financed from the Consolidated Revenue Fund with a compounded increase of 7 per cent per year – a recommendation made by the Eiselen Commission several years earlier.[176] Other similar recommendations have been made, but each is refuted by the government with the arguments that more is being spent under the present system than the Bantu contribute in direct and indirect taxes, and that the Bantu will appreciate their education only if they have a sense of financial involvement. The first argument, as has been pointed out, is redundant; the second would not be necessarily ignored if the ceiling on the contribution from the general revenue were lifted.

---

[176] Horrell, Muriel, *A Decade of Bantu Education*, Johannesburg, South African Institute of Race Relations, 1964, p. 20.

It would take little administrative ingenuity to devise means which would achieve this objective without sacrificing educational quality in the balance.

Another Bantu education policy issue centres around the small percentage of Bantu students in secondary schools. While it cannot be argued that adequate finance solves all problems, it can be soundly argued that double-sessions and the predominance of poorly qualified teachers are not conducive to an increase in the percentage of students who are prepared sufficiently to pass Standard VI examinations, and who are motivated to continue to secondary schools. Further, until conditions are improved in the primary schools, thus increasing substantially enrolments in the secondary schools, there can be little hope for a long-range solution to the problem of insufficient numbers of qualified teachers. In this sense, the instituting of double-sessions on a massive scale created a vicious cycle, the breaking of which will require measures such as the development of more comprehensive programmes of in-service training for existing teachers, especially those in primary schools, and the provision of well-planned economic incentives to prospective teachers.

Even with substantial improvement in the quality of primary education, however, so long as the South African government continues to insist upon instruction in the mother-tongue – presently the case up to Standard VI – effective secondary-level education for the majority of Bantu in South Africa will be rendered extremely unlikely. Once again, the matter is one of a sound policy carried beyond its usefulness to the point where it creates serious problems. Instruction in the mother-tongue during a child's early years of formal education is scientifically justified. But, Nationalist policy has been to extend mother-tongue instruction beyond the early years and, ultimately, it is claimed, through higher education. Many have questioned the feasibility of adapting and developing Bantu languages to twentieth century communication needs, but even with the assumption that the task is feasible, the length of time necessary to develop the vocabulary and to achieve its general acceptance and utilization would be very great indeed. In the mean time, the severe handicap caused by the abrupt shift at Standard VI, or later, from Bantu vernacular to an official language will continue to stifle Bantu educational development.

Value judgments aside, even if *apartheid* is achievable to the extent that Nationalist policy-makers maintain, it cannot be solely dependent upon the development of the Bantu languages. Since a basic objective which is stated by the Nationalist government is to assist the Bantu in developing greater respect for his cultural heritage, it logically follows that all steps should be taken which raise the level of his educational attainment. Surely, barriers or deterrents to the achievement of more effective Bantu education must be eliminated by the Nationalist government if it wishes to prove its claim that *apartheid* will work.

BIBLIOGRAPHY

Department of Bantu Education, *Bantu Education Journal*, Johannesburg, 1954.

Horrell, Muriel, *Action, Reaction and Counteraction: A Companion Booklet to 'Legislation and Race Relations'*, Johannesburg, South African Institute of Race Relations, 1963.

Horrell, Muriel (ed.), *African Education: Some Origins and Developments until 1953*, Johannesburg, South African Institute of Race Relations, 1963.

Horrell, Muriel, *A Decade of Bantu Education*, Johannesburg, South African Institute of Race Relations, 1964.

Horrell, Muriel, *Legislation and Race Relations*, Johannesburg, South African Institute of Race Relations, 1963.

Houghton, D. Hobart, *The South African Economy*, Cape Town, Oxford University Press, 1964.

Houghton, D. Hobart, *The Tomlinson Report: A Summary of the Findings and Recommendations in the Tomlinson Commission Report*, Johannesburg, South African Institute of Race Relations, 1956.

Hurley, Denis E., *Apartheid: A Crisis of the Christian Conscience*, Alfred and Winifred Hoernle Memorial Lecture for 1964, Johannesburg, South African Institute of Race Relations, 1964.

Hurwitz, Nathan, *The Economics of Bantu Education in South Africa*, Johannesburg, South African Institute of Race Relations, 1964.

Marquard, Leo, *The Peoples and Policies of South Africa*, 3rd ed., London, Oxford University Press, 1962.

South African Bureau of Racial Affairs, *Bantu Education: Oppression or Opportunity?* Stellenbosch, South African Bureau of Racial Affairs, 1955.

South African Bureau of Racial Affairs, *Journal of Racial Affairs*, Pretoria.

South African Department of Bantu Education, *Annual Reports*, Pretoria, Government Printer, 1961–.

South African Department of Bantu Education, *Report of The Commission Of Inquiry Into the Teaching of the Official Languages and the Use of the Mother Tongue as Medium of Instruction in Transkeian Primary Schools (Cingo Report)*, Pretoria, The Government Printer, 1962.

South African Department of Information, *Education – For More and More Bantu* (Fact Paper 88), Johannesburg, Dagbeek, February, 1961.

South African Department of Information, *The Progress of the Bantu Peoples Toward Nationhood*, Pretoria, Government Printer (n.d.).

South African Department of Information, *The Transkei and the Case for Separate Development*, No. 25 in the series 'Reports on the State of South Africa', London, South African Department of Information, 1963.

South African Institute of Race Relations, *A Survey of Race Relations in South Africa* (journal), Cape Town.

South African Institute of Race Relations, *University Apartheid*, South African Institute of Race Relations, November 27, 1956.

Union of South Africa, *Report of the Commission on Native Education, 1949–51*, U.G. No. 53/1951, Pretoria, Government Printer, 1952.

Union of South Africa, *Report of the Interdepartmental Committee on Native Education, 1935–36*, Pretoria, Government Printer, 1937.

Union of South Africa, *Summary of the Report of the Commission for Socio-Economic Development of the Bantu Areas Within the Union of South Africa*, U.G. 61/1955, Pretoria, Government Printer, 1955.

4· The Education of Coloureds and Indians in South Africa

RAYMOND TUNMER

There is a frequently recurring pattern in the organization of education for minority groups. The dominant group is anxious to absorb the minority as soon as possible, and, even if older generations cling to their language, culture or religion, it is hoped that younger generations will be more rapidly absorbed; education is used to hasten this process. If language, culture or religion in the minority group is very powerful, governments will often recognize this, but try to make their adherents as passive as possible. Economic integration of the minority group is often used as an encouragement for younger people to accept the assimilation inherent in the education system.

Such a pattern can be found in countries like the United States, Canada and Australia, which have absorbed large numbers of immigrants by relying heavily upon education and economic integration. Britain, where immigration from Africa, India and the West Indies has recently been discouraged, is nevertheless using the same methods to absorb the people she has already acquired. South Africa employs the same tactics to deal with immigrants from Europe. The reluctance of minority groups to abandon their language, culture or religion can be seen in countries like Canada, Belgium or Holland.

There are, however, two large minority groups in South Africa in which this pattern is not found. The Coloured people make up 9·4 per cent and the Indians 3·0 per cent of the total population of South Africa. But in these cases, the dominant group's role of urging assimilation and the minority group's frequent determination to keep something of its separate identity cannot be found. For a considerable part of South African history, the policies of the White population (itself a minority group, but one which holds both political and economic power) have been dominated by differences between peoples. Assimilation has been explicitly rejected. On the other hand, both minority groups have hoped and worked for assimilation, and have made considerable changes in their ways of life under the influence of Western European and American patterns of living which are followed by the Whites. These changes, however, have not hastened assimilation. In fact, there has been a diminution of some rights.

It is only in the present decade, when some Coloureds and Indians have (often reluctantly) accepted South African life as being dominated by group differences, that these groups have been given some limited opportunities which had been consistently denied them by all South African governments when demands for such opportunities were inspired by theories of assimilation. This is particularly clearly demonstrated in the education provision for the two groups.

There are many other reasons why the Coloured and Indian communities can be considered together in a single chapter. The Coloureds are a mixture of several peoples: Hottentots (the original inhabitants of the South Western Cape), slaves (introduced from Asia and other parts of Africa), White colonists, and, more recently, Africans from other parts of South Africa. In the Cape, Hottentots were used as herdsmen and farm labourers; slaves were used as house-servants and skilled craftsmen until emancipation in 1833. Indians were first brought to Natal in 1860 to work as indentured labourers on the sugar plantations. At the end of their indentures, most of them remained in Natal, but found other jobs. This meant that labour had to be imported regularly from that date until 1911. With the indentured Indians came smaller numbers of 'passenger' (i.e. fare-paying) Indians as traders; the origins of both groups lay in earlier periods of labour shortage.

From their origins, the present geographical distribution of the two communities stems: 88·13 per cent of the Coloureds live in the Cape, and 82·7 per cent of the Indians live in Natal.[1] Both groups are heavily concentrated in particular areas. Both groups with their traditions of skilled craftsmanship could help to reduce the country's critical shortage of skilled labour. This useful potential would not be very costly to tap as their existing educational provision is so much greater than that for the Africans.

Both population groups are expanding rapidly – they have high birth rates (47·5 per 1,000 of population for Coloureds, and 38·4 for Indians).[2] Despite high infant mortality rates (119·6 per 1,000 for Coloureds, and 56·3 per 1,000 for Indians)[3] their populations will be very much larger by the end of this century. They have at present the highest annual rates of increase of the four population groups.

[1] Republic of South Africa, Bureau of Statistics, *Statistical Year Book, 1966*, p. 89. (Afterwards cited as *Stat. Yr. Bk., 1966*.)
[2] Du Toit, J. B., *Demografiese Aspekte* in Theron, E., en Swart, M. J., *Die Kleurlingbevolking van Suid Afrika*, Stellenbosch-Grahamstown, Universiteits Uitgawers en Boekhandelaars, 1964, p. 11.
[3] *Ibid.*, p. 16.

TABLE I RACIAL COMPOSITION (NUMBERS AND PERCENTAGE) OF
POPULATION IN 1960, 1966 AND ESTIMATES FOR 2000 A.D.[4]

	Year			
	1960	*1966*	*2000 (High)*	*2000 (Low)*
White				
Number	3,080,159	3,481,000	7,033,000	5,984,000
Per cent	19·3	19·02	16·75	16·2
Coloured				
Number	1,509,053	1,805,000	5,831,000	4,606,000
Per cent	9·4	9·86	13·89	12·50
Indian				
Number	477,047	547,000	1,159,000	1,103,000
Per cent	3·0	2·99	2·76	3·00
African				
Number	10,927,923	12,465,000	27,949,000	25,222,000
Per cent	68·3	68·12	66·59	68·40

A final justification for considering the two groups together is that
from the beginning of the 1960s the administration of their social and
political life, and in particular the method of educational provision for
their children, has been almost identical.

It would be wrong to suggest, however, that there were no important
differences between the Indian and Coloured groups. Despite the Asian
origins of some of the slaves, Coloureds have largely adopted a Western
European way of life. The Indians brought with them a complex
culture, a variety of languages and religions, and a family structure,
which, despite many modifications under South African conditions,
must be acknowledged in assessing the impact on them of an education
that is entirely Western European in concept.

The Coloured population speaks Afrikaans or English as its mother-
tongue, with the large majority speaking Afrikaans (88·5 per
cent).

The most frequently occurring mother-tongue amongst the Indians
is Tamil (29·7 per cent). Another 26·4 per cent speak Hindi, 14·5 per
cent speak English and a further 26 per cent speak Gujerati, Telgu
or Urdu.[5] None of these Indian languages is taught in any state or
state-aided school – the medium of instruction being almost entirely

4 *Stat. Yr. Bk.*, *1966*, pp. A8, 10, 11, 12.
5 *Ibid.*, p. A29.

English. Formal instruction in an Indian language is given in private vernacular schools, where it is combined with religious instruction. These schools are not attended by all Indian children; they are often inefficient,[6] and because their classes are held before and after ordinary school, they can impose a heavy burden on children.

English is vital for communication between the Indian groups and with other South Africans. As a general rule, only the oldest Indians might have no spoken knowledge of English. Younger adults, even if they have had no schooling, would have learned it on the streets.

Religious practices differ widely between the two communities. Most Indians follow one or other of the two major religions of the Indian sub-continent. Hinduism is practised by 65 per cent of all South African Indians, and some 20 per cent are Moslems. Small numbers are Christians (7 per cent) or Buddhist.[7] The practices of the two major religions have changed very little in the century of Indian residence in South Africa. They require observances in the home as well as in the temple or mosque, and these agencies are mutually supporting. Indian home life is remarkably stable, and the close-knit family is held together in many cases by the regular observance of religious ritual.

Coloureds, as a result of two centuries of intensive missionary activity, are, nominally at least, members of one or the other Christian denomination. The first Coloured mission station in the Cape started work as early as 1737 and, as was so frequently the case, education was linked with religious guidance. State-aided mission schools still provide the bulk of primary education in the Cape. The largest church is the Nederduitse Gereformeerde Kerk, claiming allegiance from 29 per cent of the Coloureds. This is followed by the Anglican Church, with 17·8 per cent of the adult population as its members. Congregationalists, Methodists, Catholics, have between 7 per cent and 9 per cent of the population as adherents. Some 6 per cent of the population are Moslem.[8] Although much of the Coloured's cultural life is centred on his church, it is certainly true to say that Christianity is not as dominating a force amongst the Coloureds as Hinduism or Mohammedanism is amongst the Indians. Nor does the Coloured home provide the same support as the Indian home with its special rituals.

Family organization reveals some of the greatest differences between Coloured and Indian people. The Coloureds accept the primary or nuclear family of father, mother and dependent children as the ideal

[6] Hey, P. D., *The Rise of the Natal Indian Elite*, Pietermaritzburg, privately published, 1962 (?), pp. 25–7.
[7] *Stat. Yr. Bk., 1966*, p. A36.
[8] *Ibid.*

family organization in the same way as it is regarded by the Whites. By combining figures from the unpublished family census of 1946 and from studies of Coloured communities in different parts of the Cape Province, Steyn[9] has shown that most families in both communities consist of a man, a woman and children, although there are more childless couples amongst the Whites than amongst the Coloureds.

TABLE 2   FAMILY-TYPE ORGANIZATION AMONGST
WHITES AND COLOUREDS[10]

| Family-Type | White % | | Coloured % | | | |
	South Africa 1946	South-West Cape	South Africa 1946	South-West Cape	Knysna	Belville
Male/Female/Children	65·9	65·1	68·3	69·2	72·2	74·4
Female/Children	8·0	10·1	14·2	14·5	12·0	13·6
Male/Children	1·8	1·8	2·9	3·3	2·1	1·5
Male/Female	24·7	19·6	14·6	10·7	9·7	8·2

The second line of this table shows considerably larger percentages for Coloureds than for Whites. In many cases, these families are examples of desertion by the father, or of the mother caring for illegitimate children of one or more fathers. The percentage of illegitimate births amongst Coloured people is alarmingly high: in 1958 36·8 per cent of all Coloured births were illegitimate as compared with 1·6 per cent amongst Whites and 2·8 per cent amongst Indians. Amongst women between 15 and 19 years old, 80 per cent of their children were illegitimate; 46 per cent of children born to women between 20 and 24 years were illegitimate. Even for middle-aged women, between 16 per cent and 17 per cent of births were registered as such.[11]

It is apparent from the first line of this table, however, that most of those women do not remain the sole supporters of their illegitimate children. Many of them marry after one or more children have been born. Others set up permanent or semi-permanent unions which are not registered marriages. Those who do not form any union are represented in the second line of the table. These figures, together with those of infant mortality, suggest a serious degree of family disintegration. This is confirmed by more detailed investigations by Steyn[12] who

[9] Steyn, A. F., Gesinslewe, in Theron en Swart, op. cit., chap. 5.
[10] Ibid., p. 70.
[11] Du Toit, op. cit., p. 14.
[12] Steyn, op. cit.

investigated a hypothesis first suggested by Patterson[13] from a study by Frazier of American Negro families. Steyn looked at 50 families of the male/female/children type in each of two socio-economic groups – one high, the other low. In the higher group, 94 per cent of the families produced patterns in which either the male was dominant, or there was an equality of responsibility between man and woman. In the lower group, 42 per cent showed a pattern of female domination, and altogether 78 per cent showed this pattern or an irregular conflicting one.

Patterson suggested and Steyn confirmed that a female dominant pattern is related to the irregular or small contribution of the man to the family income, his low or non-existent level of education and the fact that in the urban areas, women can always get servant's jobs which gave them a more regular, and sometimes a greater, income than men. It is possible that lack of education and skills amongst men of the lower socio-economic classes is liable to lead to their abandoning responsibilities through frustration and despair at low wages and increasing numbers of children. Whatever factor is the main cause for the female-dominant family, its existence can hardly be doubted, and, as most Coloured families fall into low socio-economic groups, the numbers exhibiting this pattern must be very large.

Such a pattern is not of course an inevitable mark of disintegration. In the case of Coloureds, however, two factors would suggest that its operation does produce many problems. The first is the absence of any real form of extended family system,[14] which often cushions similar situations in African families, where fathers are migrant workers or are non-existent, and where the female-dominant pattern is fairly frequently found.[15] Although people additional to the nuclear family are more often found in Coloured households than in White, there is no consistent pattern of relationship to suggest that they represent either the vestiges of an extended family system or one which is gradually evolving. Interviews with Coloured families show that they would prefer a nuclear family arrangement. The traditional European pattern found in the upper socio-economic Coloured groups would seem to imply that in more normal circumstances this would be the most frequently found family type.

13 Patterson, S., *Colour and Culture in South Africa*, London, Routledge and Kegan Paul, 1953, pp. 148–51.
14 An extension of the nuclear family incorporating more distant relations: grandparents, uncles, aunts and cousins. The relationships are often minutely defined, as are interlocking rights and duties.
15 See, for instance, Pauw, B. A., *The Second Generation*, Cape Town, Oxford University Press, 1963; and Muir, R. K. and Tunmer, R., 'The Africans' Drive for Education in South Africa', *Comparative Education Review*, Vol. 9, 1965, pp. 303–22.

The second factor is that the surroundings of the Coloured community make for difficulties in a female-dominant family pattern. Employment, housing administration, social services and, above all, educational administration and values, all assume that the bulk of the money in a home is provided by the father, maternal care can be provided for most of the day by the mother, and that family decisions are made either by the father or jointly by both parents. The conflict between these assumptions and the reality which exists in a large number of Coloured families has a direct and deleterious effect on an educational system which is based on the view that home and school are complementary. When these two social agencies are at variance, education is often comparatively ineffective, as much evidence from Britain and America has indicated.[16] There is evidence that the low attainment of many Coloured children is similarly linked with poor home circumstances.[17]

The family organization of the South African Indian[18] is, generally speaking, far more effective than that of Coloureds. It is marked by the close ties between the male head and his children, even after his sons have married; there is an acceptance of marriage as a normal state for all adults; there are very few widowed or unmarried women who live alone or with their dependent children; there is still a strong tradition that married women should not work outside the household or the family business, unless they are professionally trained. The small number of illegitimate births has already been noted, and divorces are rare. Although marriages arranged by families are becoming less frequent in recent years, there is considerable family debate on proposed marriages, and much encouragement if the young people are considered to be well-matched. The break-up of such a marriage is a grave step and carries with it the disapproval of both the extended family and the community.

---

[16] See, for instance: Passow, A. W. (ed.), *Education in Depressed Areas*, New York, Bureau of Publications, Teachers College, Columbia, University, 1963; Fraser, E., *Home Environment and the Schools*, London, University of London Press, 1959; Nisbet, J., 'Family Environment and Intelligence', in *Education, Economy and Society* (ed.), Halsey, A. H., New York, Free Press of Glencoe, 1961, pp. 273–87; and in the same publication Bernstein, B., 'Social Class and Linguistic Development', pp. 288–314; Mays, J. B., *Education and the Urban Child*, Liverpool, Liverpool University Press, 1962; Jackson, B. and Marsden, D., *Education and the Working Class*, London, Routledge and Kegan Paul, 1962.

[17] Naude, J. P., *A Survey of Educational Backwardness in Selected Transvaal Coloured Primary Schools*, unpublished M. Ed. Dissertation, University of the Witwatersrand, 1961.

[18] For a brief account of South African Indian family life, see Kuper, H., *Indian People in Natal*, Pietermaritzburg, Natal University Press, 1960, ch. 6 and 7.

For most Hindus the family is the 'kutum' – the patrilineal extended family which includes 'a male head, his wife, unmarried children, unmarried brothers and sisters, younger married brothers, married sons, and brothers' married sons with their wives and children'.[19] Although this whole group does not live together, they often try to live in close proximity, and few decisions, either major or minor, are taken without consultation with other members of the kutum. The kutum relationship is not one between equals, but is strictly hierarchical with authority stemming from the single male head. A very common practice is that sons do not set up a separate household immediately after marriage, but the wife is brought to the parental house, and a joint household is set up. At one time there might be two or more married sons, their wives and children sharing the parental home. From various surveys in Natal[20] it seems that between one household in two and one in five is likely to be a joint household. More educated sons are more likely to set up separate households as soon as possible. Although wives do not break entirely from their parents, they are absorbed into their husband's kutum.

While there is nothing to equal the female-dominant family amongst the Coloured people, it would be wrong to suggest that Indians regard women as completely inferior. The Indian mother is honoured by her husband and sons, and is shown great deference by her daughters-in-law. She administers the household and often all its finances. Kuper has described her as one who 'leads by withdrawing, rules by submitting and, above all, creates by receiving'.[21]

This family structure can have a considerable effect upon education attainments. House walls are often filled with graduation-day photographs and school and university certificates. The achievements of relations are well known; they bring honour to the kutum as well as the individual; and many kutum members have made sacrifices to make the educational achievement possible. Hey's research reproduces family trees which show an extraordinary number of professional men and women in a kutum where the parents or grandparents were illiterate indentured labourers (see the diagram on page 98).

To acquire secondary or post-school education also demands considerable sacrifices on the part of the student. Although Indian society holds education in high prestige, shortage of money, overcrowded

[19] Kuper, *op. cit.*, p. 97.
[20] *Ibid.*, pp. 106–9; University of Natal, Department of Economics, *Studies of Indian Employment in Natal*, Cape Town, Oxford University Press, 1961, pp. 31, 37, 48, 91; Woods, C. A., *The Indian Community of Natal*, Cape Town, Oxford University Press, 1954, p. 101.
[21] Kuper, *op. cit.*, p. 117.

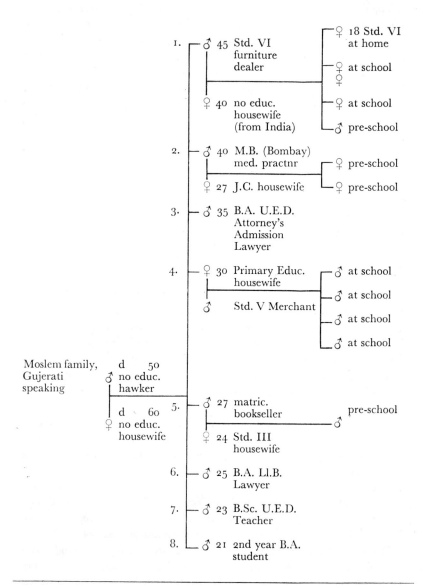

Notice the high level of education of the second and subsequent sons of illiterate parents, the much lower educational level of the daughter (No. 4) a tradition continued in the eldest daughter of the first son. This first son went to work early to assist his siblings, and No. 2 delayed his marriage to do the same. (Reproduced from Hey, *op. cit.*, p. 75.)

homes and lack of privacy do not make studying easy, as many of the Indians interviewed in Hey's study recalled. A lawyer, for instance, described his primary school days and his job in a shirt factory run by his brother: 'It was a difficult period. Early in the morning I had to get up to deliver shirts. Then I went to school and after finishing there at 2.30 p.m. I would go round to collect more material. My job was to make the buttonholes . . . I would work until it was very late – sometimes until after twelve – and then only would I settle down to my studies. I was up at seven the next day to collect the shirts again . . .'[22] After receiving higher education, it is expected that the man or woman would help younger members of the kutum to advance their studies.

In the past, there was an important exception to the Indians' regard for education: education for girls was considered a waste of time even at the primary level. Secondary and post-school education was very rare. At the large training college in Natal in 1966 for instance there were 406 men but only 179 women.[23] One father, in Hey's study, claimed that he had 'given his daughter a "good" education – Junior Certificate – and (as a thanksgiving for her early marriage) endowed a scholarship for *other* girls at the Medical School'.[24] Hey suggests that 'if the mother has had little education . . . achievements of girls in school are usually modest (even if the father is well educated)'.[25] It would seem, however, that this attitude is changing.

Of the three aspects of social organization brought from India, religion, family structure and caste system,[26] the third has undergone most change in South African conditions. Some parts of a rigid caste system were broken on the voyage across the Indian Ocean, when all castes were thrown together, or on arrival in Natal, where all did the same job. Of the four hierarchically graded caste-groups or 'varna' of Hindu organization, the lowest (Sudra caste or menial workers) was the one into which most indentured labourers fell. Many others came from the exterior or scheduled castes, but with the arrival of the 'passenger' Indians, there were representatives of all four varna in South Africa. In contrast to India itself, where the varna have been subdivided into a multiplicity of sub-castes, the tendency has been to fuse sub-divisions, and to blur the edges of each varna. Many aspects of the caste system have disappeared. There are few outward signs of

[22] Hey, *op. cit.*, pp. 30, 31.
[23] Levine, A., *The Story of Springfield*, Fiat Lux, Vol. 1, No. 3, Department of Indian Affairs, 1966, pp. 80–5.
[24] Hey, *op. cit.*, p. 17.
[25] *Ibid.*, p. 14.
[26] See Kuper, *op. cit.*, Chapter 2, for an account of the caste system in South Africa.

caste in dress or ornament. Dietary rules associated with caste (as opposed to religion) have largely disappeared. There is no longer a close relationship between caste and occupation. ('In a random sample of 84 men, 64 had taken on occupations different from their fathers.')[27] Comparatively small numbers made caste distinctions difficult to maintain, and there was no authority that could be invoked to support a threat of 'out-casting', as governments grouped all Indians together for administrative purposes.

Education is probably the most effective social agency working against caste distinctions. Western European concepts may recognize class differences but not caste differences. Those who object most strongly to the caste system are the younger more highly-educated Indians. Few secondary school pupils in Kuper's survey gave information about their families' caste.[28] Those who cling to it most strongly are the older, less educated people, and one small group – the Gujerati-speaking Hindu.

It would not be true to say, however, that no caste characteristics remain amongst South African Indians. Many Indian professional, political, and social leaders have high-caste names. But caste alone does not signal them out for leadership. They must show ability, and, in increasing measure, have had a good education. Marriage is another area in which caste ideas still seem to operate. Kuper describes one study in which in 169 out of 180 Hindi marriages and in 113 out of 120 Tamil marriages, the partners were of the same varna.[29] Yet language and culture must also influence the choice of a partner. Endogamy (limitation of marriage to members within one group, community, or tribe) is not confined to caste societies, and by itself it is not sufficient to create such a society. It would be difficult to say whether social characteristics like occupation, language and religion, or more rigid caste concepts are the more important factors in planning marriages.

It is finally necessary to point out that Christian Indians have specifically rejected caste (although it is interesting to note that many of them belonged originally to the unscheduled castes). There are no caste divisions amongst the Moslems whose religion stresses the equality of all men in the sight of God. In South Africa the caste system is unique to Indians. The Coloured people have no caste distinctions at all.

Despite these differences between the Coloured and Indian groups,

---

[27] Kuper, *op. cit.*, p. 37.
[28] *Ibid.*, p. 39, footnote.
[29] *Ibid.*, p. 31, footnote.

there are two major social factors which are helping to draw them closer to each other and to the Whites. The first of these – education in a Western European pattern – has already been mentioned, and it will be considered in more detail later in the chapter. The other factor is an economic one. Table 3 shows how both Coloureds and Indians can be found in each major occupational group.

TABLE 3   PERCENTAGE OF ECONOMICALLY ACTIVE COLOUREDS AND INDIANS IN THE MAJOR OCCUPATIONAL GROUPS[30] 1960

Occupational Group	Coloureds	Indians
	%	%
1. Professional and Technical	2·51	4·15
2. Administrative and Executive	0·22	2·04
3. Clerical	1·48	6·5
4. Sales	1·92	17·7
5. Farming/Fishing	22·85	8·4
6. Transport	3·96	5·95
7. Mining, Quarrying	0·16	—
8. Skilled trade and Production Work	35·2	29·5
9. Service	21·23	11·0
10. No occupation given or unemployed	10·47	14·88
% of total population economically active	36·7	26·4

The general reluctance of the Indians to allow married women to work accounts for the small percentage of economically active people in their group. Indians have spread themselves more evenly over the employment areas than have the Coloureds, who are still fairly heavily concentrated in two traditional work areas: agriculture and service jobs. Indians are much more concentrated in the 'white-collar' jobs (the first four categories) than are the Coloureds. In both groups, teachers make up most of the people in Category 1 (71 per cent in the Coloured group, and 74 per cent in the Indians). More than half the Coloured teachers are women, but only 29 per cent of the Indian teachers are women.

Comparatively large numbers of Indians work in wholesale and retail trade – Category 4 – and just over a third of them are classified as 'working proprietors'. Indian shops are found throughout Natal and the Transvaal. 'The obvious wealth of some . . . with well-established premises and first-class fittings and stock . . .' have helped to create the myth of the 'wealthy' Indian shopkeepers, but there is another side to

[30] Republic of South Africa, Bureau of Statistics, *1960 Population Census, Sample Tabulation: Major Occupational Groups, Whites, Coloureds and Asiatics*, pp. 26 28, 44.

the picture with 'many small back-street traders whose turnover is very low . . . the "locale" of many (shops) is in itself a serious limitation to any increase in turnover'.[31] The large number of working proprietors suggest that many of them must run one-man or one-family businesses. Only 11 per cent of the Coloureds in Category 4 are working proprietors, but since the creation, in 1962, of the Coloured Development Corporation to provide financial assistance for Coloured businessmen, most applications have been for small businesses. Both communities are short of capital and up to now Coloureds have had little business experience.

All the population groups in South Africa have been drawn towards towns and cities in the last few decades. Although the original need for Indian labour was on the sugar plantations, the Indians have almost deserted agriculture and 83 per cent[32] of them are in urban areas. Those who work in agriculture – Category 5 – are market gardeners, sugar farmers and fishermen. Surveys show that their gardens and farms tend to be small, and their investments and profits low. About one-third of them have to seek casual employment elsewhere, leaving wives and children to tend the crops. The surveys show that the educational level of these gardeners and farmers is low, so scientific farming would be impossible for them.[33]

The Coloureds still retain an important link with farming – 32 per cent of them live out of urban areas. Many of those working in Category 5 can be found in the intensive agriculture areas in the South Western Cape, and four-fifths of them are farm hands. Forty-two thousand Coloureds live on state, church or privately owned agricultural land owned or managed by Coloureds themselves. On the whole the agricultural potential of these areas is not high and many men earn extra money as migrant labourers.[34] Since 1963 government funds have been used to improve these lands with irrigation and fencing.

Coloured workers, especially women, have taken domestic service jobs – Category 9 – for many generations. Over 85 per cent of the Coloured workers in this category are women. More than half the Indian men in this category are barmen or waiters.

The largest number of Coloured and Indian employees are found in Category 8 – craftsmen and production workers – where they have helped to satisfy the needs created by the country's rapid industrializa-

[31] Woods, *op. cit.*, p. 20.
[32] *Stat. Yr. Bk.*, *1966*, p. A24.
[33] University of Natal, Department of Economics, *op. cit.*, ch. 2, especially pp. 19, 20, 38.
[34] A brief description of the Coloured rural areas appears in Muller, H., *The Role of the Coloured People in the Economic Pattern of the Republic of South Africa*, Grahamstown and Stellenbosch, University Publishers and Booksellers, 1965 (?), pp. 28–38.

tion over the last thirty years. This category includes skilled, semi-skilled and unskilled labour. It is not possible to separate the skilled and semi-skilled workers in the census statistics, but the number of labourers is given separately: 50 per cent of the Coloureds and 58 per cent of the Indians are unskilled labourers. Both groups, however, have traditions of craftsmanship and there are opportunities for apprenticeship training. In the Western Cape, by far the majority of bricklayers, plasterers, painters, plumbers and carpenters are Coloured. Many Indians and Coloureds are skilled and semi-skilled workers in textile, leather and clothing industries. Both groups can be found in the printing industry.

The numbers of White skilled workers in South Africa has not been able to keep pace with the growth of industry, and since 1955 there has been a decline in the numbers of enrolments at technical colleges and a decline in apprentices from 8,400 in 1956 to 6,600 in 1963.[35] It is therefore essential to increase the opportunities for technical training for non-Whites. Indian and Coloured adolescents could be used in the first stages as their educational systems could be fairly easily adapted for this purpose.

Long-term planning in this direction is made uncertain, however, by legislation introduced in 1956,[36] which made it possible to reserve, after investigation, jobs in certain areas for one particular racial group. By the end of 1966 nineteen 'determinations' had been proclaimed.[37] In all of them, Africans had been prevented from doing some tasks, and in most of them White workers had been especially protected. In a few (such as the building and clothing industry in the Western Cape, the Transvaal and Natal, the catering trade in Natal and in parts of the Cape) jobs have been reserved for Whites or Coloureds or Indians. It is therefore uncertain how long a particular job or skill will be completely open to Indians or Coloureds. It is difficult to defend the Act, when the shortage of skilled workers is so well documented, and when it is realized that up to 1965, 183 exemptions to the determinations had to be granted, because the workers in the 'protected' racial group were not available.[38] The Act is cumbersome and in an erratic way is liable to be a serious brake on the contribution that all non-White people can make to the country's industry.

It is also necessary to mention unemployment, which for many years

[35] 1961 Education Panel, Second Report, *Education and the South African Economy*, Johannesburg, Witwatersrand University Press, 1966, pp. 85–8.
[36] Act No. 28 of 1956.
[37] A description of each 'determination' can be found in Horrell, M., *A Survey of Race Relations in South Africa*, Johannesburg, South African Institute of Race Relations, 1962, 1963, 1964, 1965, 1966.
[38] Horrell, *op. cit.*, 1965, p. 213.

has been a problem in both communities. It is almost impossible to get exact figures, for many who are unemployed do not register as work-seekers. In the 1960 Census figures, 41,000 Whites, 89,000 Coloureds and 26,000 Indians were listed as unemployed.[39] These figures bear no relation to the proportions of these groups in the total population. The census year occurred in the middle of increasing unemployment, especially amongst Indians. This had started in the 1950s but appears to have declined after 1962. Studies in the first part of this period[40] show large numbers of young Indians who could not find work. The largest group who registered were those who had completed primary school, but had had no training in any specific skills. These are followed by those who had had no education (that is those with whom the Africans are in direct competition for labouring jobs). In 1965 some areas of heavy unemployment in the Cape and Natal were declared 'border' areas where industries employing Coloured and Indian labour would be given financial encouragement to open factories.

It is now necessary to look in more detail at the educational pro-vision for Coloureds and Indians up to the beginning of this decade. The first effective schooling for both groups was provided by missions, as it was in the case of African education. A small slave-school had been started in Cape Town in the seventeenth century, and the Moravian Mission Society started a mission in 1737, and re-established it in 1791. This set the pattern for two hundred years of religious and educational work amongst the Coloureds – a pattern followed by the Rhenish, London and South African Societies and then by the full range of Christian Churches. As late as 1964, of the 1,200 state-aided Coloured schools in the Cape (four-fifths of the total number) all but twenty were mission schools. The Dutch Reformed Church supports the greatest number, and is followed by the Anglican, Congregational, Catholic, and Methodist Churches. Similar activity, but on a smaller scale, was started in the other three provinces.

Because the numbers of Coloureds were comparatively small in other parts of South Africa, their education was linked with that of Africans in the Orange Free State, and with the Indians in the Trans-vaal. The control of the content of education was gradually assumed by the four provincial education departments and with minor exceptions was identical with that given to White children. Provincial education ordinances differ, and differences were also found in the administra-

[39] Horrell, *op. cit.*, 1963, p. 210.
[40] University of Natal, Department of Economics, *op. cit.*, ch. 5, especially p. 138.

tion of Coloured education. In Natal, after 1942, Coloured education was free and compulsory at the primary school and some money grants were available for poorer children in secondary school. It has been calculated that the average annual cost of fees, books and writing materials for a Coloured child in a state secondary school is R16.[41]

There is no compulsory education for Coloureds or for Indian children in the Transvaal, but education is free for pupils throughout the twelve years of schooling, and grants for text and library books and laboratory equipment is the same as for White schools. It has been estimated that over 90 per cent of Coloured children of school-going age attend school, but many of them do not complete the full primary course.[42] The Orange Free State also has no compulsory education for Coloured children, and progress has been slow partly because of the small number of Coloureds in this province. Secondary classes, for instance, were started as late as 1940.

The Cape Province has not been able to introduce uniform compulsory education, but in five areas there is sufficient accommodation to enforce it between the ages of 7 and 14. Although education is free and book grants are available to poorer pupils, it seems that large numbers of children are still not at school, one estimate placing the number as large as 60,000.[43]

Education for Indians also started (in 1869 in Natal and in the 1890s in the Transvaal) through missionary efforts. Like Coloured education in the Cape, Indian education in Natal is provided largely in state-aided schools, which have always been in the majority. In 1960 there were 212 state-aided schools and 29 state schools in this province.[44] Missionary activity has, however, almost entirely disappeared. The state-aided schools resulted from the initiative and financial sacrifices of the Indian community, which provided land and buildings. After 1943 the Province paid half these costs, as well as the teachers' salaries. In the post-war years, there was an acute shortage of primary school places, and a platoon system was started in which the number of children and teachers in a school was doubled. For half of each day children had lessons out of doors. In 1966 there were still more than 28,000 pupils attending such schools.[45] During these years Indian initiative was also directed to secondary education. To supplement the small number of pupils who could attend secondary school, the privately sponsored Congress High School was started in 1948, in a

[41] Horrell, op. cit., 1962, p. 193.
[42] Minister of Coloured Affairs, Hansard, Vol. 18, 1965, col. 6,983.
[43] Hansard, Vol. 5, 1963, cols. 1,741, 1,748.
[44] Hey, op. cit., p. 63.
[45] Minister of Indian Affairs, Hansard, Vol. 7, 1966, col. 2,219.

primary school. The pupils attended for an afternoon session of less than three hours, and were taught by teachers who came in from other schools. Hey suggests that 'the work of the teachers and the honorary principal [is] a significant epoch in Natal Indian education'.[46] Since then, the province has been able to increase its high school provision very considerably. The determination of parents to provide education for their children is matched by sacrifices of teachers. For many years most Indian teachers have made a voluntary monthly contribution from their salaries towards schools building funds.

In neither Natal nor the Transvaal is education compulsory. Until 1966 pupils in Natal paid school fees and provided their own books and writing materials. These costs ranged from R7 a year at primary school to R17 at secondary school, and were slightly higher in state-aided schools.[47]

It is not being suggested, however, that there has been no improvement in educational provision for Coloured and Indian pupils in recent decades. Patterson, a severe critic of racial discrimination in South Africa, described as early as 1953 the 'considerable efforts (in the Cape) to improve matters in the face of perpetually inadequate funds and indifferent or sometimes hostile European opinion'.[48] Between 1957 and 1963 the numbers of Coloured pupils increased by almost 100,000 (from 262,000 to 360,000); over the same period the number of Indian pupils increased by 35,000 (from 104,900 to 139,600). There have been slight improvements in the numbers completing the full secondary course. Of the Coloured pupils in Standard VI in 1957, 10·55 per cent of them were in Standard X in 1961. This had increased to 12·11 per cent in 1963. The percentage for Indian pupils for the same years were 13·29 per cent and 14·85 per cent.[49]

The increase in numbers has been accompanied by a slightly better distribution of pupils over the various standards.

It is evident that there have been greater changes in Indian than in Coloured education. The changing attitude of Indian parents to the education of girls accounts for part of this improvement. Table 5 shows that an Indian girl has now a slightly greater chance of receiving secondary education than a Coloured girl (see page 107).

The extent of this change in attitude can be gauged by comparing this Table with Table 10, which shows the educational achievements of adults, where the education levels of Indian women are so much lower than Coloured women (see page 107).

46 Hey, *op. cit.*, p. 29.
47 Horrell, *op. cit.*, 1962, p. 193.
48 Patterson, *op. cit.*, p. 101.
49 *Stat. Yr. Bk., 1966*, pp. E21, 22, 27, 28.

TABLE 4   PERCENTAGE DISTRIBUTION OF COLOURED AND INDIAN
PUPILS IN VARIOUS STANDARDS[50]

	Year	Sub A/B	Std. I–V	Std. VI–VIII	Std. IX/X	Total
Coloureds	1957	37·2	54·1	7·8	0·9	100·0
	1963	37·3	52·6	9·0	1·1	100·0
Indians	1957	32·5	56·7	9·2	1·3	99·7
	1963	27·2	56·2	14·4	2·2	100·0

TABLE 5   PERCENTAGE DISTRIBUTION OF COLOURED AND INDIAN
GIRLS IN VARIOUS STANDARDS[51]

	Year	Sub A/B	Std. I–V	Std. VI–VIII	Std. IX–X	Total
Coloureds	1957	37·4	54·9	7·3	0·4	100
	1963	37·4	53·2	8·8	0·6	100
Indians	1957	36·2	56·6	6·4	0·5	99·7
	1963	29·9	58·4	10·4	1·3	100

TABLE 6   AGE DISTRIBUTION OF COLOURED AND INDIAN
POPULATION – 1960[52]

Age	Coloureds	Indians
	%	%
0–4	18·0	15·5
5–9	15·0	15·1
10–14	12·2	14·0
15–19	9·5	11·7

TABLE 7   ESTIMATE OF EXPENDITURE PER CHILD ON
EDUCATION – 1960[53]

	Total	Per Capita
	R	R
Whites – primary and secondary	78,470,000	114·1
Coloureds and Indians – primary and secondary	32,208,000	74·5
Africans – primary and secondary	20,277,000	13·5

TABLE 8   ANNUAL COST TO NATAL PROVINCE PER PUPIL[54]

	State School	State-aided School
	R	R
White	158	—
Coloured	96	58
Indian	68	47

[50] *Ibid.*, pp. E24, 30. Note: These figures do not include pupils who leave school after Standard VIII and study for their matriculation by correspondence.
[51] *Ibid.*, pp. E24, 30.   [52] *Ibid.*, pp. A27, 28.
[53] 1961 Education Panel, *op. cit.*, p. 121.   [54] Horrell, *op. cit.*, 1962, p. 193.

These improvements, however, must be set against factors which hamper educational advance. Some of the sociological factors have already been described. The high birth rates of the Coloureds and Indians make the provision of places very difficult.

More than 50 per cent of both populations are under 20, and 27·2 per cent of Coloureds and 29·1 per cent of the Indians are in the primary school age groups of 5 to 14 years. If full-scale secondary education is also considered then many of the children in the age groups 5 to 19 would have to be catered for. These comprise 36·7 per cent of the Coloured people and 40·8 per cent of the Indians.

Apart from accommodating these children, teachers must be found for them. In both groups the numbers of teachers with degrees is very small.[55] In 1966 a little over 3 per cent of Coloured teachers had degrees, but over 90 per cent had some professional training. This did not mean, however, that all these teachers had completed a full school course themselves. It was still possible for women to enrol for two years of training after completing their Junior Certificate examinations. Only 2 per cent of teachers in schools, however, had neither a matriculation certificate nor a professional certificate. Amongst the Indian teachers in Natal, there was a slightly higher percentage who had degrees (over 9 per cent) but there were 10 per cent who had not finished a full school course, and had had no professional training. After 1963, students were not admitted to training in Natal without a Standard X Certificate. Large numbers of children to be educated, and teachers with poor academic backgrounds, make teaching ineffective and are likely to delay the implementation of compulsory education.

Secondary education for Coloureds and Indians is almost entirely academic in nature. Most Coloured children do history, geography, science and biology. Only 4,400 Coloured boys out of a secondary school population of 20,000 are learning book-keeping and commercial arithmetic, and 580 of these boys are doing courses of manual training or industrial arts. Only 5,100 Coloured girls out of the 16,800 in secondary schools are learning domestic science and 542 are learning typing. There is an even more limited range of subjects in Indian secondary schools. Latin is taken by over 40 per cent of the 16,000 boys and by 37 per cent of the 7,500 girls. Only 3,700 girls and 460 boys are doing book-keeping and similar subjects; 82 boys are doing manual training.[56]

One cause of this academic bias is the statutory limitation on

[55] Horrell, op. cit., 1966, pp. 254–6.
[56] Stat. Yr. Bk., 1966, pp. E26, 32.

provincial action in technical and vocational education described in Chapter 2. Another cause is the prestige associated with academic subjects. It is clear that secondary education is providing training that has little relevance to the jobs that most Coloured and Indian children will hold after leaving school. Any large scale expansion of secondary education must be accompanied by a much broader range of subjects offered by these schools.

A matter which underlies all these problems, however, is that of finance. Table 7 gives an estimate of the amounts spent per child for South Africa as a whole, averaging the sums spent in each province.

The large differences in expenditure on the education of the different racial groups has always existed in South African education. Table 8 shows the figures for one province (see page 107).

Lower salaries paid to Indian, Coloured and African teachers, as well as the lower qualifications of so many of them would account for much of these differences. In 1966, for instance, it was calculated that a Coloured teacher earned approximately 65 per cent of what a White teacher with the same qualifications would earn.[57]

A more general explanation of these differences in expenditure, however, can be found in the methods of financing education described in Chapter 2. It will be remembered that half the province's finances come from local taxation and half from central government subsidy. This arrangement was devised to ensure that provincial autonomy over roads, hospitals and education should be maintained. For many years additional subsidies have been given to the Cape, Natal and the Orange Free State which lack the wealth of the Transvaal.

The amount of money available is therefore dependent upon provincial resources, for these determine central government subsidy. The Cape, with its large concentration of Coloured people (roughly four Coloureds for every three Whites) and Natal, with its large Indian population (about three Indians for every two Whites), have many people whose poverty prevents their making large contributions, either in direct or indirect taxation, to provincial revenues. Neither province could afford to spend on non-White education the same amounts that it spends on White education. To increase the former, the money spent on White education would have to be reduced. Not only would this never receive the approval of the electorate (which is White), but it would be unwise, as South Africa is at the moment so heavily dependent upon White skills.

There is no space to examine the full implications of central government subsidies and provincial autonomy. Arguments about the best

[57] Horrell, *op. cit.*, 1966, p. 255.

TABLE 9 PERCENTAGE OF ADULT POPULATION (20 YEARS AND OVER)
WHO HAVE REACHED VARYING LEVELS OF EDUCATION[59] 1960

	No. Educ.	Sub A to Std. 2	Std. 3/4	Std. 5	Std. 6	Std. 7	Std. 8/9	Std. 10	Level not known	Total %	Total
Coloured men and women	35·9	12·9	19·3	10·5	12·6	3·53	3·56	1·15	0·76	100·2	683013
Indian men and women	33·4	11·8	18·2	9·6	15·3	2·88	4·89	2·92	1·21	100·2	208420
Coloured men	37·15	12·6	16·58	9·71	13·39	4·2	3·92	1·75	0·71	100·01	338665
Indian men	16·41	11·51	19·67	12·34	22·63	4·36	7·22	4·9	0·96	100·00	107086
Coloured women	34·48	13·16	21·91	11·21	11·79	2·88	3·19	0·56	0·81	99·99	344348
Indian women	51·10	12·13	16·77	6·59	7·45	1·30	2·41	0·82	1·50	100·07	101334

[58] *Stat. Yr. Bk., 1966*, p. A40.

subsidy system have been raging since 1910. Some of the anomolies of the present system have been described in Chapter 3, and it is necessary to add this one to the list. South Africa has paid a heavy educational price for the rivalry between the provinces and central government, and the suspicions of the provinces about loss of powers have not all been groundless.

In the face of these difficulties, how well have the provinces managed to educate their Coloured and Indian citizens in the past? Table 9 shows the percentage of the adult population (20 years and over) who had reached certain levels of education.

It can be seen from the first two lines of Table 9 that the two populations are fairly similar in their levels of attainment. About one-third of the adults have had no education, and the numbers who have received any secondary education are very small. These figures, however, mask important differences between men and women. Indian men have managed to acquire considerably more education than Coloured men. These differences are particularly noticeable in those with no education at all, and those who have completed a full primary education (Standard VI). Indian women, on the other hand, have fared particularly badly, half of them having had no education at all.

These figures do not reveal the improvements in educational opportunity that have occurred over the years. Table 10 shows the number of adults to every thousand in different age groups who have passed Standard V.

TABLE 10   NUMBER OF ADULTS PER 1,000 OF POPULATION
WHO HAVE PASSED STANDARD V OR A HIGHER STANDARD[59]

Age	Total		Men		Women	
	Coloureds	Indians	Coloureds	Indians	Coloureds	Indians
20–24	431	552	475	724	417	353
25–34	385	431	407	659	364	223
35–64	225	232	269	367	233	80
65+	88	73	82	104	93	22

It is clear that there has been a steady improvement in the educational levels of Coloured men and women. Indian men of all ages have reached higher standards than Coloured men, and Indian women have never matched Coloured women. If this table is compared with

[59] *Stat. Yr. Bk., 1966*, p. A42.

Table 5, the full significance of the revolution in attitudes towards Indian women's education can be appreciated. As early as 1954, Woods felt that 'the tide has begun to turn and soon the problem will be . . . to find employment for them.'[60]

The decade which began in 1960 will, in any future assessment of South Africa, have to be regarded as a dividing line in the history of the Coloureds and Indians. Some of these changes are political and closely linked with these are educational developments. It has already been suggested that any attempts to promote assimilation of the two minority groups were rejected by all South African governments. Indians lost the franchise for the Natal Colonial Parliament in 1896 and the municipal franchise in 1924. In 1943 and 1946 property purchases were restricted, and Indians rejected limited franchise rights to elect White representatives to Parliament. In 1953 and 1956 Indians were prevented from bringing to Natal wives whom they had married in India, and children who had been born outside South Africa. Prior to 1948, when the Nationalist government came to power, there had been little hope of the Coloured franchise rights of the Cape being applied to the rest of the country. In the 1950s, these Cape rights were removed, and the Coloureds were placed on a separate roll. In 1950 both communities were affected by the Group Areas Act, which allowed for the residential segregation of races, and threatened trading rights as well. Since 1950 many thousands of Indian, Coloured and African families have been moved to new areas.

The most determined protest against these measures came from the South African Indian Congress, but since 1956 many of the leaders have either been arrested or banned under the Suppression of Communism Act, so that Congress has lost most of its power. The more conservative Indians (mainly traders) created the South African Indian Organization which hoped to save as much as possible for Indians through discussion and compromise where necessary.

By 1960, the Nationalist government began to stress the idea of 'separate development', and made plans for a number of African 'homelands' in which some political rights were to be granted. The Transkei (described in Chapter 3) was the first to be created. Similar ideas began to be applied to the Coloured and Indian groups. For some years there had existed a purely advisory Council of Coloured Affairs. In 1961 it was announced that this was to be expanded into a representative body with its own budget and with legislative and executive powers over such matters as education, health and welfare. From this time, this apparently quiescent body seems to have become livelier,

[60] Woods, op. cit., p. 80.

and there have been reports of opposition groups linked with embryonic Coloured political parties. When the detailed changes were debated in Parliament in 1964, it became clear a major difficulty lay in the lack of any geographic area which could be made a Coloured 'homeland'. The powers of the Council would operate over Coloureds who lived in areas administered by local, provincial and parliamentary laws created by Whites for Whites. Cilliers has pointed out that it is far from clear how effective such a council could be, for 'if any population group is to develop separately, the logical outcome of such a process . . . [is] . . . political autonomy for the group . . . [this] has traditionally been associated with the development of separate states.'[61]

The Coloured Council has been linked to the Central Government Department of Coloured Affairs which has been gradually assuming control of many services for Coloureds – welfare, administration of the Coloured Development Corporation and education. Some of its middle posts have been given to Coloured people, and the government plans to extend this policy.

As the Group Areas Act is more fully implemented, local government in Coloured hands becomes more feasible than the proposals for a representative Coloured Council. By 1966, 28 consultative committees had been created, and there is a blueprint for these to grow into full local governments, with elected representatives and budgets from local rates. This has already involved far more Coloureds than the older Cape municipal franchise which had Coloureds on some rolls.

Parallel developments for the Indian community began slightly later. It was only in 1962 that the Nationalist government publicly acknowledged that Indians must be accepted as permanent inhabitants of the country[62] – a declaration which ended hopes stretching over many decades that Indians could be persuaded to return to India.[63]

In 1961 a Department of Indian Affairs was set up and, like its Coloured counterpart, began to assume control of many aspects of Indian life and to fill some of its posts with Indians.

A nominated advisory Indian Council first met in 1964 and in 1966 the government announced that it was to be transformed into an elected body with powers similar to that of the Coloured Council. As with the Coloureds, no single area can act as an Indian 'homeland', but local government has been easier to advance and by 1966 there were eleven Local Affairs Committees, four of which were elected.

[61] Cilliers, S. P., *The Coloureds of South Africa*, Cape Town, Banier Publishers, 1963, p. 65.
[62] Horrell, *op. cit.*, 1962, p. 120.
[63] Despite financial inducements, only 40,000 Indians left South Africa between 1914 and 1953. (Kuper, *op. cit.*, p. 4, footnote.)

Verulam in Natal was the first to achieve financial and executive independence when the Administration in 1967 nominated an Indian Committee. From September 1969 this committee will be elected by democratic process.

Both the Coloureds and Indians have found difficulty in accepting the implications of these political developments. They have offered Indians opportunities for responsibility which they have never had before. For Coloureds who live outside the Cape, these were also new experiences. Employment as initiators and directors of services for their own people is obviously tempting to well-trained professional Indians and Coloureds. On the other hand, it apparently means that they must abandon claims to a voice in national affairs. The Minister of Indian Affairs, for instance, announced in 1963 that the 'political rights of Indians will be limited to self-government within their own community, but there it will end'. Those who have supported these political moves, have usually done so in the hope that they are only the first stages of advance, despite governmental insistence that political integration would never be countenanced. Press reports suggest that support for the Councils is diminishing because of their failure to soften the effects of legislation such as the Group Areas Act or Job Reservation. It is likely that opposition to such measures will become more vocal when the Councils are elected.

Both Councils have been promised full control of education, and the Departments of Coloured and Indian Affairs were given control of technical and university education. Prior to 1962, branches of the Cape Technical College provided separate classes for Coloureds. From that date, these classes were merged into the Peninsula Technical College, which, when hostels have been built, will be the centre for advanced technical education for all Coloureds. Part-time technical training in Coloured secondary schools throughout the country is intended to complement the work of the College. Up to now technical education for Coloureds has been on a very small scale. In 1964, there were some 1,700 students of whom 780 were apprentices.[64] The need for expansion has already been demonstrated, as have the difficulties created by Job Reservation.

The Indian community has supported technical education as enthusiastically as it has primary and secondary. The M. L. Sultan Technical College in Durban started part-time classes in 1929. Housed in new buildings, it now provides[65] apprenticeship training, and

[64] Horrell, *op. cit.*, 1964, p. 273.
[65] Pittendrigh, A., *Tertiary Education and the M. L. Sultan Technical College*, Fiat Lux, Vol. 2, No. 5, 1967, pp. 152–6.

specialist courses in commerce, medical technology, draughtsmanship, hotel catering, public health and technical teacher training for 5,500 students (over three times as many students as from the Coloured community).[66]

University education for non-White students has been a matter of dispute since 1959 when the government prevented them from attending the 'open' universities of Witwatersrand and Cape Town, or the segregated University of Natal, unless they had ministerial permission. These universities objected because this interfered with academic freedom: their right to choose who shall be taught. The non-White peoples objected because this was yet another separation step, and prevented their benefitting from well-established university teaching. To replace these lost places, the beginning of the sixties saw a spate of university building. Apart from the three University Colleges for Africans, one was opened for Coloureds in Cape Town in 1960 and one for Indians in Durban in 1961. These Colleges offer degrees in arts, science, commerce and education, but they have not yet started courses in applied sciences like engineering or medicine or dentistry. For this reason there are still some non-White students at White universities; others are there, with special permission, because their homes are far from Cape Town or Durban.

In 1965 there were 623 full-time Coloured students in universities (346 of them in the Coloured College) and 1,406 full-time Indian students, of whom 662 were at the Indian College.[67] There were a further 466 Coloured and 893 Indians (many of them teachers improving their qualifications) doing correspondence degrees with the University of South Africa.[68] For adults who have achieved a university education, a degree is a symbol of many years of hard work and financial difficulty. With more bursaries and loans, there has been a gratifying increase in student numbers. Students in both groups have grown almost three times in the last ten years. It is again worth noting that there are more than twice the number of Indians as there are Coloured students, although they are drawn from a population only one-third as large.

Universities are short of staff and under-financed; many are still very small. (Three universities for Whites have under 3,000 students.[69]

[66] *Stat. Yr. Bk.*, *1966*, p. E4.
[67] In 1967 there were approximately 400 South African Indian students at Universities in India. Some of these have gone to India because they reject the implications of university segregation. [Information from a private communication to the author.]
[68] *Stat. Yr. Bk.*, *1966*, p. E23.
[69] Republic of South Africa, Department of Education, Arts and Science, *Annual Report*, 1966.

The non-White colleges are all below a thousand students.) As only about 28,000 pupils of all races reach the end of secondary school each year,[70] and by no means all of these enter universities, it is clear that South Africa cannot afford to run 14 universities or plan to open its fifteenth in 1968.

Primary and secondary education for Coloureds was removed from provincial control by legislation in 1963, and Indian education by an Act of 1965.[71] By 1967 the transfer was complete. The two Acts are very similar. Both accept the contribution made by state-aided schools, and this is to continue. Both Acts envisage much greater community involvement in education than existed under provincial systems – a principle already seen at work in the Bantu Education Department. Each system will have an Advisory Council, and there will be Regional Education Boards of partly elected and partly nominated members who will advise on local needs. Each school will have a School Committee of five members chosen from seven people elected by the parents. The membership of all these bodies will be wholly Coloured or Indian. Both new Departments of Education expect to make considerable use of Coloured and Indian teachers as inspectors and subject advisors.

Under both Acts, it is possible for local areas to introduce compulsory education as soon as there is sufficient accommodation. Both systems are committed to introducing a wider range of subjects into secondary education and the creation of something resembling comprehensive education. Technical, vocational, agricultural and commercial equipment will be used for part-time adult education as well.

Neither Act was passed without opposition. There was dislike of the concept of 'Coloured' or 'Indian' education being something apparently distinct from 'education' in general. There were fears about transferring responsibility from the experienced provinces to the new, inexperienced departments. There were doubts about having a total of seven separate bureaucracies (four provincial, and one each for Africans, Coloureds and Indians) to serve a mere 18 million people. There was disappointment that neither Act provided for immediate compulsory education, or set a date by which it should be introduced.

On the other hand, the Acts proposed some very necessary improvements in the education of the two communities, especially in providing a wider range of subjects. Because they enforced separation, they gave prospects of promotion to Coloureds and Indians which had never

---

[70] *Stat. Yr. Bk., 1966*, pp. E14, 22, 28, 34.
[71] Coloured Persons Education Act, No. 47 of 1963 and Indian Education Act, No. 61 of 1965.

existed under provincial control. They gave parents greater links with the education of their children and made it easier for them to indicate the kind of education they want. The re-organization of control has made possible increased expenditure on education.

It is clearly far too early to make assessments of the working of the Acts. In many cases provincial organization is still being retained, but some beginnings have been made with plans for comprehensive schools for both groups, and some Coloureds and Indians have become Inspectors of Education. A large building programme for Natal Indian schools has been started and Indian children in Natal no longer pay fees or pay for their own books. Natal Indian teachers have had salary increases. (Education for Indians in the Transvaal was ahead of Natal, and the first task is to make provision more equal.) No further moves, however, have yet been made towards compulsory education and school meals for Natal children have been stopped.

It is very difficult to guess how the education of these two groups will develop in the next few decades. The new departments have inherited from the provinces unsatisfactory and uneven levels of education. This means that it may take many years for the promises of Acts to be ful-filled. If the Coloured and Indian Councils have so far failed to remove their people's political and economic grievances, will the Advisory Councils, Regional Boards and School Committees be able to satisfy quickly enough the parents' desires for their children? Will technical education be able to reduce under-employment and unemployment if Parliament continues to legislate against the full use of skilled man-power?

Behind these doubts, however, are some that are far more funda-mental. Is the social and political separation of groups feasible if, economically, they are so closely integrated, and their education is designed to hasten economic integration? Can they be left to create their own culture, if their education seems to make younger generations more and more Western European in outlook? Can these groups be given, with governmental encouragement, more and more oppor-tunities to exercise responsibility at local level, and yet no opportunity to exercise similar responsibility at any higher level? Until these questions are answered, no one can be quite sure for what end South Africa is educating the Coloured and Indian child.

5· Education in Malawi

BRIAN ROSE

I. GENERAL BACKGROUND

Malawi (a name which is widely accepted as referring to the reflected sunlight of Lake Malawi) has been an independent state since 1964, when with Zambia (Northern Rhodesia) it seceded from the Central African Federation. It is a narrow strip of a country like a finger, 530 miles long (from North to South) and varying from 50 to 130 miles in width. As a result of its shape this rather shrunken inheritor of the former sixteenth-century Empire of Marawi [sic] has a considerable diversity of climate. It has the advantage of containing six lakes, which together amount to one fifth of its total area of 45,366 square miles. Lake Malawi covers 11,600 square miles. Carrying a population of 3,867,000, it has in fact a higher density of population than either of its two neighbouring countries, 77 persons per square mile (Rhodesia 20 and Zambia 8·5). Lake Marawi [sic] appeared on a Portuguese map in 1546, and from that time on a series of explorers and adventurers, including Father Manuel Baretto, made mention of Marawi as the centre of a former African federation. Vasco da Gama, who rounded the Cape of Good Hope in 1497, made an incursion into the delta of Zambezi, thus opening up the missionary route that was to be nsed for many years to come. Traders followed priests; and soon the Arabs, who had for generations had mercantile connections with the east coast of Africa, began to forage inland for gold and ivory. The founding of Portuguese colonies in South America, particularly of Brazil and the West Indies, created a labour shortage that was to be satisfied by slave trading, and by the 1850s records in Zanzibar show that 19,000 slaves were 'received from the Nyassa country every year'. David Livingstone asserted that not one tenth arrived at their destination, due to the appalling conditions of the journey.[1] Slave trading had been officially abolished by Britain in 1807, but it continued in Africa until the end of the nineteenth century. By 1857 although both America and Portugal had followed the British lead, Malawi was to experience no less than 29 actions against slave traders between 1877 and 1899. The second half of the nineteenth century was, therefore, a period of disintegration for the aMaravi (the people of Malawi) which might have heralded complete collapse had it not been to a large extent that

[1] Livingstone, D. and C., *Narrative of an Expedition to the Zambezi and its Tributaries, 1858–64*, Murray, 1865.

Livingstone's dedication had aroused the interest of Scots missionaries and of planters, whose presence in the country did much to give it stability and at the same time to make it the concern of the British Crown.

There is no doubt that Malawi needed support in the last quarter of the nineteenth century, for the power scramble for Africa was developing, and the little country was subject to encroachment by German interests from the north, by Portuguese from the east and by South African aspirations (personified in Cecil John Rhodes) from the south. In 1883 the first British Consulate had been established, two years before the Berlin Conference which attempted to demarcate European interests in Africa. What was achieved geographically ignored almost all demographic considerations. Nor did the agreements of the Berlin Conference effectively stabilize European aspirations, because the Portuguese tried to extend their influence by secret treaties with Malawi chiefs. When Serpa Pinto led a thinly disguised 'scientific expedition' whose political intent was obvious to everyone, Sir Harry Johnstone, then British Consul of Mozambique, decided it was time for Britain to intervene. As a result of his recommendations the Shire Highland Protectorate of 1889 was declared, to be followed in 1891 by a proclamation covering all the country adjoining Lake Nyassa, under the title of British Central Africa. Sixteen years later, re-named the Nyasaland Protectorate (Nyasaland is spelt with one 's' in the Order of Council 1907, but was often spelt with two, 'ss'), the country was headed by a Governor, under whom legislative and executive councils administered the country. This period of consolidation was short-lived, partly because of the effect of the First World War, and partly because, during the first two decades of the twentieth century, about 100,000 alien Africans entered the country from Mozambique. These people, mostly Lomwe, were slowly assimilated together with Asians who had been introduced as railway labour during the construction of the East African Railways. There was something typical of Malawi in this 'melting pot' hospitality, for almost a century earlier the Yao, originally from Tanzania, had settled down to act as middlemen for the Arabs, whilst the Ngoni had entered from the south in 1835.

Since the decline of its imperium centuries ago, Malawi had been unable to re-establish among its people a sense of national unity and national purpose. The old 'Commonwealth' (or Empire) of Maravi which had dominated Central Africa from the sixteenth century onwards, was largely a nominal force by the end of the eighteenth century, and when the Portuguese traveller, A. C. P. Gamitto

described the Marave [sic] in 1831 the former empire had been fragmented. The disorganization of the aMaravi which followed this
political breakup was worsened by the social and psychological effects
of the slave trade; and although the coming of British administration
restored to the country a measure of stability it had lacked for a century
and a half, British paternalism was not such as to develop local
autonomy.[2] There may have been many historical reasons for this
situation, despite the fact that of all countries in Central Africa Malawi
had the highest proportion of Africans (99·3 per cent; Whites, 0·3 per
cent; Asians/Coloureds, 0·4 per cent) by the middle of the twentieth
century. Undoubtedly a certain *anomie* follows the political disintegration of any dominant community, as was demonstrated in the feeling
of national hopelessness under the weak Weimar Republic, which
preceded the Third Reich. Malawi at the beginning of the twentieth
century was unable to provide work for her growing population.
Population thinning due to slave trade was replaced by voluntary
emigration which, in the twentieth century, took the form of migratory
labour to the Witwatersrand Gold Mines in the Republic of South
Africa. In 1959 some 165,500 able bodied young men left the country
to seek employment elsewhere.

Largely a pastoral people, the Malawi are matrilineal and land
tenure exhibits those conservative elements in which the tenant has in
effect little more than a *usu fructu*. This is a system which militates
against the development of land as well as against the introduction of
conservation schemes. As has been remarked elsewhere in this book
(see Chapter 1), as long as the concept of individual leasehold ownership of land is regarded as contrary to tribal custom, the prospects of
developing a progressive peasantry and of moving thence to large-scale
regional co-operatives (as a basis for a national agricultural economy),
are remote. The achievement of a more sophisticated approach to African agriculture touches issues of variance between the old tribal leaders
and the new-style political leaders which is still politically inflammable.

In Malawi, the loss of community or local initiative may result from
a psychological *ennui* more than anything else. With few mineral
resources, its subsistence agriculture was yielding £8 per head per
annum according to the Phillips Report in 1962. With the population
doubling itself every 25 to 30 years, survival as a nation to a large
extent depends on maximal returns from intensive farming – a demand
which necessitates the almost immediate break-up of conservative
tribal land tenure systems. But a realistic development of a modern
economy depends upon an informed electorate – which is hardly

<hr>

[2] Jones, G., *Britain and Nyasaland*, George Allen & Unwin, 1964, pp. 78 *et seq.*

possible when (according to the 1950 U.N.E.S.C.O. estimate) literacy was limited to between 5 per cent and 10 per cent of the population. American sources commented that optimistic local estimates of increases of literacy to 25 per cent in the early 1960s should be treated with caution. John Phillips, whose *Education Report* provides one of the key documents to the understanding of modern Malawi, commented in his special note on *Observations regarding the Economic Potentialities of Nyasaland as bearing upon the development of Education*: 'There is a definite relationship between the effort to be put into the really successful stimulation of economic, that is largely agricultural, development, for the production of local wealth, and the existence of a sufficiently large body of highly educated and well-experienced political, administrative and managerial leaders and better educated farming and industrial communities. Clearly that advancement depends upon a growing body of nationals, in all walks of life, capable of making a much more effective contribution, directly and otherwise, to conditions and forces essential to the achievement of an enhanced economy. More, better and suitably orientated education is the vital need in this quest for national progress.'[3] Phillips sums up the quandary of so many African states when he comments: 'More and better education could stimulate economic development: an enhanced national wealth derived therefrom could provide the financial and other support for a further expanding and improving of education.'

II. EDUCATION BACKGROUND

As is almost inevitably the case in southern Africa, education was initiated by missionary groups. In Nyasaland the first attempt at formal schooling was introduced by The Universities Mission to Central Africa, which started abortively in 1860. Despite initial failure, it made possible the successful work done by Bishop Steere in 1881. By 1875 the United Free Church of Scotland Mission had begun its work under Livingstone's 'successor', Dr Laws. While it operated in the north, another vigorous mission opened in the south, concentrating on Blantyre. This was the Church of Scotland Mission, led initially by the redoubtable Dr Alexander Hetherwick. Last in the field was Dr Andrew Murray (a name famous in South African religious and educational circles), who led a mission from the Dutch Reformed Church to the central areas, working in close co-operation with the Presbyterian Churches. Several other smaller Protestant groups joined in this work. By 1889 the Roman Catholic Church, through the White Fathers,

[3] *Committee of Inquiry into African Education, Report*, Government Printer, Zomba, Nyasaland, 1962, p. 293.

began their work in Nyasaland. But, as the Phelps-Stokes Commission of 1924 was to comment, education was at all times of secondary importance to evangelization. Education made people literate – and this meant that they could read the Bible. Any other secular purpose was incidental. By 1910 the United Missionary Conference proposed that a Nyasaland Educational Code be drafted, but it was not until 1924, when the Phelps-Stokes Commission accused it of neglecting its duties, that the Government of Nyasaland began to think of participating in the control of education. The first Education Ordinance was drafted in 1927, and three years later further implementation was given to the Commission's report by the institution of an Advisory Board on Education, composed of members of the government, the missions and the public. At the same time some decentralization was achieved in District Advisory Committees, and Grants-in-Aid were regularized. During the 1930s the total expenditure of the Education Department was in the nature of £16,000. Slight as it was, in an undeveloped subsistence economy it represented 4½ per cent of the country's total expenditure. Mission expenditure was accepted as being about four times that of the government. Because the government did not have the money available to take over missionary financial involvement in education, the position remained static during the inter-war period. Whilst the missions concerned themselves with primary education, the government ventured into post-primary education at the Jeanes Training School, which produced Mission School Supervisors and Welfare Workers. Control of missionary standards of teaching was largely nominal. An official primary school syllabus appeared in 1933, and by 1941 some sort of terminal standardization was envisaged in the Standard VI examination. In actual practice Malawi African education implied for most children two years teaching through the vernacular. In what were known as 'Sub-Standards A and B', the age range varied by twelve or more years.

The result of this educational format was to be disastrous for emerging Malawi. In 1940, the country got its first secondary school which, while state-assisted, was in fact interdenominational, despite considerable Presbyterian interest. Two years later the Roman Catholic Church founded another secondary school. But this tardy provision of secondary education left Malawi without an adequate educational substructure to service its Civil Service when independence was declared in the 1960s. It was of little consolation to realize that a similar irresolution in educational strategy was to be found in most countries in southern Africa that had been under British control. With an eye to funding its modest recommendations, the Phillips Commission commented: 'We are advised by the government that financially the immediate future is bleak'. Certainly the examination of the economic potential of the country in Appendix I indicates that no *early* or spectacular internal generation of extra funds can be anticipated. Views as to whether or not Nyasaland in the future 'will have a flourishing economy are widely divergent, but in the vital years immediately ahead, when the educational basis of advance must be laid, the resources will be meagre indeed'.[4]

III. FINANCING EDUCATIONAL DEVELOPMENT

Since discussion of educational opportunity is useless unless it is supported by cash earned in a surgent economy, it would be as well to ask how Malawi could fund educational expansion. The condition of the Malawi economy has been diagnosed on several occasions. In 1960 a commission headed by Professor D. T. Jack, which had investigated the economic prospects of Malawi during its period of Federal association, 1958, 1959, reported. The Jack Report[5] (as it came to be called), attributed the recent growth of landlocked Nyasaland's economy to her association with the federation. Four years later the Federation had become a dead letter. The Report noted that for the most part Nyasaland existed on a subsistence economy, and that such cash crops as existed supported a smaller number of Nyasas than those maintained by remittances from abroad. In fact, twice the amount was sent home from abroad as was taxed locally.

Being a matrilineal community, the land on the death of the tenant used to be fragmented among the nearest female relatives – most of whom were illiterate and were little concerned with improved agriculture. There was, in fact, little individual African land *ownership*. At best there existed a *usu fructu*, a right to cultivate. An enterprising male cultivator in the traditional setting had no incentive to improve land, since he could never obtain even the *usu fructu*, let alone the ownership of capital improvement. The Jack Commission recommended using parts of Magomero, an area where it was possible to utilize Trust land to make freehold grants, which could be supervized by the department of agriculture. The Commission emphasized that agriculture was the mainspring for economic development. Involved in the expansion of this sector were roads, power and water supplies. The Commission recognized that increased expenditure on education, necessary as it

4 *Phillips Report*, p. 20.
5 *Report on an economic survey of Nyasaland 1958–1959*, Salisbury, Government Printer, 1959.

might be, should relate to increased national earnings. Finance might be forthcoming, the Commission suggested, if peasant holdings could be amalgamated into co-operatives which in turn supplied processing factories, established, the Commission opined, on non-African investment capital.

The Report highlighted Malawi's 'inefficient communications and expensive transport, as being at the root of the territory's economic problems. This lack of easy communication was seen as a major problem in marketing. Of all forms of communication, the expansion of the railways had been the most spectacular although low traffic density and high operating costs had militated against the economic use of this form of transport.' The Report noted that 'an inadequate and inefficient road system was undoubtedly a vital factor in the slow pace and character of economic development. The possibilities of lake transportation were investigated. But most water transportation services were reported operating at a loss, and the lack of adequate road services blocked the use of waterways as export outlets.

With a forward look towards the Caborra Bassa hydro-electric scheme, the Commission stressed the desirability of a hydro-electric plant, which would reduce the high power charges which were 50 per cent in advance of Rhodesian costs. At that stage of Malawi's development, the Commission was forced to stress the absence of trade training facilities, which necessitated the importation of semi-skilled and skilled labour to man such light industries which were gradually being established. But as industrial development persisted, the need for the government to promote a more sophisticated infra structure became more apparent. With the establishment of trade training schemes, the development of trade unions was desirable, and the problem of the housing of labour became more and more urgent as growing points of urbanization were developed.

The main crops in Nyasaland are maize, tea and tobacco, with cotton, ground-nuts, rice and tung as subsidiaries. Tea and tobacco, the Commission noted, formed three-quarters of the total export crops, with oil seeds becoming rapidly more important. Animal husbandry was relatively undeveloped. The Commission felt that one of the most important policies for the government to pursue was the encouragement of cash crops. There was also considerable potential in forestry, where state controlled forests could supply soft woods, as well as supplying the hardwood demands of the building industry. Mining, when the Commission reported, offered little promise. The most obvious mineral available was limestone, and there was then little sign of any other viable mineral resources in the territory, despite intensive prospecting.

At the level of secondary industry, nothing had existed at all prior to 1945, except for some processing of tea, tobacco and cotton, and future development depended largely upon the expansion of agriculture. With a very small local market, local production was only likely to be able to compete with imports where it had the advantage of a local supply of raw materials. Expansion was held back not only by communications and power supplies, but by lack of trained skills in the local labour force.

The central problem that the Jack Commission was concerned with (though it is seldom stated as such) was that of transforming the Malawi economy from a subsistence economy to a cash economy. Capital is the result of savings, of even the slight difference between used and unused production, which is profit, a margin that can be created by abstinence, increased human skill in economic production, greater increments of land and resources being employed, market development or a change in world prices that is siphoned off by the state in savings. Almost all these economic measures depend upon a social attitude of mind: a willingness to learn new skills, to apply new marketing methods, to aim at a margin of 'over-production' as against mere subsistence. And it is this new attitude of mind that is achieved by some Africans who qualify as Master Farmers – and it represents a distinct and difficult break with African social tradition. Reinforcing the conservative forces that delay the application of modern techniques is the African traditional system of land holding, the concept of communal land ownership through the tribal authorities. The clash between the African traditionalist, who is in most cases well aware that, like the House of Lords in Britain, he is an anachronism in the modern age, and the new African statesman is not merely political, but is one that touches the psychological springs of personal and national identity. The power of the traditionalist, supported by magico-religious function of the Inyanga (or, as he is confusingly known to most Whites, the 'witch doctor'), lies chiefly in the chief's control of land. Whilst no African state is likely to develop a modern economy until it establishes some form of freehold ownership or perhaps some form of private ownership on a co-operative basis similar to that attempted in parts of Yugoslavia, the destruction of the old tribal aristocracy would probably prove so traumatic socially that it could easily lead to the disintegration of the community. Something of this implication was voiced – unfortunately not as a major motif – at the 1966 Conference on African Local Government held at Lincoln University, U.S.A. Professor Speck, reporting on his work in Malawi, lamented the lack of trained manpower for local governmental institutions. This was not due to lack of training, but to the fact that as soon as self-government came as a result of the final break-up of the former Federation, local government officials then in office were removed because they were regarded as 'stooges', and almost the only people left were the chiefs in their *ex officio* status. Most of these people were uneducated and not very sympathetic to modern concepts. Those who were educated represented a challenge to the newcomers in the central government. Just at the moment when local government resources reached their lowest man-power level, the central government passed to them the control of primary education in a policy of decentralization (in addition to roads, health clinics and other commitments) and at the same time the country ran into a period of economic stringency that decreased the available funds for such services. Local government in Malawi in 1965 was, in fact, starting virtually from the beginning again.[6] The Nigerian publisher, S. Okechukwu Mezu expressed the matter well: 'On the political spectrum, British officials worked with those villagers who were willing to forsake the old and collaborate with them. Often these were the least respected in the community. From the debris of this disintegrating society, where political advancement became synonymous with the disavowal of traditional bonds and mores, arose the local government that we know today.'[7] Whilst he supports the modernization of Nigeria (and his comments would, in the author's opinion, apply with almost equal force to other states in Africa) he asserts that a sound local government should grow out from within the community and its traditional structure. 'It should capitalize on the people's conception of life.' Mezu is prepared to state categorically that to govern effectively on the local government level, Africa must 'resurrect her traditional communalism . . .'' In practice his concept would involve the very interesting raprochement of the new-style politician at the helm of central government, and the old-style 'chiefly' leader, whose control over local affairs (though faded) is by no means inconsiderable. This will possibly involve generations of bargaining, in which the largely hereditary powers of the chief over land will have to be exchanged for some other status-giving role.

Nobody who does not know African life well can understand educational problems in Africa unless they are prepared to give considerable attention to the socio-economic problems which understrut the school system. Schools cost money to build and require cash to pay teacher's salaries. A subsistence economy is so called because it works basically

[6] *Proceedings on African Local Government Since Independence*, Lincoln University, Pennsylvania, U.S.A., 1966 (mimeograph), p. 7.
[7] *Ibid.*, p. 147.

on the production of goods immediately needed to satisfy village needs, or at best, as barter. Educational plans that are unsupported by the cash to pay for their development are valueless. Whilst money can be borrowed or in some cases given, for educational purposes, it is usual to ear-mark it for non-recurrent items. The daily running costs, such as salaries, have usually to be found from internally derived revenue.

Although the presence of a small European (White) population in Malawi (0·3 per cent) presents the country with no real problem in the multiracial field, the Phillips Commission noted that the European sector produced *more than half of the value of the agricultural exports of Malawi*, tea alone amounting to 40 per cent of the total exports. The Director of Agriculture estimated that the rural *per capita* income was about £8 (16 Rands) a year in 1958.

With a new start, Malawi produced a Five Year Development Plan in 1965.[8] Briefly stated, its major objectives included:

(i) Expansion of agriculture.

(ii) Better road communications and reduced transportation costs.

(iii) Educational expansion, stressing in particular secondary and post-secondary education 'so as to provide the skilled manpower that is essential for development'.

(iv) The stimulation of the private sector and especially the encouragement of industrial development.

The U.N.O. Economic Survey had predicted the possibility of considerable agricultural increases by 1970 – maize 33½ per cent, beans 100 per cent, Burley tobacco 50 per cent, cotton 100 per cent and ground-nuts 50 per cent. Turning to education, the Plan noted that since 1964, over the two-year period beginning 1964, secondary school enrolment had stepped up from 2,010 to 6,920 and should reach 11,545 places in 1969. On the basis of capital expenditure of the nature of £5,500,000, the Plan allocated this money as follows:

	Per cent
Primary schools:	6
Primary teacher training:	13
Secondary schools and technical education at the secondary level:	63
Post-secondary education:	12·4
Secondary teacher training:	5
Administration:	0·6

80 per cent (approximately) of the expenditure envisaged is to be devoted to a crash programme in secondary and post-secondary education. Under this provision, the Education Department would be

[8] *Development Plan 1965–1969,* Government Printer, Zomba, Malawi (n.d.).

able to provide some 7,800 additional places in secondary education. By 1969 the Standard VII output would be in the region of 33,000, 11 per cent of which would be able to go forward to further education. Apart from the provision of an Institute of Public Administration and a Polytechnic College, £2·4 millions was set aside for a National University.

In 1961 Professor George Seltzer of the University of Minnesota, supported by a Carnegie Grant, assessed the manpower requirements of Nyasaland (and the other Federal territories) his findings being printed as his contribution to *Manpower and Education*, edited by Harbison and Myers in 1965.[9] He presented his H.L.M. (High Level Manpower) concept as follows:

FORMULATION OF 'HIGH-LEVEL' MANPOWER CONCEPT*

Category	Representative occupational titles or descriptive phrase	Educational attainment and/or requirement
I. Administrative and professional	Responsibility for policy decisions. Ministers, permanent secretaries, top managers, and administrative in both the public and private sectors. Doctors, chemists, agronomists, accountants, lawyers, some teachers, engineers, etc.	University graduate or postgraduate.
II. Executive and technical	Middle management or top-level assistants to the above professionals. Draftsmen, qualified nurses, laboratory technicians, engineering assistants etc. Some secondary and technical school teachers.	1–3 years beyond Form IV in a college or specialized training institution.†
III. Skilled	Occupation may require trade testing or involve apprenticeship-type training. Artisans, foremen, stenographers, primary school teachers, skilled clerks, agricultural assistants, etc.	1–5 years beyond Standard 8 in apprenticeship or special training programmes.‡
IV. All others	Labourers, sales-clerks, copy typists, etc.	Below Standard 8.

* Categories I, II, III constitute the high-level manpower (H.L.M.) universe by definition.
† Form IV is equivalent to twelve years of formal schooling.
‡ Standard 8 is equivalent to eight years of formal schooling.

9 Seltzer, G., 'Highlevel Manpower in Nyasaland's Development' in Harbison, F. and Myers, C. A. (eds.), *Manpower and Education*, McGraw-Hill, 1965.

Using 1962 as base, he analysed the situation thus:

THE H.L.M. BASE, NUMBERS, RACIAL COMPOSITION, AND
SECTORAL DISTRIBUTION, NYASALAND, 1962

Sector and Race	H.L.M. I		H.L.M. II		H.L.M. III	
	Number employed	Per cent of category	Number employed	Per cent of category	Number employed	Per cent of category
All races:						
Public sector:						
Government*	300	46	875	52	3,325	25
Teaching**	150	24	250	16	4,225	32
Total†	450	30	1,125	68	7,600‡	58‡
Private Enterprise	200	30	525	32	5,500	42
Total H.L.M. in category	650	100	1,650	100	13,100	100
	Number employed	Per cent of category	Number employed	Per cent of category	Number employed	Per cent of category
Africans:						
Public Sector:						
Government*	31	11	300	34	3,200	97
Teaching**	17	11	100	40	4,100	98
Total†	48	11	400	36	7,300	96
Private Enterprise	0	0	50	10	2,100	38

Source: Based on 55 per cent sample of non-African 1961 census and survey of African employment.
* Except teaching services.   † The sum of government and teaching figures.
** Includes teachers in non-government schools.   ‡ Does not add due to rounding.

PROJECTED BALANCE OF H.L.M. REQUIREMENTS AND
AVAILABILITIES, NYASALAND, 1962–1975

Manpower projections	Period 1 July 1962–Dec. 1965			Period 2 Jan. 1966–Dec. 1970			Period 3 Jan. 1971–Dec. 1975		
	H.L.M. I	H.L.M. II	H.L.M. III	H.L.M. I	H.L.M. II	H.L.M. III	H.L.M. I	H.L.M. II	H.L.M. III
Additional requirements:									
Attrition	85	185	150	200	475	850	175	500	1,400
Wastage	90	235	1,825	180	525	3,200	300	1,000	4,800
All replacements	(175)	(420)	(1,975)	(380)	(1,000)	(4,050)	(475)	(1,500)	(6,200)
Growth	275	1,025	4,575	690	2,800	10,550	1,200	5,800	16,400
Total	450	1,450	6,550	1,070	3,800	14,600	1,675	7,300	22,600
Potential output	25	350	3,250	290	1,500	6,900	525	2,350	8,700
'Gap' between requirements and output	425	1,100	3,300	780	2,300	7,700	1,150	5,000	13,900

As Seltzer remarked, the public sector (government administration and teaching) employs the majority of H.L.M. in all categories (7 out of 10 in I and II; 6 out of 10 in III). Malawis constitute 8, 28 and 71 of each 100 employed in H.L.M. categories I, II and III respectively. Some 50 Nyasas had degrees. Seltzer's prediction of needs and supplies of H.L.M. was contained in the table on page 130.

Because of the comparatively sizeable gaps between supply and demand he concluded that for some years to come the country would be dependent on external sources of H.L.M. But this method of recruitment would only be a palliative whilst the educational and training programmes got into gear to supply manpower internally.

Education has been placed at the centre of Malawi's progress by a number of experts, and her whole future is dependent upon it. In Malawi there are two major educational problems: the provision of secondary and post-secondary education to meet the demands of H.L.M. and the need to re-think the contents of education in such a way that the hitherto narrow rote verbalism can be replaced by more generous basic skills which will provide the basis for later specialization.

Anyone in the least familiar with the problems of African education will know that the provision of H.L.M. ultimately depends upon the problem of wastage or dropout – which, if too great, minimises the number of pupils available for full secondary school training – and the ability of the teaching staff to educate the available pupils. Of course even the appropriate teaching staff necessary to produce H.L.M. I and II are often lacking. With these points particularly in mind, we pass to an examination of the problem of education in Malawi.

IV. EDUCATION

A. Teacher Supply and Qualification

The Ministry of Education Report for 1961 offered the analysis of teacher qualifications shown in the table overleaf. These figures show inter alia that about 45 per cent of all teachers in 1961 were untrained. Taking both trained and untrained teachers together, only 6 per cent had completed a secondary school course. More than 60 per cent of the trained teachers were classified as T5, that is two years' training and no academic qualifications. The pattern of teacher training found in 1954 became to some extent a prototype. There were ten Voluntary Agency teacher training colleges and one government college at Domasi, a situation which illustrated the administration's lack of funds.

TEACHING-STAFF QUALIFICATIONS, AFRICAN SCHOOLS,
NYASALAND, JUNE 30, 1961

Teacher qualification	School level			
	Junior primary	Senior primary	Secondary	Total, all levels
Approved graduate or equivalent:				
Trained	2	6	38	46
Untrained	—	1	12	13
	2	7	50	59
Completed secondary school course:				
Trained	15	374	28	417
Untrained	3	10	7	20
	18	384	35	437
Less than secondary school course:				
Trained	3,197	282	3	3,482
Untrained	3,291	14	1	3,306
	6,488	296	4	6,788
Total trained	3,214	662	69	3,945
Total untrained	3,294	25	20	3,339
Grand total	6,508	687	89	7,284

Domasi College then offered three types of courses:

T5. For Standard IV children (six years of schooling, made up of *Grades I and II, Standards I, II, III, and IV) in the vernacular only; or T4 for those who had the Standard VI certificate.

T3. With Standard VIII certificate (i.e. three years at the secondary level). The T5 was subsequently dropped. The output of Trained Teachers, 1956–60, as presented in the Phillips Report was:

OUTPUT OF TRAINED TEACHERS 1956–1960

		1956	1957	1958	1959	1960
Government:	T.2	—	—	8	6	9
	T.3	34	22	40	40	67
	T.4	—	10	20	30	18
Aided:	T.3	5	5	12	29	20
	T.4	171	170	240	267	330
Unaided:	T.4	4	10	14	5	16
	T.5	—	15	—	—	—
Total		214	232	334	377	460

* The term 'grades' has been abandoned recently; what was formerly Grade I (the entry into school) has become Standard I, the other standards following logically. Grades I and II are retained in the South African nomenclature.

In this Report, T2 training was dependent on the completion of Standard X and the Cambridge School Certificate. T3 teachers can no longer be supplied from Junior Secondary Schools. Most of these Junior Secondary schools have in any case become full secondary schools. The T3 qualification, largely redundant, is still qualification useful for upgrading T4 women. The Report predicted that with an output of 752 trained teachers in 1963, there would be *inter alia* 2 T1, 50 T2, and 630 T4. The Report comments on the lack of funds to enable colleges to employ proper staff, the use of outdated methods by indifferent personnel, the poor quality of the English language due to lack of specialist English teachers, and the inadequacy of many of the buildings, many of which are adjunct of the local primary school.

In its *Statement of Policy for Education* the Ministry states[10] that no training college shall in future be attached to a primary or secondary school. The purpose of this exclusion was probably to raise the status of training colleges. In the past there had been a progression through primary school straight into the training college, a progression that involved the same teaching staff and the same buildings. The Blantyre Teacher Training College was planned to act as a model establishment. A special *English Language Centre* was one of its features.

The Ministry was faced with the need to act as a co-ordinating factor in a situation in which a number of different religious bodies had considerable capital investment in education, among them the Roman Catholics, the Protestants and the Muslims. Lacking the funds to buy out missionary interest, the Ministry has itself invested in schools and colleges to a limited extent, often in the hope that its own establishment would serve as models for others. It has been able to increase its control of educational practice by asserting its right to inspect schools and colleges; by controlling teacher admission and qualifications; and by controlling the curriculum. The decentralization of education, which may in itself have desirable features in that it helps to develop a robust sense of local authority, is in many ways the only way in which a financially embarrassed central administration can hope to cope. 'The participation of the community in the task of developing education,' says the Ministry (perhaps making a virtue out of necessity) 'will be achieved by the devolution of responsibility for primary education to local government level.' The executive officer of each L.E.A. is a ministerial appointment. These L.E.A.s operate through Education Committees, which are empowered to control the receipt and expenditure of monies, to award scholarships and bursaries and to inspect

---

[10] *Statement of Policy for Education*, Zomba, Government Printer (n.d.).

buildings and equipment. It is broad policy to bring all schools under
L.E.A. control in the near future, and the figures quoted in the 1966
Annual Report[11] of the Ministry of Education are an interesting
demonstration of recent trends:

	1964		1965		1966	
	Boys	Girls	Boys	Girls	Boys	Girls
Assisted	152,377	82,986	163,506	93,758	152,682	78,122
Unassisted	74,153	46,159	49,344	31,405	33,883	21,369
Total	226,530	129,145	212,850	125,163	186,565	99,491

This enrolment in primary classes illustrates the attrition in the
unassisted schools, which are mainly denominational. The Ministry
itself is therefore concentrating its attention on the two aspects of
education which are in fact crucial to any developmental policy:
teacher training and secondary education. But even in these fields the
Ministry is by no means master of its own house. One of the twelve
training colleges providing for primary education is owned and
managed by the Ministry. Six fall under Roman Catholic control, four
under the Christian Council and one under the Seventh Day Advent-
ists Church, which operates without any subsidy. The single training
college specialising in secondary education is at Soche Hill. Entry to
this college is School Certificate, and the three-year course leads to the
Diploma in Education. This college has become part of the university.
  Perhaps the greatest problem that the Ministry has had to face in
the present period of educational reconstruction has been the upgrading of unqualified and inadequate teachers already in service.
The following table indicates this undertaking:

	Upgrading T4 and T5 Home Economics 2 Years/Women	Upgrading T3 and T2 One year/Women	Emergency Course for unqualified teachers	
			Men	Women
1964	—	—	44	6 (six months)
1965	—	21	—	—
1966	37	—	88	28 (one year)

By 1967 there were two government training colleges, Soche Hill, offering
a three-year Diploma of Education, and Domasi offering the T2 and T3

[11] *Annual Report of the Ministry of Education, Year 1966*, Zomba, Government Printer,
1967?

certificates. Three more national colleges are planned. At the end of 1966, 1,146 students were in training as teachers. It is noted with relief that this was the last year in which 'pupil-teaching' was permitted. This scheme (not unknown in Britain at the end of the nineteenth century) was almost inevitable when training colleges were identified with primary schools, and represented a type of educational apprenticeship.

B. Secondary Education

If the educational system is to meet the needs of High Level Manpower (H.L.M.) to a degree that the state can function properly without using expatriate skills, the need to provide sound secondary education was obvious. Except for 1966 (when the decision to make the primary course seven years was rescinded in favour of the earlier eight-year course) the enrolment figures show a steady growth in the secondary school population:

1963	3,041
1964	5,441
1965	7,578
1966	6,225
1967	8,090

The government is trying to provide one government secondary school per district and on that basis, one school was opened in 1963, six in 1964, ten in 1965 and seven in 1967. Secondary schools operate in two phases: a two year course ending in the Junior Certificate Examination, in which successful pupils may continue and will be offered places in the Boarding Establishments and a senior course which continues from Junior Certificate to the Cambridge Overseas School Certificate which, for the new secondary schools, will start developing from 1969. Students who want to enter university take the Cambridge Certificate A.

Malawi's shortage of H.L.M. affects education as much as any other sector of the economy. Effective science, maths and language teachers are in short demand the world over, but particularly so in countries such as Malawi, which has to rely to a very large extent on expatriate teachers financed by foreign aid. A steady internal improvement is seen in the fact that the number of trained graduates teaching in secondary schools rose from 34 in 1963 to 78 in 1966 – a decided improvement but one that is still completely inadequate. By October, 1966, Malawi was using the services of 222 overseas educationists sponsored under various plans such as V.S.O. Cadets from Britain, the Peace Corps from the U.S.A. and similar organizations.

Something of the immense problem facing the Ministry is seen in a breakdown of the 1966 figures, which are tabled as follows:

	Total Teaching Force	No. with qualification above T2	Other comment
Primary school	5,945	8	But 5,066 hold T4 or T5
Secondary school	219	153	13 hold T4 or lower
Technical Education	83	69	
Inspectorate	61	12	

Of the whole teaching cadre, 3,069 have no *professional* qualifications at all, 489 have no qualifications *of any sort*, and 2,226 have only got their primary school certificate. The total number employed in education at the end of 1966 was 9,528. The immediate weakness, as will be seen from the figures, lies in the general inadequacy of primary school staff in particular. By comparison, the staffing of the secondary schools and other post-primary institutions is reasonably healthy. The position of the Inspectorate gives rise to some foreboding, since 48 of the total force of 61 persons have either a T2 or a T3 certificate only.

The administration is well aware of the importance of introducing new methods of teaching in science, mathematics and languages. With the assistance of Education-Services Incorporated, an American group, a Science Centre has been established from which, it is hoped, new concepts of teaching and methodology will radiate into the primary school system. It is, however, a little difficult to see how (in its present state) the primary school sector can underwrite effective secondary education when such a large percentage of primary teachers are inadequately qualified to handle either the content or the methodology of new maths, and similar subjects which should begin shortly after the child enters schools.

As at present constituted, the Ministry of Education is responsible for primary and secondary education. All post-secondary education and training has passed to the jurisdiction of the University of Malawi, which was opened in September, 1965 with 92 undergraduates. At present The Institute for Public Administration, the Soche Hill College (which grants an educational diploma) and the Polytechnic fall under the surveillance of the University.

The University of Malawi under its Vice-Chancellor, Dr Ian Michael, comprises five institutions (which will eventually be reduced to four): The University undergraduate campus at Zomba, Soche Hill

College of Education, which specializes in training secondary school teachers, The Institute of Public Administration, which offers diploma courses, The Malawi Polytechnic College at Blantyre and the Bunda Agricultural College near Lilongwe in the Central region.

C. The Primary School

The fact that Malawi has a reasonable educational basis on which to build is due to missionary enterprise in the first place, and the administration has never really been financially in a position to take over completely from private enterprise, as has the Republic of South Africa. But the growth of state control in the interests of a unified educational system is inevitable and the figures reflect a decline on the ability of the churches to carry the growing financial weight implicit in efficient modern educational committment.

Whilst the Ministry is able to provide much leadership and considerable control, it has been forced by lack of funds to delegate much of its work to local authorities, especially in the primary school sector. These L.E.A.s receive funds from the following sources:

(i) Grants in aid from the government – amounting to £1,145,000 in 1966.

(ii) Local rates – often difficult to collect in an economy in which cash circulation is limited.

(iii) Tuition fees – (£7 10s 0d, tuition; £10 0s 0d, boarding) which, like rates are not always easy to collect.

The 'no fee, no enrolment', policy is being followed rigorously at present. Inability to pay is partly linked to inadequate harvests.

L.E.A.s pay all teachers, distribute school supplies to assisted schools, control book orders and supervise buildings and equipment. Although the L.E.A. executive officer is a government nominee, there is such an acute shortage of people capable of this level of administration and financial control that considerable inefficiency and occasional lapses of public morality do occur. It is difficult to establish a unit cost for Malawi primary education – say on a 'per pupil per year' basis. Many African countries lack the facilities for data collection at present – let alone its subsequent statistical analysis. The 1966 Report states that a sum of £1,636,838 was spent to educate some 286,056 children in the primary school system – which gives an approximate unit cost of £5·7 (R11·4). This may be compared with a per capita 1960 expenditure of R13·5 in the Republic of South Africa.[12] The Malawi figure may be nearer to R12, because of hidden contributions (i.e. as when parties

---

[12] *Education and the South African Economy*, the 1961 Educational Panel, 2nd Report, Witwatersrand University Press, 1966, p. 123.

give their labour to help build classrooms, or missionaries give adminis-trative skills free).

Although the figure of R11·4 as a per capita annual cost must be taken as tentative and subject to later correction when more accurate figures are available, it may be useful to assess the financial loss to Malawi of wastage by dropout in the primary school system. It is a moot and probably controversial point as to the number of years a child should remain in the educational system so that its dropout is not complete wastage. It is generally accepted that if a child has not acquired a basic literacy – the skills of reading and writing at least in his mother tongue – he will fall back into illiteracy very rapidly, especially in a subsistence economy in which he has no stimulus to maintain such basic skills as he may have acquired. Even basic literacy will probably be in jeopardy with less than four years at school. The figures below illustrate a most serious problem in primary education in Malawi – and one typical of many African states. In June 30, 1962, 95,926 children had begun in (the now) Standard I: by June 30, 1966, 32,496 children of the 1962 intake remained in Standard IV.

Over this four year period there had been a *loss* of 63,430 children which represents a dropout from the 1962 beginners of 66·1 per cent.

Or again, taking a different group over a slightly longer period, we find: in June, 1960, 101,694 children started school; by June 30, 1966, 23,423 remained from these original starters. Over this six year period, there had been a loss of 78,271, which represents a dropout of 67 per cent. This is an alarming state of affairs. If we take up the shorter term dropouts, and if we accept that the dropout rate is 50 per cent or over (so as not to overstate the argument) we are left with some 48,000 whose educational gains are very slight (when they exist at all) and who probably represent an investment loss of over R500,000 which is very approxi-mately 15 per cent of total expenditure on primary school education.

The teacher pupil ratio continues to be 1 : 50 in the first two classes and 1 : 45 in most others. At present the primary course is an 8 year course followed by a 4 year secondary course. An attempt at a 7/5 system was abandoned in 1965/6, and a return was also made to a more rigorous examination system at school certificate level on com-pletion of the eighth year of primary school, and then again at Junior Certificate level, two years later in secondary school. The Ministry is aware of the 'besetting sin' of much African education – learning by rote, and the 1966 report notes: 'The opportunity is being taken in the setting of (examination) papers at least at the Form II level (Junior Certificate) to encourage in the school's teaching methods which make pupils think rather than merely learn facts by rote'.

GENERAL EDUCATION ENROLMENT BY LEVEL OF EDUCATION
AT JUNE 30, 1966
(A) GOVERNMENT AND AIDED SCHOOLS
SECONDARY SCHOOLS

	Std. 1	Std. 2	Std. 3	Std. 4	Std. 5	Std. 6	Std. 7	Std. 8	Total
Male	24,368	18,506	19,342	18,032	18,775	18,312	16,335	19,012	152,682
Female	15,764	12,487	11,806	10,238	8,879	7,261	6,677	5,010	78,122
Total	40,132	30,993	31,148	28,270	27,654	25,573	23,012	24,022	230,804

SECONDARY EDUCATION

	Form II	Form III	Form IV	Form V	Form VI (2 year course)	Total
Male	1,732	1,121	1,091	628	39	4,611
Female	632	409	324	277	2	1,644
Total	2,364	1,530	1,415	905	41	6,255

(B) UNASSISTED SCHOOLS
PRIMARY EDUCATION

	Std. 1	Std. 2	Std. 3	Std. 4	Std. 5	Std. 6	Std. 7	Std. 8	Total
Male	11,391	7,830	5,818	4,482	3,249	409	303	401	33,883
Female	7,665	5,501	3,795	2,458	1,593	139	108	110	21,369
Total	19,056	13,331	9,613	6,940	4,842	548	411	511	55,252

SECONDARY EDUCATION

	Form II	Form III	Form IV	Form V	Total
Male	103	45	45	24	217
Female	38	18	6	5	67
Total	141	63	51	29	284

NUMBER OF CLASSES AND PUPILS BY CLASSES, JUNE 30, 1966

1	2	3	4	5	6	7	8	9	10
		Unassisted			Assisted			Government	
		Pupils			Pupils			Pupils	
	No. of classes	Boys	Girls	No. of classes	Boys	Girls	No. of classes	Boys	Girls
Standard 1	830	11,391	7,665	1,280	23,195	14,785	34	1,173	979
Standard 2	815	7,830	5,501	1,276	17,673	11,794	33	833	693
Standard 3	765	5,818	3,795	1,253	18,546	11,175	32	796	631
Standard 4	561	4,482	2,458	1,237	17,339	9,743	32	693	495
Standard 5	368	3,249	1,593	1,179	18,147	8,496	28	628	383
Standard 6	23	409	139	1,081	17,755	6,930	27	557	331
Standard 7	12	303	108	985	15,771	6,386	24	564	291
Standard 8	20	401	110	836	18,286	4,723	24	726	287
Total Primary	3,394	33,883	21,369	9,127	146,712	74,032	234	5,970	4,090

1	2	3	4	5	6	7	8	9	10
	Unassisted			Assisted			Government		
	No. of classes	Pupils		No. of classes	Pupils		No. of classes	Pupils	
		Boys	Girls		Boys	Girls		Boys	Girls
Form II	3	103	38	25	538	265	43	1,194	367
Form III	2	45	18	25	534	229	23	587	180
Form IV	2	45	6	25	549	208	23	542	116
Form V	1	24	5	25	506	189	8	122	88
Total	8	217	67	100	2,127	891	97	2,445	751
Form VI (two years)	—	—	—	2	39	2	—	—	—
Total	—	—	—	2	39	2	—	—	—
Total Secondary	8	217	67	102	2,166	893	97	2,445	751
Grand Total	3,402	34,100	21,436	9,229	148,878	74,925	331	8,415	4,841

6· Education in Zambia

JAMES ROBERTSON

The country we now call Zambia was until 1964 known as Northern Rhodesia, and the change in name coincided with a change in political and national status which had repercussions at every level of national life. The changes initiated are seen most vividly in the national system of education. Before October 24, 1964, the organization of education had been the responsibility of men and women acting as the instruments of a colonial government, centred in Great Britain, in bringing a Protectorate to self-governing and independent nationhood. Thereafter the fundamental responsibility lay with the indigenous people themselves, and the educational system we see today, while owing much to the structure built by its western originators, has both its impetus and its direction determined by the aspirations of the Zambian nation and its leaders in the present century.

For the sake of clarity, and constrained by the need for brevity, the following plan has been adopted for this study of Zambian education:

I Background
  A The Nation and the Country.
  B The Economy.
  C Political History.
  D Educational History, till 1963.
  E The Transitional Years.
II The Structure of Zambian Education in 1965.
III Education in the First National Development Plan 1966–70.
IV Policy Problems in Education.
V Conclusion.
VI Bibliography.

It will be noted that the pivotal year for the purpose of the analysis to be made is 1964. It was then that the national will began to be precise in planning and execution. The social service that had helped the nation to be born became a principal instrument of the national will.

I. BACKGROUND

A. The Nation and the Country

The people of the land belong to approximately 70 tribes of Central Bantu, welded together in 'One Zambia – One Nation'. The 1965 estimate[1] of the population is given as 3,700,000 Zambians and 82,300 others. These latter comprise approximately 70,000 Europeans, 9,700 Asians, and 2,600 people of mixed racial descent. There are many among the 'others' who look upon themselves as permanent Zambian citizens, but probably the majority do not see themselves and their children as identified permanently with the nation whom they serve.

The Zambians themselves[2] divide (in one sense) into 764,200 settled in urban areas and 2,866,000 in rural parts of the country. But the tribal, clan, family, language, district, provincial, economic and religious ties which bind the urban and rural areas are manifold, despite the emergence of urban dwellers who are second and third generation townspeople and comparatively detribalized. This binding together has been emphasized politically with the emergence of nationhood. The people of the 70 tribes mentioned above lived, until the colonial penetration of the country, in valleys and areas where the local languages flourished and remained differentiated. With the need for communication that came from mission, trade, travel, war and western administration, these languages were eventually grouped into five roughly geographical sectors:

  (i)   North – Bemba.[3]
  (ii) East – Nyanja.
  (iii) South – Tonga.
  (iv) West (Barotseland) – Lozi.
  (v)   North-West – Lunda/Lovale.

Two points are worth noting. First, the language Nyanja used in the East had its principal roots in Malawi (Nyasaland). The period after the Second World War saw a great increase in the use of newspapers and radio, and the official vernaculars used were the first four named above. At the same time English became the *lingua franca* of the country. The importance of these facts will become more evident later when we note the educational problems involved in providing a school system which takes account of the interaction of English and four agreed vernaculars.

---

[1] Table 1, *Ministry of Education, Annual Report, 1965*, p. 29.
[2] *First National Development Plan, 1966–7*, p. 5.
[3] The short form of the name of the language, without the Ci- prefix has been adopted, without prejudice to the purist.

The country itself lies almost symmetrically round the intersection of latitude line 14 degrees south and longitude line 28 degrees east, and is completely landlocked. Starting with the Congo in the north and moving in a clockwise direction, Zambia's neighbours are Tanzania, Malawi, Mozambique, Rhodesia, South West Africa, and Angola. These seven are almost joined by Botswana, which juts in between the Caprivi Strip of South West Africa and Rhodesia, quite close to the Victoria Falls on the Zambezi River. The only railway line running from the Falls in the south to the Congo in the north, bisects the country. The bulk of the non-African population lives in the towns along the line of rail, with the highest proportion centred in the Copperbelt towns just south of the Congo border, and in the capital city of Lusaka, which lies at the junction of the east-west and general north-south lines of communication.

Most of the country is part of a flat plateau at an average altitude of 4,000 feet above sea level, but it has a few places in the river valleys of the Zambezi, Kafue and Luangwa where the altitude drops to 2,500 feet, and correspondingly fewer ridges where over 5,000 feet is reached.

B. The Economy

1. Agriculture

Along the railway line are to be found productive farms owned and developed largely by Europeans, about 700 in number. In 1964 it was reckoned[4] that from 182,000 acres they produced £7,700,000 worth of agricultural sales, over and above their own family needs. Three million pounds of this came from tobacco, and maize accounted for £2·5 millions. The rest came from cattle and subsidiary crops. In marked contrast, the rest of the huge rural population, numbering about 450,000 African families, from an acreage of approximately 5,000,000 was able to produce only £3·2 m. sales evenly spread over maize, cattle and other crops, with the rest coming from the production of £200,000 worth of tobacco. These figures are given to indicate the principal products, and the magnitude of the problem of agricultural education involved, and they form a vivid contrast with the finance coming from mining.

2. Mining

This comparatively dominant industry is concentrated in the Copper Belt, contiguous with the Congo, with subsidiary workings at Broken

4 *F.N.D.P.*, p. 2.

Hill and in scattered small mines elsewhere. The principal product is copper, of high quality, and it is from this product's world sales that the Zambian government derives its principal resource for educational development. It will be understood that the amount of money available for national economic growth is dependent both on production and world prices. The estimated gross output[5] from copper mining in 1965–6 was £199 m. from which an expected government revenue of £72 m. was likely to accrue. The £199 m. figure is a vivid contrast to the £11 m. (approx.) agricultural sales in 1964, and probably the comparison of government revenue from these two sources would be even more disparate.

It is hard to get exact figures of comparison, as the above extract shows, but the published figures of the gross output of the major sectors of the economy for 1964 indicate the problem in another way. Agriculture provided[6] £12·7 m. while mining provided £154·4 m. out of a total of £320·5 m.

Perhaps a better indication of the resources available for education come from Government Revenue figures abstracted[7] from Table 29 of the official 1967 statistics.

CENTRAL GOVERNMENT REVENUE (FIGURES IN £M.)

Year	Total	from Income Tax	from Minerals, Royalties and Copper Export Tax
1963/4	31·859	15·086	3·131
1964/5	78·537	33·550	21·170
1965/6	108·297	40·171	41·237
1966/7 estimated	122·965	36·820	58·880

At this stage it is important to notice that the great increase in funds from mining since 1963–4 is made possible by the royalties now accruing to government and not to the former chartered companies. Later we shall take note of the proportion of government revenue being applied to education.

3. Other Industries

It will be evident from the table above that income tax, mining tax and royalties in 1966–7 alone accounted for £95·7 m. of the £122·965 m.

[5] *F.N.D.P.*, p. 31.
[6] *F.N.D.P.*, p. 6.
[7] Volume IV, No. 4, April, 1967.

estimated revenue. This is an indication of the proportionately small contribution made by other industries. It will suffice that the most important for growth are tourism, small industrial and commercial services, and electrical power. An indication of prospects can be found in the current National Plan. For our purposes we note that agriculture and mining are the mainstay of an economy which for obvious reasons is ready to put a great deal of money – proportionately – to education.

C. Political History

From the death of David Livingstone onwards Zambia was penetrated from the south by both missionaries and traders in the latter part of the nineteenth century. A detailed description of their early journeys, and negotiations between them and the Barotse nation in Zambia can be found in the relevant literature.[8] Francois Coillard of the Paris Evangelical Mission established himself as an intermediary between the traders and the Barotse King Lewanika, and from 1889 onwards the major concessions were being negotiated. In the same year the British South Africa Company, founded by Cecil Rhodes, was granted a Royal Charter and began to see the country north of the Zambezi river as the next stage in the growth of empire.

In 1890 the concession of the mineral rights was made by King Lewanika and his council and the commercial bridgehead, leading to eventual administrative control, was made a growing reality. In 1892 the Protectorate status of Barotseland was recognized by the Queen and notice given of the eventual arrival of Her Majesty's representative.

It was not until 1897 that the British South Africa Company sent Major Robert Thorne Coryndon as British Resident Commissioner in Barotseland, he having the dual role of company respresentative and Queen's representative. We cannot follow the whole story of gradual infiltration by the Company into complete administrative control of what became known as North-Western Rhodesia, but by 1900 Barotseland and the bulk of the Southern Province were being systematically administered, and in the next few years control spread northwards in the direction of the railway line.

In 1891, when Nyasaland (Malawi) came under the control of the British Government, it was agreed that the British South Africa Company would be entrusted with the development of the area known as North-Eastern Rhodesia, with Her Majesty's Commissioner in Nyasa-

[8] See Bibliography.

land exercising political control through the Company's Administration. In 1898 the formative control became more precise with the appointment of Robert Edward Codrington as Deputy Administrator, and the administrative centre was founded near the present Fort Jameson. In 1890 Codrington became full Administrator and district government was inaugurated.

In both North-Western and North-Eastern Rhodesia settlement by Europeans became a steady practice and these settlers began to ask for more and more say in an advisory capacity to government. They were vociferous and by 1921 there were[9] 8,634 of them in North-Western Rhodesia. The High Commissioner of South Africa, representing the U.K. government listened to their point of view, and in the years immediately after the First World War political agitation grew. Negotiations on the future depended on the issue whether or not North-Western and North-Eastern Rhodesia would amalgamate with Southern Rhodesia. The 1922 Advisory Council elections showed that the settlers were against union with Southern Rhodesia. In 1923 the latter country, by referendum, decided against union with South Africa, and in the same year the Advisory Council to government in Northern Rhodesia asked for unitary status under the Crown. The appropriate Order-in-Council was made establishing rule through a Legislative Council and Governor in 1924, and so Zambia gained its first stage of political unity under the Crown.

Gradually the Legislative Council became liberalized racially, and by 1945 key church leaders held membership of the Council 'as representing African interests'. The next stage was the nomination of African members of Legislative Council for the same purpose, after election by the African Representative Council, which had its roots in tribal and district councils.

Eventually the franchise was widened, ordinary and special electoral rolls were compiled, and in the 'Federal Years' there gradually emerged limited and full internal-self-government. From 1963, with the dissolution of Federation, the way was paved for full political independence and the nation was born.

Out of the original company administration there grew up the division of the country into Provinces and Districts. From 1924 onwards District Officers, within the Colonial Service, built up the administrative structure of Provincial and District Government closely allied both with local government by chiefs and headmen in the mainly rural

---

9 Aelfand, M., *Northern Rhodesia in the Days of the Charter*, Blackwell, 1961. The whole of this section is indebted to this work, and also to Cann, L. H., *The Birth of a Plural Society*, Manchester University Press, 1958.

areas, and with municipal local government in European-dominated towns and townships.

The educational system in the African sector was closely linked with local government in the rural areas, and central government took the major responsibility for education in the towns. The fact that municipalities did not themselves enter the field of education (in the schooling sense), meant that there was lacking, both in the African and European sector, local contribution of a significant nature to education, that can be found in a country like Great Britain. This lack in towns, combined with a corresponding lack for different but obvious reasons in the rural areas, had its effect when the Local Education Authorities were formally established by ordinance in 1952.

In this short section one can notice the links between political and educational development, between church and state, and between administration of local government and education.

D. Educational History

1. *1885 to 1925*

During these years education in any systematic sense was in the hands of the missionary societies of many denominations. In 1885 Francois Coillard of the Paris Evangelical Missionary Society received permission to found a Mission Station in Barotseland, and this enterprise was the forerunner of many other Christian missions, in all the provinces. The early missionaries started evangelically based schools out of which the formal educational system grew, and the importance and the continuity of this influence is clearly visible up to the present day.

The first secular enterprise in education came with the foundation of the Barotse National School in 1907. Money came from the Barotse National Trust Fund, which had been established as a result of an agreement between the British South African Company and Paramount Chief Lewanika. But it was not until 1925 that any government[10] money was made available for helping African education.

The impetus for governmental participation came from the work of the Phelps-Stokes Commissions in Africa which resulted in the publication of the *Memorandum on Education Policy in British Tropical Africa*, in 1925. At the same time the General Missionary Conference in Northern Rhodesia made a formal request that the government establish an education programme. The result was that a sub-department for

[10] The B.S.A. Company helped European Education. See later, p. 172.

'Native Education' was started under the aegis of the Department of Native Affairs and the foundations of governmental enterprise in education in Zambia were laid. It is chastening to note that in 1925 a contribution[11] of £348 was made to the mission schools, and yet the average attendance in 1924 was recorded as approximately 40,000. Admittedly 'attendance' did not imply what would be expected today, but the figures quoted make interesting comparison with the millions of pounds rightly spent today.

2. 1925 to 1953

(i) Were we attempting a detailed history of this period we should split it up into several periods which correspond to discernible planning programmes related to economic and political growth. But in order to devote as much space as possible to the current educational system 1953 has been chosen to mark the end of the second period.

The year 1930 saw the formation of the African Education Department as a separate entity. A five-year plan was formulated which did not materialize because of economic depression. The approach was to consolidate the missionary work by the provision of 'grants-in-aid', and the heavy dependence of government on the voluntary agency is exemplified by the fact that in the annual expenditure[12] of the fifth year of the plan it was envisaged that out of a total of £71,346 the missions would receive £31,940. In point of fact government expenditure on education did not reach £30,000 p.a. till 1938. More important however in the early part of the period under review is the fact that Superintendents of Native Education were appointed. These were succeeded by Education Officers who formed the core of the administrative machinery to be described later. Emphasis was given to the training of teachers, community supervisors and agricultural leaders. Trades school training was also established. The institutions set up by the government parallel to those founded by the missions were to have a seminal effect on later development.

With the advent of the Second World War there came the beginning of a remarkable expansion of primary education, which in its very success, created, as we shall see, many future social, economic and educational problems. By 1946 expenditure[13] by government on education for Africans had risen to £192,922 p.a. and in 1,168 schools we find that 135,167 pupils were enrolled. It would be tedious to be more specific about statistics for the succeeding years. These are readily

[11] *Annual Report on Native Education*, 1926.
[12] *Triennial Survey, N. Rhodesia*, Ministry of Education, 1963, p. 1.
[13] *Triennial Survey*, 1963.

accessible in the government reports. The important factors are rates of expansion, primary emphasis, and the beginnings of the secondary system in both an academic and vocational sense.

In the latter part of the period there appeared a great increase in planning and in capital investment in education, both from territorial resources and also from the Colonial Development and Welfare Funds, but the pattern still emphasized the growth of primary education.

During the period we are considering it is essential to remember that European education had become an important part of the formal system of education and we need now to review its growth and size.

(ii) In the early part of this century, with the coming of settlers, and their families, scattered groups of European children began to receive instruction in small schools. These started as a mixture of church and parental enterprise in the years 1906 to 1910, in Fort Jameson, Livingstone and Lusaka district, supported by grants from the Beit Trust and the B.S.A. Company. Between 1912 and 1925 these grew in number and enrolment, and in many cases had small boarding hostels attached.

There is a short but detailed account in M. Gelfand's *Northern Rhodesia in the Days of the Charter*, which also has some illuminating details of the Barotse National School. The relevant chapter referring to Europeans only, ends thus:[14]

> No facilities for secondary education existed as yet in Northern Rhodesia, so the older pupils had to be sent south with the help of the Beit Trust and an annual grant by the administration. In 1921 there were 528 children of school-going age resident in Northern Rhodesia, but only 239 were at school. In spite of this expenditure on education rose from £6,900 in 1920–21 to £7,500 in 1924–25, and the government was already facing large deficits in this department.

The first Director of European Education[15] served from 1926 to 1948, and during this period numbers rose, secondary education was introduced (1927), an advisory board formed (1935), and compulsory education introduced (1942). From 1946 to 1949 enrolment doubled to 4,033 pupils, with 72 Coloured and 100 Asian pupils.

An important commission, led by the late Professor T. Williams* of Johannesburg, Rector of the College of Education, investigated education in 1948 and one of its recommendations was that European and African Education be merged. Government agreed in principle but a decision to implement the idea was deferred.

[14] *Op. cit.*, p. 252.
[15] See Department of European Education, *Annual Report*, 1953.
* Sir Thomas was subsequently Speaker of the Legislative Assembly in Zambia.

From then until 1953 the Department of Education became responsible for higher education, for Indian education, and for the selection
of candidates for teacher training in Southern Rhodesia. By 1953 there
were 9,429 European and 492 Asian and Coloured children enrolled.
The great majority of the teachers were expatriate Europeans, and the
organization was largely parallel to that obtaining in Southern
Rhodesia. This enabled the changeover to Federal responsibility to be
made easily in 1953.

The abstract (Tables 1–4, p. 153) from the Annual Report for
1953 (q.v.) summarizes the extent of the work.

(iii) The end of the period under review saw the publication of
*African Education – A Study of Educational Policy and Practice in British
Tropical Africa*. This volume summarized the work of Study Groups
set up by the Colonial Office and the Nuffield Foundation in West
Africa and in East and Central Africa, which culminated in the Cambridge Conference of 1952. This study provided the major part of the
stimulus which inaugurated the final phase of development in education in Zambia before independence. This is not to say that the recommendations of the Report were a blue-print for development. They were
rather vivid examples of the ideas that were eventually to be implemented in the light of the political and nationalist pressures beginning
to drive the emerging nation.

It has already been noted above that 1953 saw also the foundation
of the Federal experiment which was to end in 1963, when European
and Asian education became the responsibility of the Federal authorities and not the territorial authorities. African Education remained
a territorial responsibility, and it was not until 1964 that the educational system of the territory came under actual unitary direction.

3. *1953 to 1963*

To prepare for the description of education on Zambia in 1963 it
seems wisest to treat the ten years prior in a slightly different fashion.
It is worth while looking more closely at the background to educational
development and the major influences that paved the way for the
current system.

(a) *Legislation*
(i) In 1952 the African Education Ordinance was published and this
provided for 'the establishment of local education authorities in all
provinces and districts, a unified African teaching service, the appointment of school councils, closer management and regulation of schools

TABLE I EUROPEAN EDUCATION 1953

ENROLMENT

	Government and Aided Schools	Private Schools	Total
Pre-school	—	271	271
Primary	7,045	1,171	8,216
Secondary	1,316	118	1,434
Total	8,361	1,560	9,921

With 90 Correspondence pupils, the final total was 10,011.

TABLE 2

	Estimated Population	Scholars	Percentage
European	50,000	9,519	19
Coloured and Asiatic	5,000	492	9·8
Total	55,000	10,011	18·2

Types of Schools	No.
Government	29
Private-Aided	2 (Mission-Schools)
Private-Unaided	7 (Convent Schools)

Of these one went to Form VI; two went to Form V; five went to Form IV

TABLE 3 TEACHERS IN GOVERNMENT SCHOOLS

	Certificated		Uncertificated		Total	
	No.	%	No.	%	No.	%
Graduates	93	29·2	3	0·9	96	30·1
Matriculants	205	64·5	12	3·9	217	68·4
Non-matriculants	2	0·6	3	0·9	5	1·5
Total	300	94·3	18	5·7	318	100

Teacher-Training
27 grant-aided students studying in Southern Rhodesia and South Africa.

University Education
Students numbering 81 in South Africa and 24 in the United Kingdom assisted by scholarships and loans.
General assistance given to these totalled £16,645.

TABLE 4 EXPENDITURE (FOR COMPARISON)

	1953	Increase over 1952
African	£744,440	£135,299
European	£564,346	£105,207
Coloured and Asiatic	£30,488	£716

and proper financial control designed to ensure that the best value is obtained for the public funds spent on education'.[16]

(ii) In 1953 the Federal government became responsible for 'the education of non-Africans and for the higher education of all races, while the territorial government was responsible for the education, other than higher education, of Africans. One government could only assume responsibility in a sphere allocated to the other government with the consent of that government'.

(iii) In 1959 the Department of African Education became the Ministry of African Education, and the way was paved for the foundation of the Ministry of Education in 1964.

(b) *Voluntary Agencies*
These were principally the missions, native authorities in rural areas, a few farmers, with the missions preponderating in numbers, resources and influence. With the advent of legislation in 1952 gradually the system saw local authorities take over from Native Authorities, and by 1963 schools were to be found in four categories, viz.,

(i) Government.

(ii) Local Education Authority.

(iii) Grant-aided, managed by voluntary agencies.

(iv) Unaided, managed by voluntary agencies.

It is important to note that in 1963 the government had no direct work in primary schools in the African sector. However, the running of the Local Education Authority Schools was made possible through Government Education Officers and their staffs taking over the management of these schools on behalf of the L.E.A.s. In that year the voluntary agencies managed primary schools where the enrolment was between 42 per cent and 60 per cent of the total number in school. The latter years of the period were marked by a number of the missions handing over the management of their schools to the Local Education Authorities.

Similarly in the secondary sector, and teacher training, the voluntary agencies were responsible for a greater number of pupils than government and L.E.A.s combined. These facts are a measure of the close link between government and mission that is an essential feature of the growth of the system.

(c) *Teacher Training*
(i) Until 1955 the colleges involved in the training of teachers had

16 *T.S.*, 1963, pp. 2 and 3.

been numerous and small. As a result of the 1953 report on African education negotiations were begun with the voluntary agencies to reduce the number of small colleges and establish in the first instance five larger colleges with numbers in the region of 250–300 students in two-year courses. Those missions belonging to the Christian Council of Northern Rhodesia were allotted two, the Roman Catholics one, the Local Authority one, and the fifth was the Government College, which had originally started as the Jeanes Training Centre and was concerned with the training of community workers as well as teachers. For some years a few smaller colleges persisted for denominational reasons, and for reasons concerned with the education of girls.

(ii) By 1963[17] there were 7,164 teachers employed in the schools, and 96·8 per cent of these had been trained, in varying degrees. 229 of the rest were graduates. However only 596 (8·3 per cent) had completed the full secondary course. These statistics show to a remarkable extent the emphasis that had been placed on training in the forty years previously.

(d) *Advisory Committees*

(i) From 1925 onwards Advisory Boards had been in operation, which enabled the government to seek the advice of the general public, and those engaged in education, missions, commerce, industry, etc. in policy problems. Both the African and European sectors of education had separate Boards.

(ii) Correspondingly within the teaching and administrative sectors there grew up professional committees on female education, secondary education, trades training, primary education and teacher-training. It would be impossible in a short compass to follow the curricular developments which flowed from this work, but they represent a remarkable example of professional enterprise and co-operation.

(e) *The Organization of Teachers*

(i) In 1953 there was introduced a Unified African Teaching Service, to which all (or by far the majority) of teachers belonged. The rest were either members of the European or African Civil Service. In 1961 the position was made much more rational by the establishing of the Northern Rhodesia Teaching Service which was non-racial in composition. However, those who had begun as Civil Servants continued mainly within their traditional service. The developments described did much to prepare the way for a fully national system, and one marked benefit, perhaps often lost sight of, was the stopping of wastage

[17] Cf. *T.S.*, 1963, tables in Appendix.

when teachers were attracted into other forms of employment which offered better wages. The new conditions, including defined scales, promotion definitions, and the long-term pension benefits brought a relative stability.

(ii) Correspondingly the teachers themselves in 1953 formed their Teachers' Association which in 1962 became the Northern Rhodesian Union of Teachers, formally registered as a trade union. This period marked a time of great debate about wages and conditions, but there began a professionally based interest in standards and self-help that was to be important in developing national consciousness.

(f) *Local Education Authorities*
In the earlier years prior to 1953 there had existed Local Education Committees at provincial and district levels which had advised on expansion policy, and local matters like the allocation of building funds. These were transformed by the 1952 legislation into statutory Local Education Authorities, widely representative. They depended heavily on departmental staff and had considerable authority in the allocation of funds at provincial level. It was originally hoped that 'within a few years these would become an integral part of local government, developing into education committees or district or provincial councils'.[18] This hope did not materialize, and this was due to the need for central financial control, the inability of the authority to raise its own local funds, and the dearth of comparable competence in general local authorities, particularly in the rural areas.

(g) *Managership of Schools*
For many years the expatriate missionaries were the only people with the training and tradition to enable them to lead in school management, which involved much of the function that would be performed in a developed society by heads of schools. The formation of the Local Education Authority schools at this time started the movement for the training of African managers and gradually the whole system began to be transformed with the emergence of African managers and more important, the kind of Head who managed his own school and staff.

(h) *Miscellaneous*
To end this section it must suffice that we note the development of higher education, overseas bursary systems, experiments in compulsory education, co-education, education for girls, a publications bureau, technical education bureau, technical education, further education, health services, youth work, community service, and social service.

---

[18] *Annual Report*, 1953.

TABLE 5
DIAGRAM TO ILLUSTRATE THE GENERAL ORGANIZATION OF THE
MINISTRY OF AFRICAN EDUCATION, 1963

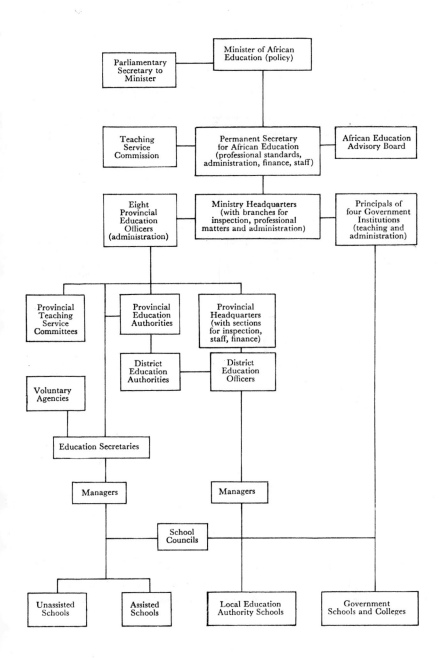

TABLE 6

DIAGRAM SHOWING THE GENERAL STRUCTURE OF THE
FORMAL AFRICAN EDUCATION SYSTEM, DECEMBER, 1963

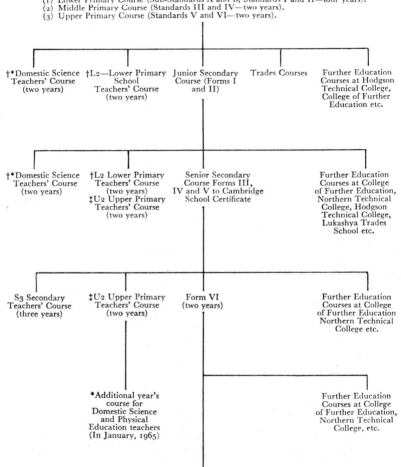

PRIMARY SCHOOLS

(1) Lower Primary Course (Sub-Standards A and B, Standards I and II—four years).
(2) Middle Primary Course (Standards III and IV—two years).
(3) Upper Primary Course (Standards V and VI—two years).

†*Domestic Science Teachers' Course (two years)

†L2—Lower Primary School Teachers' Course (two years)

Junior Secondary Course (Forms I and II)

Trades Courses

Further Education Courses at Hodgson Technical College, College of Further Education etc.

†*Domestic Science Teachers' Course (two years)

†L2 Lower Primary Teachers' Course (two years)
‡U2 Upper Primary Teachers' Course (two years)

Senior Secondary Course Forms III, IV and V to Cambridge School Certificate

Further Education Courses at College of Further Education, Northern Technical College, Hodgson Technical College, Lukashya Trades School etc.

S3 Secondary Teachers' Course (three years)

‡U2 Upper Primary Teachers' Course (two years)

Form VI (two years)

Further Education Courses at College of Further Education Northern Technical College etc.

*Additional year's course for Domestic Science and Physical Education teachers (In January, 1965)

Further Education Courses at College of Further Education, Northern Technical College, etc.

Degree Courses

† It should be noted that these refer to the same course. It was intended that the course would be a two-year post-Junior Secondary but because there were insufficient numbers it was found necessary to admit a number of students with post-Standard VI qualifications.
* In 1965 it is intended that the course for Domestic Science teachers will consist of one additional year following the normal U2 course.
‡ It should be noted that these refer to the same course but a number of students admitted have in fact completed a senior secondary course.

These areas of education will be described in detail later. Everything that has been sketched so far depended on the gradual evolution of a Ministry of Education, formally organized, and the structure of the Ministry of African Education in 1963 set out in the previous table,[19] together with the table[20] illustrating the formal system in the same year is a convenient summary on which to build a picture of the contemporary setting of education in Zambia.

As was indicated at the end of the previous main section, European education was a Federal and not a Zambian responsibility during this period and reference should be made to the chapter on Southern Rhodesian education. It was a tremendous growth period both at the level of enrolment and capital expenditure.

The summary[21] extracts from the 1962 Federal Education report gives a picture of the expansion when contrasted with the 1953 figures.

TABLE 7

Enrolment	Primary		Secondary		Total
	Boys	Girls	Boys	Girls	
European	6,049	5,245	2,524	2,233	16,050
Asian	828	822	200	81	1,931
Coloured	155	160	43	31	390
Total	7,032	6,227	2,767	2,345	18,371

Total number of pupils in the Federal System, 1962:

European	63,065
Asian	7,670
Coloured	4,530
	75,265

Northern Rhodesia enrolment is approximately 25 per cent of Federal enrolment. Total Recurrent Federal Education Vote 1962–63 amounted to £8,403,636. On an approximate percentage basis the Northern Rhodesia cost would be approximately £2,100,000.

In a sense this section (I) is one of parenthesis, bringing the information on European education into perspective and enabling us to study present day Zambian education as a fully integrated system, both administratively and racially.

[19] See Table 5.
[20] See Table 6. These figures are taken from pp. 10 and 11 of T.S., 1963.
[21] Table 6, *Federal Annual Report*, 1963.

TABLE 7A PRIMARY SCHOOL ENROLMENT 1965
(OFFICIAL REPORT TABLES VII TO X CONFLATED)

Grade	(i) Non-Fee-Paying			(ii) Unaided			(iii) Fee-Paying			(iv) Private			(i)+(ii)+(iii)+(iv)
	B	G	Total	B	G	Total	B	G	Total	B	G	Total	
I	41,960	39,560	81,466	504	425	929	1,058	886	1,964	223	280	503	84,862
II	38,215	34,267	72,482	467	374	841	1,192	985	2,177	201	225	426	75,926
III	38,334	32,019	70,353	314	224	538	888	812	1,700	140	219	359	72,950
IV	38,958	30,209	69,167	309	210	519	818	776	1,594	109	192	301	71,581
V	22,396	14,099	36,495	631	377	1,008	822	719	1,541	94	173	267	39,311
VI	20,321	11,747	31,978	480	159	639	863	659	1,522	74	177	251	34,390
VII	10,989	5,145	16,134	324	23	347	767	569	1,336	84	189	273	18,090
VIII	8,819	3,733	12,552	367	30	397	—	—	88	—	—	—	12,949
ESN	—	—	—	—	—	—	53	35	88	—	—	—	88
Totals	219,902	170,725	390,627	3,396	1,822	5,218	6,481	5,441	11,922	925	1,455	2,380*	410,147*

PRIMARY SCHOOL—DISTRIBUTION BY RACE—1965
(OFFICIAL REPORT—TABLE XVI SLIGHTLY RE-CAST)

Type	African	Asian	Eurofrican	European	Total
I	390,594	9	18	6	390,627
II	5,218	—	—	—	5,218
III	1,132	2,383	630	7,777	11,922
IV	174	66	195	1,948	2,383*
Total	397,118	2,458	843	9,731	410,150*

* Slight discrepancy in official figures.

TABLE 7B PRIMARY SCHOOLS—NUMBER OF TEACHERS 1965 (ABSTRACT FROM OFFICIAL REPORT TABLE XXVI)

Zambian

School Type	Trained								Untrained								Total
	Graduate		Secondary		Non-Secondary		Total		Graduate		Secondary		Non-Secondary		Total		
	M	F	M	F	M	F			M	F	M	F	M	F			
I	—	—	110	7	5,552	1,420	7,089		—	—	—	—	148	57	205		7,294
II	—	—	4	—	79	9	92		—	—	—	—	31	3	34		126
III	—	—	3	—	2	1	6		—	—	—	—	—	—	—		6
IV	—	—	—	—	—	1	1		—	—	—	—	—	1	1		2
Total							7,188								240		7,428

Non-Zambian

School Type	Trained								Untrained								Total
	Graduate		Secondary		Non-Secondary		Total		Graduate		Secondary		Non-Secondary		Total		
	M	F	M	F	M	F			M	F	M	F	M	F			
I	—	—	3	52	—	—	55		—	—	—	—	—	—	—		55
II	—	—	8	1	—	—	9		—	—	—	—	—	—	—		9
III	14	38	81	254	6	20	413		11	22	7	8	—	—	52		465
IV	3	12	—	34	—	4	53		—	1	1	15	—	—	26		79
Total							530								78		608

	Trained	Untrained	Total
Zambian	7,188	240	7,428
Non-Zambian	530	78	608
Total	7,718	318	8,036

Overall pupils : staff ratio 51.04:1 (Note teachers in Grades I to IV in schools Types I and II work a double session daily).

II. THE STRUCTURE OF ZAMBIAN EDUCATION IN 1965

A. PRIMARY EDUCATION

In 1964–5 there emerged four categories of primary schools:

(a) *Non-Fee-Paying Maintained and Aided Schools*
Managership in the hands of L.E.A.s and voluntary agencies.
Number: 1,852.

(b) *Unaided Schools*
Managed by voluntary agencies, not qualifying for grants-in-aid.
Number: 45.

(c) *Fee-paying Government Schools*
Schools carried over from the former European education system, but now integrated racially.
Number: 50, including 3 under special conditions.

(d) *Fee-paying Private Schools*
Sponsored by voluntary agencies.
Number: 13.

A study of the enrolment figures in Tables 7A and 7B, pp. 160–1, against the pre-independence statistics, elicits the following matters of interest:

(i) The Transitional Development Plan had aimed at increasing enrolment in the first year and in the fifth year, corresponding to the entry points in the former lower primary and upper primary classes. This increase is marked. Grade I in category (a) schools accepted 8,995 more pupils than in 1964, and Grade V increased entry by 3,438. The total percentage increase in category (a) was 9 per cent which means 32,376 more pupils.

(ii) Category (b) schools would seem to be steadily reducing in numbers.

(iii) The former 'European' schools [category (c) mainly] derived their increase in numbers from the integration policy. Seven hundred less European children entered the schools, but African numbers on entry increased from 204 in 1964 to 1,132, mainly in Grade I.

The official report for the year draws attention to other important factors.

(i) Seven per cent of the places available in category (a) schools were not taken up, principally in remote areas.

(ii) In this year the two former systems approached parity in the number of years devoted to primary education. Formerly the African sector had an eight-years grading, and the European system a seven-year course, plus a reception class. Now the system is approaching standardization on a seven-year pattern throughout.

(iii) Schools in categories (a) and (b) made special arrangements for Grade VII and VIII pupils to take the secondary selection 'examination' on a quota system which ensured reasonable justice to both groups.

(iv) A decision of policy was taken this year which will result in the abolition of the African Primary School Leaving Certificate, replacing it by a headmaster's report.

(v) The management of over 390 schools was handed over by several missionary societies to the Local Education Authorities. This was done at the request of the voluntary agencies (all non-Roman Catholic societies) and is an interesting example of the growth of the L.E.A.'s capacity to absorb the managerial strain previously borne by missions.

B. Secondary Education

Although this year saw an unprecedented expansion of secondary school facilities the leeway that is still to be made is enormous, before there can be said to be a reasonable balance between the primary and secondary sectors. (See Tables 8A and 8B, pages 164–5.)

Using the same categories as were named for the primary system we note the following:

		Numbers
(a)	Non-fee paying: Maintained and Aided	55
(b)	Non-fee paying: Unaided	9
	(These V.A. schools are, in the case of boys, often seminaries sponsored by the R.C. Missions)	
(c)	Fee-paying Government Schools	11
	(From the former European sector)	
(d)	Fee-paying: Private	7
	Total:	82

In commenting on the statistics for the year the *Annual Report* makes the following observation: 'Total enrolment in the non-fee-paying secondary schools rose from 8,177 in 1964 to 10,615 in January 1965, an increase of almost 30 per cent, clear evidence, indeed, of the Ministry's determination to expand secondary education as rapidly as possible. Girls, regrettably, made up only 22 per cent of the secondary school enrolment, and it is apparent that it will be several years before the

TABLE 8A SECONDARY SCHOOL ENROLMENT 1965
(OFFICIAL REPORT—TABLES XII TO XV CONFLATED)

Form	(i) Non-Fee-Paying			(ii) Unaided			(iii) Fee-Paying			(iv) Private			(i) + (ii) + (iii) + (iv)
	B	G	Total	B	G	Total	B	G	Total	B	G	Total	
I	3,092	1,009	4,101	330	17	347	1,212	705	1,917	52	184	236	6,601
II	2,225	704	2,929	252	9	261	646	490	1,136	42	128	170	4,496
III	1,367	316	1,683	45	—	45	625	376	1,001	30	96	126	2,855
IV	763	160	923	15	—	15	446	283	729	24	63	87	1,754
V	634	122	756	13	—	13	168	69	237	26	1	27	1,033
VI M	—	—	—	—	—	—	57	26	77	—	—	—	77
VI L	123	15	138	—	—	—	60	19	79	—	13	13	230
VI U	82	3	85	—	—	—	32	19	51	—	5	5	141
Totals	8,286	2,329	10,615	655	26	681	3,240	1,987	5,227	174	490	664	17,187

TABLE 8A SECONDARY SCHOOLS—DISTRIBUTION BY RACE—1965
(OFFICIAL REPORT—TABLE XVII SLIGHTLY RE-CAST)

Type	African	Asian	Eurafrican	European	Total
I	10,584	15	14	2	10,615
II	681	—	—	—	681
III	1,466	731	171	2,859	5,227
IV	89	33	44	498	664
Total	12,820	779	229	3,359	17,187

TABLE 8B SECONDARY SCHOOLS—NUMBER OF TEACHERS 1965 (ABSTRACT FROM OFFICIAL REPORT—TABLE XXVII)

Zambian

School Type	Trained							Untrained							Total
	Graduate		Secondary		Non-Secondary		Total	Graduate		Secondary		Non-Secondary		Total	
	M	F	M	F	M	F		M	F	M	F	M	F		
I	13	2	42	5	28	1	91	—	—	—	—	2	—	2	93
II	—	—	2	—	5	—	7	2	—	—	—	—	—	2	9
III	1	—	—	—	—	—	1	—	—	—	—	—	—	—	1
IV	—	—	—	—	—	—	—	—	—	—	—	—	—	—	—
Total							99							4	103

Non-Zambian

School Type	Trained							Untrained							Total
	Graduate		Secondary		Non-Secondary		Total	Graduate		Secondary		Non-Secondary		Total	
	M	F	M	F	M	F		M	F	M	F	M	F		
I	176	69	53	34	—	1	333	64	23	4	7	—	1	99	432
II	17	1	14	—	4	—	36	9	—	2	1	—	—	12	48
III	88	66	47	46	—	—	247	16	21	6	1	—	1	45	292
IV	8	11	1	14	—	2	36	—	1	—	9	—	—	10	46
Total							652							166	818

	Trained	Untrained	Total
Zambian	99	4	103
Non-Zambian	652	166	818
Total	751	170	921

social and economic forces militating against the education of girls has been completely overcome.'

It can also be discerned that the large increases are in Forms I and III, i.e. in those forms where previous selection procedures had been particularly rigid in operation. This trend paves the way for the eventual lengthening of the secondary course to five years, for all pupils who desire to continue.

Among the other matters of interest we can make brief mention of the following:

(i) A decision was taken in 1964 to abolish fees in Form I in category (c) schools. This is part of a plan to abolish fee paying in these schools by 1969. Consequently the category 'Government: Fee-Paying' will begin to disappear. Probably categories (a) and (c) will merge; category (b) disappear and/or merge with category (d). In this way the system will be closer to that of more developed countries.

(ii) In 1960 the mining companies established the Northern Rhodesia Educational Trust which became a voluntary agency establishing and managing day secondary schools in several mining towns. (It also helped to establish some primary schools, and one large training college, to which reference will be made later.) These second-ary schools were handed over to L.E.A. in 1965, and were a valuable increase in the capital and professional resources available to the local authorities.

(iii) In town day secondary schools great problems were evident concerning the poverty of the homes from which many secondary pupils came. This had serious consequences for standards. There were no facilities for work at 'home', and often meals were inadequate and irregular. School heads made great efforts to provide preparation facilities in schools and in some cases to help with mid-day meals.

(iv) Mention must be made of the number of people outside the school system who were studying for junior secondary (Form II) qualifications privately. It is recorded that 6,377 candidates sat the External Form II Examination in 1965. This compares astonishingly with 4,496 enrolled in Form II, and is a vivid measure of the hunger for secondary education. Incidentally, of the external candidates 464 gained full certificates and 987 completed the subjects necessary for the award of certificates.

3. Teacher Education

Reference has been made above[22] to the rationalization of teacher-training that took place from 1953 onwards and the statistical tables[23]

[22] p. 155.   [23] Cf. Table 9.

TABLE 9 TEACHER TRAINING ENROLMENT—1965 (OFFICIAL REPORT—TABLES XVIII AND XIX CONFLATED)

School Sector	Pre-Service Courses									In Service Courses			
	First Year			Second Year			Third Year			One year trained teachers	Craft trained teachers		Domestic teachers
	M	F	Total	M	F	Total	M	F	Total	M	M	F	F
Primary Lower	175	204	379	129	163	292	—	—	—				12
Primary Upper	337	111	448	219	273	492	—	—	—	75	55		—
Secondary	—	—	—	3	3	6	10	2	12	—	—		

Pre-service enrolment 1,429   In service enrolment 142   Total enrolment 1,571

Large Colleges

	M	F	Total
Board of Governors (Government) (1)	120	54	174
Lower Education Authority (2)	355	53	408
Voluntary Agencies:			
Christian Council (2)	266	168	434
Roman Catholic (1)	262	—	262
Total	1,003	275	1,278

Small Colleges

	M	F	Total
Voluntary Agencies:			
Dutch Reformed (1)	—	55	55
Roman Catholic (4)	—	238	238
Total	—	293	293

(Abstract from Official Report Table XXVIII)

Staffing	Trained	Untrained	Total
Zambian	38	2	40
Non-Zambian	84	3	87
Total	122	5	127

Overall Students: Staff Ratio—12.37:1

show the enrolment in the large and small colleges. Basic training was on a two-year pattern for primary teachers, and a three-year pattern for secondary teachers (non-graduate). In an effort to prepare for primary and secondary expansion it was decided to change the pattern to that of one-year training, followed by a year's supervized training as serving teachers, before reaching fully qualified teacher status. The colleges thus sent out in December 1965 from their pre-service training enrolment a total of 1,342 primary and 17 secondary teachers, approximately 55 per cent being one-year trained. It will be noted that this coincided with the planned large double entry from Grades VII and VIII in the primary schools, prior to their re-organization on a seven-year pattern. This prepared the way for larger expansions in the upper primary sector and in secondary Form I, in 1966.

In 1965 the number of teachers in the primary and secondary sectors was increased to a total of 8,956, and the percentage expansion possible in 1966 was approximately 15 per cent.

The balance between trained and untrained teachers in the schools as a whole remains remarkably high in favour of the trained teacher. In 1962 for example[24] the trained : untrained ratio for primary teachers in the African sector in Zambia was 6,027 : 174. Only Uganda of all the Commonwealth territories in Africa had a comparable ratio. (In Western Nigeria alone the ratio was 13,393 : 26,756.) In 1965 we see the proportion as 7,188 : 240 for Zambian teachers, and this is exceptionally commendable.

Within the secondary sector the amount of indigenous teacher training for that range of pupil has been very tiny, and in 1965 there was no entry to the courses provided. It had been seen that this would need to be tackled again in relation to university studies, and in fact, as we shall trace later, this was a case of 'reculer pour mieux sauter'.

The expansion of the secondary schools at this time was made possible by the recruitment of 213 teachers from outside Zambia, 81 inside Zambia (many married women), and 42 new teachers trained under the U.N.E.S.C.O. scheme in conjunction with University College in Salisbury. These were graduates from the U.K. and other Commonwealth countries who did their year's professional training in Africa. In fact the scheme came to a precipitate end in Salisbury in November, 1965 with the illegal declaration of independence in Southern Rhodesia, and as we shall note when we record the development of the University in Zambia, this gave an impetus to university-based secondary teacher training.

[24] Burns, D. G., *African Education*, Oxford University Press, 1965, p. 150.

4. *Technical and Commercial Education*

The relevant statistical tables (Tables 10a and 10b) give a concise picture of the scope of work being attempted in this field. But it is necessary to make a historical digression to understand the functions of the institutions whose enrolment is tabulated.

The definitive document that needs detailed study is known as the Keir Committee Report, *A Survey of Technical and Commercial Education in Northern Rhodesia* (1960). Sir David Lindsay Keir was Chairman of the commission sponsored by the Northern Rhodesian government, the Federal government, and the Copperbelt Technical Foundation. The latter had the backing and influence of the mining companies.

TABLE 10A   VOCATIONAL TRAINING: TRADES SCHOOL
ENROLMENT, 1965

Centre		Trade or Craft				
	Carpentry	Brick-work	Electrical	Mechanical	Com-mercial	Total
Lukashya						
Trade School	18	14	27	28	12	99
Livingstone						
Trade School	21	15	—	—	—	36
Mukobeko						
Trade School	27	60*	—	—	—	87*
	Building Crafts		Engineering Crafts			
Lusaka						
Craft Courses†	—	71	—	31	—	102
Total	66	160	27	59	12	324

* Includes 30 students on Short Courses (6 months).
† Final year of Craft Courses held at David Kaunda Technical School.

FURTHER EDUCATION AND TRAINING: ENROLMENT, 1965

I. Full-time and Block Release	*Enrolments*
Northern Technical College:	
Craft and Technician Apprentices (Engineering)	440
Evelyn Hone College of Further Education:	
Commercial and Technician	162
Lusaka Centre:	
Craft Courses	102
Kasama, Broken Hill, Livingstone:	
Trade Schools	222
Total	926

II. *Part-time and Block Release*	*Enrolments*
Northern Technical College:	
Technician, Craft, Commercial	1,004
Evelyn Hone College of Further Education:	
Commercial, Technician	1,114
Adult Education:	
General, Primary, Secondary, Commercial	13,785
Total	15,903

Reference, p. 49, *Annual Report*, Ministry of Education, 1965.

TABLE 10B   COLLEGE OF FURTHER EDUCATION: ENROLMENT, 1965

	Term 1	*Term 2*	*Term 3*	*Average*	*Total*
Intramural:					
Full-time	125	177	183	162	
Day release	38	66	71	58	
Evening	1,311	1,096	750	1,052	
	1,474	1,339	1,004	1,272	1,272
Extramural:					
General					2,036
Upper Primary					4,598
Junior Secondary					1,584
G.C.E.					142
Vocational					146
Total					9,777

Reference, *Annual Report*, Ministry of Education, 1965, p. 48.

In the analysis made in the earlier paragraphs of the report of the facilities available in the territory it becomes clear that this sector of the educational system suffered greatly from its bi-partite roots in the pre-national political, social and industrial European and African worlds. Paragraph 110 of the Report says pithily: 'The division of responsibility between the two governments, each having its own policy, a lack of integration between what is being separately attempted by government departments and private bodies, and the various objectives, methods and standards which they respectively accept, presents an urgent need and opportunity for change.'

For the general reader it is hoped that the following summary will make the picture reasonably clear.

(a) *Trades Schools*

These had grown mainly from 1950 onwards to give training in bricklaying and carpentry to lads with only six or eight years' primary education behind them. By 1960 there were 20 of them scattered through the country. They helped to produce the artisans among Africans for the building expansion of the post-war years. Standing high above these schools, and only minimally related to them, was the Government Training Centre in Lusaka, which eventually became known as the Hodgson Training Centre. It had itself evolved from the earlier Munali Training Centre in Lusaka, the secondary wing of which established itself, on another site in Lusaka, as the leading territorial secondary school. At the Hodgson Training Centre, where the entry was more selective, and at a higher level, including post-secondary, the artisan training work moved into the fields not only of bricklaying and carpentry, but also into tailoring, mechanical and electrical engineering, and painting and decorating. In addition the best students were encouraged to stay and be trained as instructors for other trades schools. In the period just before independence the institution became known as Hodgson Technical College and was preparing African students for City and Guilds Diplomas. Because of its relationship with industry, and the difficulty of penetrating the trade union barriers and standards which were European-centred, and for less easily visible reasons, this institution became the focus of a great deal of disciplinary trouble. In the end it ceased to be. Its buildings were used for the foundation of the country's first technical secondary school named 'David Kaunda Technical School' in memory of the President's father. In 1965 it also provided hospitality for vestigial building and craft courses.

Correspondingly the whole trades school approach was revised and only three remained in 1965, pending the national planning of technical education.

(b) *Northern Technical College*

Another root of technical education was to be traced to the work of the Copperbelt Technical Foundation, aimed originally at facilitating the training of European young men in preparation for work in the mines. It was established by a deed of trust in 1956, and a gift of £400,000 initially made possible the building of centres in Kitwe, Chingola, Luanshya and Mufulira where tuition could be given on a day release and part-time basis to mining aspirants. This dissipation of capital over several centres appears to have produced institutions poorly equipped for the task, and this factor, coupled with the difficulty of recruiting suitable teaching staff, seems to have held the training to a kind which crammed students for Institute and other examinations based on South African and Southern Rhodesia. (Keir Report, para. 82.) To be fair, the trust deed did not differentiate between European and African, but in practice, tradition, and politics, prevented the Africans from participating.

Towards the end of its reign the Federal government gave £8,000 towards the founding of a Technical College in Ndola (the 'port' of the Copperbelt), and when the influence of the Keir Report became dominant eventually this institution became the Northern Technical College, 'with the former C.T.F. institutes in the mining towns as an integral part of the College'.

By 1965 this College had a new board of governors appointed, and the extent of its current work is concisely seen in the table (Table 11).

TABLE II   NORTHERN TECHNICAL COLLEGE ENROLMENT: 1965

Block Release Courses (Apprenticeship):	
Engineering and Applied Science (average per term)	440
Part-time Day Release Courses (Apprenticeship):	
Engineering and Applied Science	40
Full-time Courses	145
Part-time and Evening Courses	819
Total	1,444

Abstracted from Table XXIII, *Annual Report*, 1965.

(c) *Evelyn Hone College of Further Education*

In the year before independence this College was built in Lusaka with funds provided by the territorial government, the British and American governments, the British South African Company and the mining companies. It began with work in the following departments: commerce and general studies, audio-visual media and art, home economics, hotel work and catering, physical education, librarianship and extra-mural studies. Great help was given by the American Agency for International Development and U.N.E.S.C.O. in staffing the courses. Since then it has expanded enormously and it has taken under its wing the technological training originally begun at Hodgson Training Centre (cf. p. 171 above). Communication studies in broadcasting, language teaching, journalism, and electronics have been inaugurated, and at the same time the college deals with adult education in the Lusaka region.

Table 10b (Table XXII – Annual Report 1965) shows that extra-mural work is a major part of its contribution to national growth.

5. *General Adult Education*

By 1965 this had been brought under central control of the Ministry, and between 1964 and 1965 it is noteworthy that there was a remarkable increase in enrolments, from 4,498 to 13,785. This was made possible by the foundation of Adult Education Centres in Ndola and Luanshya in the Copperbelt area. Table XX[25] of the Annual Report

[25] See Table 12.

TABLE 12   ADULT EDUCATION ENROLMENT, 1965
(CLASSES DIRECTLY SPONSORED BY THE MINISTRY)

	Lower Primary	Middle and Upper Primary	Junior Secondary	G.C.E. and Other	Total
Northern	60	295	195	—	550
Eastern	371	391	136	21	919
Southern	626	2,670	801	267	4,364
Western	733	1,390	1,069	464	3,656
Central	1,038	1,460	542	—	3,040
Barotse	—	77	135	—	212
North-Western	407	245	110	—	762
Luapula	72	82	128	—	282
Totals	3,307	6,610	3,116	752	13,785

Reference, Table XX, *Annual Report*, 1965.

shows the interesting fact that 80 per cent of the enrolments were to be found in the three line-of-rail provinces. However, large increases proportionately were made in many rural provinces, and the whole pattern emphasizes the surge of national feeling in the post-independence year, expressing a desire that manpower should be as fully-trained as possible, and that those born in an age when education was difficult for all but the few should have a second chance, no matter how belated.

Up until 1965 correspondence education had been the work of many private firms, several operating in South Africa and Southern Rhodesia. In 1964 a unit was set up in the college of further education to sponsor this work officially. It met with great success and in 1965 the unit moved to the Copperbelt and plans were made to sponsor this service at G.C.E. as well as junior secondary level.

6. *Technical and Professional Services*[26]

(a) *Library Service*
The headquarters of this service is in Lusaka, housed in a building made possible by a gift from the Ford Foundation in New York. The building, completed in 1961 does not act as a library for the local area. It is a place from which library centres, regional libraries, mobile libraries, postal library services, and librarian training may be organized. By 1965 it had begun to open regional libraries in rural areas, and its relationship to the previously mentioned Adult Education work is very strong. Its book stock had reached 57,476 by 1965.

[26] For the rest of this section see *Annual Report*, 1965, from which the material is taken.

(b) *Publications Bureau*
From 1962 the Bureau ceased being the Joint Bureau of Northern Rhodesia and Nyasaland. It had been established to promote the publication of indigenous literature in 1948 with the help of a grant from British Colonial Development and Welfare Funds. It has a remarkable unobtrusive record that would well repay careful and detailed study. The Zambian Bureau in 1965 had 309 sponsored books in print in at least fifteen different languages. It made available a total of 42,000 volumes, some directly printed, and others (60 per cent) guaranteed through commercial publishers. The schools are heavily dependent on the Bureau for the sort of literature that makes vernacular study possible.

(c) *Audio-visual Aids*
This service had its roots in one developed under the European education ministry. Its central distribution is done from Lusaka, and all schools with facilities, such as electricity, can make use of the equipment.

(d) *Psychological Service*
This was re-established in 1965, and succeeds the original European education service. It is concerned with testing development at the attainment and diagnostic level, and provides limited clinical facilities.

(e) *Educational Broadcasting*
Prior to 1965 the ordinary sound broadcasting facilities had been used by schools on a very haphazard and unplanned basis, except where individual teachers had been able to use material. There now came into being an Educational Broadcasting Council which inaugurated adult education programmes and the first experimental term of schools broadcasts. 2,000 radios were distributed to upper primary, secondary schools and training colleges, and plans were laid for an educational broadcasting wing within the Zambian Broadcasting Corporation.

Television had reached only the densely populated Copperbelt and the public transmissions were used for educational television. These were dependent on overseas material, but 1965 was an important year in that special staff were seconded to production and the mining companies made available £10,000 to provide equipment enabling the service to plan and transmit its own programmes.

7. *Higher Education*

(This is most conveniently treated in the following section.)

C. Education in the First National Development Plan 1966–70

No sooner had independence become a reality than the government produced its transitional development plan[27] for the period January 1965 to June 1966. The references made to the 1965 education achievement above indicate the intensity of the national determination, and point the way for a study of the first full plan. At the time of writing no report has been issued for 1966 and indeed the 1965 figures were only published in mid 1967.

It is clear that the plan for education is related to the whole national plan in terms of several cardinal principles:
  (i)   Total planned economy.
  (ii) Manpower projections.
  (iii) Social justice, current and retrospective.
  (iv) Technological and agricultural revolution.
  (v)   National unity.
  (vi) Competitive international status.
Readers are urged to consult the original for a clear picture of the planned growth. The following summary tables set the pattern:

1. Fundamental Aims

(i) To provide sufficient places for primary education for every child aged seven in Zambia in 1970.

(ii) To provide opportunities for all upper primary school children in urban primary schools and 75 per cent of children in rural primary schools to complete a seven-year primary course.

(iii) To improve the quality of primary education by expanding teacher training, and upgrading the standards of existing teachers.

(iv) To expand secondary schooling to provide the manpower in the numbers and with the skills required for national development. This includes preparing people for higher education, teacher training and technical training as well as for direct entry to employment in the public and private sectors.

(v) To provide the resources for the University of Zambia to enrol

[27] *Transitional Development Plan*, Republic of Zambia, 1965.

over 1,600 students in 1970 and develop it to take a leading part in the educational, professional and cultural life of the nation. Professional training in engineering, medicine, agriculture, administration, teaching and law will be started. A broad range of useful research and scholarship will be encouraged and a National Council for Scientific Research established.

(vi) To develop the facilities for adult education (including classes for women, regional libraries, educational broadcasting) in order that the opportunities of education are available to Zambians of every age in every part of the country. Every agency contributing to education – missions, mines, industry or individuals – are assisting the educational development of the nation and are, therefore, welcomed.

TABLE 13   PROJECTED PRIMARY ENROLME

Number of Classes

	1966 (actual)	1967	1968	1969	1
Grade I	2,550	2,878	3,249	3,581	3
Grade II	2,156	2,550	2,878	3,249	3
Grade III	2,018	2,156	2,550	2,878	3
Grade IV	1,954	2,018	2,156	2,550	2
Total Lower Primary	8,678	9,602	10,833	12,258	13
Grade V	1,416	1,581	1,636	1,740	2
Grade VI	944	1,416	1,581	1,636	1
Grade VII	850	944	1,416	1,581	1
Total Upper Primary	3,210	3,941	4,633	4,957	5
Grand Total (all Primary)	11,888	13,543	15,466	17,215	18

Notes:
   * Figures from C.S.O. estimates.
   † Rounded up to nearest 1,000; both figures are slightly in excess of the age gr
allowing some margin for achieving universal enrolment.
Assumptions:
   (i) Grade I enrolment—38 (worked out from historical data on enrolme
Grade V enrolment—39.
   (ii) The progression in enrolments from grade to grade has been worked out

2. *Primary Education* (see Table 13)

The following significant features are to be noted:

(i) The double-session system for teachers in the first four grades continues.

(ii) By 1966, 75 per cent of urban children will have entered a full seven year course.

(iii) The relatively high numbers coming out of primary schools by the mid 1970s will not be absorbed in urban employment. This will mean a need 'to adapt the primary school syllabus and system so that primary school leavers are introduced to the skills and attitudes needed to make a useful start on the land'. There are problems raised for teacher training here.

ON-FEE-PAYING SCHOOLS, 1966-70

		Enrolments			Total Age Group*		% Age Group Enrolled	
56 *al*)	1967	1968	1969	1970	1966	1970	1966	1970
234	109,364	123,462	136,078	140,000†	108,000	136,000	93	100
643	96,024	104,771	118,277	130,000†	102,000	127,000	80	100
491	80,663	94,871	103,514	116,858	97,000	119,000	76	98
721	75,086	81,308	95,629	104,342	92,000	113,000	79	92
089	361,137	404,412	453,498	491,200	399,000	495,000	83	99
346	61,659	63,804	67,860	79,326	89,000	105,000	62	75
774	54,516	61,289	63,421	67,453	85,000	100,000	44	67
159	35,928	53,262	59,879	61,962	79,000	94,000	43	66
779	152,103	178,355	191,160	208,741	253,000	299,000	50	70
368	513,240	582,767	644,658	699,941	652,000	794,000	70	88

rent continuation rates calculated from historical data: thus assume 95·8 per cent
nue from Grade I to Grade II, 98·8 per cent from Grade II into Grade III and
per cent from Grade III into Grade IV. Of those in Grade V, 99·4 per cent
Grade VI and 97·7 per cent move from Grade VI into Grade VII.
) Enrolments in Grades I and V have been worked out on the total intake
ity per class – see (i) above. The resulting continuation rate between Grade IV
Grade V, worked out on data in table above, averages 84·4 per cent.
ference, p. 56, F.N.D.P.

TABLE 14A   EXPANSION OF SECONDARY SCHOOL PLACES
DURING THE PLAN
(ENROLMENT IN NON-FEE-PAYING SCHOOLS)

	1966	1967	1968	1969	1970
Form I	8,250	12,425	14,000	15,575	17,150
Form II	4,154	7,885	11,880	13,380	14,890
Form III	2,049	3,290	5,460	8,610	9,310
Form IV	1,543	1,960	3,150	5,210	8,240
Form V	847	1,480	1,870	3,010	4,990
Total	16,843	27,040	36,360	45,785	54,580
Estimated enrolment in existing fee-paying, private and unaided schools	6,960	8,000	8,400	8,700	8,700
Grand Total Secondary	23,800	35,040	44,760	54,485	63,280

Reference, *F.N.D.P.*, Table II.

3. *Secondary Education*

In this sector manpower needs are predominant at the technician and technologist level (see Table 14B).

TABLE 14B   OUTPUTS OF AFRICANS FROM THE SCHOOL SYSTEM
DURING THE PLAN AT END OF YEAR SHOWN

	1966	1967	1968	1969	1970
Primary:					
Grade IV	11,100	11,300	13,500	16,300	13,600
Grade VII	18,700	19,300	35,100	39,700	40,000
Secondary:					
Form II	—	700	1,600	2,900	3,200
Form V	875	1,600	2,100	3,690	5,720

The following features are notable:

(i) Schools are moving to a standardized 840 enrolment pattern.

(ii) The syllabus will be diversified to meet technical and commercial needs.

(iii) There will be a new emphasis on science teaching.

(iv) Complete unification of the system is expected by 1969.

(v) Not till after 1970 will employers be able to find enough manpower for industrial and commercial needs.

(vi) Note is taken of the need to keep costs under control.

(vii) An effective teacher : class ratio of $1\frac{1}{2}$: 1 is envisaged. (The report reverses the ratio which hardly seems feasible.)

(viii) The problem of supply of secondary teachers is huge.

About 2,500 secondary school teachers will be required by 1970. By that time the new secondary teacher training college and the University of Zambia will together have produced only about 200 Zambian teachers. The balance will have to be made up by expatriates. . . . Recent experience in recruiting has been favourable, but the recruitment agencies must prepare themselves for an annual recruitment building up to some 800–1,000 new teachers by 1970.[28]

TABLE 15 ENROLMENTS, NEEDS, OUTPUTS OF TEACHERS FROM PRIMARY TEACHER TRAINING COLLEGES*

	1966 (actual)	1967	1968	1969	1970
David Livingstone	216	300	300	300	300†
Chalimbana	177	300	300	300	300†
Charles Lwanga	221	300	300	300	300
Chilubula	73	—	—	—	—
Chikuni	26	25	—	—	—
Katete	36	—	—	—	—
Kitwe	175	175	175	300	300
Kasama	86	200	300	300	300
Fort Jameson	74	200	300	300	300
Malcolm Moffat	181	300	300	300	300
Mongu (women)	75	150	150	150	150
Minga	68	—	—	—	—
Mufulira	204	300	300	300	300
Solwezi	—	—	50	100	150
Fort Rosebery	—	—	150	300	300
Mongu (men)	—	—	—	150	200
Total Capacity	1,612	2,250	2,625	3,100	3,200
Total intake: Beginning of year	1,612	2,250	2,375	2,300	1,700
Total output: End of year	1,500	1,900	2,050	1,500	1,500
Additional Needs:					
For new Schools	1,600	1,464	1,635	1,096	749
Wastage‡	400	400	400	400	400
Total	2,000	1,864	2,035	1,496	1,149

* Enrolment and output figures assume one-year training carrying on until 1970, but it is intended to return gradually to the two-year training. A continuation rate of 94 per cent is assumed.
† Includes fifty in-service trainees.
‡ A 4 per cent wastage rate has been assumed for 1966 (the Ministry's teacher strength is 10,000). The absolute figure (400) rather than the percentage rate has been assumed for subsequent years as it is thought that the wastage rate will decrease progressively.
Reference, F.N.D.P., Table IV.

[28] F.N.D.P., p. 57.

It is clearly recognized that 'Zambianizing the syllabus is obviously more difficult when relying so heavily on teachers from other countries'.

4. *Teacher Training* (see Table 15)

In Section B 3. above mention was made of the emergency changeover to one-year training for teachers in primary sector, and to the pause in the training of secondary teachers. 1967 saw the establishing of a higher teacher training college at Broken Hill (now called Kabwe), under the aegis of the Institute of Education of the University of Zambia. This is planned to take 100 students per annum, for a three-year course. Most entrants will have three or four 'O' level passes, and will train for secondary teaching in the lower forms. An interesting development will be the training of women on this deeper basis for infant work. These will be a powerful force for carrying on the tradition set by former expatriate teachers within the so-called European infant classes in primary schools. They will form an interesting pressure point towards the removing of the double session system in the majority of primary schools.

Table 15 clearly summarizes the projections aimed at in the primary teacher training colleges, and by 1969 there should be a surplus of graduates from the colleges which will help to tackle the problems of primary education for all, and the abolition of the two-session system in Grades I to IV.

Hidden within the table is the problem of the probationary year, adequately supervized, and the continuing meritorious attempt to provide some in-service training.

The upper classes in secondary schools will be taught by university trained graduates (cf. pp. 184–7 following).

5. *Technical and Commercial Education*

The key institutions being used are the Trades School, the David Kaunda Secondary Technical School, the Northern Technical College and the Evelyn Hone College of Further Education, the history and development of which was traced in section B 4. above. The incentive to provide manpower for industrial and commercial expansion is obvious. Among the developments currently planned are the following:

(i) The introduction of sandwich courses in the building and construction trades which will enable on-the-job training to march in step with trades instruction of a more formal kind.

(ii) The United Nations Development Programme has been asked for assistance in getting construction workers.

(iii) There is to be a return to a larger number of provincial trades schools more closely geared to local manpower needs.

(iv) The experimental David Kaunda Secondary School is intended to foster a vocational bias to technical and science studies leading to engineering study of a graduate nature at the university, or to technician training at the Northern Technical College or the Further Education College.

(v) The latter institution is expanding its Department of Technology, its residential facilities, and is relating its training to the needs of technicians within civil engineering.

(vi) A measure of the new emphasis is to be seen in the earmarking immediately of £350,000 for urgent expansion in these fields.

6. Adult Education

Six new centres, in addition to those described in B 5., are under way, and there have been important increases in the staffing of this work.

In conjunction with the Department of Community Development, adult literacy classes are being expanded, and this is a remarkable rebirth as it were, of the mass literacy campaigns begun in the period 1949–53, which did not have a lasting success.

7. Technical and Professional Services

Following the description given in B 6. we can note the significant changes:

(i) Six provincial (regional) libraries are under way. Branch libraries are planned for centres of population of 2,000 upwards in many rural areas.

(ii) Municipal libraries are being expanded and 50 per cent recurrent grants offered to municipalities erecting their own buildings.

(iii) A centralized service for secondary schools is being organized to provide a minimum of 5 library books per secondary pupil and three per upper primary pupil. One notes with pleasure the precise definition of target, and the million volumes involved.

(iv) Educational broadcasting is steadily being established as a normal concomitant to classroom instruction. The emphasis currently is on teacher training, secondary and upper primary schools and later the provision will extend to all sectors of primary schools.

(v) The national television service now extends to Lusaka and the pioneering work in the Copperbelt is ready for further extension.

8. *Higher Education: Historical*

Until 1965, with the foundation of the University of Zambia, virtually all higher education for the territory took place outside its borders. For years bursaries for teacher training, university, and many other sectors of professional education had been awarded for study in the United Kingdom, U.S.A., Southern Rhodesia, South Africa, India and Pakistan, West Germany, Italy, Soviet Union, many African countries like Uganda, Kenya, Basutoland, and elsewhere in the world. These awards had been channelled through the territorial and Federal governments, the political parties, churches, and extra-territorial agencies. A detailed analysis is available in the 1965 Annual Report of the Ministry of African Education.

Within the territory the principal nibbles at the problem had been made through the Oppenheimer College of Social Service in Lusaka, the secondary teacher training at Chalimbana, and some departmental efforts in agriculture administration, and medical-ancillary services.

More important still, in many ways, was the post-graduate research work centred in the Rhodes-Livingstone Museum at Livingstone, and the Rhodes-Livingstone Institute in Lusaka. The latter organization had been taken in as a constituent part of the University College of Rhodesia and Nyasaland after 1953, and became the original 'ready-made' unit of the national university. It was originally set up to investigate the 'Social and Psychological Problems of Man in British Central Africa'. This statutory body was brought under the aegis of the Ministry of Education in 1959, while preserving its scholarly independence. By then its aims[29] were:

> To analyse scientifically the social and economic life of modern man, indigenous and immigrant, in Central Africa. To provide accurate scientific information on the social (and economic) life of man for Governments and other persons working with human beings in this area. To disseminate this accurate information as widely as possible to the public.

Between 1963 and 1965 its practical function turned partly away from the field of social anthropology to that of educational research in connection with a Mental Ability Survey, carried out with funds provided by government and the mining companies. It also gave great practical help to the Ministry of Education in planning secondary selection at the time when the school system was integrated.

In the later years of Federation, when national independence began to be seen as an imminent reality, the idea of a university, more fully

[29] See preface, end-papers of any Rhodes-Livingstone Institute publication.

expressing national needs and inspiration received several stimuli. A clear account of these is to be found in para. 131 of the 1963 *Triennial Survey*. The eventual Advisory Council under the chairmanship of the late Sir John Lockwood, Master of Birkbeck College, London University, published its report in 1964, and a Provisional Council was quickly established. The University of Zambia Act was passed in 1965, and came into operation 13 months after the Independence celebration. The act defined its functions thus:

> To encourage the advancement of learning and research throughout Zambia and to hold out to all persons whatever their race, places of origin, political opinions, colour, creed or sex the opportunity of acquiring higher education.

It had as its fundamental premises two practical aims:

> To be responsive to the real needs of Zambia, and to be an institution which, on merit, will earn the respect of the university world.

9. *The University of Zambia*

Prior to the formal Act which constituted the university, there had been formed a Provisional Council which set about raising funds and making the necessary preparations for recruiting staff. Under the Chairmanship of Sir Thomas Williams (who had been previously the head of the Commission on European Education in 1948, and later Director of European Education), the Provisional Council in addition to its administrative and inspiriting function, arranged for the transfer of the Rhodes-Livingstone Institute from Salisbury University College, and the Director became the first Professor. In July 1965 the Vice-Chancellor, Dr D. G. Anglin was formally appointed, and the first core of staff was gathered. When U.D.I. took place in Southern Rhodesia the U.N.E.S.C.O. education unit there was withdrawn to Zambia, and so formed a nucleus of an education faculty. In the latter part of the year the Oppenheimer College of Social Service (later Social Science) was also incorporated within the University, and this establishment provided the first premises in which formal teaching was to begin in 1966.

Income for the university came in the first instance as follows:

Government	£1,000,000
Independence grant from the U.K. Government	1,000,000
Private funds, including nationwide contributions	450,000
B.S.A. Co.	100,000
Anglo-American Corporation	60,000
Rhodesia Selection Trust	60,000

A site on the periphery of Lusaka was acquired and plans prepared.

The important recommendations of the Lockwood report centred round the concept of a post 'O' level university; four-year pass degree courses; an extra year for an honours course; vocational bias to provide teachers and other professional people; a two-stage degree system in two units of two years each; and a cross-over point at the end of Part 1 for those moving say to technology from arts, or vice-versa. In addition emphasis was laid on extra-mural studies, extension work and correspondence education. The one thing to note at this point was the end of the sixth form tradition in the secondary schools, fully implemented by 1966, but probably an idea that one day might revive.

In March, 1966[30] the University formally opened with 312 students, in temporary accommodation in the Oppenheimer College. It founded in the first instance Schools of Humanities; Social Sciences; Natural Science; and Education. It hopes to add Schools in Administration, Agriculture, Law, Medicine and Engineering. The Rhodes-Livingstone Institute, founded in 1937 within the Social Sciences School, formed the new Institute of Social Research, and is the embryonic part of a future centre for African Studies.

The first degrees are the B.A. and B.Sc., and these are not marked as general, special, ordinary or honours studies. Each student has to complete 16 courses (not subjects), doing four per annum. He will specialize in two subjects (or one subject with two subsidiary subjects), one of which may be education. Science students must take English, mathematics and chemistry in the first year, and African studies or education in the following year. Conversely, arts students take English, a science course and African studies in the first year. This emphasis on a broad basis of topics in the early years is significant. Eventual entry to medical, engineering and agricultural studies is from first year natural science, and from the humanities and social science course students may proceed to administration, law and social work.

(a) *Developments in 1966*

(i) The Institute of Education was formally established with a special concern for in-service training, and liaison with territorial training colleges.

(ii) At the social level house councils were inaugurated together with the usual student societies, and the Students' Union was formed.

(iii) Deans of the Schools were appointed.

(iv) Departments of Correspondence Studies and of Extra-Mural Studies were formed, and great use was made of the buildings during vacation courses in topics as varied and vivid as writers' workshop,

[30] This section is compiled from mimeographed material published by the University. The first Calendar is awaited.

TABLE 15A ENROLMENT 1966

The following figures summarize the first entries:

Degree	Schools	Year	Numbers
B.A.	Humanities and Social Sciences	I	122
	Social Sciences	II	29
B.Sc.	Natural Sciences	I	82
			233
Diploma	Social Sciences	I	15
	Social Sciences	II	22
			37
Postgraduate	Education		42
Total (includes 63 women)			312

The second-year entries indicate people entering from VIth Forms (degree), and from the former Oppenheimer College.

A small internal survey of the Natural Science School showed the following career intentions of the first students:

Engineering	30
Medical	30
Agriculture	9
Teaching	5
Pure Science	4
Unsure	4
	82

Note: An interesting footnote, indicative of standards in degree studies, is that in the year examinations 52 per cent passed in all courses and 26 per cent were referred till March 1967, just before the new term began. (The university year is for two long terms between March and December.)

adult education, Voluntary Service Overseas orientation, secondary teachers of English, extra-mural tutors' training, radio scripting and social welfare field work.

(v) Building on the new site went ahead but was not ready for 1967.

(b)[31] *Enrolment 1967*
Full-time students rose to 536, made up thus:

Humanities and Social Science	269
Natural Science	157
Social Service Diploma	60
Postgraduate Certificate of Education	50

Part-time students numbered 550, made up thus:

Degree Correspondence Courses	150
Extra-mural courses	400

It is noteworthy that a Director of Correspondence Studies has been appointed and the part-time study for degrees offered three courses, and there is one course for a part-time P.C.E. The tutorial material distributed is the product of the same tutors doing internal teaching, and students are required to attend Residential School in August-September during the short vacation.

(c) *Research*
Apart from material produced by the Institute for Social Research, with its roots in the Rhodes-Livingstone publications of previous years, the Natural Science School reports that in 1966 28 research papers were published, and there were 26 research projects pending.

(d) *Staffing*
In addition to the key University Officers of Vice-Chancellor, Pro-Vice-Chancellor, Registrar, Bursar, Librarian, Dean of Student Affairs and their Assistants, the following numbers of Academic Staff are shown as of September 1966:

TABLE 16   PROJECTION OF ANNUAL ENROLMENTS IN THE
UNIVERSITY OF ZAMBIA, 1966–71

	1966	*1967*	*1968*	*1969*	*1970*	*1971*
1st year	205	200	335	517	657	1,185
2nd year	29	189	160	268	414	525
3rd year	—	25	180	152	255	393
4th year	—	—	24	171	146	242
5th year*	—	—	—	—	43	36
Post Graduate	42	50	50	60	70	70
Diploma	36	50	60	70	80	90
Totals	312	514	809	1,238	1,665	2,541

* Fourth-year students continuing in Medicine, Engineering, Law and possibly Agriculture.
Reference, *F.N.D.P.*, p. 60.

[31] Compiled from *Newsletters*, sponsored by the University. See also Table 16.

	Full-time	Part-time
School of Natural Science	26	4
School of Humanities and Social Sciences	35	1
School of Education	15	8
Department of Extra-Mural Studies	1	—
Department of Correspondence Studies	1	—

(e) *The Schools and Departments*
  (i) *School of Humanities and Social Sciences*
Subjects: economics, English, French, history, geography, mathematics, political science, sociology, psychology, law and social work. (The last two are within this school temporarily.)

  (ii) *School of Natural Sciences*
Subjects: biology (leading to botany and zoology in year II), chemistry, geography, mathematics, physics, psychology.

  (iii) *School of Education*
Education is an option in years II, III and IV for B.A. and B.Sc. students. The Postgraduate Certificate work follows a traditional pattern.

  (iv) *Department of Correspondence Studies*
Students are required to be qualified for matriculation, and follow the same courses as full-time students. To be eligible an applicant must also satisfy the university that he cannot attend as a full-time student, but is able to attend the compulsory residential courses.

  (v) *Department of Extra-Mural Studies*
This has been formed to enable adults to have an opportunity to share university teaching as part of national extension work. Certain subjects, 'conducive to national unity and a sense of national identity' (e.g. African and Zambian history, languages, economic development), are to be emphasized. It makes use of radio broadcasting regularly. It also arranges the vacation courses of the university.

  (vi) *Library*
The new building is due for completion by March 1968, on the new campus and will hold over 300,000 volumes and be designed to serve 1,650 readers. In its structure it will closely pattern the 'schools' concept of the whole university.

  (vii) *Centre for African Studies and Institute for Social Research*
The second of these two units forms part of the larger whole. It flows from the Rhodes-Livingstone Institute described above, and it has

expanded greatly its inter-disciplinary approach. Later it is hoped that other Institutes in fields including history, human geography and demography will form part of the Centre for African Studies.

(viii) *Student Finance*

For those normally domiciled in Zambia fees are £60 per annum for tuition, and £90 per annum for residence. Those who live outside Zambia are charged correspondingly £300 and £150. Special bursaries of a generous nature are available, and for the P.C.E. student who commits himself for a tour of work in Zambia, after qualifying, the conditions are very attractive.

(ix) *Future Plans*

The Development Plan lays stress on the following needs:

Zambianization on both the public and private sectors of the country.
Manpower for further expansion of the economy.
Replacement manpower to make up for death and retirement.[32]

The enrolment projections in Table 16 summarizes the intentions.

They are based on the assumption that half those completing secondary education will qualify for university. Till 1970 arts and science will take 50 per cent shares. Thereafter science students will increase their proportion.

Capital costs for the period ending in 1970 are estimated at £8m. Recurrent costs by 1971 will be £2·5m. per annum. Together these costs represent 1 per cent of the gross domestic product.

10. *Other Education*

In this survey little or no mention has been made of key institutions such as the College of Natural Resources, the Agricultural Research Station, Medical Training School, Staff Training College, Clerical Training School, Military Training School, Police Training School, Co-operative training schemes, Zambia Youth Service, etc. They are of too specialized a nature to come under the heading 'Education in Zambia', where the unifying principle has been a special relationship with the Ministry of Education. In addition there have been noteworthy private ventures like that of the Ecumenical Centre at Ndola, and numerous small church-centred educational enterprises. The reader is referred in the first case to the Development Plan as it affects other ministries, and it will probably be an early function of the new university to trace the wider roots of all that can be called education in Zambia.

[32] *F.N.D.P.*, pp. 50–1.

D. Policy Problems in Education

At the risk of repetition elsewhere it is perhaps pertinent to enumerate the following:

1. Lingua Franca

At present English fulfils this function but it is most difficult for the true emotion of an African National to be expressed in a western tongue. One wonders which, if any, vernacular, will eventually predominate, and what will be the conditions that pre-empt one rather than another. Or will there emerge a composite vernacular like Swahili in East Africa? The schools and university have problems about how many vernaculars are to be encouraged. The historians and sociologists have much to contribute in preparing for the years of decision.

2. Music and Drama and Art

There has been a great dearth of real research or even conservation within these areas of human creative enterprise in Zambia. One wonders how far the emphasis on manpower, production etc. coupled with the early domination by mass media, has increased the facility with which these activities, in their distinctive sense, die.

3. Philosophy and Religion

The humanism and vigorous humanity of the present President Dr Kaunda have helped to produce a national unity that one day must take a more structured form which will have its roots in a philosophical and religious way of thinking that stems from some syncretism between the Bantu and the West. The task for education within this is so imprecise that it is seldom even thought of.

4. Status of Women

The efficiency of the nation alone would seem eventually to imply a revolution in the rate at which girls and women are educated, and there is bound to be a period of delicate balance in which male unemployment might be exacerbated by the need for special incentives for women.

5. Agricultural Revolution

The changeover from subsistence agriculture to something nearer that pertaining in western countries, involves problems of Land Tenure, Local Authority competence, traditional tribal authority changing, etc., requiring a mode of education that eventually aims at the transformation of society's structures. The industrial advance in mining is finding the finance to initiate educational change, but at the same time it introduces social stresses because of a money economy which creates elites who lose understanding of other groups' problems.

6. *Teacher Training*

The present pattern of one-year training has within it the seed of a later problem, viz. that of in-service training to meet rapidly changing needs of a new society, served by teachers who will not have had the depth of training that will enable them to adapt. The move of correspondence education at the university level based on the pattern of the Armidale[33] unit in Australia is one hopeful attempt to make up the lack. So too is the emphasis on the use of radio and television. But these areas need much more personal inter-action, as between tutor and student, and eventually this will have to be provided.

7. *Curriculum Reform*

Experience in other emergent countries has shown the need for Zambianization of the curriculum throughout every sector of the school system. There would appear to be, in the recruitment of a huge number of secondary teachers from other countries to permit initial expansion of the system, a risk that there will be little opportunity to do other than replicate the examination dominated patterns of western nations. However, there is a deep and important national sensitivity about this issue that will keep the necessary vigilance.

8. *Miscellaneous*

No mention has been made in detail of the quantity-quality debate, or of the manpower-expansion problems. These will have been amply illustrated in many cognate contributions within the present volume. As one reads the Zambian politicians' and civil servants' ideas one feels that they are ready to learn from contemporary history and ultimately the compromise will evolve into some distinctive contribution to international living.

E. Conclusion

The present writer served 20 years within the Zambian educational system and remembers in 1945 that the per caput grant for a child in the first grade of a bush school was 6d per annum, and that the

---

[33] Sheath, H. C., *Report to Federal and Territorial Government*, 1963.

present leaders reached their eminence in a process of sifting that that was socially unjust and nationally divisive. One has no doubt that Zambia is relatively lucky in that within limits, the finance is there, the system is there, and the national will is there. The last table shows the financial resources and they are exciting (see Table 17).

TABLE 17   ESTIMATED RECURRENT EXPENDITURE ON EDUCATION
IN ZAMBIA, 1966-7—1969-70

		1966-7	1967-8	1968-9	1969-70
Primary*	(£M.)	6·3	7·1	7·8	8·4
Secondary*		3·4	4·6	5·7	6·9
Technical†		0·6	1·0	1·2	1·3
Teacher Training		0·4	0·5	0·6	0·7
Adult Education		0·4	0·5	0·6	0·7
Administration, educational broadcasting and miscellaneous educational services		1·2	1·2	1·3	1·4
University		1·0	1·1	1·7	2·7
Grand Total Recurrent		13·3	16·0	19·0	22·1
Estimated additions for rising salaries‡		0·00	10·6	0·8	1·1
Capital expenditure		9·6	9·7	10·2	10·3
Grand Total		22·9	26·3	30·0	33·5
Percentage of Gross Domestic Product (excluding subsistence)		6·6	7·2	7·4	7·5

Notes: Reference, *F.N.D.P.*, p. 60.
   * Includes fee-paying schools.
   † Includes further education.
   ‡ Follows main assumptions of Plan.

Many nations have rallied to provide skilled professional help and one awaits with eagerness the fruits of a practical wisdom that will raise up the really creative Zambian educators, without which the long-term ideals of the present nation cannot be fulfilled.

BIBLIOGRAPHY

A. OFFICIAL PUBLICATIONS

From: Government Printer, Lusaka (many now out of print).
Annual Reports and *Triennial Surveys* of the Department (later Ministry) of African Education, 1925 to 1963. (Earlier material in Annual Reports of Department of Native Affairs.)
Annual Reports of Department of European Education, 1939 to 1953.
Annual Reports of Ministry of Education, 1964 onwards.
Approved Syllabuses, primary and secondary, 1956.

Minutes of Advisory Boards, African and European, prior to 1964.
Government Gazette, published weekly, contains index of all legislation,
   1911 onwards. See especially years 1956, 1960, 1961, 1965.
Hansard Reports on Legislative Council, Assembly and Parliament.

B. STATISTICAL MATERIAL (General)

(This is obtainable from the Central Statistical Office, P.O. Box 1908,
Lusaka, Zambia.) Of particular value one may mention the following:
National Accounts and Balance of Payments, 1954–65.
Reports on the 1963 Census.
African Population Map, 1964.
Migration Statistics, 1966.
Monthly Digest of Statistics (Annual Subscription).

C. MAJOR REPORTS

1925, *Memorandum on Education Policy in British Tropical Africa* (Phelps-
   Stokes Commission).
1947, Gwilliam, F. H. and Read, M., *Report on Education of Women and
   Girls*, Lusaka, Government Printer.
1953, Nuffield Foundation and Colonial Offices, *African Education*,
   London, Oxford University Press.
1960, Keir Committee Report, *A Survey of Technical and Commercial
   Education in N. Rhodesia*, Lusaka, B.S.A. Co. Management Services
   Ltd.
1963, U.N.E.S.C.O. Report, *Education in Northern Rhodesia*, Paris,
   U.N.E.S.C.O.
   Sheath, H. C., *Report on Correspondence Education at University Level*,
   Salisbury, Government Printer.
1964, *Lockwood Report on the Foundation of the University of Zambia*,
   Lusaka, Government Printer.
1965, *Provisional Report on National Development*, Lusaka, Government
   Printer.
1966, *Manpower Report*, Lusaka, Government Printer.
1967, *First National Development Plan*, Lusaka, Government Printer.

D. MAJOR JOURNALS AND REFERENCE WORKS

1. *Overseas Education*
Benson, Sir Arthur, 'On Education in Northern Rhodesia', Volume 27,
   No. 1, April 1955.
Clarke, M. G., 'Secondary School Selection in Northern Rhodesia',
   Volume 31, No. 3, October 1959.

Cottrell, J. A., 'Compulsory African Education in Broken Hill', Volume 19, No. 1, October 1947.

Good, R., 'Intelligence and Attainment in Northern Rhodesia', Volume 28, No. 1, April 1956.

Milne, F. D. and Stevenson, P. K., 'Selection for African Secondary Schools in Northern Rhodesia', Volume 31, No. 2, July 1959.

Robertson, D. M., 'Jeanes Training Centre, Chalimbana', Volume 17, No. 3, April 1946.

2. Rhodes-Livingstone Institute Papers and Journals

Now titled *African Social Research* and *Zambian Papers*, obtainable from The Registrar, University of Zambia, P.O. Box 2379, Lusaka.

These are too varied to list, but they represent a major record of anthropological work, with an emphasis latterly on socio-economic problems in education. A more popular publication is the *Northern Rhodesian Journal*, which dates from 1950 onwards. (See Section F.)

3. Various References

Arnold, G., 'The Zambia experiment', *New Commonwealth*, April 1965.

Drake, H., 'A Bibliography of African Education', *University of Aberdeen Anthropological Museum Publication*, No. 2, 1942.

Etheredge, D. A., 'The role of education in economic development, The example of Zambia', *Journal of Administration Overseas*, Volume 6, No. 4, October 1967.

Hay, H., 'Mass literacy in N. Rhodesia', *International Review of Missions*, July, 1946.

Irvine, S. H., 'African Education in N. Rhodesia: the first forty years', *Teacher Education*, Volume 2, No. 2, November 1961.

Jolly, A. R., 'Education Planning in Zambia', *World Yearbook of Education*, Evans, 1967. See Chapter 18.

Parker, F., 'African Education and Manpower in Zambia', *World Yearbook of Education*, Evans, 1966.

Parker, F., 'Early days in the Department of African Education in Northern Rhodesia', *Northern Rhodesia African Education Journal*, Volume 7, 1962.

There are also many duplicated typed records in libraries like that of the Institute of Education, London University, and the Commonwealth Office Library, London.

A useful first source book is the Education Libraries Bulletin Supplement Five and Supplement Nine *Education in Africa: a select bibliography*, University of London, Institute of Education, 1962, 1965.

E. General Works

Baldwin, R. E., *Economic Development and Export Growth, 1920 to 1940*, Los Angeles, University of California Press, 1966.

Barber, W. J., *The Economy of British Central Africa*, Stanford University Press, 1961.

Barnes, J. A., *Politics in a Changing Society*, Oxford University Press, 1954.

Colson, E., *The Plateau Tonqu of Northern Rhodesia*, Manchester University Press, 1962.

Cunnison, I. G., *The Luapula Peoples of N. Rhodesia*, Manchester University Press, 1959.

Dohe, C. M., *The Lambas of Northern Rhodesia*, London, Harrap, 1931.

Fagan, B. M. (ed.), *A Short History of Zambia*, Nairobi, Oxford University Press, 1966.

Gelfand, M., *Northern Rhodesia in the days of the Charter*, Oxford, Blackwell, 1961.

Gann, L. H., *A History of Northern Rhodesia*, London, Chatto & Windus, 1964.

Gann, L. H., *The Birth of a Plural Society*, Manchester University Press, 1958.

Gluckman, M. and Colson, E., *Seven Tribes of British Central Africa*, Manchester University Press, 1959.

Hall, R., *Zambia*, London, Pall Mall Press, 1965.

Richards, A. I., *Land, Labour and Diet in Northern Rhodesia*, London, Oxford University Press, 1939.

Richards, A. I., *Chisungu*, London, Faber and Faber, 1956.

Smith, E. W. and Dale, A. M., *The Ila-speaking Peoples of Northern Rhodesia*, London, Macmillan, 1920.

Taylor, J. V. and Lehmann, D. A., *Christians of the Copperbelt*, London, S.C.M. Press, 1961.

Watson, W. *Tribal Cohesion in a Money Economy*, Manchester University Press, 1961.

Wilson, G. H., *History of the Universities' Mission to Central Africa*, London, U.M.C.A., 1936 (and a later revision).

7· Education in the Former High Commission Territories of Bechuanaland (Botswana) Basutoland (Lesotho) and Swaziland

BRIAN ROSE

The former High Commission Territories of Swaziland, Basutoland and Bechuanaland came under the surveillance of Great Britain during the nineteenth century. All three territories are landlocked, economically underdeveloped and to a considerable extent dependent on the Republic of South Africa in such matters as trade, banking, communications and postal services.

Britain's annexation of the territories, although made under differing circumstances during the nineteenth century, was motivated almost entirely by the political determination to contain the Boer Republics. As a result Britain had little interest in or intention of developing these comparatively large areas or of exploiting their natural resources. They constituted, until the end of the Second World War, rural Imperial slums. During the 1950s, when Britain decided to divest herself of colonial responsibilities, there was much belated activity aimed at lifting the educational systems to a slightly higher level of efficiency than had hitherto appertained, as well as at laying the foundations for a viable national economy that could be continued after independence had been achieved. A degree of education has been achieved in all these territories, which is due almost entirely to missionary enterprise.

Each territory requires separate treatment. The (often unconsciously accepted) idea that negritude makes Africa a single homogeneous community is unsupported by fact. In culture, history, natural resources, educational development, governmental experience and domestic custom, African communities differ from one another considerably.

I. BOTSWANA

A. Historico-Cultural Survey

Schapera accepts 1600 A.D. as the probable date when the Bechuana people began to settle their present homeland.[1] Eight new tribes were formed by a process of fragmentation, so that today the 593,000* Botswana (unlike the Lesotho to whom they are related) have no Paramount Chief even though the Bamangwato tribe has achieved considerable dominance.

When, during the second half of the nineteenth century, an element of expansionism made its appearance in British Colonial policy in Africa[2,3,4] the concept of federations of Central and Southern African states under the suzerainty of the British Crown was advocated by one proconsul after another.[5] If suspicion of British intentions made Boer co-operation impossible, a certain expansionism of their own created in the minds of British administrators a determination to contain the two republics.[6,7] The proclamation of the Protectorate of Bechuanaland in 1885 was a strategic move to block Boer infiltration into the north which might seriously embarrass imperial intentions. The first High Commissioner explained the proclamation in words that were to typify the subsequent British policy: 'We have no interest in the country north of the Molopo, except as a road to the interior; we might therefore confine ourselves for the present to preventing that part of the territory being occupied either by filibusters or foreign powers, and doing as little as possible in the way of administration.'[8] Rhodes, some years later concerned with a railroad through Bechuanaland to Bulawayo as a logical development of the imperial plan, noted that he took for granted the surrender by the Colonial Office of their

---

* The figure for 1967, projected from the 1964 Census Report.

[1] Shapera, I., *The Tswana*, London, International African Institute, 1953, p. 15.

[2] Goodfellow, C. F., *Great Britain and South African Federation*, Oxford University Press, 1966, p. 10.

[3] C.O. 48/306 D. 104 Smith to Earl Grey, July 12, 1850.

[4] C.O. 48/491 D. 379 Frere to Hicks Beach, Dec. 1, 1879.

[5] Spies, F. J. du T. (ed.), *Die Dagboek van H. A. L. Hamelberg, 1855–71*, Cape Town, 1962, p. 173.

[6] Goodfellow, *op. cit.*, p. 183.

[7] C.O. 48/468 D. 29 Carnarvon to Barkly, April 25, 1874; Disraeli Papers Box XII Carnarvon to Disraeli, April 11, 1874, etc.

[8] *Basutoland, Bechuanaland Protectorate and Swaziland*; Report of Economic Survey Mission, 1960, H.M.S.O., p. 37.

interests in the Protectorate to the British South Africa Company[9] and it was only due to the intervention of a delegation led by Chief Khama in 1895, and the ceding of land for the railway, that the continued protection of the Crown was assured.

Bechuanaland continued placidly enough during the first twenty-five years of the present century, a colonial backwater that attracted no capital except in areas of White settlement and in sporadic attempts at mining, and even less administrative talent. In 1926, owing to the minority of Seretse Khama, his uncle, Tshekedi Khama became Regent of the Bamangwato. In what was to be a stormy career stretched over 22 years, he clashed almost immediately with the administration which required his signature to a mining concession negotiated without his knowledge. Backed by the *kgotla* (tribal council), Tshekedi began a bitter legal battle to defend tribal rights, which was successfully concluded in the London courts. When the administration challenged the legality of his decision under tribal law, he appealed to Privy Council and once again won his case. But when in 1933 he tried before a tribal court a White man charged with *crimen injuria*, the Acting High Commissioner, Admiral Evans, with much melodrama, deposed him. Two weeks later Tshekedi was restored after an exchange of recognizances and the British government sent Sir Alan Pim to report on conditions in the three Protectorates. What with a world depression, a prolonged drought and the outbreak of foot-and-mouth disease, it is hardly surprising that Sir Alan could do little more than underscore the bankruptcy of Bechuanaland. With a certain poignancy he noted that the educational provision made by the British government of the day included £1,000 for 180 White children, and £100 for 8,000 Botswana annually.[10]

In 1920 a small step towards local responsibility was taken when Advisory Councils, which met once a year, were set up under the chairmanship of a senior civil servant to advise the Colonial authorities. Almost twenty years later, in 1938, Tribal Treasuries were inaugurated to receive 25 per cent of the yearly $2·4 tax levies. The expenditure was subject to tribal control, and at the same time chiefs were placed on a salaried basis and no longer required to reimburse themselves directly from the taxation for which they had hitherto been responsible.

In 1948, Tshekedi had been Regent for 22 years. As his nephew was not only a graduate of a South African university, but had studied at Oxford and was now completing his law studies at the Inns of Court,

[9] Sillery, A., *The Bechuanaland Protectorate* (Rhodes to Lord Ripon, 1894), p. 66.
[10] Halpern, J., *South Africa's Hostages*, Penguin, p. 271.

the Regent decided that the moment for his re-call had come. The news of his impending marriage to an English woman created tremendous initial opposition in the kgotla, and Tshekedi himself led the movement to oust the heir. Seretse gradually won the tribe to his side, and the Regent's rigidity led to suspicion of his own ambition and his final exile.[11] In 1950 Seretse was summoned to London and offered a pension of £1,000 a year if he would relinquish all claims to the Bamangwato chair, and when he refused he was banished for five years. After a reconciliation, both leaders returned as private individuals, Tshekedi in 1952 and Seretse in 1956, at which date he could hardly have known that he had just ten years in which to create a social structure in his country that would be able to support the Botswana Republic that was to be proclaimed in 1966. The first political party, the Bechuanaland Protectorate Federal Party, issued its largely traditional manifesto in 1959, to be followed by the militant Bechuanaland People's Party in 1960. Strongly Pan-African in sentiment and therefore anti-traditional, the B.P.P. soon divided into three parties and thus dissipated its forces. Mr Seretse Khama's Bechuanaland Democratic Party met no serious opposition when it was founded in 1962. In that year he took office on the Executive Council, and was clearly being groomed for the post of Prime Minister. In the national elections for the Legislative Assembly held before self-government was granted in 1965, B.D.P. captured 28 of the 31 seats, and Mr Khama became Prime Minister. Shortly afterwards he was knighted.

B. Land and Resources

Completely landlocked, Botswana, with its 225,000 square miles is a little bigger than Metropolitan France. Only the eastern areas provide good cattle grazing and a sufficient rainfall for a subsistence agriculture which is gradually being converted to cash cropping. Much of the central and southern parts of the country are Kalahari desert, whilst 6,500 square miles of the north-west are taken up by swamps formed by the Okovango River delta. The possibility of directing the 9,000 cusec inflow into irrigation and hydro-electric power (investigated by the U.N. Development Programme in 1966) lies in the future. Botswana is cattle country at present. As in many other parts of Africa the land is communal to the tribe and is the gift of the chief who can demand its return. For this reason there is not much fencing and little has been done until recently to improve the fertility of soil which may not be to the

[11] Halpern, op. cit., p. 276.

present user's ultimate benefit. To the African pastoralist, cattle are wealth, and he does not easily surrender his animals to the market. If he is persuaded to do so, he often withholds his prime beasts and sells those which are in poor condition. The following table indicates the distribution of labour in Botswana:

Activity	Number of Workers
Agriculture, forestry, hunting and fishing	227,649
Mining and quarrying	1,940
Manufacturing	2,420
Construction	2,704
Electricity and water services	120
Commerce	2,468
Transport and communication	2,315
Services	9,798
Ill-defined activities	1,264
Total	250,678[12]

By the end of 1966, before the widespread rains, the drought had reduced the national herd by at least 33 per cent and in some areas by 50 per cent. With a year's calves lost it would take at least five years to recover. One fifth of the country was dependent on famine relief. The financial implications of this disaster meant that over 40 per cent of internally generated government revenue had to be devoted to rehabilitation measures.[13]

There are possibilities of mining brine and salt, asbestos and manganese, a great deal of low-grade coal and some iron ore. The presence of diamonds and oil is suspected but not proved. The little mining of asbestos and manganese that was in operation had ceased at the end of 1965.[14] In February 1967 Roan Selection Trust announced publically that copper deposits in Botswana had been identified.

At the end of 1964 meat exports were worth R9·7 million, which amounted to 85 per cent of the national exports. Mining necessitates not only investment capital but power, water and accessibility to markets, which are problematic in Botswana. The railway to some extent ameliorates the problem of communication, but water and power supplies remain undeveloped. The improvement of the Shashi complex by the installation of a power generating plant which will supply copper mining at Matsitamma is intended.[15]

[12] Transitional Plan for Social and Economic Development, Government of Botswana, 1966, p. 2. Henceforward known as T.P.S.E.D.
[13] Ibid., p. 5.   [14] Ibid., p. 2.   [15] Ibid., p. 27.

C. EDUCATION

The Transitional Plan reports that the total number of persons in the Category I manpower (persons with a degree or a diploma) for whom posts are available is about 370, of which 10 per cent are occupied by Botswana; the total number of Category II (minimally School Certificate) posts is 1,600, of which less than 25 per cent are filled by Botswana. To achieve self-sufficiency within 25 years the secondary schools must from 1975 produce at least 250 School Certificate holders a year. In 1966 45 matriculants were anticipated. Present and projected enrolments are shown as follows:

	1961	*1966*	*1967*	*1971*
Primary	39,000	75,000	73,159	80,000
Secondary	618	1,499	1,854	2,500
Teacher Training	109	296	310	660
University	6	80	86	140[16]

1. *Primary Education*

247 primary schools accommodate 75,000 (1966) children, which is approximately half the number of children of school-going age. The teacher : pupil ratio is 45 : 1, wastage is 60 per cent and more than 200 classes have more than 80 pupils. Many schools are nothing more than a single room, some of which accommodate six classes. Forty and a half per cent of the children of primary age are able to find places in the schools.[17] Half the teachers who are employed at fixed salaries of £84 p.a. (men) and £66 p.a. (women) are unqualified (628 out of 1,364 in 1964). But these salaries have since been improved. The output of teachers from the training colleges amounts to about 80 per annum, whilst losses from the schools amount to 150 p.a. This loss is made more acute by a pupil increase:

1962	46,500
1963	54,800
1964	62,000
1965	65,000

[16] *Ibid.*, p. 33.
[17] Lewis, L. J., *Teacher Training for Primary Schools in Bechuanaland* (duplicated pamphlet), pp. 3-4.

As Professor Lewis comments, the shortage in 1964 was estimated at 400 teachers and 1,000 classrooms.[18] The U.N.E.S.C.O. Educational Planning Mission of 1964 expressed another facet of the problem when it commented that the school population had risen by 55 per cent, school buildings by 20 per cent and the teaching force by 18 per cent since 1960.[19]

2. Secondary Education

During his Regency, Tshekedi Khama raised £100,000 to build a new secondary school in the country at Moeng, in 1947. Further developments waited until 1954, until which time secondary pupils went to schools in South Africa, notably Tigerkloof. The *Bechuanaland Government Handbook on the Five Year Development Plan* (1963–8) commented that the weaknesses of the secondary school system included: '. . . unsuitable siting and planning, single-form entry, courses stopping short of Cambridge School Certificate examination level, lack of adequate science courses, wastage of pupils . . . inadequate number of suitably qualified teachers . . . etc'. It was intended then to centralize secondary education in six schools, although this number has since been raised to nine. Despite the fact that preference is given to younger applicants, 62 per cent of those in Form I are over 16 years of age. Forty-two per cent of those who entered Form I failed to complete Form III in 1965. The completion of Junior Certificate (end of Form III) marks the entry into the civil service. The medium of secondary school education is English. The following table[20] shows the target numbers required to meet manpower needs, and the actual 1966 and 1967 position:

	Proposed (1975)	Actual (1966)	1967
Form V	350	77	84
Form IV	360	81	163
Form III	735	308	467
Form II	750	498	486
Form I	775	535[20]	631

[18] *T.P.S.E.D.*, pp. 33–6.
[19] U.N.E.S.C.O., Bechuanaland Educational Planning Mission, 1964, p. 73.
[20] *T.P.S.E.D.*, p. 34.

3. *Higher and Vocational Education: Teacher Training*

Two government teacher training colleges exist at Lobatsi and at Serowe which offer diploma courses in lower primary and higher primary teaching. Entries for lower primary teaching have increased since 1961 from 35 to 89, whilst entries for higher primary have fallen 11 to 10. In 1965 80 new teachers qualified. Quite rightly, the government intends to develop teacher training considerably, aiming at an output of 200 a year by 1970.[21] At the same time the urgent necessity to raise the qualifications of most in-service teachers has been acknowledged in a number of reports, the latest being that of Professor L. J. Lewis who proposed, *inter alia*, an in-service course for uncertificated teachers that would begin with a four-week residential course to be followed by full-day seminars once a month organized locally by a headmaster or field officer as follow-up support. At the end of the second year a two-week residential course would round off the work and qualify the teacher as a certificated elementary teacher. After a further three years' work in the schools, he would be eligible to present himself for the three-year residential course.[22] Professor Lewis advocates the encouragement of group techniques and programmed learning assignments and specialized studies in such fields as teaching technique in the lower primary school. This plan has been largely accepted, and in-service courses are now centred on Francistown. In 1967 the government of Sweden made 400,000 dollars available for this project through U.N.E.S.C.O. which has promised assistance and will probably help subsidize staff and equipment costs.

Attention has already been drawn by the present writer to the effect upon educational policy of using boys and youths as herdsmen for cattle,[23] a practice that largely accounts for the fact that three-quarters of the pupils in Forms IV and V are twenty years and more in age.[24] The advanced school entry age conditioned by these socio-economic factors puts a brake upon higher education. Thirty-one Botswana students are at present studying at the University of Botswana, Lesotho and Swaziland at a cost to the government of R3,600 each. In 1967–8 Botswana paid a R122,000 subvention to U.B.L.S., plus fees, travel and boarding costs, which worked out at between R800 and R1,000 per

---

[21] *T.P.S.E.D.*, p. 36.
[22] Lewis, *op. cit.*, p. 6.
[23] Rose, B. W., 'Educational Policy and Problems in the Former High Commission Territories of Africa', in *Comparative Education*, Vol. I, No. 2, March 1965, pp. 113 *et seq.*
[24] *T.P.S.E.D.*, p. 34.

student. Botswana needs at least sixty graduates a year to man her high level posts.[25] The problem of qualified school leavers threatens not only the local public service, but the existence of the U.L.B.S. (University of Lesotho, Botswana and Swaziland, in Maseru, Lesotho, formerly Roma University.) By 1975 Botswana may be able to send forward 100 students. To be an economic proposition the U.L.B.S. needs ten times that number.[26]

II. EDUCATION IN LESOTHO

A. Historico-Cultural Survey

Towards the end of the seventeenth century the forerunners of the present Basuto began to settle near Ficksburg[27] but the effective foundation of the mountain kingdom probably dates from the time when Moshesh, fleeing before Chaka's bloodthirsty onslaughts, established himself high in the Maluti mountains. The Paris Evangelical Missionary Society sent in its first representatives in 1833 and they immediately established elementary schools and were followed in 1862 by the Roman Catholic Mission. During the 1860s there were sporadic border incidents in which the Basuto were involved with Boer forces, whose incursions forced Moshesh to ask the English government to be treated as 'the lice under the Queen's blanket'. In 1868 the country of Basutoland was placed under the control of the High Commissioner, and the frontiers with South Africa have remained unchanged for almost a century. In 1871 the Governor of the Cape, Sir Henry Barkly, used his discretionary powers and placed Basutoland under the Cape government, where it remained until increasing dissatisfaction led to the gun war of 1880–1 and another appeal to the British government to assume control, which was granted in 1884. Governing indirectly through the Paramount Chief, British officials seem to have hoped for a time when this mountainous 'island' country would once more be integrated with South Africa, but when the chance came during the discussions about South African union in 1910, the Basuto sought British permission to remain under imperial protection.

[25] *T.P.S.E.D.*, p. 34.
[26] *T.P.S.E.D.*, p. 34.
[27] Coates, A., *Basutoland, Corona*, H.M.S.O., 1966, p. 15.

B. Economic Resources

Basutoland is a small country of 11,716 square miles, with a population of about one million. Without significant natural resources, other than water and manpower, and with appalling soil erosion which is to some extent accelerated by a communal system of land tenure, Basutoland would be bankrupt if it were not for minimal external support. Labourers in 1957 employed in the Basutoland Administration were earning between 43 cents to 72 cents per day,[28] working a 54-hour week. Dr Munoz of the World Health Organization reported that 44·5 per cent suffered from endemic thyroid goitre, that infant mortality was 116 per thousand and that 75 per cent of all Basuto were undernourished to a significant degree.[29] Only one million acres in Lesotho is considered to be arable.

C. Land Tenure

All land is vested in the Paramount Chief, and the use of it is allocated in theory by him to those who need it. In practice this allocation is the prerogative of the chiefs. Most families subsist on allotments of 5–10 acres, which is all that is available for the 150,000 families that have a right to land appropriation. The allotment is often made in separated smaller parcels of land. Because no land is owned by its cultivator but is merely on loan from the tribe through the Paramount, improvements are seldom made, not only because there is no firm tenure, but because the planting of trees or the erection of fences could be construed as initiating claims to security of holding, which would lead to immediate social retaliation. This consideration illustrates the interdependency of social structure and educational provision. Without fences, herdboys are necessary. There are estimated to be some 66,000 herdboys minding cattle, at an age when their peers in other communities would be at school. Of a population now estimated at 975,000, 90 per cent is engaged in subsistence agriculture.[30] This lack of tenure also militates against the erection of factories or the installation of commercial undertakings, since (from the time of Moshesh, who was trying by the continuance of this traditional Basuto policy to

[28] Halpern, J., *South Africa's Hostages*, Penguin, 1965, p. 172.
[29] Munoz, J. A. and Anderson, M. M., *Report and Recommendations on a Nutrition Survey conducted in Basutoland*, W.H.O. Regional Office for Africa (mimeograph), 1951–60.
[30] Henry, G. N. in Stevens. R. P.. *Lesotho, Botswana and Swaziland*, London, Pall Mall Press, 1967, p. 106.

preserve the territorial integrity of his people from exploitation by adventurers) the freehold ownership of land is not part of Basuto tradition. Eleven thousand seven hundred households hold no land at all, 35·6 per cent of those who do have land grants hold less than 4 arable acres, and 75·5 per cent hold less than 8 acres, leaving 4·5 per cent with 15 acres or more. Grazing is communal. Henry[31] points out that a further vexation in Basuto land-usage is involved partly in the opposition of agriculture to cattle farming, and partly in the insistence that land must be cultivated for seasonal crops such as maize or sorghum. In effect the agriculturist, having harvested his crop, ceases to have rights over the land, which then returns to commonage. This custom makes harvested lands available grazing for cattle. The cattle owner would therefore feel cheated out of his traditional perquisite of feeding his animals in harvested lands, if for instance, cash crops such as potatoes followed up the seasonal crops. The communal nature of land makes tree planting as a remedy for soil erosion impossible. Cattle owning is intricately associated with personal prestige and lebola or bride-price (a type of African dowry paid by the groom to the bride's family, traditionally in an agreed number of cattle), rather than with a marketable commodity. Agricultural products such as maize, and sorghum, together with mohair, wool and hides, form the bulk of Lesotho's exports.

The small diamond deposits are not on a scale to attract international attention.[32] Henry[33] expresses some doubt about the reliability of previous surveys of diamondiferous ore in Lesotho, and he quotes a confidential report of 1962 which has since become available, which he feels supports Basuto belief that the real resources have been underestimated. The very thorough investigation carried out by the Biemans Committee, which first met in October 1963 and which had among its members Mr V. H. Osborne, former Secretary for Mines in the then Union of South Africa, found evidence of small diamond deposits, but not of any major deposit. The cost of recovery and the amount of profit likely to accrue led the Committee to recommend the Paramount Chief to allow private prospecting to continue, but not to involve state funds. Annexed to the report are a number of assessments of diamond deposits, not one of which was thought to amount to more than a quarter of a million rands in value, and many to much less.[34] The most immediate prospect that would improve export earnings

[31] *Ibid.*, p. 108.
[32] *Report of the Diamond Investigating Committee* (mimeograph), Maseru, 1964 (n.d.).
[33] Henry, *op. cit.*, p. 102.
[34] *Report of the Diamond Investigating Committee.*

would be the building of the Oxbow scheme to supply cheap water and hydro-electric power to the Republic of South Africa and more especially to the mining areas of the Orange Free State.

D. Education—Problems of Missionary Approach

It was to a large extent traditional among non-Christian Basuto that 'formal' education should coincide with the *initiation school*, which takes place between the ages of 14 and 16. Initiation represents the traditional introduction to the mysteries of adult sexuality and the inculcation of concepts of male superiority and tribal obedience, which culminates in the rituals of circumcision. The Roman Catholic Church will not under any circumstances re-admit the pupil who has taken part in initiation except in those rare occasions where the boy can prove he was coerced. Girls also have their initiation schools. Of modern Basuto, the 1956 census showed that 33 per cent are Roman Catholics, 21 per cent French Protestants, 9 per cent Anglicans and 5 per cent other Christians.[35] If the church is concerned about the tremendous spiritual counter-attraction of pre-Christian custom, its opposition to the initiation lodges supports educationists in their attempts to bring Basuto boys to school at an earlier age.

1. *Primary Education*

James Walton, a former Deputy-Director of Education in Lesotho, has reported that whereas 78 per cent of all girls in the 6–16 year age group attend school, only 45 per cent of the boys in the same age group are at school.[36] The explanation of this figure is to be found in the fact that because land in Lesotho is communal and unfenced, boys play a vital part in the economic life of the community as herds. The reduction of school entry age of boys to anything like European or American standards will probably take time. Night classes for herdboys, though attempted, are palliative.[37] Nor, in the case of Basutoland, is the problem eased by the mountainous terrain which makes schoolgoing not only erratic, due to climatic conditions, but even physically dangerous. In many parts of Lesotho parents are reluctant even to consider attendance for children under 10, who, with little or no provision for boarding must walk several miles to and from school over rough countryside.

[35] Halpern, *op. cit.*, p. 208.
[36] Walton, J., 'Factors affecting attendance in Basutoland schools', reprinted from *Teacher Education*, Vol. II, No. 2, Nov. 1961, p. 33.
[37] Walton, *op. cit.*, p. 34.

(a) *Drop-out and literacy*

The facts that 95 per cent of all Basuto children go to school *some time* in their lives, and that, *per capita* the Lesotho school attendance is one of the best in Africa,[38] needs closer examination. Opinions vary, but it is generally accepted that a child must have at least four years of continuous education in order to achieve a basic literacy. In other words, the child who drops out of the school system after, say, two years, is *not literate*, and has cost money and professional attention which is useless. The 1960 figures of drop-out are as follows:

1st Year Primary	41,978
3rd Year Primary	23,316
6th Year (end of Lower Primary)	8,858
8th Year (end of Upper Primary)	2,900
1st Year Secondary	792
3rd Year Secondary	306
5th Year Secondary (who will write matriculation)	67[39]

(b) *Expenditure*

It is estimated that 98 per cent of Lesotho schools are church foundations[40] and as Walton noted in 1961, there were 1,050 schools in existence. Since 1948 the government of Lesotho has assumed overall control of Lesotho's education, and salaries of teachers are paid from government funds in all recognized schools. Education in 1960 accounted for 12 per cent of government expenditure. To the government figure of 51*s* per pupil per year another 34*s* was added from voluntary agencies, bringing the total to 85*s*.[41] Primary tuition is free. But pupils are required to pay for books and personal equipment. Those who come from long distances have to find boarding fees.

The term 'African' refers to a continent and is incapable of the generalizations so often ascribed to it. When Mason states that 'it is well known that in *nearly all* African countries there is a much smaller proportion of girls attending school than there is of boys',[42] he might have supported *his qualification* by referring to Lesotho. The 1964 figures for primary school attendance were:

	1964
Primary: Girls	100,057
Boys	64,984
Secondary: Girls	1,304
Boys	1,448

[38] Halpern, *op. cit.*, p. 205.
[39] *Ibid.*
[40] *Report of an Economic Mission (Morse)*, H.M.S.O., 1960, p. 251.
[41] Walton, *op. cit.*, p. 31.
[42] Mason, R. J., *British Education in Africa*, O.U.P., 1959, p. 105.

Expressed in percentage, 90 per cent of all girls between the ages of 8 and 16 were at school, and 60 per cent of the boys in the same age group.[43] The 1964 Annual Report on Education showed that some 165,036 children were in 1,060 schools, with an average 155 children per school. Many of these schools are one-room schools, of 45 by 20 feet, in which double session timetabling is the only way to offer even rudimentary education. Since 1960, when the ratio of children to teachers was 54 : 1, this unhealthy position has worsened, and the 1964 figures showed 61 : 1.[44]

2. Secondary Schools

(a) *Outline*

With the deepening realization of the importance of secondary education in providing the technical, administrative and scientific understructure for the independent community of Lesotho, expansion of primary school facilities was 'frozen' as from 1960 in order to allow the government to concentrate its energies on secondary and higher education. In 1960 the number of schools was stated under denominational ownership as:

Paris Evangelical	454
Roman Catholic	452
English Church	141
Other Missions	16

These church schools form part of a state-aided scheme. The state was at that stage directly responsible only for the Lerotholi Artisan Training Centre, some technical schools, three night schools for herdboys and a small school for the children of lepers. Although children are permitted to enter primary school at the beginning of the year in which they turn six, most of them delay until their eighth and ninth year, and hence finish their primary education in their sixteenth or seventeenth year. The course is an eight-year one, divided into six years of lower primary and two years of higher primary. The intention is to make primary education compulsory and free as soon as this becomes economically feasible. With no centres of urban concentration, the operation of compulsory education would be difficult and in any case would meet with considerable opposition as long as parents require boys for herding duties.

[43] *Lesotho*, British Information Services pamphlet, 1966, p. 29.
[44] *Education in 1964*, Annual Report Summary of the Permanent Secretary, Maseru, 1965, p. 3.

(b) *Curricula*

In the primary schools, the curricula include Sesotho, English, arithmetic, history and geography (with singing, religious education and similar ancillary subjects) in the lower primary; and with the addition of domestic science, elementary science, agriculture and nature study in the higher primary. A departmental examination is set at the end of Standard VI. In regard to medium, English becomes a medium in primary schools at the Standard III level, the main medium in Standard IV and the sole medium in Standard V.[45] When the child passes his Standard VI examination, he is able to proceed to one of the 24 (1964) secondary schools. Most of these offer three-year courses, whilst eight (1964) offer a full five-year course. After three years, pupils may sit the High Commission Territories Junior Certificate Examination. In 1964, 464 sat and 318 passed. If a candidate gets a 'W.E.' (without English) he is not eligible to proceed further in higher education or to train as a teacher. One of the biggest stumbling blocks, which the department is attempting to remedy, is science teaching. Aided by Colonial Development and Welfare Funds, a pioneer science laboratory has been constructed in the Basutoland High School and plans for the construction of several others are going ahead. The problem of integrating laboratories, equipment, teaching and teacher training is a long-term one.

The function of the Department of Education is in the nature of a partnership with private enterprise (mostly church). The department retains the control of syllabuses, external school examinations and teacher training, using its inspectorial staff.

3. *Higher Education and Vocational Training*

The former Pope Pius XII University College which now (as U.B.L.S.) serves the three territories which once came under the High Commission, received its charter from H.M. the Queen in January 1964. Together with teacher training colleges and an artisan training school (which is post-primary) these institutions are responsible for higher education in Lesotho. Entrance to the university is gained by a good pass in the Cambridge Overseas School Certificate examination with a credit in English. In 1964, 53 of the 184 students at the university were Basuto. Despite the proud claim of a 60 per cent literacy rate in Lesotho, this literacy is felt to be on a low level which is not adequate to support the quality of secondary education necessary to develop

[45] Annual Report of the Permanent Secretary for Education for 1963, Maseru, Lesotho, 1964, p. 20.

advanced skills that are economically viable. Henry maintains that 'the standard of 90 per cent of the literates is not high enough to produce efficient teachers . . . farmers, accountants . . . typists . . . technical assistants . . . or any other of the middle level skills so indispensable to efficient production and industrialization, let alone high-grade skills . . .'[46] 'As we have noted, 90 per cent of the population of 975,000 is engaged in subsistence agriculture. Less than one quarter of one per cent of the population is provided with commercial and industrial skills, and about one-half of one per cent has professional skills in fields (such as) teaching, medicine, nursing, law and the lower-echelon jobs in the civil service.'[47] So severe were the strictures of this authority that local officials regarded him as biased. The reader must differentiate between fact and opinion.

III. SWAZILAND

A. Historico-Cultural Survey

Almost encircled by South Africa except to the east, where the territory is bounded by Mozambique, Swaziland has an area of 6,705 square miles, and, as four major rivers flow through it, it comprises one of the best-watered regions in Southern Africa. Some 8·8 per cent of the country is used for agriculture.[48]

The traditional communal tenure of land that impedes Lesotho's economic and social progress has not operated quite so extensively in Swazi practice. In the late nineteenth century the Paramount Chief, Mbandzeni, not only continued the earlier practice of granting concessions to White prospectors and adventurers, but so enlarged the practice that he and his councillors were receiving the (for the times, not inconsiderable) amount of £12,000 yearly. Not only had the Paramount dealt in mineral rights, but, as Shepstone (junior) was to discover when he became Resident Adviser in 1886, much of the land had been alienated by the rapacious chieftainship as well. Soon after Mbandzeni's death an attempt was made to sort out the incredible muddle of his reign and in 1890 the Regents approved a Chief Court which confirmed 352 of the 364 concessions.[49]

Swaziland continued to be a diplomatic counter in the struggle between Boer and Briton till the end of the century, British policy

---

[46] Henry, op. cit., p. 106.
[47] Ibid., p. 107.
[48] Ibid., p. 243.
[49] Stevens, op. cit., p. 180.

being directed to blocking the landlocked South African Republic from access to a seaport. At various times Swaziland has been under Transvaal suzerainty, the protection of Britain or briefly self-governing. In 1907 the Swazis were shocked to find that under British Proclamation through the Governor of the Transvaal, only one-third of their land was reserved to their own exclusive use.[50] The plea that Mbandzeni had not understood the alienation of tribal land involved freehold usage was not accepted in London, and from this time forward young Swazi were encouraged to offer a portion of their earnings from the Witwatersrand gold mines to a fund for the repurchase of Swazi land. After his installation in 1921 as Paramount Chief, Sobhuza II (the reigning king) made the reclamation of land his main objective, and some 52 per cent of the area is now Swazi-owned.[51] Swaziland for half a century was a dual state with what one investigator, Sir Alan Pim, referred to as a permanent legacy of distrust from the 'partition period'.[52] But the partition was a patchwork, with Whites developing farms alongside Swazi peasant holdings. Despite the many tensions emerging into the present from the confusions of history, Swaziland's duality had this favourable outcome, that it not only broke down the feudal organization of land tenure but it provided through 'White' management and development, models of farming practice. That such models might excite envy rather than emulation until the mass of Swazi agriculturalists are able to effect savings through cash cropping and more productive use of their land, cannot be gainsaid. An inchoate realization of this situation partly explains the 1964 election results.[53]

As in other African territories, Swaziland is ruled by an aristocracy of chieftains headed by the Paramount or *Ngwenyama*, who, although theoretically subject to advice and control through his councils, also occupies a magical role in his powers of fertility control which gives him much of the prerogative formerly accorded to Divine Kings. The National Council, theoretically composed of the head of each household (the Libandla), has an inner council or Liqoqo which is a type of Privy Council. Under this central organization there are 172 chiefs. Political opponents have accused the indigenous aristocracy of being only concerned to protect itself from the invasion of modern democratic progress, a situation that they contend could become politically explosive. When Sobhuza, from his position of prestige decided to

50 *Ibid.*, p. 186.
51 *Ibid.*, p. 187.
52 Cmd. 4114, *Financial and Economic position of Swaziland* (Pim Report), p. 8.
53 Rose, B. W., 'Swaziland: A Contemporary Survey' in *African World*, May, 1965.

head his own party in the 1964 election, Sir Brian Marwick, the retiring Queen's Commissioner commented that in some quarters there was evidence of 'an impenetrable conceit, a clutching at crutches to support limping traditions'.[54] But for all that, the Ngwenyama's party, the *Imbokodo*, swept into power.

B. Land Tenure

The landowning position, although improved, may still prove to be a flash point. Of Swaziland 45·9 per cent[55] is owned by the approximately 10,000[56] White Swazilanders, half of whom are South African citizens, together with a small number of Eurafricans and a handful of individual Africans. White ownership in Swaziland includes land belonging to missions and mining groups.

C. Mineral Resources

Unlike Lesotho, Swaziland has considerable mineral wealth. In one of the five largest mines in the world, asbestos is mined at Havelock by a firm predominantly British controlled. Sales for 1965 were R5,793,501. Tremendous reserves of iron ore are being exploited in the Bomvu Ridge and exported to Japan under contract for ten years at the rate of 1,200,000 tons a year – an enterprise that led to the building of rail connection with the Mozambique system so as to reach the port of Lourenco Marques. This export was valued at close on R4½ million in 1965.[57] The Morse Commission reported coal in both the north and south,[58] some of which is high-quality anthracite, which may be mined now that the rail link has been established. Other minerals waiting development include kaolin, barytes and tin. The development of extensive forests to supply pulp factories is also a source of income.

Discussing the economic backwardness of the Swazi themselves, Henry lists three contributing factors:

(i) the autocratic rule of a conservative chief dedicated to traditionalism;

[54] Halpern, J., *South Africa's Hostages*, Penguin, 1965, p. 362.
[55] *Ibid.*, p. 338.
[56] *Ibid.*, p. 339.
[57] *Swaziland 1965*, H.M.S.O., London, 1966, p. 52.
[58] *Basutoland, Bechuanaland Protectorate and Swaziland*, Report of an Economic Survey Mission (The 'Morse' Commission), London, H.M.S.O., 1960, p. 440.

(ii) the illiteracy and ignorance of the vast majority of Swazi who find their security rooted in tradition and custom rather than in individual enterprise, initiative and change, and

(iii) the very limited opportunities provided for acquiring skills and for employing them in the prevailing industrial and social environment.[59] He adds: 'the literacy rate is lower in Swaziland than the other two countries (Botswana and Lesotho): an estimated 75 per cent of all the Swazi are illiterate.[60] However, the 1960 estimates were:

Urban: 35 per cent illiterate,
Rural: 75 per cent illiterate.

Senior members of the Administration would estimate it at below 70 per cent today.

D. Primary Education

With independence, Swaziland will either have to find ways of attracting outside capital or she will have to induce social changes that will ultimately lead to the generation of capital necessary not only to expand her economy but to provide funds for education. At present the control of effective production is in non-Swazi hands. Since the Second World War, when Britain decided to increase her aid from the nominal support she had previously given, most post-war funds have been used to exploit natural resources to the neglect of the human potential of the territory. As the Director of Education commented: 'The main educational problem in Swaziland is . . . lack of finance. We have only two-thirds of our children at primary age in primary school, and about a fifth of those in primary school are taught by professionally unqualified teachers.'[61] In addition, the wastage during primary schooling is alarming. The 1962 figures showed that 1·99 per cent of the total initial school intake in the three territories survives into the secondary system.[62] But this figure improved to about 10 per cent in 1966.

In 1965 the primary system operated with 1,376 teachers and 49,513 pupils, giving a teacher : pupil ratio of 1 : 36. Entry into the system is now fixed at a maximum of eight years, except in specially designated schools.

[59] Henry, *op. cit.*, p. 245.
[60] *Ibid.*, p. 246.
[61] Day, D. R., private communication to author, Swaziland, 1966.
[62] Rose, B., 'Educational Policy and Problems in the Former High Commission Territories of Africa', *Comparative Education*, Vol. I, No. 2, Oxford, 1965, pp. 113–18.

E. Secondary Education

Of the 8,500 children who entered the primary system in 1958 1,370 entered the secondary system in 1966 (about 16 per cent). Seventy-two matriculated in 1965.[63] Of these 41 were of university standard.[64]

The 31 secondary schools comprise:
(i)   12 full five-year high schools leading to matriculation.
(ii)   18 three-year junior high schools.
(iii) 1 one-year high school (1967 figures).

The teacher ratio is 1 : 17, to be stepped up to a maximum of 1 : 25. Of the 205 (1966 figures) high school teachers, 125 were graduates. In the Junior Certificate Examination 554(+) candidates were entered and 344 passed, a situation partly explained, comments the Director, by the fact that 1965 was the first year in which a full pass in English was obligatory.

1. *Medium*

From Grade I to the end of Standard II (four years) children are taught through the vernacular. From Standard II onwards the medium is English.[65] But as only approximately 41 per cent in the early 1960s of the initial intake of 11,803 continued into Standard II, approximately 60 per cent have acquired a doubtful vernacular literacy and have no knowledge of English at all. About 50 per cent of the vernacular classes, in fact, complete a four-year course.[66] This position has been improving. 1966 figures, for instance, show that of the 10,564 children who entered Grade I in 1963, 6,917 reached Standard II in 1966. Assisted by a grant from the Carnegie Corporation, a new approach to English teaching has been initiated in the William Pitcher College, at present (1968) headed by Mr L. M. Arnold, by which a much more functional and highly motivated approach to English teaching was initiated in Grade I (a similar level of entry to that used in the Lanham experiment in the teaching of English in Bantu schools in South Africa. The Lanham method was entirely different, but has recently

[63] *Annual Report of the Director of Education* (Swaziland), 1965, Annexures, 9.
[64] *Ibid.*, p. 3.
[65] *Ibid.*, p. 3.
[66] Arnold, L. M., *Report on an experiment to improve the standard of English in African schools in Swaziland*, duplicated 8 pages.

been shown to be most successful). 45 schools have so far been involved in Swaziland, and by 1967 the first classes to reach Standard V
were tested in an attempt to provide validation for this approach. Dr
James Hemming, who approved the additional time given to *using*
English by Swazi children, felt that the scheme provided both variety
and incentive.

2. *Literacy*

Literacy rates are higher for the urbanized Swazi (65 per cent) than
for the rural Swazi (28 per cent*).[67] It should be borne in mind that
only 13 per cent of the Swazi are urbanized;[68] 221,000 or 87 per cent
live in Swazi areas. The 1965 Annual Report, using later figures than
those available to Henry, estimated that some 61,700 Swazi[69] could be
classed as literate (in the sense that they could read and write at least
one language). This would represent, in a population of 287,000,[70] just
about 21 per cent. With financial assistance from the Calouste Gul-
benkian Foundation in London, the *Swaziland Sabenta Society* started
literacy classes for adults, and a year later more than 100 Swazi had
completed vernacular literacy classes. With the backing of the government and of industries, Sabenta has expanded rapidly.

3. *Mission Influence*

According to the Annual Report (1965) of the Director of Education,
there were 370 educational institutions in Swaziland, of which 45 were
government-owned. 44 are Local Authority schools, generally erected
and supported by national or tribal authorities, and the rest are known
as voluntary agency schools. 174 receive aid which comprises salaries
of all teachers. Building and equipment grants are also available from
the government and 107 are completely private. 297 of the 332 primary
schools are non-government. It will be noticed that these reflect educational institutions (teacher training colleges etc.) other than schools as
well as the general school system.[71]

---

* This is higher than the Administration's estimated figure (1967) quoted on
p. 213.
[67] Henry, *op. cit.*, p. 246.
[68] Halpern, *op. cit.*, p. 393.
[69] *Swaziland, 1965*, H.M.S.O., 1966, p. 11.
[70] *Ibid.*, p. 5.
[71] *Annual Report of Director of Education, 1965*, Table I.

Although the Methodists were in the territory by 1847, it was not until 1880 that a permanent mission was established at Mahamba. By 1890 the Lutherans and Anglicans had also established themselves, and were followed by various Scandinavian missions, the Church of the Nazarene (1909), and the Roman Catholics (1914); the Dutch Reformed Church arrived somewhat later. By 1924 there were over one hundred mission schools in existence. From about this time some of the chiefs became concerned about education and several schools were initiated by them. Typical of missionary concern for education was the work of Bishop Watts. It was he who founded St Marks School in Mbabane for the education of White children in the territory, one of several schools that he initiated for different racial groups in Swaziland.[72] Waterford School, founded in the early 1960s, is an example of modern enterprise. Owing its existence to the initiative of a former Johannesburg teacher and headmaster, Mr H. Stern, it provides residential non-racial education and is supported by a number of funds in South Africa and overseas. Recently, its academic results have been outstanding by any criterion. All schools in Swaziland are now non-racial (or integrated). Some Africans have been admitted to St Marks, formerly an all-White school. The conditions governing admission are that the applicant must: not exceed seven years of age on January 1st; satisfy the headmaster that he knows enough English to enable him/her to follow the teaching; satisfy the headmaster that he is in a position to observe the school rules. At present only a fractional number of Africans will qualify for entry to formerly White schools. As Halpern comments 'Few would suggest that any useful purpose would be served either by swamping beyond their absorptive capacity the handful of White schools with African pupils or by lowering the standards of White schools to those of the African. The answer would seem to lie rather in raising the level of African primary schools . . .'[73] In 1967 the situation had altered to the extent that about 30 per cent of the children in former 'White' schools were African or Eurafrican.

4. Teaching Staff

The 1965 Departmental Report showed that of a total teaching staff of 1,376, only 77 teachers in the primary schools had completed a secondary school education.[74] This can be re-stated in the form that 1,299

[72] Annual Report of the Director of Education, 1963, p. 2.
[73] Halpern, op. cit., p. 414.
[74] Annual Report of the Director of Education, 1965, Table 4.

teachers out of 1,376 in the primary school *have not matriculated*. Of these, 375 have no professional training certificate. These facts point again to one of the great weaknesses in the educational systems of the three territories: *the secondary school system*. The position of teacher qualification in the secondary school system in Swaziland is better, for of a teaching force of 182, 101 are graduates. But even here, 20 teachers have themselves failed to complete a full secondary education.

5. Secondary Education Problems

Examining the 1965 figures one finds the following enrolments:

Grade I	11,803 (average age 8·1)
Standard 6	2,378 (average age 16·2)
Standard 7, Form I	1,060 (average age 16·2)
Standard 11, Form V	72 (average age 19·4)[75]

It is noted that the Swaziland African school structure has one more year than is found, say, in the structure of South African White education, though it is the same as the Bantu education system. Children entering the secondary school system at an average age of 16·2 years already face many situations of social conflict, of which tribal initiation, increasing social pressure to productive work and a growing feeling of incompetence when faced with the syllabus demands (new maths, English etc.) are typical. In 1968, Standard 6 was taken from the primary school, so that the system has become a 7-year primary followed by a 5-year secondary course, in all schools.

F. Higher and Vocational Education

Teacher training in Swaziland is conducted at the William Pitcher College and at the Nazarene College, both of which train students for primary lower and primary higher certificates, as well as sharing in the training for primary higher. The 1965 figures show that 73 candidates presented themselves for examination and that 34 passed completely, 11 failed and the rest (28) had partial or supplementary passes.[76]

Vocational Training

Despite the provision of vocational training as part of the function of the Department of Education, there has been much criticism of its

---

[75] *Annual Report of the Director of Education, 1965*, Table 9.
[76] *Ibid.*, p. 4.

value, particularly by industrialists who would be willing enough to use Swazi labour at a semi-skilled or skilled level, if it existed. Henry has commented that graduates from the trade school are turned out annually with 'some knowledge of building, carpentry, motor-mechanics and electrical installation. None of these graduates appear to meet the specific requirements of industry',[77] a conclusion reached in the Morse Report (p. 449). From 1965 the Trade Training Centre was moved from the Ministry of Education to that of Labour as the Swaziland Industrial Training Institute.

In 1965, following a visit to Swaziland by Professor T. N. Tolani of the International Labour Organization, vocational training was transferred from the dual control of the Education Department and the Department of Labour to the Department of Labour, and in 1966 the Trade Training Centre was upgraded to the Swaziland Industrial Training Institute.[78] Improvements in this area may therefore be expected under his leadership.

G. RELATIONSHIP WITH SOUTH AFRICA

As is the case of the other territories considered in this section, Swaziland has special and inescapable bonds with South Africa.

(i) Some 25–30 per cent of her active labour force works in South Africa, injecting about 10 per cent of the total income for the territory annually.

(ii) Her trade is closely associated with South Africa. The 1962 import–export position was as follows:

	£
Imports:	
From South Africa	6,390,000
From Other Countries	811,500
Exports:	
To South Africa	4,721,000
To Other Countries	2,853,000

(iii) Currency, banking, postal control and most transport originates in South Africa.[79]

(iv) The customs union between South Africa, Botswana, Lesotho and Swaziland is a source of revenue for Swaziland.

---

[77] Henry, op. cit., p. 246.
[78] Annual Report of the Director of Education, 1965, p. 4.
[79] Halpern, op. cit., p. 418.

Educationally Swaziland is faced with the need to:

(i) Reorganize secondary education in such a way that the present fall-out is at least partially eliminated.

(ii) To restructure secondary education so that it provides a better basis for (a) vocational training, (b) teacher training, and (c) university training.

(iii) To follow improvements in secondary education by an upgrading of teacher training.

(iv) To gear vocational training into the realities of the existing job situation in terms of the Tolani proposals. The replacement of non-Swazi labour by Swazi labour in semi-skilled and skilled work should be accepted in principle even though some competition during a transition period might be permitted.

(v) Because of its value in reducing cultural isolation, renewed efforts should be made to produce fluency in English ultimately leading to literacy.

(vi) Integrate educational policy into the overall socio-economic plan.

IV. CONCLUSIONS

The future of the former High Commission Territories is difficult to prognosticate. Three fields of employment are available at present:

(i) Migratory labour in the mines of South Africa, a type of work that not only introduces some industrial discipline but offers access to semi-skilled and skilled work. Although the social effect on back-home families is disruptive, the contribution made to community resources in terms of human capital is considerable.

(ii) Peasant-subsistence agriculture and cattle-husbandry, which forms the predominant African occupation.

(iii) An inadequately supplied sector of professional, clerical and administrative workers many of whom are, in any case, insufficiently trained to cope adequately with the work they are expected to do.

In most states of Africa the demand for education is vociferous, and it is frustrated by two major factors:

(i) lack of funds, and

(ii) lack of trained teachers and adequate 'plant'.

The problem facing many African administrations is to find not only the initial capital, but funds to cover the running costs which tend to increase over the years. Unlike some investments in which the original capital is largely returned through profits in five or seven years, investment in education is a long-term operation. A teacher only begins to show some return on capital outlay after at least twelve years, and, in the case of a graduate teacher, after sixteen years. Most emerging African states are based on a subsistence (or near-subsistence) economy almost completely incapable at present of generating the revenue to expand their educational services. Manoeuvering an inadequate budget, even the most conscientious politician is loath to ignore demonstrable current improvements in other sectors (such as roads) for educational advantages that will only become apparent in twenty years' time. The principle that 'a little bread is better than no loaf' accounts for the willingness of many African Ministries of Education to accept financial and other aid almost indiscriminately – a policy of expediency, in which temporary gains are offset by lack of stability of policy and planning. Where undeveloped mineral resources occur, their exploitation may provide the state with funds that would not otherwise be available. Because most new African states have neither the capital, manpower or the skills necessary to create industrial revenue, they may have to countenance a type of neo-colonial economic exploitation for some decades to come.

With the creation of funds for educational use, the priority will be teacher training, and a dual strategy involving both in-service training of present teachers as well as the expansion and modernization of normal training facilities will have to be planned. Before such a programme could be undertaken two essential pre-requisites must be considered. Firstly, the teaching profession must be upgraded, not only by salary scales linked to qualification and experience, but by improved conditions such as pensions. The pupil-teacher ratio, which often soars to over 60 : 1 must be drastically reduced. Secondly, in order to justify better salaries a *minimal* entrance level of Standard VIII must be required. But this will mean the provision of more secondary schools and the encouragement of pupils to remain in them long enough to qualify for teacher training.

Despite the African's urgency to participate in modern education, he is strongly integrated emotionally into the traditional social structure. Less individualistic (and far more group orientated) than most Western Europeans, he accepts tribal authority and custom uncritically. The spirit of enquiry that underlies modern science and the pragmatism encouraged by New Maths, are at present alien to his cast of thought. But although the present hierarchical society, personified in the quasi-magical priest-king, would appear increasingly anachronistic, the problem of achieving a transition to a new African society with an increased capacity for modernization is an urgent one.

Economic and social links with South Africa are considerable. The territories under consideration not only offer investment possibilities for South African capital but represent markets (not yet mutual) as well. The agricultural produce of all three territories finds a ready market in South Africa. Lesotho is so poorly endowed with natural resources that without the economic co-operation of South Africa she could hardly survive at all. The continuance of South African employment of her manpower and the possible sale of water and hydro-electric power (when it is commercially available), may help Lesotho to maintain her independence. Both from an economic and from an educational point of view there is much to be said for the creation in the near future of a Regional Co-ordinating Authority in Southern Africa, since almost inevitably a solution of local problems involves near-neighbours. A number of pointers in this direction have been apparent not only in the government's Good Neighbour Policy, but in the massive blue-prints for water conservation and power generation in Southern Africa advanced by Dr van Eck of the Industrial Development Corporation and by the Odendaal Commission on South West Africa, *inter alia*. The Customs Union that at present exists between South Africa and the three Territories might well be used as a basis for such a regional authority. At this level of co-ordination, South Africa's economic and educational experience would be invaluable to her neighbours.

8· African Education in Rhodesia

FRANKLIN PARKER

I. INTRODUCTION

African education in Rhodesia must increasingly be viewed in the context of that country's controversial international position. Rhodesia's Unilateral Declaration of Independence (U.D.I.) from Great Britain on November 11, 1965, was a significant world political incident, eliciting economic sanctions from Great Britain and the United Nations and evoking hostile opinion from neighbouring countries under African rule. Despite rationing and belt-tightening, Rhodesia has appeared to be confidently weathering the many pressures to return her to British rule. A basic issue is the constitutional question of African majority rule, which Britain required as a condition for independence and which has been resisted by the European-controlled government under the Rhodesian Front Party. White Rhodesians insist that they must rule until a sufficient number of Africans have reached a responsible stage of development. Such a stage of development for an increasing African majority with accompanying political sophistication requires education. Thus, a key element to Rhodesia's future is education—its quantity, quality, speed, and direction—mainly for the African majority, but also for the other racial groups.

A. GEOGRAPHIC AND ETHNIC FACTORS

Located in south-central Africa between the Limpopo and Zambezi Rivers and lying north of the Tropic of Capricorn, landlocked Rhodesia is bounded by Zambia on the north and north-west, on the south by the Republic of South Africa, on the east and north-east by Portuguese Mozambique, and on the south-west by Botswana. Most of the country lies over 1,000 feet above sea level, more than four-fifths is above 2,000 feet, and less than a twentieth is above 5,000 feet. While it is hot, arid, and unhealthy in the low areas, the climate is mild and healthy in the high veld, the main area of development. The average annual rainfall of about 30 inches is concentrated in a rainy season from November to April.

The African population[1] of 4,080,000 (94·24 per cent of the total population) belongs to various Bantu tribes, the two largest being the Mashona, concentrated around the capital of Salisbury and in the east, and the Matabele, living around the second largest city of Bulawayo and in the west. The 224,000 Europeans (5·17 per cent of the population) are mainly recent immigrants from Great Britain and South Africa. The 8,100 Asians (0·19 per cent of the population) are mainly storekeepers and traders. There are 13,000 Coloureds and others of mixed parentage (0·30 per cent of the population). The African-to-European ratio is 19:7. Separate school systems exist for the four racial groups, although the government has permitted integration in a very few private schools.

B. Brief History[2]

Africans have lived in Rhodesia for over 2,000 years. They had early contact with Arab traders and are believed to have built the great stone structures of Zimbabwe between the eleventh and fifteenth centuries. The Mashona lived in eastern Rhodesia for several hundred years until they were conquered by the stronger and more militant Matabele under Mzilikazi, who crossed the Limpopo River from South Africa in the mid-1830's. Missionary Robert Moffat of the London Missionary Society station in Kuruman, Bechuanaland (now Botswana), established the first permanent mission station in Matabeleland at Inyati in 1859. His son-in-law, missionary-explorer David Livingstone, explored central Africa.

The discovery of gold in Mashonaland in 1868 heightened European interest in the area and brought German, Portuguese, and other hunters after mining concessions. To head them off and to secure south-central Africa for Great Britain, Cecil John Rhodes, Prime Minister of Cape Province, secured concessions from Lobengula, son of Mzilikazi, sent about 200 British and Boer pioneers from South Africa to hold the land (1890), and secured a royal charter authorizing his British South Africa (B.S.A.) Company to administer the territory. Rhodesia, as the territory was named, was administered by the B.S.A. Company and

---

[1] Population statistics as of December 31, 1965, from Central Statistical Office, Salisbury, Rhodesia.

[2] For historical account see Mason, Philip, *The Birth of a Dilemma*, London, Oxford University Press, 1958, Part II; Evans, Ifor L., *Native Policy in Southern Africa*, Cambridge, Cambridge University Press, 1934, Part III; Brelsford, W. V. (ed.), *Handbook to the Federation of Rhodesia and Nyasaland*, Salisbury, Government Printer, 1960, Chapter 4; Lord Hailey, *An African Survey*, London, Oxford University Press, 1957; and Hanna, A. J., *The Story of the Rhodesias and Nyasaland*, London, Faber and Faber, 1960.

invariably at a loss. When the anticipated gold mining proved to be less extensive than expected, the pioneers sent for their families and settled as farmers on the best land. Rebellions by the Matabele and Mashona in 1893 and 1896 were put down.

Rejecting incorporation as a part of the Union of South Africa in a referendum held in 1922, European Rhodesians were given largely self-governing status under a legislative council and a governor in 1923. Britain retained veto power over legislation affecting Africans, a power never used, and over foreign affairs. Long talked-about amalgamation with neighbouring Northern Rhodesia, which has profitable copper mines and with which Rhodesia had long shared communication and transportation services, and with Nyasaland, came about in 1953, despite opposition from African nationalists. Critics have cited the ill-fated ten-year-long Federation of Rhodesia and Nyasaland (1953–63) as a white Rhodesian inspired arrangement to enhance their own financial position with Northern Rhodesia's copper wealth and Nyasaland's cheap migrant labour. Britain had insisted that poverty-stricken Nyasaland be included in the Federation. Whatever history may say to revise or justify this charge, African nationalists in the two northern territories, following independence patterns set elsewhere in West and East Africa, succeeded in gaining independence for Nyasaland (now Malawi) and Northern Rhodesia (now Zambia) in 1964.

Faced by critical African governments to the north, by internal African nationalist agitation, and by criticism from the Afro-Asian bloc in the United Nations, the Rhodesian government became increasingly conservative and outlawed successive African nationalist parties when their protests became a threat. Fearing Great Britain's pressure for constitutional changes that would so liberalize the franchise as to make for what white settlers considered premature and dangerous African majority rule, the Rhodesian government under Prime Minister Ian Smith of the Rhodesian Front Party unilaterally declared its independence from Great Britain on November 11, 1965. It is in this context of crisis that education in Rhodesia must be viewed.

C. Economic Factors and Income[3]

Rhodesia is mainly an agricultural country with minor but growing secondary industries. Tobacco and cattle are the chief agricultural products. Rhodesia is the world's second exporter of tobacco, after the United States. Its flue-cured Virginia tobacco is the chief export

[3] From Central Statistical Office, Salisbury, Rhodesia, as published in *Central African Examiner*, IX, No. 3, October, 1965, pp. 8–9.

earner, the profit accruing mainly to European tobacco growers. Africans employed in the cash economy numbered 621,000 in 1964, or 15 per cent of the total African population. Almost all of the remaining working adult Africans are on an agricultural subsistence economy.

While the average annual income of working Europeans in 1963 was £1,216 ($3,404·80), the comparable figure for Africans working in the cash economy, including housing and food often added to cash wages, was £115 ($322·00). The figure for 1964 of average earnings of Africans in cash employment was £121 ($338·80); a breakdown of types of employment and wages that year is shown in Table 1.

TABLE 1   AFRICAN WAGES AND EMPLOYMENT IN RHODESIA, 1964

Sectors	Per Head £	$	Number Employed	%
Agriculture	67	186·60	273,000	44
Mining	144	403·20	40,000	6
Manufacturing	198	554·40	66,000	11
Construction	162	453·60	29,000	5
Electricity, water, etc.	168	470·40	4,000	1
Commerce	180	504·00	33,000	5
Transport and Communications	292	817·60	16,000	2
Domestic Services	110	308·00	94,000	15
Other Services	180	504·00	66,000	11
All Sectors	121	338·80	621,000	100

Europeans' much higher wages and standard of living can be seen in a government pamphlet published in 1966 intended to encourage immigration to Rhodesia:

> Wages are good. A fitter and turner averages 10s per hour ($1·40), a buyer in a large departmental store £70–£120 per month ($196–$336), a shorthand typist £50–£75 per month ($140–$205), and a newly qualified male teacher, as a non-graduate with three years' training, would commence at £900 per annum ($2,520), or, with an honours degree and training certificate, at £1,200 ($3,360). The cost of living is roughly comparable with that in Great Britain. The cost of food is similar and in the larger centres rents are generally lower in Rhodesia. Cigarettes average 3s 10d ($·54) for fifty, and the excise on liquor is a good deal less than in Great Britain. Income tax is substantially lower also—a married man with two children earning £1,400 a year ($3,920) would pay £17 ($47·60) income tax per annum.[4]

As an overview, it may be convenient to note the present structure of African education.

4 *Rhodesia in Brief, 1966*, Salisbury, Government Printer, 1966, p. 7.

TABLE 2 RHODESIA
African Education

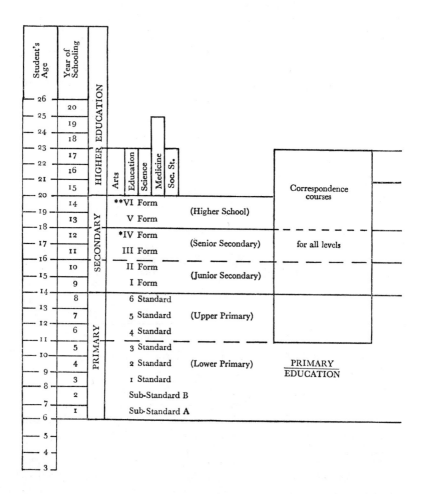

Compulsory education: 6–11 years of age (urban)
School year: Late January – Early December (3 terms)
Grading: 1–100
      50 pass mark

Teacher Tech. Tr.	Agricultural College	Technical Colleges	
Teacher Training	(Adv. Agric.)	Technical Tr. (Intermediate)	(post-Camb.)
			Commercial Training
(P.T.H.)	(Spec. Tr.)	(second)	(post-Jr.)
(P.T.L.)	(Jr. Tech. Bias Agric.)	(Jr. Tech.)	(Jr. Sec.)

TABLE 3   AFRICAN EDUCATION STATISTICS, RHODESIA, 1965

Class of school	Number of schools	Enrolment Government		Enrolment Mission and other schools		Total Enrolment		Total
		M	F	M	F	M	F	
A Teacher Training—								
Lower P.T.L. T.4	21	—	—	828	481	828	481	1,309
Higher P.T.H. T.3	18	133	46	841	279	974	325	1,299
3-year course T.1	1	115	19	—	—	115	19	134
2-year course T.2	1	47	3	—	—	47	3	50
Domestic Science—2-year	1	—	27	—	27	—	27	27
B and C Primary	3,099	30,618	27,283	318,002	251,903	348,620	279,186	627,806
D Community	94	3,764	1,013	3,691	747	7,455	1,760	9,215
E Special	6	—	—	432	208	432	208	640
F Post Primary—								
Industrial	7	290	—	142	—	432	—	432
Secondary and Commercial	75	2,575	606	6,058	2,256	8,633	2,862	11,495
G Homecraft	9	—	—	—	400	—	400	400
J (A) Primary: Aided Farm	129	—	—	6,041	4,523	6,041	4,523	10,564
1965 Totals	3,461	37,542	28,970	336,035	260,884	373,577	289,794	663,371
1964 Totals	3,403	39,083	31,259	321,447	250,807	360,530	282,066	642,596
1963 Totals	3,387	37,790	30,405	312,236	244,095	350,026	274,500	624,526

II. PRESENT STRUCTURE OF AFRICAN EDUCATION

1. *School Ladder*[5]

Table 2 shows the present African school structure, consisting of the following stages: five-year lower primary, ages 5 to 10 (Sub-Standards A and B and Standards 1, 2, and 3); three-year upper primary, ages 11 to 13 (Standards 4, 5, and 6)—the full eight-year primary stage terminating in a Standard 6 Certificate examination; two-year junior secondary, ages 14 to 16 (Forms 1 and 2)—terminating in the Rhodesian Junior Certificate examination; two-year senior secondary, ages 16 to 18 (Forms 3 and 4)—terminating in the Cambridge School Certificate examination; two-year higher school, ages 18 to 20 (Form V and a two-year Form VI)—terminating in the Higher Certificate examination required for university entrance; and higher education beyond. Described later is the new policy plan for African education, now in process and to become effective after 1970; the eight-year primary school will be reduced to a seven-year primary school, followed by a two-year junior secondary school and senior secondary school of four years leading to the Cambridge and Higher School Certificates.

2. *School Statistics, 1965*[6]

Table 3 presents the statistics for African schools and enrolments in 1965 below the university level. A total of 663,371 pupils (373,577 boys and 289,794 girls) are taught by 18,544 teachers (17,923 Africans and 621 Europeans) plus 421 part-time teachers in Grade D community and evening schools. The non-government (mainly mission) schools contain 90 per cent of the total enrolment (596,859 out of the total enrolment of 663,371). Of the 75 secondary schools, 61 are mission secondary schools and 14 are government secondary schools. Non-government or mainly mission schools are divided into the following ten grades:

[5] Sasnett, Martena, and Sepmeyer, Inez, *Educational Systems of Africa*, Berkeley, University of California Press, 1967, pp. 915–62.
[6] Secretary for African Education, *Annual Report for 1965*, Salisbury, Government Printer, 1966, p. 18.

Grade	Kind of School
A (1)	Teacher training lower; two-year post-Standard 6 course
(2)	Teacher training higher; two-year post-Junior Certificate
(3)	Domestic science
B	Central Primary; Sub-Standard A to Standard 6, including boarders
C (1)	Lower primary; Sub-Standard A to Standard 3
(2)	Higher primary; Standards 4 to 6
D	Community schools; adult classes in night schools Unaided upper primary classes attached to existing schools
E	Special schools for blind, deaf, and dumb
F (1)	Post-primary industrial
(2)	Secondary
G	Homecraft and domestic training
H	Correspondence schools
J	Schools established in European areas for primary or community classes
(1)	Aided farm schools
(2)	Unaided farm schools
K	Unaided schools providing classes or courses to meet special needs

A. New Plan for African Education

1. *Major Provisions*[7]

On April 20, 1966, the Minister of Education, Mr A. F. Smith, presented to Parliament a new policy statement on African education. He proposed that 2 per cent of the Gross National Product be allocated annually to African education and that teacher's salaries be raised as recommended in 1965. He pointed out that about 45 per cent of the school children left school after the five-year lower primary stage (i.e., after Standard 3) and that of those completing the full eight-year primary course (i.e., Standard 6), just under 25 per cent entered secondary schools. He proposed that the eight-year primary school be reduced by one year to a seven-year primary school (with the term 'Grade' to be substituted for 'Standard' and Grades 8 and 9 to designate the junior secondary years of Forms I and II) and that by 1969 the full seven-year primary course be available for every child who can reach a school; that 37·5 per cent of primary school leavers be offered two years of secondary education (to begin in 1970 and be fully attained

[7] Statement by Minister of Education to Parliament, April 20, 1966, in *Teacher in New Africa*, III, No. 4, June, 1966, pp. 4–8.

by 1974); and that 12·5 per cent of primary school leavers be offered four years of secondary education, with academically able students going on for further education. Thus, 50 per cent or half of the graduates of the seven-year primary school would have access to secondary education. He also advocated additional correspondence courses, paid for by the students, as an avenue for those of the remaining 50 per cent who could not be accommodated in secondary school. This plan implemented the recommendations of the Judges Report of 1962, to be discussed later.

The transition from the eight-year to the seven-year primary school will be accomplished as indicated below.[8]

TABLE 4

1966	1967	1968	1969	1970
Sub A	Grade 1	Grade 1	Grade 1	Grade 1
Sub B	Grade 2	Grade 2	Grade 2	Grade 2
Std. 1	Grade 3	Grade 3	Grade 3	Grade 3
Std. 2	Grade 4	Grade 4	Grade 4	Grade 4
Std. 3	Grade 5	Grade 5	Grade 5	Grade 5
Std. 4	Std. 4	Grade 6	Grade 6	Grade 6
Std. 5	Std. 5	Std. 5	Grade 7	Grade 7
Std. 6	Std. 6	Std. 6	Std. 6	

Pupils in Sub Standard A in 1966 entered Grade 2 in 1967; pupils in Standard 2 in 1966 entered Grade 5 in 1967. Pupils in Standard 3 in 1966 continued in Standard 4 in 1967 and will enter Standard 6 in 1969. In December, 1969, Standard 6 ceased to exist and was the last output of the eight-year primary school. In 1969 there were a full range of classes, Grades 1 to 7. In December, 1969, there was in fact a double output of primary school leavers—from Grade 7 and Standard 6. The year 1970 will see the seven-year primary course established in Rhodesia.

To finance the seven-year primary schools for all children as from 1969 and still maintain other African educational developments, it was necessary to increase fees from pupils, beginning in 1968, the new fees being called registration fees, as distinct from school fees. Those new fees, however, could be avoided if local communities themselves could raise the needed finances.

The Minister pointed out that to the present partners in African education—the government, missions, and parents—there ought to be added the local government councils. They needed to assume

[8] *Ibid.*, p. 27.

responsibility for primary schools and later on for junior secondary schools while the Government would be responsible for senior secondary schools.

The eight to seven-year primary school transition will require revising the syllabuses and will also require changes in the qualifications and training of teachers. He proposed that Grades 1 and 2 be taught by women teachers specifically trained in infant methods for two years after leaving Grade 9 (or Standard 6 for the time being). Grades 3 to 7 will be taught by teachers who have had three years of training following their Junior Certificate (after Grade 9 or junior secondary level). Junior secondary pupils will be taught by teachers who have had two years' training post-Cambridge School Certificate (after their fourth year of secondary school). Senior secondary pupils will be taught by teachers who have had three years' training after attaining a first-class Cambridge School Certificate. Pupils in higher forms of senior secondary school (former Form V and the two-year Form VI) will be taught by B.A. graduates and honours graduates, mostly from the University College of Rhodesia.

The Minister proposed that the present 33 African teacher training colleges (2 government and 31 mission) be reduced to six colleges (2 government and 4 non-government United Colleges), which with the University College of Rhodesia and concerned teacher education advisory bodies would be organized under the umbrella of an 'Institute of Education'.

To achieve more effective job placement of African school leavers, the Minister urged a policy of emphasizing trade and industrial training for urban youth and agricultural training for rural youth. Noting that critics of Rhodesia's racial policy had pointed to the lack of African secondary education, he mentioned the 45 new secondary schools established since the Rhodesian Front Party under Ian Smith had won the 1962 election. 'We have managed to give secondary education to nearly 25 per cent of those leaving the primary schools,' he said. The immediate problem, he noted, was to reduce the ever-increasing cost of primary education in order to devote more money to secondary education. The ways thought of to do this included encouraging more responsibility in primary education by local African government (strongly advocated by the Judges Commission) and by voluntary (mainly mission) bodies; improving teacher education so as to be able to reduce primary education from eight to seven years; introducing some double sessions in primary schools; and introducing small registration fees. 'Under this new policy,' he said, 'we are giving an opportunity for about half our African population to remain in school until they are at least 16 years of age.' 'I understand that in Britain,' he added, 'only 34 per cent continue to go to school after the age of 15.' He pointed out that in 1946 Rhodesia had only two African secondary schools with a total enrolment of 48, that in 1966 about 6,000 Africans a year were being admitted to secondary schools, and that by 1971 under the new policy about 23,000 a year would enter secondary schools. Such was the Minister's explanation of the new plan which has been accepted as the government's policy on African education.

2. Commentary on the New Plan

Following the announced new policy for African education, Mr M. G. Mills, Secretary for African Education, gave a speech on the topic, 'After School, What Then?'[9] The expansion phase of the new plan, he said, to seven years of primary school for all, with 37·5 per cent of these going on to two years of junior secondary schools and 12·5 per cent of primary school leavers going on to four years of secondary school, is in accord with recommendations made by the Judges Report (published in 1963), the U.N.E.S.C.O. Planning Mission (it completed its work in Rhodesia in October, 1964, but no report has been published), and the Ministry of African Education. Very few difficulties could arise for the 12·5 per cent who go on to 4 years of secondary school and some beyond. 'It is from this group,' he said, provided that they could be taught by qualified teachers, 'that there will emerge the professional men and women, the technologists, the high-level manpower of the Rhodesia of 1978.' His concern for the 37·5 per cent who would receive nine years of school was that their education fit them for earning a living. He suggested that two-thirds of their school week be spent on academic subjects leading to the Junior Certificate examination and one third on handiwork, industrial work, and vocational preparation.

'The 12·5 per cent, the 37·5 per cent, they're all right,' he said. 'The other 50 per cent, the lower half of the pool of ability, these will be the unskilled workers of the future, just as they would be in Birmingham, Chicago, Nairobi, Gwelo. Seven years of primary school will have done all that Rhodesia can do for these folk. They take their proper place in society, be it rural or urban, industrialized or ranching country. There is no racialism or colour in this, just plain economics and the age-old relationship of capital and labour.'

9 Speech given at a conference of the Council of Social Services.

3. *Government Reply to Criticism of the New Plan*

The government attempted to reply[10] to misunderstanding and criticism of the new plan. For example, the 'double sessioning' phrase in the new plan had been misinterpreted to mean that teachers would have to do double work without an increase in pay. The intention, a government report stated, is that Grades 3 and 4 be bracketed together under one teacher, but these grades would be taught different subjects by other teachers and for specified periods would be taught under a 'programmed learning' process. While it is true that a teacher would be saved in each school, the report continued, as the plan develops 'so will the need for increases of trained teacher staff'. Only untrained teachers will be among those eliminated, 2,500 or more as early as January, 1967. Yet, the report observed, each year at least 2,000 teachers leave because of resignations, dismissals, maternity and other reasons. Also, many of the affected younger untrained teachers will be eligible for teacher college training. 'It is expected that by 1967 the country will have 85 per cent trained teachers in all grades of schools— this is a high ratio by African standards.'

An immediate cry had been heard in some quarters that the reduction of the primary school from eight to seven years was intended to make it more difficult for Africans to qualify as 'B' Roll voters. The report denied that this was intended or would be the effect, since the primary school franchise requirement would be met by the new seven-year primary school and the secondary school Junior Certificate franchise requirement would hold for the new junior secondary schools after nine years of education.

Some critics had charged that teacher training under the new plan would have the effect of lowering standards. The report explained how the new plan would improve teacher preparation: Grades 1 and 2 would be taught by women teachers with two years of training after Grade 9, an improvement over the old primary training lower in which two years of training were taken after Standard 6. Grades 3 to 7 would be taught by teachers trained for three years after Grade 9 (Junior Certificate level), i.e., teachers with a total of twelve years of education, which the report asserted 'is a very high level in most parts of Africa'. The specially trained vocational teachers for Grades 8 and 9 to provide vocational education and guidance for the 37·5 per cent of primary school leavers 'are something new for Rhodesia and indeed for

[10] 'Current Reaction to Plan for Education', *Rhodesian Commentary*, I, No. 15, August 22, 1966, p. 6.

Africa' and 'are sufficient to give the lie to suggestions by the critics of lowered standards'.

To doubts expressed by the churches about the role of their mission schools under the new plan, the report stated that, 'At primary level the Churches are welcome to stay'. In teacher training 'it is planned that "United Colleges" with many participating denominations will produce our teachers for the next 50 years'. The new junior secondary schools would be under the care of the missions or of local African councils with the government paying grants for teachers. Senior secondary schools will continue as at present with the missions mainly responsible in rural areas. 'From 1970 Government will assume responsibility for all *new* Secondary Schools and a Church, if it wants to set up its own school, will be eligible for *per capita* grants which at present are paid to 'private' schools in the European sector'.

4. *Government's claimed accomplishment in African Education*

(a) *Ratio of Children in School to Total Population*

To counter criticism of its racial policy and to defend its effort in African education, the Smith government has made several comparisons with other countries. England, with its more productive workers, has three adults to every child in school while in Rhodesia, where half of the total African population is under 17 years of age and where the workers are much less productive, there is one adult per child in school. Despite this fact, Rhodesia estimates that it enrolls 95 per cent of eligible African children in lower primary school. Rhodesia also claims to have at school almost as high a ratio of African children in relation to her total population as does Great Britain and more than many African countries:[11]

Rhodesia	1 in 6
Malagasy Republic	1 in 10
Ghana	1 in 11
Algeria	1 in 12
Liberia	1 in 14
Tanzania	1 in 18
Dahomey	1 in 22
Guinea	1 in 26
Mali	1 in 64
Ethiopia	1 in 71

[11] *African Advancement in Rhodesia; Information Paper No. 3*, Salisbury, Government Printer, April 1966, pp. 8–9; *Progress in African Education*, Salisbury, Government Printer, 1966, pp. 3–5.

(b) *Literacy*

Citing U.N.E.S.C.O. figures, the government has pointed out that of the world population, 55 per cent are literate. In Africa and India 10 per cent to 15 per cent are literate. In Rhodesia, about 30 per cent of Africans are literate.[12]

(c) *Reasons for Expenditure Discrepancy between European and African Education*

Amounts spent on African education have risen dramatically in recent years: just over £500,000 ($1,400,000) in 1949; just under £3 million ($8,400,000) in 1956; £6·45 million ($18·06 million) in 1965. Critics, however, have pointed out that while the government spent £6·45 million ($18·06 million) in 1965 on 643,592 African pupils—£10 ($28) per African pupil, it spent that year £6·12 million ($17·14 million) on 58,769 European pupils—over £100 ($280) per European pupil.

The government offers several justifications for this discrepancy.[13] First, over 95 per cent of African pupils are in primary schools which cost a fraction of the cost to build and run compared with secondary schools. Second, though European pupils receive no better education in Rhodesia than they would get elsewhere, the government stresses that their parents, who represent 5·17 per cent of the population, pay over 98 per cent of the country's income taxes and that these taxes also pay for the bulk of African education. Third, Africans have shown interest in education for their children only in the last thirty years; in light of their relatively recent influx into schools, the government believes the expansion of facilities has been quite significant. Fourth, to equalize per pupil expenditures for Africans with that for Europeans would cost Rhodesia twice its entire budget. Fifth, 90 per cent of African schools are in rural areas where the African people with the help of the Christian missions build their own schools. Sixth, to spend less on European education in order to spend more on African education would cause many Europeans to leave Rhodesia, with a resultant fall in revenue, and would also discourage expatriate teachers from coming to Rhodesia.

The aim is to raise the standard of African education, stated a government report, and to do this calls for more expatriate staff who are now

12 *Ibid.*
13 *Ibid.*

difficult to recruit. Of the 666 qualified secondary teachers in African education today, 130 are African and 536 are Europeans. The report bluntly stated that Rhodesia's progress and African advancement rest on European enterprise and capital, 'with, of course, the help of largely unskilled [African] labor'; and without this combination of effort, 'the country would fall back into an abyss'.

(d) *Efforts made in Secondary Education*

Within established standards for entry and advancement in secondary schools, Rhodesia claims to be meeting Africans' needs. A government report[14] pointed to the selective character of secondary education everywhere in the world and noted that it is not normal anywhere for the whole school population to expect secondary education, that only 34 per cent of pupils in Great Britain continue schooling beyond age 15, and that even in the United States there are 23 million adults who have fewer than eight years of schooling. In the Rhodesian Standard 6 certificate examination passes are graded 1, 2, 3, 4, and 5. About 25 per cent who receive the higher passes in grades 1 and 2 find places in secondary school and this 25 per cent 'roughly corresponds with the rate of progression to secondary schools elsewhere'. Of the 27,513 pupils who took the Standard 6 certificate examination in 1965, about 25 per cent or 7,009 received grades 1 and 2 passes, and of these 6,059 went on to secondary school. 'The places available are roughly equal to the number of students qualifying to enter,' stated the report. In 1956 there were 1,756 African pupils in secondary schools. In 1966 the number had increased to 13,600 (with a like number taking secondary courses by correspondence). 'This surely demolishes the argument that secondary education is being held back.' The report also stated, 'As far as sixth form places are concerned, there are at present more available than there are African students offering themselves'.

5. *Challenges made of Government Claims*

In a journal article on African education, mission representative W. A. Hoskins expressed concern over the reduction of almost 25 per cent of trainees in teachers colleges in 1966.[15] He feared that fewer

---

[14] *Ibid.*
[15] Hoskins, W. A., 'Burying Our Talents', *Central African Examiner*, IX, No. 3, October, 1965, pp. 4–5; Ross, L. C., 'Readers' Reply to African Education', IX, No. 4, November 1965, p. 10 (and Hoskins' reply, pp. 10–11).

teachers would limit educational opportunities for African pupils. A
government spokesman, L. C. Ross, explained that the reduced intake
of teacher trainees had not been made on racial or political grounds
but because funds and expansion plans required an average annual
intake of 1,050 into teachers colleges. He pointed out that the government intended in six years to attain universal primary school enrolment.
Hoskins' reply was to estimate that universal primary education in
six years would require 10,000 *additional* teachers, rather than a reduced
number. The government plan for universal primary education thus
could only become a reality by using untrained teachers. He pointed
out that four-fifths of the present teachers had only two years' training
beyond Standard 6 and that if a further dilution took place it 'would
expand the present large gap in educational opportunity between
European and African in Rhodesia to an unbridgeable gulf'.

Hoskins challenged the government's contention that European
school fees in 1964 of £1,100,000 ($3,080,000) were almost five times
as much as African school fees of £200,000 ($560,000). He pointed out
that the £200,000 ($560,000) in fees referred only to the 10 per cent
of African children in Government schools and added that the fees,
books, and building costs paid by the remaining 90 per cent of African
children in mission and other schools (i.e., paid by African parents) would
amount to another £1 million ($2,800,000) per year, considerably
exceeding European fees. He pointed out further that besides this direct
contribution by Africans, their personal and sales taxes together with
the estimated £2 million ($5,600,000) per year contributed by the
missions disproved the government's contention that Europeans pay
for the bulk of African education.

Harsher criticism to which no government response has been found
has come from some students studying for the Post Graduate Certificate
of Education at the University College of Rhodesia.[16] In a series of
four articles on education they pointed out that while every European
youth is given secondary education, only 25 per cent of Standard 6
African school leavers enter secondary school. Entrance requirements
for teachers colleges show further the differences between the two
school systems: five subjects passed at General Certificate Ordinary
level for Europeans (Form IV or 11 years) in contrast to a Standard
6 pass for Africans (or only 8 years). These students pointed out that
because of the high drop-out rate, half of every 100 African children
entering primary school will drop out midway in the course, only 25

---

[16] *Central African Examiner*, VIII, No. 10, May, 1965, pp. 13–14; VIII, No. 11,
June, 1965, pp. 10–11; VIII, No. 12, July, 1965, pp. 12–13; IX, No. 1, August 1965,
pp. 11–12.

will complete Standard 6, and only 1 will reach Form V of secondary school. Few Africans are qualified to enter the University College of Rhodesia. They pointed to the government's annual expenditure of £100 ($280) per European pupil and only £9 10s ($26·60) per African pupil. They pointed to the greater amount voted in 1964–5 for African primary schools, £4,814,000 ($13,479,200) or 78 per cent of the total African education vote, and the smaller amount for African secondary schools, £729,210 ($2,041,788), as compared to the smaller proportion for European primary schools, £2,372,800 ($6,643,840), and the larger proportion for European secondary and higher education, £3,110,500 ($8,709,400). They wrote that 'education in Rhodesia has always had political overtones,' implying that education for Africans is designed to keep them from attaining franchise qualifications and from competing with White youths for jobs.

An even harsher critic who has taught in Rhodesia, Lester K. Weiner, wrote of the new (1966) plan for African education:[17] 'Unmentioned in this plan for the 'expansion' of African education is the government proposal to eliminate 3,500 lower qualified teachers through 'proficiency examinations' at the end of 1966. Unmentioned is the fact that African teacher training colleges were ordered to cut their intake in half in January, 1966.' He charged that the proposed vocational courses, to be financed by local African communities and designed to equip African youths to be useful in the reserves, 'is a cheap imitation of the Republic of South Africa's apartheid policy'. 'In essence,' he wrote, 'what the new post-U.D.I. plan for African education amounts to is an attempt to save money at a time when Rhodesia's economy is being strained by economic sanctions. The financial burden is being transferred to the African people, who are already suffering the most from low wages and unemployment.' Weiner concluded: 'The Rhodesian claims of advancement on merit will only have meaning when Africans receive senior secondary and higher education in the same proportions as whites'.

So run some of the counter-claims made by critics of Rhodesia's policy on African education. These criticisms, as well as the positive claims made by the government, may well be coloured by political bias. In the context of a continent dominated by countries under African majority rule, Rhodesia's White government is often suspect. It may be useful to place the African education aspect of this controversy in a more understandable framework by examining its history.

[17] Weiner, Lester K., 'African Education in Rhodesia Since U.D.I.', *Africa Today*, XIV, No. 2, 1967, pp. 14–15.

III. HISTORICAL REVIEW OF AFRICAN EDUCATION[18]

1. *Missionary Beginnings*

The missions began African education and today in rural areas, aided by government grants, still provide the bulk of educational services. As mentioned above, Robert Moffat established the first permanent mission station at Inyati in 1859 and the first mention of a school at that mission was in 1883. Cecil Rhodes and the B.S.A. Company encouraged recognized missionary activity for their Christianizing effect on Africans. By 1900 ten missionary societies had been given 325,730 acres for mission stations. The missions provided religious instruction, simple manual instruction in building and trades, and some reading and writing in the vernacular and English.

2. *Early Government Support*

The first education ordinance of 1899 created an education department and an inspectorate, mainly for European, Asian, and Coloured schools, but also set grant qualifications for Africans in mission schools. The first grant was $2·40 per pupil per year up to a maximum of $240 per school when fifty or more pupils attended 200 days per year and had at least two hours per day of industrial training. The first payment was made in 1901 when three schools enrolling 265 pupils earned £133 ($638·40). A new ordinance in 1903 raised the maximum grant per school to £125 ($600) and required teaching habits of dis-

---

[18] Parker, Franklin, *African Development and Education in Southern Rhodesia*, Ohio State University Press, Columbus, 1960, Chapter IV; 'Early Church-State Relations in African Education in Rhodesia and Zambia', in *Church and State in Education. The World Yearbook of Education, 1966*, New York, Harcourt, Brace & World, 1966, pp. 200–16; 'African Community Development and Education in Southern Rhodesia, 1920–35', *International Review of Missions*, LI, No. 203, July, 1962, pp. 335–47; 'African Education in Southern Rhodesia', *Foreign Education Digest*, XXV, No. 3, January-March, 1961, pp. 13–19; 'Education of Africans in Southern Rhodesia', *Comparative Education Review*, III, No. 2, October, 1959, pp. 27–32; and 'An African School in Southern Rhodesia', *Phi Kappa Phi Journal*, XXXVIII, No. 2 Summer 1959, pp. 23–6.

cipline and cleanliness, industrial training, and for the first time the teaching of English—on the approval of a visiting inspector.

Deliberations of the first of the biennial missionary conferences in 1906 resulted in a new ordinance of 1907 which divided grant-earning schools into three classes: first class boarding schools under European supervision at mission stations, second class outlying day schools under European supervision, and third class village schools under African teacher supervision. The education of girls was also encouraged by special grants. Further ordinances following missionary conference recommendations brought additional schools under grant-earning conditions. These conditions directed African education along agricultural and industrial rather than academic lines. After 1912 the Director of Education was authorized to close independent and spurious schools.

3. Conflict over Industrial versus Academic Education

An African Affairs Inquiry of 1910–11 noted the keen desire of advanced Africans for academic education, adding that 'we . . . should retain control of this kind of education'. The committee insisted on European missionary supervision and opposed further education outside the territory except in the Union of South Africa. The Europeans' preference for an industrially and agriculturally biased education for Africans was reflected in this statement: 'I do not consider it right that we should educate the native in any way that will unfit him for service. He is and always should be a "hewer of wood and drawer of water" for his master.' A legislative member said in 1905 that an 'uneducated native was the most honest, trustworthy and useful'. A civil servant native commissioner said, 'The native in his ignorance almost invariably abuses a purely "book" education, utilizing it only as a means of defying authority and oppressing his "raw" fellows'. Another official wrote, 'A purely literary education should not be considered for years to come'.

The 1899 ordinance had directed that industrial training be offered; the 1903 ordinance required that it be systematically taught. The 1907 ordinance prescribed industrial training to include farming, brickmaking, road making, building, carpentry, ironwork, and for girls, domestic work. The 1910 ordinance made specific grants to European teachers of industrial and agricultural work and those engaged in teacher training. Grants for industrial education were increased in 1914, 1917, and 1921. Matching grants were provided for industrial equipment. While most missions favoured industrial training, they also believed that some academic education was inevitable, first because the African needed to know how to read the Bible and understand sermons, and secondly because the Africans demanded academic education. While this inevitability was recognized in the 1919 Department of Education report, the problem has persisted in Rhodesia and is reflected in today's pattern of mass education at lower school levels with relatively few reaching full secondary and higher academic levels.

4. First Government Schools

In 1918 native commissioner H. S. Keigwin interested the government in developing village industries such as basket-making, chair-making, pottery, tilework, and other crafts which would not compete with European trades and products. His plan was accepted and in 1920 he was appointed Director of Native Development, a sub-department of Native Affairs. Africans trained in Government schools were to go out as demonstrators to develop village industries. The belief was that better work habits would result and Africans' earning power would increase. Such schools were opened at Domashawa in the Chindamora Reserve in 1920 and at Tjolotjo in the Gwaii Reserve in 1921.

In 1922 the missions complained that the two government schools had received $35,700 or about $190·40 per pupil while their 1,002 mission schools had received $77,621·24 or only about $1·38 per pupil. Officials explained that capital outlay required the high initial cost and countered with often-voiced criticism of the missions, chief of which that denominational rivalry proliferated inefficient schools. The missions' reply was that if their third class schools were inefficient it was because of inadequate government support. The legislative council, concerned about self-government in 1923, also saw the impracticability of Keigwin's scheme. Education for village industries had not worked out. In fact Africans at the two government schools had demanded academic education as in first class mission schools. Keigwin found this demand hard to refuse.

To study the dual government-mission African school system, a Native Education Inquiry Commission was appointed in 1925. The report of this Inquiry Commission supported the agricultural and industrial emphasis of African education, noted that the steady influx of Africans to towns would soon require government-built urban schools, proposed to substitute grants based on teacher qualifications rather than on student enrolment as a way to curtail mushrooming third class schools and to make them more efficient (enacted in 1939), and pointed out that African education was important enough to be removed from Native Affairs and placed under a department and director of its own.

5. *Education for Community Development, 1927–35*

The first Director of the new Department of Native Education was Harold Jowitt, a professional educator with 14 years' experience in Natal Province, Union of South Africa. He reflected the community development emphasis advocated by Lord Lugard's principle of indirect rule by the Phelps-Stokes Commission Reports of 1920 and 1924, by the 1926 African cultural development conference at Le Zoute, Belgium, and by the early policy statements of the newly formed Colonial Office Advisory Board on African Education. With the passage of the Native Development Act of 1929 and Jowitt's appointment as Director of Native Development (temporarily replacing the Department of Native Education), he was given power to pursue community development with avidity. An enthusiast and publicist, Jowitt began the unification of the Shona dialect, emphasized the vernacular in village schools, published a vernacular newspaper for teachers, organized Jeanes teachers as community improvement demonstrators and as supervising master teachers in village schools, and promoted maternity care, child welfare, irrigation, health, and agricultural improvement. The Depression years limited Jowitt's community development approach. His large powers incurred the hostility of the Chief Native Commissioner. Jowitt's forced resignation ended this phase of the experiment of adapting the African to his rural and cultural milieu.

6. *George Stark, Director 1935–54*

The Department of African Education was reactivated in 1935 and placed under the Chief Native Commissioner. The new director was George Stark, one of three professional educators who had come from South Africa to Rhodesia as inspectors of African education in 1928. His administration saw the advent of government-managed urban primary school, the establishment of secondary schools, improved teacher education, and other developments. Urban primary schools, foreshadowed as necessary in 1925 and accepted in principle as a Government responsibility in 1932, were postponed due to lack of funds. Under pressure from the influx of Africans into towns, leading missions submerged their differences and in 1942, aided by Government grants, established united or non-denominational primary schools in several urban centres. Towards the end and after World War II the Department of African Education was able to finance, administer, and staff urban schools, steadily increasing the intake of pupils until the majority of urban children could find a place at the age of 6. Similarly, secondary education, accepted in principle as a government responsibility in 1938, was started by one mission without government aid in 1939 and by two other missions with government grants in 1944. The first government secondary school, Goromonzi, was opened in 1946.

Untrained teachers were a serious obstacle. Out of a total of 1,659 African teachers in 1934, 1,500 or 94 per cent were reported as untrained and they averaged only five years of education. The average monthly salary for trained male African teachers that year was $9·52. There was no uniform salary scale. In 1950 untrained teachers comprised 70 per cent of the total African teachers and in 1958, 50 per cent. The entrance requirement for teacher training was raised to Standard 4 in 1934. A two-year post-Standard 6 teacher training course was agreed to in 1936 and put into effect in 1939. The Beit Trust foundation established thirty annual teacher training scholarships in 1937 and the government offered teacher training scholarships in 1948. It also helped to have grants based on teacher qualifications rather than on pupil enrolment. At the urging of the missionary conference of 1942 a unified annual salary came into effect in 1945 ($169·26 for trained men teachers and $145·08 for trained women teachers). In 1949 a two-year post Form II teacher training course was instituted to prepare teachers for Standards 4, 5 and 6. On the recommendation of the 1951 African Education Inquiry Commission a long overdue government teacher training school was opened at Umtali in 1956.

7. H. C. Finkle, Director 1954–63

After World War II the shortages of staff and building materials led to increased African pressure for school expansion. Africans criticized mission education, demanded urban education, and asked the Government to assume responsibility for all schools. To meet criticism and to aid future planning, an African Education Inquiry Commission was held in 1951 and made 144 recommendations.[19] One of many recommendations put into effect included the preparation of detailed syllabus scheme books to aid teachers, many untrained, in lower primary schools from Sub-Standard A through Standard 3.

Expansion under a five-year plan, 1956–61, was instituted under Director of African Education H. C. Finkle, who like his predecessor George Stark and his successor C. S. Davies (1963–7), had come from South Africa in 1928 to work in African education in Rhodesia. The main aim of the plan was to achieve primary education up through Standard 3 for all children in urban areas and for as many as possible in rural areas. Tied to this aim was the phased growth of teacher education and secondary education.

Without adequate African census-gathering facilities, the government sensed but underestimated the growing population explosion.[20] The influx of job-seeking Africans from Nyasaland (now Malawi) and Mozambique, plus natural population increase because of better health and a higher birth rate exacerbated the school situation. It was not known in the 1950's as it is known now that the African population was increasing annually by 3 per cent. With its budget limitations two choices seemed open to the government in the 1950's:

(i) to provide full eight-year primary education in urban areas or

(ii) to provide universal lower primary education to Standard 3 in every village. In this choice between quality and quantity the Government at first gave priority to numbers. While success in numbers enabled successive conservative governments to claim high African enrolment in lower primary schools (95 per cent claimed), it is only fair to note that the Ministry of African Education did pursue its second priority of quality in upper primary and secondary schools. Rhodesia's economic growth rate declined, however, and this fact coupled with the population explosion halted capital grants for buildings. It was the more expensive upper primary and secondary schools that had to take the squeeze.

This picture of a broad base and a tiny apex in African education is illustrated by figures recently given by A. V. Judges, who chaired the Rhodesian Education Commission of 1962: of 540,000 enrolled in primary school, 83,000 finished Standard 6, but of these only 2,819 or 4·4 per cent of the 13-year-olds could be transferred to Form I of secondary school, and only 45 entered lower Form VI. Lack of places forced out the majority of pupils.

[19] Southern Rhodesia, *Report of the Native Education Inquiry Commission, 1951*, Salisbury, Government Printer, 1952.

[20] Judges, A. V., 'Racial Discrimination Within a Policy of Expansion – Rhodesia', in *The Education Explosion. The World Year Book of Education, 1965*, New York, Harcourt, Brace & World, 1965, pp. 463–79.

TABLE 5   RHODESIA
European Education
(Including Asian and Coloured)
and for
Northern Rhodesia and Nyasaland (Years of Federation)

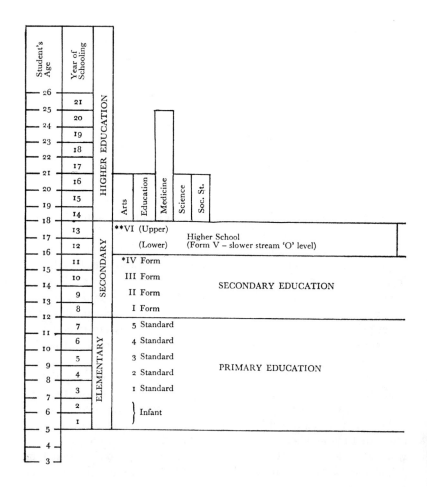

Compulsory education: 7–15 years of age
School year: Late January – Early December
Secondary grading: 1–100
50 pass mark

			Technical Institutions	
Teacher Training	Commerce	Agriculture	and Apprenticeship	
	Commercial Courses		(Tech.) High School	Craft

N.B.: While this paper describes mainly African education, Table 5 is included to indicate the structure of European, Asian, and Coloured education. At the end of 1965 the Central Statistical Office, Salisbury, Rhodesia, listed 231 non-African schools enrolling 59,344 students. In addition there are two vocational-technical multi-racial schools enrolling 1,820 students. The multi-racial University College of Rhodesia had an enrolment of 847 students in March, 1967, 300 of whom are Africans and Asians. See Sasnett and Sepmeyer, *op. cit.*, and *Rhodesia Herald*, March 20, 1967.

8. *The Rhodesia Education Commission of 1962*[21]

It was the seven-member Rhodesia Education Commission of 1962 which pointed up the statistical fact that half the African population was under 17 years of age and that the total population would be doubled by 1986. Chief among the commission's 147 recommendations were those calling for reduction of the eight-year primary school to seven years followed by three years of junior secondary school, more initiative for local African government with the missions remaining as partner under government leadership in secondary education, and a national system of teacher education in a few consolidated centres. Three years after publication of the report the Government announced its new policy for African education, based largely on but somewhat modifying the commission's main recommendations.

Thus, Rhodesia has embarked on an African education policy that aims in some ten years' time to enable 50 per cent of its African youth to achieve secondary education of two years and more. The implication of this policy seems to be to increase the number of educated Africans who can qualify for the franchise as well as to provide better trained manpower. The Government seems to be setting a ten-year educational pace in which to work out a political accommodation with its African majority.

Political conditions in Africa and the world are such that the present Rhodesian Government is suspect by people within and outside its borders. Its plans for African progress and education have never satisfied critics that its motives are generous or even honourable. We have yet to see whether or not circumstances allow the present government to have ten years' grace to work out the destiny it conceives for Rhodesia. The storm of economic sanctions and the weight of opposing Afro-Asian opinion are at present formidable obstacles.

---

[21] —, *et al.*, *Report of the Southern Rhodesia Education Commission, 1962*, Salisbury, Government Printer, 1963.

9· English Teaching in African Schools[1]

L. W. LANHAM

I

Much has been made of problems connected with the inclusion of science and mathematics as subjects in mass education in Africa. In fact, the achievement of acceptable levels in spoken and written English for the purposes intended, and on the scale now envisaged, poses inherently greater problems. One of the greatest difficulties is, paradoxically, the fact that the teaching of English has an established tradition in Africa. For half a century or more teaching methods, materials and syllabuses – which even at the outset were inappropriate – have been entrenched and are held today as a vested interest by many teachers and the senior inspectorate. With few exceptions, the recent revolution in language teaching has made little impression on the teaching of English in Africa. Teaching methods do not seem to have changed radically and realistic goals are still missing. Whereas emphasis should be placed on the spoken word and, in writing, on skill in the use of expository, descriptive English, the prestige of literary studies has been effectively transferred from British education to African, and the language has been severely neglected as a basic means of communication. It is not uncommon for young Africans to be obliged to wrest the sense from Shakespeare before they are capable of writing meaningful, grammatically correct sentences in English.

Related to this first disadvantage of an established English-teaching tradition is a second which derives from the very nature of second-language learning. In learning a language there is a considerably greater quantity of information to be assimilated in an organized way and stored in the mind than is necessary when learning mathematics. Much of what is learned must be so thoroughly absorbed that it is committed to the level of habit, e.g. sentence patterns, pronunciation, orthographic conventions; a good deal needs a thorough intellectual grasp, e.g. the referential and connotative meaning of words. The

[1] Section I is based on an article written in 1964 for *Optima*. Section B was written later and describes experiments carried out in Southern Africa aimed at arresting the deterioration of English teaching in primary schools, relying on methods which are practicable in the context. A full report on these experiments has been published by the English Academy of Southern Africa, *Teaching English in Bantu Primary Schools*, Johannesburg, 1967.

major obstacle to accurate learning is, however, the fact that the acquisition of a vast range of new components and the intricate conventions of their ordering and arrangement proceed alongside the established model of the mother tongue which, in its workings and the overall frame of its organization, matches what is being learnt. Equivalents, usually false, can readily be found at points where the learner has either not learnt, or has forgotten, the required components. By contrast, the teaching of arithmetic or mathematics starts with a clean slate. There are no false transfers to be made from a previously learnt system; decimal numeration, the processes of multiplication, division, and so on, have international currency.

In every major linguistic area in the world where English is learnt as a second or foreign language, there is a characteristic set of deviations from authentic English, each of which is a point of easy transfer from the mother tongue into English. With the passage of time these deviations become institutionalized and give a specific stamp to Indian English, African English in its various forms, Spanish English, and so on. In an area where one generation supplies the English teachers to the next, mother-tongue interference can be cumulative so that, with time, English in that area may deviate more and more from accepted norms. The pronunciation system usually suffers greater disruption than grammar or vocabulary: authentic *written* English is available anywhere in the world, and because the units of grammar and vocabulary are adequately differentiated in written symbol, such threats as the loss of the pronouns *she* and *her* in African English have, at least for the present, been kept at bay.[2] The learner, already initiated in the phonetic orthography of, for example, a Bantu language, can find little logic in the written symbolization of English units of pronunciation. At points of major disparity – for example, the 21 vowels and diphthongs of South African English, compared with but five equivalents in Zulu – there is nothing to curb gross mother-tongue interference. As a result, African English has only 12 distinctions in vowel and diphthong and, in a dictation test given to a class of African matriculants, there is an even chance that *buck* will be written down as *bark*, or *heat* as *hit*.

It is wasteful and completely impractical to attack mother-tongue interference at every point. There is no objection at all to African dialects of English, provided that, like all other dialects of English, they share the same basic standard English 'design' such as underlies

---

[2] The use of *he* and *his* in reference to both male and female is a feature of spoken African English at quite high levels. This aberrancy arises from the absence of sex distinction in pronouns in Bantu languages.

American, Australian and South African English. The vocabulary must consist of words that have, substantially, English rather than African meanings. The interference of the mother-tongue has already gone too far in all varieties of African English, and, as the dilution of the main stream of effective English teaching continues, greater inroads are imminent.

The extent to which each major linguistic area in Africa has produced its own particular form of aberrant English is not generally realized. If present trends continue, spoken English in various territories in Africa may well be reduced to little more than a local patois. In South Africa, well-educated African teachers already find great difficulty in following a tape-recorded discussion on mathematics by a Liberian colleague. The social and political implications of unchecked mother-tongue interference can be serious. In 1959, the following statement was made at a conference called by the British Council: 'And so, it's no exaggeration to say that the vast majority of those responsible for teaching the English language in East Pakistan are themselves incapable of understanding a single sentence spoken by a native speaker, or of producing – orally or on paper – a single correct sentence, however simple'.

No lesser objective can be set for the African schoolchild who studies English for several years in a primary school than that he should understand simple standard English, and be understood when talking to English speakers from overseas or from other areas in Africa. Reading and writing skills advance rapidly and effectively if based on an adequate mastery of the *spoken* language. It follows that teachers must be equipped to identify and counter the aberrancies of African English that derive from mother-tongue interference. Applied linguistics now has the task of specifying major points of interference in each main variety of African English.

At this stage let us adjust the focus on African English generally, and bring in details of how it is learnt, taught and used in South Africa at present. In broad outline, the pattern is similar to that in all former British territories in Africa: here, as elsewhere, English teaching is in the hands of Africans; and Africans will continue to teach other Africans.

There are two basically different ways of acquiring a second language that are not necessarily mutually exclusive; they may be effectively combined. The first is by 'natural assimilation' from a new social environment, and matches in many ways the learning of the mother-tongue. The second is by being taught by a teacher using particular methods and materials. In the first, objectives are identifiable, rewards obvious and motivation high (the most important prerequisite for successful second-language learning); in the second, rewards and objectives are less obvious, and motivation often low, particularly in young people whose language learning forms part of enforced education.

The first situation requires, for accurate learning, a processing and ordering of randomly selected linguistic material which is fed into the mind, and the human brain is best able to cope with this task up to the age of puberty; thereafter the ability to learn a language in this way usually diminishes fairly rapidly. It is no mean feat to learn a language and learning it by natural assimilation requires intense, if largely subconscious, mental activity, sustained for long periods. The environment in which it is learnt is stimulating and real-life situations make words and sentences meaningful in a way impossible to achieve in a classroom.

The second language-learning situation is usually, however, artificial, discontinuous and far less stimulating. It allows for a deductive as well as inductive approach: that is to say, an approach that relies both on data supplied by the teacher and data that the learner obtains for himself. Because of mental attitudes, restrictions on time, and the very nature of the learning process, this approach requires an effective organizing of the linguistic material before it is presented to the learner. The fact that generations of English schoolchildren, after five or more years of French, are able to conjugate irregular verbs, but lack even an elementary ability to communicate orally with a Frenchman, testifies not only to the ease with which false objectives can be set, but also to the need for expertise in preparing the teacher and his materials.

Until the Second World War, the African schoolchild learning English in South Africa had considerable advantages over his counterparts farther north because of the opportunities afforded him to learn by natural assimilation. These advantages derived from contact with the largest concentration of mother-tongue speakers of English on the continent and, more effectively from the presence of English-speaking teachers in the classrooms. Although teaching methods and materials were as inappropriate as anywhere else in Africa, there was a fair chance, in post-primary education, that there would be an English-speaking teacher to provide a continuous flow of authentic English for eager young ears to absorb. This situation produced several generations of Africans who had the excellent command of English so often commented on by English-speaking visitors who have travelled through Africa. Today, however, such opportunities for learning are little better in South Africa than they are farther north. Social and political trends have served to isolate children at the best age for learning a language. In addition, of the teachers – whose numbers have increased three- or four-fold to match the enormous increase in school-going population – probably less than twenty are now English-speaking.

Recent research indicates that almost all children have their first real contact with English when they enter a primary school – including children in large English-speaking cities such as Johannesburg. From the beginning, therefore, they learn by being taught, and for a year and a half are subjected to aural-oral learning, and have no contact with written English. This is the age of high receptivity for language learning and the die of African English is cast during the first two to three years of schooling. The English they acquire derives from the African primary-school teacher and the materials and methods at her disposal. It is now necessary to examine each of these.

Only a very small percentage of older primary-school teachers, located mainly in the English-speaking cities, belongs to a generation that commands the best African English on the continent. The majority are younger women produced by one of many training institutions in this country. A measure of the deterioration of English is obtained from a comparison of the two generations. A specially devised test of proficiency in spoken English[3] applied to teachers in training in six institutions in all parts of the country, yielded results such as the following: of 178 trainees, 153 could not name correctly the hands of a clock (although telling the time is normally taught in primary schools). Their answers revealed such gross points of mother-tongue interference as the 'horns', or 'wings', or 'sticks', of a clock. In a test devised to ascertain their grasp of the meaning of *carry*, in contrast with that of *hold*, 62 failed to use the word correctly. The examiner, carrying a box from one end of the classroom to the other in a deliberate fashion, was said to be 'sending', 'putting', 'walking', the box. More than half insisted on a difference in pronunciation in such pairs of words as *their* and *there*, *too* and *two*, which they effected either by resorting to sounds of their mother-tongue, or, in the first pair of words, pronouncing *r* in one and not in the other. Teacher trainees do not lack keenness or interest, but the English of more than 70 per cent of them is totally inadequate for an oral-aural approach in the primary-school classroom. With a number of the trainees tested, the simple enquiry: 'Where did you go to school?' had to be recast and repeated several times before it was understood. This tallies with the report presented by the recent Transkei Commission of Inquiry which said:

[3] Established examinations are poor tests of the adequacy of the teachers' spoken English. Concentration is on the written word, and major points of mother-tongue interference (the acid test of second-language achievement) are largely ignored.

The Commission found many pupils in both Standard 6 and Form I (the desired level of education for the primary-school teacher) unable to express themselves coherently in the simplest English. The writing of English is on the whole very poor. . . . In Form I, teachers who have to use English as a medium of instruction (in subjects other than English) are forced to use the greater part of the year to teach the language. . . .

This situation is certainly no worse than in other countries in Africa.

Emerging from training college, the primary school teacher brings very little with her to the highly specialized task of aural-oral language teaching. For materials, she has the English syllabus for primary schools, but this is probably a mere listing of the type of item to be taught: it is not intended as a teaching plan. (The teacher has, until quite recently, been left to devise her own vocabulary of 100 words in the first year, and 150 words in the second.) Teacher training institutions concentrate, perforce, on bolstering the inadequate English of the trainees, and provide very little that is likely to be effective for aural-oral language teaching. Once in her own classroom, the average teacher quickly resorts to such time-worn practices in African education as the endless repetition (in her own aberrant pronunciation) of the same word or sentence, and speech and action games in which such activities as lighting a fire are described in a fixed set of memorized sentences. Both these techniques are of minimal effectiveness. Mere repetition of the same item, and the mouthing of memorized sentences, contribute nothing at this stage to the main objective, namely, to inculcate the sentence forming devices of the language. This kind of teaching sets a deviant pattern of linguistic behaviour which is carried beyond the primary-school stage into the speech of many adult Africans. If situations are completely stereotyped, it is possible to communicate by having available for recall a limited, fixed set of sentences, combined with a restricted ability to substitute a few nouns as subjects or objects. Situations that are in any way unique, and call for creative linguistic ability, bring about a more or less complete break-down in communication. Early evidence of this parrot-like linguistic behaviour has been found in recent tests carried out in first-year primary-school classes in Johannesburg. In response to the question: '*What is this/that?*' (the examiner pointing to some object) the answer is frequently, '*My name is nose/shirt/table*'. The child, recalling the response '*My name is John/ Sipho/Mary*' to '*What is your name?*', simply recalls the one meaningful piece of English he has effectively memorized. For many children this is the sum total of their English learning after one and a half years.

In schools and universities all over southern Africa, there is evidence that English essays, reports, etc. are constructed from memorized pre-encoded stretches rather than an internalized grammar and vocabulary. This completely non-creative use of language may, when combined with the African flair for mimicry, gives a superficial impression of competence that has been known to deceive even senior managers in industry who have denied that their working force finds difficulty in communicating. It is our belief that many Africans in unskilled and semi-skilled occupations in industry who have had a primary school education, use English in this way. Tests conducted in industry in Johannesburg have revealed severely limited vocabularies, virtually no command of important sections of English grammatical structure (such as the verb conjugation), and frequent misunderstanding of what is said.

Observations up to now have been directed at the aural-oral learning stage in the early years of primary school. (Of the total number of children entering primary school, over 50 per cent leave school by the beginning of the fifth year.) Contact with written English, which begins in earnest in the third year, undoubtedly enriches the learning experience of the child; but it also places further obstacles in the way of effective mastery of the spoken language. The havoc wrought on English pronunciation by mother-tongue interference is aggravated by the habit of pronouncing written English words as they are spelt. (Reading and writing in the mother-tongue with its phonetic orthography have already been learnt.) English pronunciation is never taught systematically; sound is not separated from symbol, and the African teacher has no frame of reference to apply when coping with aberrancies which creep in from the two main sources of interference. The irregularities of English spelling place a heavy burden of learning on the child, and this may be the reason why general progress often falls off at this stage. The average teacher, whose own meagre resources in spoken English have been exhausted, now begins to seek her teaching materials in the written word. 'Grammar' (of a minimally instructive sort) and 'composition' (a particularly futile exercise in early stages of language learning) chiefly occupy her attention. 'Conversation' (i.e. what remains of the aural-oral approach) is very often based on the reading book, and this establishes the practice of using literary English in speech. African English is permanently marked with this feature at an early stage.

The primary-school teacher is clearly the keystone in the structure of English education in Africa. Nothing that is written here should be taken as a condemnation of her; many are good teachers, but they lack the resources with which to teach. More than anything, the present situation demands materials; comprehensive, thoroughly programmed courses, presented in a rigid framework, that provide every item for pattern drills, language games, etc. In recent years, English courses designed for use in African primary schools have become available, usually in the form of sets of books for pupils, matched by a set of teachers' manuals. The use of these courses would certainly improve the present position, but visits to African schools soon show that the availability of courses and their effective implementation are two different things. If course materials do exist in a school, the headmistress usually takes some time to locate the books in a dusty corner of some cupboard.

The teacher's reliance on her own resources is the consequence of her training. Frequently there is a haphazard, inadequately formulated approach to 'teaching method', which is based on theoretical notions that have little practical efficacy. Training institutions would probably do better if they trained teachers to teach a specific course that they have learned to know thoroughly, and to rely on the techniques and teaching aids prescribed for it.

Currently available courses fail to meet one or more essential requirements of the oral-aural approach to English teaching in Africa. Much of the total substance of classroom lessons has to be provided by the teacher; for example, only the skeleton of pattern drills is generally given. Mother-tongue interference as the major disruptive force in the learning of English in Africa, is barely recognized in most courses. Any course which provides instructions such as: 'The pupil . . . must frequently hear the correct sound or pattern before he can say it correctly; and the teacher must repeat any new word or pattern several times . . .', fails to take into account the realities of English teaching in Africa. Not one per cent of African teachers has a sufficient grasp of English pronunciation to meet this requirement, even if there happens to be an authority such as a dictionary close at hand. They lack any descriptive frame even for discussing English pronunciation, and the great disparity in systems between English and the Bantu languages makes any rough set of equivalents unacceptable for adequate communication. To meet the need for authentic models of pronunciation it seems that a tape recorder or similar sound-producing instrument providing pre-recorded lesson material would be a powerful teaching aid in the hands of the primary-school teacher.

To say that the development of materials is the main objective for English education in Africa does not imply the relegation of the teacher. The best possible materials can be rendered ineffective by bad presentation. The re-education of teachers is certainly necessary, but their time in training college would be more profitably spent learning to *implement* expertly devised teaching materials, to use modern teaching aids, and to understand the rudiments of inductive learning.

II

The language teaching revolution, which began some 25 years ago, continues to produce men, materials and ideas in ever increasing quantities, concentrated mainly in the field of 'teaching English to speakers of other languages'. The general impression is, however, that little real impact has been made on the general teaching of English in Africa. It is pertinent to find reasons for this because some education departments have been prepared to experiment with new approaches and several major experiments in English teaching have been in progress for some years. Enthusiastic reports of initial successes in these experiments are seldom followed by evidence of the successful extension of the experimental method and materials to the education system in general. Any attempt at an educational revolution in Africa encounters intractable difficulties and the first lesson that has to be learnt is the need to work within the limitations of the African context. The test for any new approach is whether it can survive intact after two or three years in schools outside the experimental group. Building new methods and materials around available teacher talent and general resources, is more likely to bring success than an attempt to implement an elaborate theory of language learning and teaching without adequate assessment of these local resources.

One rock on which the best laid schemes may founder is the established tradition of English teaching in Africa. A peep into one of the ten thousand classrooms soon reveals what the accepted practices of this tradition are. The children (possibly an unmanageably large number, but well-behaved as only African children can be) stand or sit in neat rows responding to the teacher by chorusing the sentences she offers or answering the questions she asks. It is unlikely that the ranks will be broken during the lesson – small-group work is not part of the tradition and a dozen small groups of primary school children working purposefully is not easy to organize or maintain. So the English lesson remains a parade ground affair with very little individual activity or response. Perhaps a dozen English questions or commands and a dozen responses will emerge during the lesson, probably less; it is even possible for the lesson to begin and end with the same sentence. The main technique is choral practice with a few leaders, many followers, and some non-participants. Repetitions *ad nauseam* are likely and in the lower grades a typical feature is the disjointed sentence 'it – is – a – book' with each word isolated and bearing a high level of stress.

Probably more Xhosa (or Shona, etc.) than English will be spoken in the form of cajolings, translations of the English, threats, etc. The teacher may take her sentences from prepared materials, but she is more likely to rely on her memory and there is, in consequence, little structural relationship between them. She has, in any event, been trained to be self-reliant in her teaching and an instruction in a course or syllabus such as: 'revise prepositions', will spur only the most conscientious to prepare a well-ordered set of preposition phrases and devise situations in which to use them.

If there is any discernible method or approach underlying English teaching in primary schools in Southern Africa, it is the situational-contextual approach (with some lip-service paid to direct method). Effective and impressive in the hands of an enthusiastic English-speaking teacher in a North London school, it takes on a very different appearance in the average African lower primary school.

In 1963, a small group of academic linguists and educationalists in the University of Witwatersrand and a senior inspector of African schools initiated experiments to develop new approaches to teaching English in primary schools, without exceeding the resources of the average teacher and classroom. The following main objectives were set in preparing the experimental method and materials:

(i) A step-by-step teaching programme which prescribed in carefully judged progression, every next teaching activity both in its form and content, and was sufficiently comprehensive to permit little deviation if the daily programme was to be completed in the time available.

(ii) The provision in detail of all drill and practice material so that there was no instruction such as: 'Revise prepositions' without a set of drill sentences bringing in all the appropriate prepositions, situations and vocabulary suitable for revision at that stage.

(iii) The provision of a tape recorder and regular weekly tape lessons providing not only models and drills in authentic English, but also (in conjunction with a teacher's lesson sheet giving the text of the tape lesson in full) a means of controlling the progression of activities in the English lesson.

(iv) A strictly limited amount of in-service training to prepare primary school teachers for using the method and materials.

To implement (i) above, a recently published English course for primary schools was provided for 8 schools. The course specified the material content of each day's lesson in terms of sentence and phrase patterns, vocabulary, etc., presented in several main 'steps', but did not confine the teacher too closely as regards procedure and left the actual wording of drills, language games, etc. to her. Only a few hours were necessary to prepare teachers for using this course, but adherence to the pace and content of the course was insisted upon. This requirement called for brisk progress with structured materials, rather than a haphazard selection of time-worn items which an occasional glance at the syllabus might suggest. In 4 of the 8 schools (termed 'experimental schools') the experiment went a step further in constraining the teacher in the content of her teaching, her methods and procedures, and attempted to make up for an inadequate command of spoken English. Tape recorders were provided and weekly tape lessons and accompanying teachers' sheets were delivered regularly to the schools. Sheets and tape lessons indicated the form of each teaching activity corresponding to the 'steps' in the course and filled them out with drill material, model sentences, etc. in a way which compelled adherence from the teacher. The extent to which materials of this kind could dictate the form and content of a lesson were investigated during this phase of the experiment.

This comprehensive programme of daily teaching was intended as a means of ousting undesirable teaching practices and a way of making up for inadequate and insufficient English in the classroom.

After some 12 months of teaching, specially designed objective tests of achievement in spoken English (based on the prescribed syllabus) were administered in the 8 schools. In addition, 4 other schools outside the experiment following the traditional pattern of teaching were also tested. They matched the 8 schools in economic and social background and taught according to the same prescribed syllabus. In the tests, the experimental schools were superior to the 4 schools who had received only the course (mean score of 53·7 per cent against 44·2 per cent), but not at a significant level. In the 4 schools teaching along traditional lines, however, the tests proved far too difficult and were discontinued because of the inability of the children to answer the questions and the consequent embarrassment of the class teacher. At this stage the highest ranking school had a mean score of 12·8 per cent.

The results of this experiment provided fairly conclusive evidence that a detailed daily programme followed implicitly by the teacher was a major step towards overcoming the inherent weaknesses of primary-school English teaching. Unattractive as it may be to those who cherish language teaching as an art, there is little doubt that the tradition of English teaching in Africa remains resistant to innovations which rely heavily on the initiative and resources of the teacher. It follows that an element of compulsion must be built into any detailed, structured course for primary schools, and the inspectorate must ensure the compliance of teachers.

The Johannesburg experiment went a stage further in investigating the extent to which it is possible for a comprehensive course with suitable teaching aids to control content and procedure in the English class. A tape recorder (or similar sound-producing instrument), regarded as indispensable in the type of course envisaged in the experiment, is able to 'talk' to the teacher as well as provide good models, etc. As may be imagined, there is a limit beyond which a prepared course cannot go in controlling classroom teaching. It seemed that the optimum was a teacher's lesson plan which could be read at a glance, showing the content and progress of the lesson step by step. The lesson sheet indicated where the tape lesson could be used to lead a pattern drill, introduce a point of pronunciation, or rehearse responses in anticipation of a small-group activity, but content was not itemized on the lesson sheet.

In time, the tape lesson provided about one third of a lesson and the opportune moment for using it lay at the discretion of the teacher, who was well-versed in the course and the use of the machine. The tape lesson therefore remains a teaching aid in the hands of a trained teacher, an aid more powerful than most in its ability to fill out a lesson with 'live' material, which overworked and undertrained teachers are seldom able to assemble on their own. It provides, moreover, authentic models of English; many primary school teachers are acutely aware of their own inadequate command. Possibly more important is the teacher-educating potential of well-prepared 'live' materials on tape or disc, particularly when the points of weakness in African English are made known during a period of training.

Implicit in our belief in a structured, comprehensive English course is an assurance of wide acceptance on the part of primary school teachers. In our experience there is a willingness to accept a new pattern of teaching in this form; teachers are much more apprehensive about new methods when they call for a redeployment of their own resources. As evidence of teacher enthusiasm is the fact that ten or more Johannesburg schools outside the experiment have bought tape recorders from their own limited funds and sought permission to use the materials of the experiment as they stand. The results of this experiment in primary-school English teaching suggest that teacher-training institutions would contribute more to English teaching in primary schools if trainees spent their time learning the content and methods of an approved course. The strenuous efforts to repair and supplement the desperately inadequate resources of the average trainee would be made more purposeful; there is clear evidence that structured, comprehensive course materials, followed up by well-designed objective tests concentrating on known areas of weakness, are highly effective as teacher education.

Tests of achievement during the course of the experiment described above brought the realization that the transfer of classroom learning to real-life communication is currently the great challenge for the English teacher in Africa – as it is for all language teachers. The unhappy truth that the skilful manipulation of words and structures in live and machine-led language drills carry no implication of an equal facility in responding to natural linguistic stimuli in real-life contexts, has only recently become evident to the enthusiastic proponents of language teaching based on modern linguistics. Even the highest scoring classes in the Johannesburg experiment scored poorly in tests which approached the conditions of normal conversation and one is impressed by the need for a dimension of language teaching which involves overt responses to reinforce communicative activities based on meaningful situations. Obviously, more physical activity in language learning is called for and this is one aspect of teaching most difficult to control in the lower levels in primary school. It may, of course, be claimed that situational learning is a feature of 'traditional' primary school teaching. It requires, however, only the briefest acquaintance with primary school teaching to realize that theory and practice are two very different things, and that 'situational-contextual' method developed in Britain demands too much of the average teacher in Africa.

Two experiments currently taking place in Africa hold promise of a practicable means of introducing 'communication' ('contextualization') in primary school teaching. In East Africa, Professor Gerald Dykstra's experiment in 'New Concepts in Language Learning' stresses 'non-predictable, purposeful communication' from the beginning of English teaching and uses such techniques as carefully devised language games in which graded components can be presented in stimulating contexts and thus evoke meaningful responses. In Swaziland, the 'English Through Activity' experiment directed by Mr L. Arnold stresses physical involvement and 'having fun' while using contextually meaningful utterances. 'English Through Activity' complements more rigidly patterned classroom teaching along the lines of the comprehensive, structured course which we have advocated. The latter, in its vocabulary and grammatical structures, anticipates to some extent the corresponding 'English Through Activity' session. This complementation we believe to be an essential feature for contextualizing activities of the Arnold and Dykstra type. Firm guidance is essential in the presentation stage of the primary school lesson and the best safeguard against the disintegration of open-ended 'contextualizing' activities is the inescapable control of a programmed course. The encouraging response from teachers and inspectors in the course of the experiment already described led to the extension of the project to other aspects of English teaching apart from the oral-aural approach in the first two years of primary school. The teaching of reading was recognized as another weak link in the chain of primary school English teaching and results obtained with the use of a modified orthography are worth brief mention.

In South Africa, African children are introduced to English reading in about the tenth week of the second primary-school year. They come to it after mastering reading in the mother-tongue with an orthography almost completely phonemic ('phonetic'). The introduction to English reading is mainly 'look-and-say' and phonic to a lesser degree, and comes as something of an intellectual shock to 7- and 8-year old Africans. In part this is due to the unsuitable content of reading materials; more serious, however, is the quantity and type of learning necessary to control the capricious conventions of English spelling, which overtax even young mother-tongue speakers – hence the success of i.t.a. reading, which could be a powerful reinforcement of the oral English lesson, and a means of reaching beyond the meagre resources of many teachers, is reduced to a travesty by the practice of reading in order to memorize, i.e. memorization exercises in which page numbers, key words and illustrations serve as cues to memorized stretches of text. Among the many disadvantages of the English orthography in second-language teaching is spelling as a source of aberrant pronunciation – African children are sometimes encouraged by teachers to pronounce words as they are spelt as means of remembering the correct spelling.

In 1965, four experimental schools took a calculated risk in agreeing to withhold normal English spelling and to introduce reading by the phonic method using a completely phonemic spelling[4] of South African English representing consonants, vowels and stresses. Called 'pronunciation spelling' (p.s.) this orthography endeavoured to retain some of the commonest phoneme-grapheme correspondences of traditional orthography (e.g. /ee/ to represent *ea* in *lead*, *ee* in *seed*, etc.) while keeping them on a one-to-one basis. It avoided unfamiliar letters as far as possible – only 3 were necessary. With reading material printed in p.s., children in the experimental schools learned to read more quickly and completed their first reader in between one-half and one-quarter the time taken by children reading the same material in

---

[4] I.t.a., as the best known modified alphabet for introducing English reading, is not fully phonemic and most words retain in part their traditional spelling (notably in the unstressed syllables). This is done in anticipation of transfer to traditional orthography.

control schools. The experimental schools were able to reach the half-way mark in their third-year (Standard 1) reader in the same grade 2 year and, in Standard 1, finished this reader and continued with supplementary reading amounting, in quantity, to approximately half as much again.

The supplementary reading was provided as a 'library' with children reading in class as individuals and proceeding to the next book in the 'library' only after passing a comprehension test on the book they had read. Some three-quarters of the children in the experimental schools finished 5 small supplementary reading books and passed the comprehension tests in 5 hours reading time. Supplementary reading opens up a new dimension in English reading in the primary school – reading in order to understand rather than to memorize. In assuming false goals for English reading, the primary school teacher seldom succeeds in finishing the one class reader for the year and English reading never realizes its full potential as a means of reinforcing and extending the oral English of the classroom. Supplementary reading as described here does not necessarily depend on a modified orthography because some control schools in the experiment were able to complete nearly the same quantity of reading. It does require, however, that both the class reader and the supplementary readers are suitable in content, that close attention is paid to grading the latter and that oral and written materials intercorrelate in vocabulary and grammatical structures.

The reading experiment ended with transfer from p.s. to traditional orthography at the end of the Standard 1 (third) year. Transfer was problem-free and successful beyond expectations. It was made to coincide with the introduction to English writing and, as planned, the latter proved to be a powerful reinforcement for transfer. Techniques used in transfer included the reading of parallel texts, blackboard discussion of p.s.-t.o. correlations, and concentration on some of the more bizarre spellings such as 'one'. The success of transfer was apparent in the results of the final tests administered entirely in traditional orthography in both control and experimental schools in April of the fourth primary school year (Standard 2). Children who learned to read in p.s. were slightly superior in spelling and in reading accuracy and very significantly better in reading comprehension. It seems, therefore, that there are definite advantages in the use of a modified 'phonetic' orthography in the teaching of English as a second language at primary school level, and, of significance to all concerned with use of modified, 'initial training' alphabets, transfer to traditional orthography poses no insuperable difficulties.

10· Education in Angola and Mozambique

EUGENIO LISBOA

A. An Historical and Cultural Survey

It has been customary to divide the policy of education in the Portuguese Overseas Territories into three main periods:[1] the first being from the era of the Discoveries until 1834 (when education overseas, almost exclusively under the care of the religious orders, became extinct); the second covering the period 1834 to 1926 when (on October 13) the João Belo Decree (Fundamental Regulations of the Portuguese Catholic Missions in Africa and Timor) was published; the third being from 1926 to the present.

Portuguese education in Africa began with the experiment made in the old Kingdom of Congo during the reigns of Joao II, Manuel I and Joao III 'in a period which may be placed between the discovery of the river Zaire (1482) and the middle of the sixteenth century.'[2] Afonso, King of Congo, requested the King of Portugal to send him people capable of co-operating with him in the 're-organization of his kingdom', and Manuel responded by sending an embassy headed by Simao da Silva and provided with orders which, with meticulous care, stated the object of the missions and the means at its disposal. According to the orders, the principal function of the Ambassador would be to create a ' "new" Christianity in those lands, not only to serve God, but also, through the safeguards of the Christian religion, to establish stronger and more secure links between the two monarchs'.[3] Professor

---

[1] Belchior, Manuel Dias, Evolucao Politica do Ensino em Moçambique, in *Moçambique – Curso de Extensao Universitaria, 1964–5*, Lisbon, 1965, pp. 637–45; and also Freitas, Joao da Costa, 'Politica do Ensino em Angola', in *Angola – Curso de Extensao Universitaria, 1963–4*, Lisbon, 1964, pp. 407–20. In this same connection may also be quoted: Azevedo, Avila de, *Politica de Ensino em Africa*, Lisbon, 1958, pp. 111–41. The first two books were published by the Instituto Superior de Ciencias Sociais e Politica Ultramarina, Lisbon; the third book was published by the Junta de Investigacoes do Ultrama of the Portuguese Overseas Ministry.

[2] Azevedo, Avila de, 'Duçăcao em Africa', in *Estudos Ultramarinos*, No. 3, Lisbon, p. 109, 1962.

[3] Freitas, João da Costa, *Politica do Ensino em Angola*, p. 408.

Silva Rego adds in this connection that King Manuel 'did not, of course, overlook the need for artisans and teachers to assist the Kingdom of Congo in their great undertaking. He finally advised Afonso to organize an embassy to be sent to Rome.' Later, Henrique, son of the King of Congo, was to rise to the dignity of a bishopric. The cultural ties between the two kingdoms were further strengthened by the fact that, as well as missionaries, Portugal sent to Congo 'masters in reading and writing' and also the artisans required to train craftsmen. On the other hand, Portuguese boats regularly brought African Congo youths to Portugal and, throughout Lisbon, they were placed in monasteries and private homes where they studied 'philosophy, the arts and Portuguese customs', which knowledge they would then take back to the Congo.[4] Nevertheless, this influence of Portuguese culture in the Kingdom of Congo was rapidly lost and, in the middle of the seventeenth century there was practically no trace of it: when in 1624 Father Mateus Cardoso, Rector of the Luanda 'Liceu', visited S. Salvador in Congo he found very few Africans who could still speak Portuguese. The reasons for the failure of the experiment with Congo are complex and probably multiple, but they are no doubt connected with the demographic upheaval caused by the slave trade conducted from San Tome, which depopulated, almost completely, certain areas of the Kingdom.

In the seventeenth and eighteenth centuries, education penetrated into Angola and Mozambique mainly through Jesuit Missions. Along the banks of the Buanza River in Luanda they founded schools not in any way inferior to those then existing in Europe.[5] Apart from the Jesuits and, on a very small scale, that of the Capuchin monks, the remaining religious orders contributed in no way towards the diffusion of education, their activity having been entirely devoted to catechism (that is, in so far as Angola is concerned since, in Mozambique, the Dominicans had an even more remarkable influence).

In 1605 the Jesuits already held a 'rudimentary school' in their college in Luanda, and in 1622 they started teaching literature, theology and ethics.[6] Avila de Azevedo states, when quoting the historian Ralph Delgado, that 'around the school, there lived numerous servants who engaged in various jobs known to be useful, such as tailoring, shoemaking, pottery, cooperage, ceramics and caulking. The negro workers were people of a certain respectability and some of them even enjoyed the luxury of having their own slaves'.[7]

[4] *Ibid.*
[5] 'Educãçao em Africa', pp. 111–12.
[6] Azevedo, Avila de, *Politica do Ensino em Africa*, p. 119.
[7] *Ibid.*

According to Avila de Azevedo this first attempt to obtain professional qualifications must have been the oldest ever tried south of the
Equator.[8] Alongside missionary education, the government attempted
only very tentatively (and exclusively in Luanda) to complete such
action. D. Francisco de Sousa Coutinho initiated two geometry classes
and, in 1798, Miguel Antonio de Melo encouraged the preparation of
professions equivalent to those of present day accountants and topographers, by means of the teaching of arithmetic, geometry and trigo-
nometry.

Towards the end of the eighteenth century, because the Jesuits had
been driven away from all Portuguese territories, education declined
considerably in spite of the fact that the Franciscans, Carmelites,
Capuchins and some secular monks still remained in Luanda. The
expulsion of the Jesuits, which took place in the eighteenth century
during the time of the Marquis of Pombal, was followed by a decree
issued by the Minister Joaquim Antonio de Aguiar (1834) which
abolished religious orders and expelled all the monks from Portuguese
territories, thus completely destroying missionary education.

The situation in Mozambique at first appeared to be somewhat
different since, in certain areas, the work of the missionaries was contested by a strong Islamic influence; in the areas where this influence
had not penetrated the same factors which had hampered its penetration also hindered that of the Portuguese missionaries.[9] However, in
areas such as the Zambezi Valley which were outside the influence of
Moslem religious action and, after initial resistance dramatically
symbolized by the martyrdom and death of the Jesuit Father D.
Goncalo da Silveira in 1560, Christianity finally took root with the
conversion of Monomotapa to Christianity in 1629.

The Dominicans established their base in Vila de Sena, influencing
an area where the Jesuits had not been successful.[10] They settled on the
island of Mozambique, near the seat of government, founded a school
– Colegio S. Francisco Xavier – and expanded their missionary action
throughout Luabo, Tete, Sena and Quelimane. Father Luis Mariano
went deeper up country along the Chire River, reaching the shores of
Lake Niassa.[11] The appearance of churches throughout the whole of the
Zambezi Valley was just as rapid as their decline from the beginning of
the eighteenth century. With the expulsion of the Jesuits by the
Marquis of Pombal and upon the abolishment of all religious orders, it

[8] 'Educaçao em Africa', p. 104.
[9] *Evol. Polit. do Ensino em Moç.*, pp. 638–9.
[10] *Politica do Ensino em Africa*, p. 122.
[11] *Ibid.*

was found that in 1835 'only ten priests lived in the remote parts of Eastern Africa'.[12] Only a few secular members of the Diocese of Goa remained to represent educational activity in Mozambique but, after all, their influence was restricted to the coast.[13] It must be pointed out that, despite their missionary and educational activity, the Jesuits, in so far as their action in Angola was concerned, were frequently accused of taking active part in slave trading with South America, which became so notoriously scandalous that it greatly affected the Angolan economy. The Society of Jesus even had its own ships which engaged in the slave traffic between Angola and Brazil.

The true beginning of the second period of the political evolution of education in the Portuguese Overseas Provinces may be considered as having taken place not in 1834 (when the religious orders were abolished) but in 1845 (August 18) when the Liberal Minister Joaquim Jose Falcao issued a decree which determined the establishment of the public school in the Portuguese Overseas Provinces. In the terms of this decree education was divided into two degrees: the *first degree* which was given in the so-called elementary schools and the *second degree* in the so-called *main schools*. *Elementary* schools operated where necessary; the main schools were only operated in the capitals of Mozambique, Angola, San Tome, Cape Verde and India. The programmes followed for the elementary schools were reading, writing and arithmetic, besides Christian doctrine and history of Portugal; in the *main* schools, Portuguese grammar, drawing, geometry, book-keeping, economy of the Province and knowledge of physics applied to industry and commerce.[14] On November 30, 1869, that is, 24 years later, the Navy and Overseas Minister, Luis Augusto Rebelo da Silva, promulgated a new decree which completed that of Falcao: the elementary grade of primary tuition was divided into first and second classes and tuition became compulsory for all children living within a distance of not more than three kilometres from an elementary school; sexes were separated and the number of subjects in the main schools was increased. It should be pointed out here that the so-called main schools proved to be a complete failure as there was no explicit equivalent to the tuition administered in Metropolitan Portugal:[15] for instance, the only main school which operated in Luanda could not attain an attendance of more than 30 pupils and closed shortly after it had been founded.[16]

[12] *Ibid.*
[13] *Evol. Polit. do Ensino em Moç.*, p. 639.
[14] *Polit. Ens. Af.*, pp. 124-5.
[15] *Ibid.*, p. 126.
[16] *Polit. Ens. em Angola*, p. 411.

The decrees issued by Falcao and Rebelo da Silva had not excluded future support to missionary activity which had ceased with the above mentioned abolishment of the religious orders. Therefore, on December 17, 1868 a Decree was promulgated whereby various advantages were offered to priests who carried on their activities in San Tome, Angola, Mozambique and Timor. As the Berlin and Brussels Conference assured 'the free and public practice of all beliefs and the right to organize missions belonging to any religion, in the territories dependent on the States participating', the Portuguese government, through fear of the influence of Protestant missions on the African masses, were led to give Catholic missionaries stronger measures of protection.

From a general point of view, public tuition founded on the basis mentioned above did not turn out to be a great success. As a matter of fact in Angola, where 24 primary schools existed in 1863, only 16 remained in 1869 with a total attendance of 584 pupils.[17] On the other hand, Lourenco Marques only had its first official primary school in 1907.[18]

On November 22, 1913, following the proclamation of the Republic, with the publication of the law which separated the state from the churches and with the enforcement of this law overseas, religious missions were substituted by lay missions which the republican government considered more effective 'to the native races'. Nevertheless, on October 13, 1926 – that is, under the present political regime – the Minister Joao Belo published a decree (Fundamental Regulations of the Portuguese Catholic Missions in Africa and Timor), which abolished the lay missions in favour of Catholic missions. However, only after the publication of the Missionary Regulations (April 5, 1941) governing the 1940 Missionary Agreement, was the education of natives placed completely in the hands of the missionaries. 'In places where, on the date of publication of the Regulations, no missions had yet been established or when these could not yet undertake their activity, native education continued in the care of the state but then only until such time as the missions were in a position to take charge'.[19] This, as may be seen, was specially intended for the natives.[20] Although under the care of the missions, the state kept control since it reserved the right to draw up plans, programmes and tests through the governments of each colony. The teachers and monitors were also under the missions' charge and not considered as government officials, but the

[17] Ibid.
[18] Evol. Pol. Ens. Moç., p. 643.
[19] Ibid., p. 644.
[20] Estatuto Missionario, articles 66 and 74.

government could always veto the transfer of a teacher from one place to another.

In brief, going back to the analysis of the decree which created this tuition, originally called *rudimentary* tuition, and later (as from 1956), entitled adaption tuition (*ensino de adaptacao*), Avila de Azevedo indicated the following policy:

(i) Existence of well-defined tuition for the natives;

(ii) Native tuition to be entirely entrusted to the Catholic missions as official tuition;

(iii) The state would only intervene in the tuition of natives by indicating the plans and curricula and by providing the examination certificates. [21]

In schools, the teaching of the Portuguese language became compulsory and the teaching staff, when African, would necessarily have to be of Portuguese nationality. Twenty years after the publication of this decree (1960) the number of missions and parishes had multiplied from 44 to 167.

This system of adaptation tuition was not well received generally and was, in fact, greatly criticized, amongst other reasons, for the manifest discriminatory character of rudimentary education 'specially intended' for Africans. Placed as it was in the hands of the missions, under the state's protection, it no doubt gave rise to a higher school attendance which increased, in Mozambique, from 95,444 (in 1942) to 385,359 (in 1960). However, if we look into the question of schooling progress and not just mere attendance, the former proves to be frankly disappointing.

Manuel Dias Belchior does not hide this fact when he stated in his work already mentioned: [22] 'No table relative to the results obtained in this system of education was drawn up. The figures indicated by official statistics are, in general, quite incomplete and, therefore, any table drawn would be misleading. In any case these figures, although partial, leave no margin for doubt as to the low level of progress, not only on the part of male but also of the female pupils'. [23] James Dufy in the book which he published in 1962, *Portugal in Africa* indicates the progress obtained in this type of education as being of one in forty but we are unaware on what statistics the results were based.

With regard to secondary school education, the first 'Liceu' created

[21] *Pol. Ens. Afr.*, p. 131.
[22] *Evol. Pol. Ens. Moç.*, p. 659.
[23] *Ibid.*

in Angola was the 'Liceu Central de Salvador Correia', in Luanda in 1919, due to the steps taken by Filomeno da Camara. In Mozambique we have already noted that the first Liceu, named 'Liceu 5 de Outubro', in Lourenco Marques, was created by decree dated March 2, 1918.

Finally, by decree of August 21, 1962 the universities of Angola and Mozambique were officially created; these started to operate during the 1962/63 academic year, with the following courses: pedagogical science, medicine-surgery, engineering, veterinary medicine, agronomy and silviculture. The University of Mozambique opened with an attendance of 290 students.

2. *Social and Economic Structures*

(a) *Mozambique*

This overseas province, with a surface of 784·032 sq. km and a population which should at present be in the region of 7,251,200, of which around only 200,000 are non-Africans, is characterized by a relatively low density of population (9 inhabitants per sq. km). The population is widely dispersed and added to this fact is its great ethnical diversity and a plurality of languages as well as the most varied social and cultural traditions.

In short, Mozambique has already been pointed out to be a 'heterogeneous society, characterized by the existence of three distinct social and economic traits', namely:

(i) A minority of the population (2·5 per cent of the whole population) comprising Europeans, Asiatics, Coloureds and some Africans, concentrated in urban areas, farming and mining. It is a westernized minority which is almost completely civilized. It engages in modern activities and provides the state with most of its public revenue.

(ii) A numerical minority (3·5 per cent) composed of elements of various races but, above all, Africans, with a tendency to gather at the perimeter of the most important centres of population. The Africans of this type of population are of rural origin, with a tendency either to attract their distant relatives to their side or to leave their tribes and therefore, at least partially, abandon the cultural and social system from which they originate.

(iii) A great majority (94 per cent) of Africans, composed of farmers living 'basically on a subsistence level of economy, supplemented by paid labour of a migratory nature and by some profit-making farmers'.[24]

The diffusion of a common language, Portuguese, throughout the territory, continues to be insufficient.

In a publication presented in 1967 at the First Portuguese-Brazilian Symposium on Contemporary Portuguese Language, Dr Manuel Saraiva Barreto estimates that in the three provinces of Guinea, Angola and Mozambique, probably 70 per cent of the population do not speak Portuguese. And he ends by stating: 'It is in these extraordinary circumstances that the problem of teaching Portuguese to native populations of our Overseas Provinces will be framed'. We might add that this is not only the problem of Portuguese education but also of education *tout-court*.

On analysing the social and economic structures of Mozambique, Professor Jorge Dias draws attention to three fundamental points which are: the dispersion of population (in connection with scanty demographic density; only two districts have more than 10 inhabitants per sq. km., there being certain areas where the number is 1 per sq. km.); the great mobility of the African population who are not bound by the land; and, 'quite an ethnical heterogeneity'.[25] Professor Jorge Dias sums up the situation as follows: 'It is, therefore, an immense land, about nine times the size of Portugal, practically unoccupied. In some districts there may be found endless forests, cut by hundreds of kilometres of bad roads linking the most important centres and, here and there, small villages lost in the vastness of the bush.'[26]

Agriculture, as it is practised in almost all of Africa, is 'an itinerant agriculture, consisting of clearing land, burning of fields and hand sowing . . . which is still seen today in so many parts of Mozambique' and 'prevents the closeness between man and his land which, as a matter of fact, is the principle of private property or possession of land. Man does not take root anywhere and his settlement is imperfect because, whilst adopting an economy of depredation, he is, to a certain extent, an outlaw'.[27]

At first the arrival of the Portuguese had very little influence on the life of the hinterland population since their occupation was restricted

[24] Carvalho, A. Lima de, 'Reflexoes para uma analise dimensionalda Estrutura de Moçambique', in *Moçambique – Curso de Extensao Universitaria (1964–5)*, p. 127. Lima de Carvalho quotes, in his article, from another book: 'Promocao Social em Moçambique', Lisbon, J.I.U., 1964, pp. 9, 21–2.
[25] Dias, Jorge, 'Estruturas Socio-Economicas em Moçambique', in *Moçambique – Curso de Ext. Univ.*, p. 83.
[26] *Ibid.*
[27] *Ibid.*, pp. 84 and 85.

mainly to coastal areas. Nevertheless, the Portuguese brought food products from South America, such as maize, beans, manioc, groundnuts, sweet potatoes, pineapples, two types of pumpkin, tomatoes, avocado pears and pawpaws, products which were ultimately channelled into the interior. Some of these products still comprise the staple food of the Mozambique people.[28] In this connection Professor Jorge Dias comments as follows: 'Although, on the one hand, the food situation, improved by the importation of new types, must have contributed towards the increase in population, on the other hand the pursuit of slave trading, which became more intense with the Arabs from Zanzibar and Ibo, constituted a great population drain which was overcome only after many years.'[29]

The disruptive influence of the Europeans upon the traditional African way of life took varied forms. In the south, for instance, the typical village of the tsonga-changanes 'with huts built in a circle around the corral . . ., comprising a large clan'[30] originally formed by the amalgamation of the old farming populations with Swazi and Zulu cattle-herding peoples, became, as mentioned by Professor Jorge Dias, a fragmented family 'in small groups of two or three huts with their own cattle, each group with its own Head'[31] when men emigrated to the Rand Mines in the Transvaal and made their way to urban centres where they looked for better-paid and less hard work.

It was in the cities, both in Angola and in Mozambique, that the major portion of the White and Coloured population concentrated and became what Professor Tenreiro[32] called the ideal places for inter-racial contacts: it is therefore mainly in the cities that miscegenation abounds, to such an extent that, still quoting Professor Tenreiro, the city of Luanda (capital of Angola) was referred to as the 'mulatto city' more than fifty years ago.[33] As the result of their contact with the White man, money started to circulate amongst the Negroes, causing them to lose their sense of values completely. Cattle were no longer considered indispensable for the payment of 'lobolo' (Bride price), and eventually lost their mythical significance altogether.[34]

In the north of Mozambique, economic development resulting from

---

[28] Murdock, George Peter, *Africa, its Peoples and Their Cultural History*, quoted by Prof. Jorge Dias in his above article, p. 90.

[29] *Ibid.*, p. 91.

[30] *Ibid.*, p. 93.

[31] *Ibid.*

[32] Tenreiro, Francisco, 'Problemas de Geografia Humana', in *Angola – Curso Ext. Univ.*, p. 53.

[33] *Ibid.*

[34] *Estruturas Soc. Econ. Moç.*, p. 93.

the production of and trading in products such as sisal, also gave rise to the payment of salaries in currency and brought about changes in culture. Traditional values lost their influence. A notorious relaxation in the sexual habits of a society of farmers, until then very much restrained in this sector, resulted.[35]

(b) *Angola*

Angola, with a surface of 1,246,700 sq. km. (almost 14 times the size of Metropolitan Portugal) and a population which should be in the region of 5,500,000 inhabitants, shows a demographic density of four inhabitants per sq. km., which places it 'amongst the least densely populated territories of Black Africa'.[36]

The population of Angola, divided into somatic types, according to estimates and the census taken from 1900 to 1960, is indicated on the following table:

Years	Total	White	Coloured	African	Other types
1900	2,716,000	9,000	7,000	2,700,000	—
1910	2,921,500	12,000	9,500	2,900,000	—
1920	3,131,200	20,700	10,500	3,100,000	—
1930	3,343,500	30,000	13,500	3,300,000	—
1940	3,738,010	44,083	28,035	3,665,829	63
1950	4,145,266	78,826	29,648	4,036,687	105
1960	4,830,449	172,529	53,392	4,604,362	166

As seen in the case of Mozambique, Angola shows a great ethnical diversity, a large variety of language and very varied social and cultural traditions. The same three social and economic traits may be classified: two small minorities; the first one, constituted by Europeans, Coloureds and some Africans (no Indians), concentrated mainly in urban areas occupied by farming and mining is a largely urbanized group. Almost 70 per cent of the European population is concentrated in cities. The second of these two minorities is composed mainly of Africans about to leave their tribes and concentrated near the boundaries of large centres. Finally, a great majority of rural Africans living on a subsistence level of economy devoted entirely to farming. In certain areas, but especially in the southwest part of the province,

[35] *Ibid.*, pp. 95–6.
[36] Barata, Oscar Soares, 'Aspectos das condicoes demograficas de Angola', in *Angola – Curso Ext. Univ.*, p. 125.

'cattle breeding plays an important part in the way of life of the various populations'.[37]

According to Professor Jorge Dias, 'The native Angolan communities are still unaware of the spirit of individual economic competition. Work is a necessity because, in order to survive, man requires food and shelter'.[38] However, Professor Dias goes on to say that 'the sudden transformation through which we are going is being rapidly transmitted to the Angolan native communities. Slowly, the opportunities to obtain new and varied articles in city markets with money obtained more easily from paid labour, rouses in many the urge to earn money. New requirements turn up which call for the acceptance of new forms of work. . . . Sooner or later no one escapes the cultural influence of those who guide the economy.'[39]

In a brief synopsis of the principal native social and economic systems existing in Angola, Professor Dias mentions the following four ethnical groups:

(i) The Bushmen – primitive hunters having no technical knowledge.

(ii) The Lundas-Quiocos from the northeast, the Quicongos and Quimbundos from the north and northeast: groups of a farming economy, capable of raising excess produce for barter. They raise small domestic animals but without pastures for grazing.

(iii) The Hereros, who live on animal husbandry.

(iv) The Ambos, the Nhaneca-Humbe and the Ovimbundos, people who live on farming and animal husbandry.

3. Economic Development

Both the Provinces of Angola and Mozambique show, without any doubt, the typical characteristics of marked economic underdevelopment. In a report by the Chairman of the Board of Directors addressed to the shareholders of Banco de Credito Comercial e Industrial de Moçambique, the gross domestic product per capita, in 1963, in Angola and Mozambique, is indicated as being U.S. $155 and U.S. $147 per annum respectively (it should be noted that the total average for the whole of Africa, in 1958, was U.S. $121 and Mozambique U.S. $139). In that same year, 1958, *per capita* earnings in Africa varied

[37] Sarmento, Alexandre, *Enciclopedia Verbo, II*, Lisbon, Verbo Ed., 1964, p. 322.
[38] 'Estruturas Socio-Economicas em Angola', in *Angola – Curso Ext. Univ.*, p. 191.
[39] *Ibid.*, p. 193.

between U.S. $40 (Ethiopia) and U.S. $300 (South Africa). The above mentioned earnings, although bearing comparison with the majority of African areas are, nevertheless, excessively low, if we take into account the fact that in Metropolitan Portugal the gross domestic product per capita is very low (U.S. $400 per year). This however is almost treble that prevailing in Mozambique.

The economy of Angola and Mozambique is, as stated above, mainly a subsistence level economy. Non-monetary activities, typical of this type of economy, represented, in 1963, 42·1 per cent of the gross domestic product, and in 1958 the gross domestic product corresponding to the non-monetary channels was in the region of 45·5 per cent in Angola and 47·5 per cent in Mozambique. A marked tendency to increase monetary activities to the detriment of the non-monetary, is nevertheless noticeable. In the same report it is stated that the gross domestic product, estimated at constant prices in 1964, and as far as Angola is concerned, reflected an annual rate of increase of 4·6 per cent during the period 1958–63 and 5·4 per cent during the period 1960–63. In Mozambique, during the same periods, the rate of increase per annum was 7·1 per cent and 9 per cent, respectively.

A report drawn up by the Investigation Committee of the Industrial Association of Mozambique, setting out the Third Development Plan (1958–73) recommends to the architects of the plan as follows:

On the basis of an economic diagnosis of the Province, the main target for action is the rural sector, taking into consideration the strong recommendations of specialized organizations such as the F.A.O. whose report on Africa states: 'an increase of productivity in the rural sector constitutes the only way to guarantee widespread economic progress.'

In the process, industry would emerge as the means of raising the overall level of productivity. As the plan progresses and manual labour on the marginal level of efficiency in agriculture becomes worthless, this source of labour will have to be used at the highest levels of productivity.

In support of agriculture there are factories producing agricultural implements, fertilizers and other products on the one hand. On the other hand flour mills, rice husking plants, factories canning fruits, and fruit and vegetable juices, derivatives of dairy products and meat, and industries processing raw materials, such as cotton, cashew, and oil seeds. To help with the balance of payments there is sugar, sisal, tea, fishing and the tourist trade.

However, industrialization would not be the main object of this plan. The basic aim would be productivity at all levels and in all sectors. Starting the plan at the subsistence level and with the attendant expansion of the internal market, it would then be possible to consider the programme of industrialization seriously as foreseen for the following stage (of development).

Also, within the proposed scheme another point of structural strength must be that of supervision. Re-organization would include financial administration, transport, education, health and welfare.[40]

These same ideas, with small and unimportant variations, may equally be applied as far as Angola is concerned.

B. Present Attitudes Towards Education As Reflected in Current Policy

1. Primary Education

(a) Education Principles

The two main principles of the policy of education – not only primary but also secondary – are: the separation of sexes in schools and the uniformity of education. The first principle – separation of sexes – dates back from 1869, by order of the Minister Rebelo da Silva. On July 5, 1941, the Regulations covering government primary education, approved by a special decree, again declared that primary education in Mozambique would, as far as possible, follow the system of separation of sexes. The first primary schools for girls were created in Mozambique in 1940.

As far as the principle of uniformity of education is concerned the special characteristics of each one of the Overseas Provinces should be taken into account (such as economy, social and economic structures, demographic density, climate, etc.); The whole policy of education in the Portuguese Overseas Provinces, attempting to fuse the principles of unity and diversity, was increasingly inclined, owing to political unity, towards the principle of educational uniformity throughout Portuguese territory. The desired principles of a regional education which seem to us should be followed more and more were neglected.

The creation of rudimentary education which was also called 'adaptation' ('adaptacao'), intended specially for natives, was somewhat in conflict with the principle of unity since it created, in the Overseas Provinces, a type of education which did not exist in Metropolitan Portugal and which was expressly designed for natives. In principle, of course, the requirement for this type of education – preparatory to primary education – cannot be contested, if it is borne

[40] *Estudos*, No. 4 (Lourenco Marques), G.E.T. A.I.M., 1967, 02.08.

in mind that the African masses do not speak Portuguese and normally live amongst primitive unskilled peoples. Upon reaching school age they are not at the same level as European children, so they cannot join them in ordinary primary education. This is one aspect of the problem. The other is that the low level of this education, owing to a shortage of duly qualified teachers and monitors, also contributed to the deep-rooted idea that it was a second grade education for natives only. The very small salaries paid to teachers and monitors of these schools no doubt contributed to this impression. The cost, per capita, was very much lower than that, per capita, of the government primary education. This is why missionary education – to whom the system of 'adaptation' was entrusted – is somewhat unfairly criticized, considering that the means at their disposal were in no way commensurate with their task. This, of course, is no excuse for the often serious errors made by those who administered this type of education in mission schools.

Later on we shall see that this anomaly of a special system of education, existing overseas and not in Portugal, together with the criticism of the very weak results, gave rise to a reform of primary education, promulgated by the decree published on September 10, 1964.

Another strong reason for criticism made of the system of 'adaptation' is that although to a certain extent it is a kind of preparatory education for normal primary education, the African pupil had no access to government schools unless he possessed the right to citizenship as an 'assimilated' African. This right was not conferred upon him for having attended school, but through a long administrative process.[41] The same position holds in respect of secondary education and here with stronger reasons, since this was available mainly in government schools. Analysing the statistics it is found that the number of assimilated Africans both in Angola and in Mozambique was always insignificant, which further accounts for the discriminatory nature of this type of education. With the abolishment of the Native Law in 1961 and with the publication of Decree 45,908 of September 10, 1964 these problems were given their first solution.

(b) *Attendance and results obtained in the 'adaptation' system of education*
In 1940 the index of illiteracy in Mozambique was 99·9 per cent (for Angola, Avila de Azevedo[42] stated that he could find no statistics in this respect but, taking into consideration that Guinea showed 99·7 per cent we possibly are not far from the truth by saying that Angola probably showed a similar figure).

[41] *Polit. Ens. Af.*, p. 162.
[42] *Ibid.*, p. 164.

Going through the statistical tables published by Manuel Dias Belchior in his work mentioned above we find that in the ten-year period which spans 1951 to 1961, the number of pupils registered in the 'adaptation' system of education in Mozambique rose from 161,371 to 348,265 which represents, taking into account normal primary education (13,043 pupils in 1951 and 140,063 in 1961), an increase in the enrolment rate from 20 per cent to over 30 per cent (these are percentages of students actually enrolled compared to the school age population). It is, therefore, found by taking figures only into account that, in 10 years, there was an increase of 315·9 per cent in school attendance. Nevertheless, as Belchior states, the highest point in school attendance does not correspond to the year 1961–3 but to the period 1958–9, when 392,796 pupils were registered, which represents an increase of 243·5 per cent in eight years. This may, in part, be attributed to the increased number of normal primary schools from 1961 which would have transferred a certain number of the more evolved Africans from the 'adaptation' system of education to primary schools.[43]

Another point of interest is the separation of the sexes in schools. The proportion is approximately two boys to one girl. The causes for this are many:[44]

(i) Dispersion of habitat is nearly always made more difficult by the lack of roads and transport. Dwellings are normally far from schools, thus forcing the pupil to walk long distances. (According to information obtained from people who live in the bush, there are certain pupils who do not object to walking up to 15 km to school.) This factor of distance affects the girl more than the boy.

(ii) Premature marriage of girls is frequent.

(iii) Economic factors are such that, apart from performing domestic chores, women and girls work on the land in this type of community, since their contribution is vital for the survival of their group. Girls, therefore, usually work more than boys.

Another fact to be concluded from the statistics given by Belchior is that in the 'adaptation' system practically all education was placed in the hands of Catholic missions: 93·4 per cent in 1951–2 and 98·3 per cent in 1958–9. The remaining institutions (government and private schools and foreign missions) were attended by a percentage which varied between 6·6 per cent and 1·7 per cent in the period 1951 and 1958.

---

43 *Evol. Pol. Ens. Moç.*, p. 655.
44 *Ibid.*, pp. 655 and 658.

As stated before, this 'adaptation' system of education proved, in so far as progress is concerned, to be a failure. The reasons are multiple: the religious character of the education which could have driven away the African who was afraid that a religion different from his own might be imposed upon him; social and economic reasons; but above all the scarcity of means at the disposal of the missions to cover the schooling of the territory. Within the overall poor results, the boys made better progress than the girls, for the same reasons which caused the substantially lower female attendance.

(c) *Normal Primary Education*
Alongside the system of 'adaptation' there was the normal primary education, comprising four classes, for pupils from the ages of 7 to 12. This education was compulsory for children of the ages mentioned but, as stated before, only the children whose parents held full citizenship were allowed in official (government) schools. The principal subjects taught were: Portuguese, arithmetic, geometry, history of Portugal, geography and nature study, drawing, handiwork, ethics and religion, physical training, music and domestic science. This education was provided at official schools, missions and other private schools.

After a brief analysis of figures we find that, in Mozambique, school attendance increased from 13,043 pupils in 1951–3 to 40,063 in 1961–1963 which corresponds to an increase of 207·1 per cent in 10 years.[45] The largest increase, however, took place between the school years 1960–1 and 1961–3 since the number of pupils then increased by 10,000. If the analysis is made according to sexes it is noted that male attendance went up from 7,890 to 25,944 during the period in question, that is, an increase of 173·9 per cent. It is also found[46] that in this type of education official schools are, by far, those which show a higher attendance (with percentage between 51·1 per cent and 67·3 per cent during the same period) as compared with the Catholic missions (34·3 per cent and 27·7 per cent), the foreign missions (6·0 per cent and 0·4 per cent) and private schools (8·6 per cent and 4·6 per cent). It should be noted that although the percentage dropped from 34·3 per cent to 27·7 per cent, the true number of pupils which attended Catholic missions increased from 4,469 in 1951–2 to 11,101 in 1961–2. The same thing happened with private schools (1,126 to 1,847). With regard to foreign missions, the attendance dropped from 785 pupils to 151, which discloses an incontestable retrogression.

45 *Ibid.*, p. 660.
46 *Ibid.*, p. 662.

In respect of Angola, unfortunately, the tables available through the *Synthesis of Activities* issued by the Provincial Secretariat of Education (1964–5) are so vague, so lacking in detail that they point out neither to which type a private school belongs, nor the distinction between the system of 'adaptation' and normal primary education (an absolutely essential distinction since these types of education are necessarily attended by different ethnic types), nor the separation of the sexes.

The table follows on page 281.

Assuming that the population of Angola was 4,500,000 inhabitants in 1955 and 5,216,000 in 1964–5 (which figure should not be far wrong), we note that the rate of enrolment in schools rose from 9·3 per cent to 23 per cent (percentage of pupils actually enrolled compared to school-age pupils) in that period (considering the school age as being between 6 and 12). As stated, unfortunately the above table includes the system of 'adaptation' and normal primary education, which is evident if we compare the number of pupils shown therein with the non-native population of Angola in the same years. Taking into account, therefore, the two types of education we see that there was an increase of 186 per cent in school attendance which caused the rate of enrolment to rise from 9·3 per cent (a low figure) to 23 per cent.

From the point of view of progress in education, 5,910 pupils of both sexes, that is 45·3 per cent of the pupils registered, passed through the normal primary school in Mozambique, in 1951–3, this percentage having risen to 57·8 per cent in 1960–1. Male and female progress is similar in this type of education, contrary to what happened in the system of 'adaptation'. This may be explained by the fact that normal primary education is mainly urban and in the cities girls are not faced with the disadvantages they find in the bush.

For Angola we have no data that might allow us to reach conclusions. Apparently, however, results should be similar to those of Mozambique.

As mentioned before, with the publication of Decree No. 45,908 of September 10, 1964, there was a reform in primary education in the Portuguese Overseas Provinces, which eliminated the separation between the system of 'adaptation' and 'normal primary education' which therefore became available to all Portuguese without distinction of race (note that, with the abolition of the 'Native Law' (*Estatuto do Indigenato*) there ceased to be a distinction between assimilated Africans and non-assimilated Africans, for which there is no official impediment to Africans attending any official schools). Primary education became compulsory, general and common to all Portuguese.

School years	Schools			Teachers			Students		
	Official	Private	Total	Official	Private	Total	Official	Private	Total
1955	981	302	1,283	1,445	666	2,111	47,070	19,874	66,944
1955–6	1,063	308	1,371	1,640	610	2,250	50,141	18,617	68,758
1956–7	1,088	372	1,460	1,441	711	2,152	49,044	20,170	69,214
1957–8	1,013	415	1,428	1,411	714	2,125	60,795	22,265	83,060
1958–9	1,025	614	1,639	1,415	1,051	2,466	58,637	27,139	85,776
1959–60	1,083	649	1,732	1,842	1,094	2,936	71,898	32,129	104,027
1960–1	1,388	623	2,011	2,092	798	2,890	71,906	33,875	105,781
1961–2	1,442	589	2,031	2,346	797	3,143	77,596	34,730	112,326
1962–3	1,582	747	2,329	2,351	1,005	3,356	85,061	38,580	123,641
1963–4	1,697	663	2,360	2,766	1,040	3,806	111,207	41,881	153,088
1964–5	2,036	459	2,495	3,259	1,038	4,297	148,597	43,096	191,693

However, compulsory education cannot be put into practice except where the government itself has the necessary means to enforce it, i.e., when the number of schools in the territory is adequate and free transport assured. Therefore, article 62 of the above-mentioned decree states that: 'Minors living at a distance of more than 5 km from primary school, official monitorial school or free private school, are exempt from enrolling for primary education if they are not provided with free transport, and at more than 6 km whenever there is a school canteen near the school or monitorial school, when the journey is easy and free from danger and the children are at least 9 years old on date of enrolment.' These conditions reduce considerably the stringency of the decree mentioned.

Normally the system of the separation of sexes continues to be adopted and girls are preferably taught by women teachers.

Elementary primary education administered in the Overseas Provinces is similar to that in force in Portugal, adapted to local conditions (Art. 1). This education is administered in monitorial schools (*postos escolares*) and official (government) primary schools, schools given official status (officialized) and private schools, comprising 4 classes preceded by a pre-school class (Art. 2). The main object of this class is to teach the Portuguese language and other preparatory activities to assimilate the school syllabus – obviously this class is specially intended for Africans who, in the majority of cases, have no knowledge of Portuguese at the time when they enter school. However, a child who is less than 6 years old and does not become 7 before December 31 (according to more recent legislation [Decree 47,480] it is now March 31 of the following year) of the year when first enrolled, independent of race, must be registered in the 'pre-school' class. Only children of 7, or those who reach this age before December 31, are exempted from attending the pre-school class at the specific request of parents, provided Portuguese is their home language and they are sufficiently developed mentally to attend First Class. From what has been said it may be concluded that in a large number of urban schools, where the percentage of African pupils is negligible, the pre-school is not really warranted (although it exists). In any case, even in some urban schools the percentage of African pupils is very high. An example of a primary urban school attendance in a poor area of Lourenço Marques is as follows:

White pupils	8·4%
Indian pupils	1·5%
Coloured pupils	12·5%
Negro pupils	77·6%

Nevertheless, in other zones of the same city, considered wealthier, the percentage of Negro pupils can be very low as, for instance, that of the following school operating in a good suburb of Lourenco Marques:

White pupils	90·7%
Indian pupils	2·4%
Coloured pupils	2·8%
Negro pupils	4·1%

Although attendance is compulsory until the final examination for children of both sexes between 6 and 12 years of age, children up to the age of 14 who have not concluded primary education by the age of 12 are allowed to enrol provided there is no disadvantage to education.

The co-operation given by Portuguese Catholic missions to the government has been officially acknowledged. The exclusive responsibility of administering a specific type of education, as was the case of the 'adaptation' system has been withdrawn. Primary education schools governed by the missions were granted official status. This means that the curriculum taught is supervised by the government. The missions participate in the training of teachers and the government provides for their schools the teachers and monitors (*professores de posto*) which they may require. It is expected that the monitorial schools and primary schools will be closely linked to the communities where they operate, participating in the activities which are predominant there through meetings between the teachers and pupils' families, visits to farms, factories and guidance in social games (Art. 3). Primary schools are located in urban centres and other places considered appropriate. Monitorial schools operate in the remaining population centres (Art. 50). Tuition in monitorial schools of rural environment must necessarily include the first three classes of primary education, preceded by a 'pre-school' class. Such schools may be developed into primary schools when considered to be of high enough standard. Primary education administered outside official schools or semi-official schools, i.e., in private schools or private monitorial schools, must adhere to the rules and regulations governing this form of education in official schools.

There are three types of teachers: primary elementary education teachers; monitorial school teachers (*professores de posto*); and school monitors. The first named are those who hold diplomas from the 'Escola de Magisterio Primario' (teachers training college). The monitorial school teachers are those who obtain their qualifications at special training centres or have been contracted for the post. This course for the qualification of monitorial school teachers lasts four years and, in Angola and Mozambique there should be one of these schools for each district (9 in Mozambique and 15 in Angola). For a prospective student to be considered for enrolment for training for this type of teaching, it is necessary to have completed, at least, primary education. Monitors may be male or female. Some may be allowed to undertake primary school teaching in rural centres. (Monitors do not teach in urban centres.)

Where the number of classrooms on the premises is insufficient, groups rotate lessons in morning and afternoon sessions. In some schools there are even three groups, two in the morning and one in the afternoon.

The syllabus to be followed and books to be used require the official approval of the Minister responsible in Lisbon.

From the above résumé it can be concluded that the quality of education and its relevance to the people of a particular area (fundamental in the case of rural people) depends greatly on the quality of the monitorial school teacher – his background and the level of his salary. A monitorial school teacher, in Mozambique, earns a salary of between $2,700 and $3,000 and monitors are paid salaries from $7,000 (Mozambique) to $1,200 (Angola). On the other hand a semi-official monitorial school teacher earns, according to a declaration made by Father Carvalho Araujo to the Legislative Council of Mozambique on May 11, 1967, a salary between $800 and $1,200 and monitors get no more than $600.[47] It was also Father Araujo who drew attention to the discrepancy between the cost of tuition in the semi-official monitorial schools (rural) and the cost of tuition in official schools. In the first case, the 355,447 pupils who attended monitorial schools in 1963–4 cost $23,750, i.e., $70 per pupil per annum, whilst the 31,804 pupils who, during the same period, attended official schools, cost $51,824,714, i.e., $1,600 per pupil. This gives an idea of the poor level of rural tuition provided in semi-official monitorial schools compared with the tuition given in official schools (the greater number of which are in urbanized areas).

Tables I and II[48] show the population per district (Angola and Mozambique), the school-age population per district, the number of pupils in fact enrolled and the rate of enrolment per district and in total. It is seen that in Mozambique (1965–6) the rate of enrolment varies, between districts, from 22·9 per cent (Zambezi) to 55·6 per cent (Mozambique), with a general average of 37·6 per cent. In Angola (1964–5) the above rate varies between 6·9 per cent (Cuando-Cubango)

[47] *Noticias* (Daily Newspaper – Lourenco Marques), May 12, 1967.
[48] See pages 310, 311. Part of the information included in Table II is from *Estatistica da Educacao (1964–1965)*, Angola. The figures included in Table I are still not published but are official.

and 62·9 per cent (Cabinda), with a general average of 23·9 per cent (this figure is slightly higher than that formerly mentioned – 23 per cent, in view of the fact that the number of pupils indicated in the table – 199,307 – is a little over the 191,693 mentioned in the previous table. It should be noted that both tables are taken from official publications).

It should also be pointed out that a certain number of children between the ages of 11 and 12 attend secondary school and, therefore, the rate of enrolment should really be somewhat higher than in the figures given.

An analysis of the 1966 issues of *Education Statistics* covering the period 1964–5 leads to the following conclusions:

(i) Mozambique: The total number of pupils enrolled in primary schools (of all kinds) is 348,378[49] (35,001 in official schools, 32,379 in semi-official schools – missions – and 3,098 in private schools), of which 237,277 are male and 121,101 female, i.e. in a proportion slightly lower than 2 boys to 1 girl (see Table III). Table IV shows establishments of education and teachers per district. From this, we find a total of 4,486 teachers (and monitors) for 358,378 pupils, that is, an average of 80 pupils per teacher, which is high. There are 1·4 teachers per establishment, which denotes a large majority of monitorial schools with only one teacher.

Reviewing the allocation of pupils per class, and their progress we conclude as follows:

Of the 358,378 pupils in the whole of primary education, only 106,498 made any progress, i.e. 29·7 per cent.

Of the total school population (358,378) 241,462 pupils are in preschool education, i.e., a percentage of 67 per cent. Therefore, only 33 per cent are distributed from the first to the fourth class, i.e., between the classes which constitute primary education (pre-school represents, mainly, as seen before, first instruction in the Portuguese language). Of the 241,462 pupils in the pre-school class 52,334 obtained a pass, i.e. 21·7 per cent.

The allocation of pupils per class was as follows:

Pre-school Class	241,463
First Class	66,316
Second Class	26,824
Third Class	13,994
Fourth Class	9,882

[49] The figure 358,378 does not include, due to lack of information, the students from officialized schools in the Gaza and Lourenco Marques districts. We estimate these as being 60,000. As this figure does not substantially alter the results, we worked only with the above 358,378.

The number of pupils enrolled in the fourth class was 9,882, i.e., 2·8 per cent of the population in the five classes. Of these 5,386 passed their examination, i.e., 54·5 per cent of fourth class pupils and 1·5 per cent of the total school population (note that many pupils prefer not to sit the fourth class examinations so that if they fail in the test for admission to secondary school they may be able to repeat fourth class). Of the 348,378 pupils, 333,699, that is, 96 per cent are African. Since almost all the pupils attending pre-school classes are African, we may quite safely say that 72 per cent of the African pupils in primary education attend pre-school class and only 28 per cent are spread throughout the other four classes.[50]

> Of the 333,699 African pupils, 240,890 attend pre-school class, 58,554 First Class, 21,026 Second Class, 8,301 Third Class and 4,929 Fourth Class.[51]
> Of the 106,498 pupils who obtained good results in the five classes, 74,040 were boys and 32,458 were girls, i.e. a slightly higher proportion than 2:1. With very little fluctuation this proportion, as far as results are concerned, is maintained throughout the five classes. In the above figures we did not take into consideration 9,751 (adolescents and adults) or 92 'backward'.

(ii) Angola: The total number of pupils enrolled in primary education, in the same year (1964–5), was 199,307 (154,459 in official and semi-official schools and 44,848 in private schools) of which 134,905 were boys and 64,402 girls, i.e., a proportion slightly above 2 boys to 1 girl (girls in Angola are somewhat more affected by social and economic conditions than in Mozambique). Table VI shows that the 199,307 pupils are taught by 4,434 teachers, that is, 45 pupils per teacher, which is better than in Mozambique; it also shows the existence of 1·8 teachers per school, a little higher than in Mozambique (1·4).

On analysing the allocation of pupils by class and their progress, we come to the following conclusions:

> Of the pupils enrolled (199,307), 111,141 passed, i.e., 56 per cent (more than the 29·7 per cent for Mozambique).
> Of the total school population (199,307) 76,930 pupils fall under the pre-school class, i.e., 38·6 per cent (a figure very much lower than the 67 per cent in Mozambique).
> We are not given any figure covering pre-school passes, but it is

---

[50] *Estatistica da Educação (1964–5)*, No. 2, Moçambique, p. 33. The distribution of students according to races is the following as far as primary education is concerned: Asiatic – 155; Whites – 10,672; Indians – 3,307; Africans – 333,699; Coloured – 10,545.
[51] *Ibid.*, p. 33.

known that in the pre-school and First Class combined there were 106,239 pupils who passed. As the number of pupils enrolled in these two classes is 135,763, we may say that the percentage of passes was 78·3 per cent. The number of pupils enrolled in the Fourth Class (the last year of primary education) was 13,570, i.e., 6·8 per cent of the population spread over the five classes (which is better than in Mozambique and this is explained, in part, by the very much higher percentage of pupils in the pre-school class in Mozambique).

The allocation of pupils, according to class, was as follows:

Pre-school class	76,930
First Class	58,833
Second Class	31,184
Third Class	18,790
Fourth Class	13,570

It is a pity that in official statistics published in Angola no indication is given as to allocation of the school population according to ethnic groups.

In the above mentioned figures neither the number of adolescents and adults, 4,047, nor the number of 'backward' pupils[52] were taken into consideration.

As mentioned before, there are at present no difficulties from an administrative point of view, to prevent any African from attending any official school. Attendance and enrolment of the African *en masse*, however, is hampered by their own social and economic backwardness and the government's difficulty to provide more schools (which would involve expenditure not commensurate with the relatively small budget for the Province).

2. *Secondary Education ('Liceu')*

The curriculum of secondary education is identical throughout Portuguese territories, whether Metropolitan Portugal or the Overseas Provinces. Secondary education consists of three stages. The first and second stages combined constitute the so-called General 'Liceu' course. This course is considered a sufficient qualification for admission to the various government departments. The third stage consists of

[52] *Panorama of Education in the Province of Mozambique*, 1964 (originally published in English by the Board of Education of Mozambique). Also, *Panorama do Ensino na Provincia de Mocambique*, 1965 (published by the Board of Education of Mozambique).

eight different choices and is intended to give a pre-university preparation (or Junior College) to those who wish to further their studies.

Secondary education may be provided in government or private
establishments and on an individual and private tutorship system.

The subjects taught are: First stage: Portuguese history and language; French, geographical and biological sciences; mathematics and
drawing; Second stage: Portuguese, French, English, history, geography, biology, physics-chemistry, mathematics and drawing; Third
stage, and in the 8 choices or groups, the following subjects are given:
Portuguese, Latin, Greek, French, English, German, geography,
history, biology, physics-chemistry, mathematics, drawing, philosophy
and political and administrative organization of the nation (civics).
Each one of the eight groups has a maximum of six subjects, of which
two are compulsory for all groups: philosophy and political and
administrative organization of the nation. Apart from the subjects
mentioned, the following subjects are also part of secondary education:
religion and ethics, physical training, choir singing and handiwork.[53]
Those pupils whose parents or tutors object are not compelled to
attend the religion and ethics class.

Admission to secondary education takes place by means of an
examination to which children who have reached the age of 10 by
December 31 and who prove to have attended the fourth class of primary school with good results may be admitted. To pass from the first
stage to the second and from the second to the third and to graduate,
examinations are required. In the first two instances, however, such
pupils attending official schools, who obtain average marks of not less
than 14 (70 per cent) in their respective stages, may be exempted from
examinations.

Essential qualifications in order to become a teacher (*efectivo*) in
the 'Liceu' are a licentiate in the subjects to be taught, followed by a
probationary period which ends with a government examination.

Nevertheless, with reference to the 1967 academic year, for instance,
of the 204 teachers of the official 'Liceus' in Mozambique, only 43,
that is 21 per cent, hold the above-mentioned required qualifications.[54]
There is a very great shortage of qualified teachers (*efectivos*) which
is not a phenomenon peculiar only to Mozambique or Angola. The
contracted teachers who, in Mozambique, comprise 39 per cent of the
teaching staff, hold a university degree but did not pass a government
examination. Some of the non-established (*eventuais*) teachers (40 per

53 *Panorama do Ensino na Prov. de Moc.*, pp. 19–20.
54 From a statement made at the 'Assembleia Nacional' in Lisbon by one of its
members (Custodia Lopes) – in *Noticias*, March 18, 1967.

cent of the total in Mozambique) do not even hold a university degree, although they do so in the majority of cases, at least in the government 'Liceus'.

The first 'Liceu' was established in Mozambique in 1919 (liceu 5 de Outubro) and it was the only one that existed in the whole Province until 1954. In 1954 and 1955 two further 'Liceus' were created, one in Beira and the other in Lourenco Marques. But it was no doubt due to the dynamic initiative of the Governor General Sarmento Rodrigues that the number of 'Liceus' has now doubled, three new 'Liceus' having been created in 1961: one in Lourenco Marques, for girls only, one in Quelimane (Zambezi district) and another one in Nampula (Mozambique district). The Nampula 'Liceu' only started to operate in 1962. Since 1959 qualifications granted by the various secondary education establishments scattered throughout the Province have been given full official recognition. The table[55] below gives an indication of the official secondary education in Mozambique from 1956 to 1963:

Years	'Liceus'	Teachers	Students
1956–57	1	58	1106
1957–58	3	85	1831
1958–59	3	100	2052
1959–60	3	106	2251
1960–61	3	101	2553
1961–62	5	117	2888
1962–63	6	155	3430

Investment (not taking into account the expenses incurred with the erection of new buildings) increased from Esc. 6,838,180 ($81,407) in 1956 to Esc. 26,536,583 ($325,912) in 1962, that is, fourfold.[56] After the foundation of 'Liceu Salvador Carreia' in 1919, in Luanda (Angola) and 'Liceu Diogo Cao', in Da da Bandeira (Angola also), in 1929, the only new 'Liceu' (for girls) was founded in 1954 in Luanda. In Angola, there are now nine official 'Liceus', the school population having risen from 1,510 (in 1955) to 7,491 (in 1964). The scale of progress in this type of education is indicated in the table overleaf.[57]

Going through the last tables of *Education Statistics* relative to the period 1964–5 we find that, in Mozambique, the picture is as follows:

The total number of pupils in secondary schools is: 7,827, of which

[55] Boleu, Oliveira, 'O Ensino em Mocambique', in *Ultramar*, Lisbon, 1964, No. 18, p. 104.
[56] *Ibid.*, p. 105.
[57] *Sintese das Actividades dos Servicos*, Secretaria Provincial de Angola, 1964–5.

Years	Schools			Teachers			Students		
	Official	Private	Total	Official	Private	Total	Official	Private	Total
1955	2	18	20	47	145	192	1,510	1,610	3,120
1955–6	3	21	24	65	147	212	1,730	1,899	3,729
1956–7	5	26	31	96	172	268	2,009	2,034	4,043
1957–8	5	27	32	108	172	280	2,457	2,248	4,705
1958–9	5	26	31	122	219	341	3,006	2,355	5,361
1959–60	5	32	37	137	241	378	3,568	2,894	6,462
1960–1	5	35	40	138	244	382	3,959	3,527	7,486
1961–2	7	37	44	173	254	427	4,917	3,500	8,417
1962–3	9	37	46	210	266	476	3,955	3,745	9,700
1963–4	9	36	45	258	298	556	7,500	3,947	11,447
1964–5*	9	42	51	265	313	578	7,491	4,479	11,970

* As at 31/12/1964.

5,408 are in official establishments, 1,626 in mission schools, 793 in private schools.

The number of secondary education establishments, in the whole Province, comprises 39: 6 official, 6 mission schools given official status, 19 non-official mission schools and 8 private ones.

The number of teachers is 564: 267 in official schools (including those given official status), 207 in missions and 90 in private schools. The number of pupils who obtained a pass was 4,942 (i.e., 63 per cent of the total enrolled): 3,242 in official schools (60 per cent),* 1,154 in mission schools (71 per cent)† and 546 (69 per cent)‡ in private schools. It is noted that the majority of secondary school pupils (4,147, i.e., more than half) is concentrated in the district of Lourenco Marques; the district of Manica and Sofala has 2,030. Next comes Sambezia with 750 and Mozambique with 415. In the other districts the number varies between 94 and 191 (very low figures). In the Niassa district there is not one secondary school pupil in spite of a population of 319,000 inhabitants (1966). The number of male students is 4,103 and female 3,724, i.e., practically the same. This proportion is maintained throughout the whole of secondary school education.

The number of pupils enrolled in the 7th year (the last) was 467, of which 322, i.e., 4 per cent of the total number of students enrolled in the 'Liceu' education, graduated.

The ethnic division is as follows: of the 7,827 pupils, 5,817 (74·3 per cent) are white, 648 (8·3 per cent) are Indian, 636 (8·1 per cent) are African, 615 (7·9 per cent) are Coloured and 111 (1·4 per cent) are Asiatic.

It is also noted that the division, according to sexes amongst the various races, was made in the proportion of 1/1 amongst whites (2,876 boys/2,941 girls), slightly less than 2/1 amongst Indians (402/246), 3/1 amongst Africans (474/162) and a little less than 1/1 amongst Coloured (284/331).

With regard to Angola, the position is as follows:

The total number of pupils is 12,560 (higher than the 11,970 which we indicated in the above table, but these referred only to the beginning of the academic year, as also indicated), of which 7,966 were in official schools (also more than the figure of 7,491 mentioned in the table given) and 4,594 in private schools.

The number of secondary schools is 52, of which 9 are official and 43 private.

The number of teachers, 591; 265 being official and 326 private.

* Percentage of pupils in official schools who obtained a pass.
† Percentage of pupils in missionary schools who obtained a pass.
‡ Percentage of pupils in private schools who obtained a pass.

The number of pupils who obtained a pass was 7,827 (i.e., 62 per cent of the total registered): 4,626 in official schools (58 per cent)* and 3,201 in private schools (69 per cent).†

It is noted that the great majority of secondary school pupils (5,527, i.e., almost half) is all concentrated in one of the 15 districts of Angola (Luanda) and that some districts, as for instance Lunda, practically have no pupils (25)—the Lunda population is 267,057. In 9 of the 15 districts of Angola there is still no secondary school education and in 3 districts there is not any official or private 'Liceu'. The number of male students is 6,322 and female students is 6,238 (a proportion of 1/1). This proportion is maintained throughout the whole of the 'Liceau' education.

The number of pupils enrolled in the 7th year (the last) was 517. 388 graduated—note that this figure includes tutored pupils who applied to undergo exams and who do not come under the figure of 12,560 comprising the school population. The 'Education Statistics of Angola' do not indicate the distribution of the school population according to races.

3. Technical-Professional Education

This covers preparatory technical schools, schools for crafts and trades, commercial and industrial schools, commercial and industrial institutes, agricultural training schools and training schools for civil service.

(a) Preparatory Technical Schools
First stage: consists of two years (preparatory) common to both commercial and industrial schools (second stage) . . . Curriculum includes: Portuguese history and language, geographic and biological science, mathematics, drawing, handiwork, religion and ethics, physical training, choir singing.

(b) Commercial and Industrial Schools
Second stage: Apart from the preparatory stage given at preparatory technical schools, all or some of the following courses are provided at these schools:

(i) *Commercial Schools*: general commercial course (three years for day scholars, or six years of night school); shorthand-typist course (three years); domestic science (four years); preparatory section for commercial institutes (one year).

---

* Percentage of pupils in official schools who obtained a pass.
† Percentage of pupils in private schools who obtained a pass.

(ii) *Industrial Schools*: Training for electricians (three years for day scholars, or six years of night school), metal worker course (three years for day scholars or six years of night school), carpentry and cabinet making course (three years for day scholars or six years of night school), commercial art course (four years for day scholars, or six years of night school), laboratory assistant course (three years day), mechanic course (three years day), master builder course (four years night), preparatory section for Industrial Institutes (two years), draughtsman for civil construction course, preparatory section for fine arts. Commercial and industrial schools may be followed by Intermediate Instruction (commercial and Industrial Institutes) which one may enrol after attending the relative preparatory section.

(c) *Intermediate Institutes* (Commercial and Industrial)
These are technical schools of higher standard following graduation from industrial and commercial schools. There are 4 in Angola and 4 in Mozambique (if we take as two the Commercial and Industrial Institute in Beira).

(d) *Crafts and Trades Schools* (basic professional education)
There are rural schools at which various trades are taught, apart from a preparation for literacy at the level of the preparatory stage. There are at present 3 of these schools in Mozambique and 5 in Angola. The courses provided are, for example, metal working, tailoring, shoemaking, carpentry, typesetting, spray painting.

(e) *Agricultural Training*
For those majoring in agriculture there is one school in Angola; one will shortly be operating in Mozambique.* Meanwhile in Mozambique there is the 'Limpopo Practical Agricultural School' ('Escola Pratica de Agricultura do Limpopo') and 3 preparatory agricultural schools have been created.

(f) *Training Schools for Civil Servants*
The school population in technical-professional education in Mozambique, as of 1964–5, was 12,100 of which the majority (11,224) attended preparatory technical schools (a) and commercial and industrial schools (b). The attendance in intermediate institutes (c) in that same year was 370 pupils; crafts and trades schools; (d) 185; agricultural training schools (e) 61 pupils and training schools for civil servants (f) 260 pupils.

The total school population – 12,100 – comprised 8,439 boys and 3,661 girls. It is split up as follows, according to ethnic groups:

* This will probably be operating by the time this work is published.

	Male	Female
Yellow	186	84
White	4,357	2,163
Indian	822	309
African	1,923	438
Coloured	1,151	667
Totals	8,439	3,661
Total	12,100	

That is: 22 per cent Asiatics, 53·9 per cent Whites, 93 per cent Indians, 19·5 per cent Africans and 15·1 per cent Coloured.

From this it can be observed that the percentage of Africans enrolled in technical-professional education is more than double the percentage of those attending 'Liceu' education.

African students (Table VIII, page 320) are spread as follows throughout the various forms of technical-professional education:

(a) + (b) Preparatory technical schools and commercial
and industrial schools 2,020
(c) Intermediate Institutes 7
(d) Crafts and Trades 171
(e) Agricultural Training........................... 13
(f) Training for Civil Servants 150

2,361

If we consider the 'Liceu' education and the technical-professional education combined the following figures are arrived at:

Total number of pupils 7,827 ('Liceu') + 12,100 (Technical) = 19,927.

Number of African pupils: 636 + 2,361 = 2,997.

Percentage of African pupils in the two types of education — 15 %

In Angola, taking into consideration the same types of technical-professional education, we obtain a school population of 11,905: 10,686 (a) + (b); 383 (c); 498 (d); 207 (e) and 131 (f).

	Male	Female	Ratio
a+b (10,686 students)	7,340	3,346	2:1
c (383 students)	310	73	4:1
d (498 students)	289	209	1·5:1
e (207 students)	162	45	4:1
f (131 students)	62	69	1:1

In Mozambique, the total number of pupils who concluded their course in all forms of technical education in 1964–5 was 1,461 (as seen before, the school population, in that period, was 12,100). In Angola, for instance, in the courses (a) and (b), where the great mass of technical-professional students is registered, there were 1,797 pupils who concluded their course in the academic year 1964–5, as against 10,686 pupils, of which 1,075 were boys.

4. Teachers Training Colleges and Training Centres for Monitorial School Teachers

Teachers training colleges produce qualified primary school teachers. Graduation from the fifth year of the 'Liceu' is required to enrol in these colleges. The duration of the course is two years.

In 1964–5 there was one of these colleges in Mozambique with 11 teachers and 89 students and 3 in Angola with 24 teachers and 210 students.

Monitorial school teachers qualify from training centres for monitorial school teachers. There were 9 in Mozambique (1964–5) with 752 students and 54 teachers, and 6 in Angola with 39 teachers and 550 students. The proportion of male/female pupils is approximately 2 : 1.

5. University Education

This form of education only started in 1963–4, both in Angola and in Mozambique, priority being given to what were considered the most important courses and which were referred to before. There is one university in Angola (Luanda) and another one in Mozambique (Lourenco Marques). In Angola the University started with 286 students spread as follows: 112 (education), 45 (medicine and surgery), 97 (engineering), 18 (agronomy), and 14 (veterinary medicine). In the academic year 1966–7 the total number of pupils had increased to 590: 21 (education), 21 (assistant teachers for technical schools – eighth group), 9 (assistant teachers for technical schools – eleventh group), 158 (medicine and surgery), 93 (civil engineering), 18 (geology and mining), 39 (mechanical engineering), 60 (electrical engineering), 78 (industrial chemical engineering), 39 (agronomy), 54 (veterinary medicine). The number of professors rose from 28 in 1963 to 77 in 1966.

The progress chart for Mozambique is as follows:

Courses	1963/64		1964/65		1965/66		1966/67	
	M	F	M	F	M	F	M	F
Education	62	70	37	39	32	42	36	34
Medicine and Surgery	22	9	40	15	61	42	79	73
Veterinary Medicine	10	2	14	5	21	12	28	13
Agronomy	4	3	10	5	21	9	20	13
Engineering	90	16	138	21	167	41	195	54
Assist. Prof. Technical School – 8th group	—	—	—	—	7	14	7	32
Assist. Prof. Technical School – 11th group	—	—	—	—	7	5	15	13
Other courses	2	—	4	8	10	12	11	7

As seen, the percentage of male students varies between 62 per cent (1966–7) and 70 per cent (1964–5).

As far as Mozambique is concerned in the period 1967–68 students are ethnically grouped as follows: 625 Whites, 73 Indians, 36 Coloured, 8 Africans and 6 Asiatics, i.e. 83·5 per cent Whites, 9·8 per cent Indians, 4·8 per cent Coloured, 1·1 per cent Africans and 0·8 per cent Asiatics. Of the 8 Africans, 5 are studying medicine and 3 are studying engineering (for greater detail see Table IX).

Engineering and medicine are the longest courses (six years), followed by veterinary medicine and agronomy (five years); assistant professors for technical schools courses (two years); education (one year).

C. FINAL COMMENTS

In a general way, it may be concluded that education in Portuguese territories, including Angola and Mozambique, is not diversified, but is clearly uniform and strictly controlled by the government. Even private tuition is subject to strict control by the official provincial inspectorate, private schools being called upon to furnish all kinds of information of a bureaucratic nature. Apart from this, as mentioned before, textbooks must be approved in Lisbon and tuition can only be based on these books. Almost all primary education and secondary education is practically official, and teachers are more or less under the direct control of the state. This control is greater in the case of secondary education, since most of the teachers are under contract. Their services may easily be dispensed with should they, at any time, deviate from the official programme or from officially approved policy. Another means which the government uses to influence the minds of the young is through the 'Mocidade Portuguesa' (Portuguese Youth Movement) which seems to the government to be the most efficient method of educating them to be loyal to the regime. The object of this organization is to preside over all extra-curricular activities. It faithfully reflects the political philosophy adopted by the 'New State' ('Estado Nove'). For example, no students' meeting may be held unless it is under the supervision of the 'Mocidade Portuguesa'.

The school population has increased, as seen, in all branches of education but the rate of enrolment in primary education has not yet reached 40 per cent in Angola or in Mozambique. It is acknowledged in many African countries that acceleration in educating the masses, at all costs, may not be the most advisable policy. Although in Mozambique, for instance, only 10 per cent of the primary school population is given first rate tuition, which is available in official schools, there is no doubt that the rate of enrolment has increased in the last 20 years. On the other hand, amongst the pupils who complete primary education, the percentage of those who enrol in secondary education is still too high (in Mozambique it is in the region of 40 per cent or more). At the U.N.E.S.C.O. meeting held in Addis Ababa in 1961, the percentage considered ideal was 30 per cent. Some African governments, to avoid the alarming drop which was noted in the level of secondary education, decided to adopt an even smaller percentage than the established 30 per cent, as was the case with Nigeria which decided not to allow more than 15 per cent of the pupils who complete primary education to proceed to secondary education.[58] Algeria also brought the percentage down from 70 per cent to 22 per cent which appears to be an abrupt decrease but, as pointed out by B. Girol de l'Ain in a most interesting article published in Le Monde,[59] from which we have extracted this information, it should be noted that even in France itself, just before the last war, only 20 per cent of those who completed primary school enrolled in secondary education.

Education is expensive, especially from the point of view of the gross domestic product per capita. In Mozambique, the per capita G.D.P. is about Esc. 400 per month and the salary of an official primary school teacher is in the region of Esc. 4,800 i.e., 12 times more, whereas in the United States, for example, the salary of a primary school teacher is only 1·5 times the gross domestic product per capita.

[58] De L'Ain, B. Girod, 'L'école dans de "tiers monde" – III', in Le Monde, December 8–14, 1966.
[59] Ibid.

This does not mean that the salaries of our teachers are high, on the contrary, it means that, with the low gross earning per head, an exaggerated number of schools is not commensurate with the budget. When it comes to secondary education the picture deteriorates; a permanent 'Liceu' teacher earns, in Mozambique, Esc. 7,250 $00 per month which, although a very low salary is, almost 20 times the gross domestic product per capita (in the United States it is only twice). In the case of a university professor, his monthly salary is estimated to be around 40 or 50 times the gross domestic product per capita (in the United States it is only five times). It is believed that in the Portuguese Provinces the cost of a university education is not less than at least 10 times the cost of a 'Liceu' education. The buildings too are expensive. In spite of the fact that the disparity between the cost of education and the product per capita in Angola and Mozambique (and in Africa in general) cannot be entirely solved by a drop in the cost of school buildings, the truth is that much can be achieved in the field of low cost construction. It may be added that in certain cases, in Mozambique, one classroom alone has cost Esc. 300,000 $00! In Portugal, where the product *per capita* is at least 3 times higher than that in Mozambique, one classroom has cost an average of only Esc. 100,000 $00 according to information given by the Sub-Secretary for State for Public Works.[60] Also in the United States, the maximum outlay permitted for the construction and equipment of primary and secondary schools is Esc. 9,000 $00 per pupil. However, the construction of the Beira 'Liceu', 'Liceu Antonio Enes' in Lourenco Marques and the Prep. Technical School 'Governador Joaquim Araujo', amounted, respectively, to Esc. 25,000 $00 and 18,000 $00 and 12,000 $00 per pupil, which is excessive in a country with budget difficulties.[61] If the schooling of large and scattered masses is, in itself, expensive, it will be even more so until such time as more modest buildings are constructed. It has been suggested, for instance, that as far as possible, 'an improved prototype of the traditional or native type of building be used for schools with voluntary unpaid work done by the people, which would be possible only when they begin to realize the benefits to be gained from the work they are called upon to carry out'.[62] 'The creation of boarding schools for the poor children from rural areas'[63] has also been suggested, and also that improved native resources be used as a means of accelerating the spread of schools throughout the territory.

---

[60] F. M., 'A Realidade na Construcao de Edificios Escolares', in *Voz de Moçambique*, No. 171, March 24, 1965.
[61] *Ibid.*   [62] *Ibid.*   [63] *Ibid.*

Taking into account the high cost of education, the question of priority must be considered in relation to its various levels and characteristics. There are many who – quite rightly – for political, economic and social reasons, advocate the idea of spreading adequate instruction, on a large scale, to the underdeveloped population who still live on the most primitive system of agriculture at a pure subsistence level of economy.[64] The plan for schooling should, therefore, give priority to the rural masses, bearing in mind, as a fact of major importance, 'the technique connected with cultivation of the soil, since agriculture, animal husbandry and fish breeding, etc., have been and will for a long time continue to be the main sources of rural wealth'.[65] That is, this form of education would have a distinctly practical character. We are aware that, at the end of 1964, a Group for Social Improvement made recommendations to the government in this respect. If the present Reform of Primary Education gives heed to the 'linking of education to environment', the principle of 'Unity' of teaching must still be a predominant feature to avoid any resentments. In our opinion, the danger of the inevitable accusation of there being a 'distinction' between rural and city education should be faced unflinchingly. The cost of education is so high, its value as an investment is so important, that all precautions taken to guarantee an adequate and productive investment are justified. Primary education as it stands now runs the risk of causing, as it did before, the creation of bureaucratic ambitions and consequent drainage of demographic capital from the fields to the city without benefit to anyone.

Secondary education, although showing an increase in school population, is still very modest in level. The percentage of the African population who attend this form of education has greatly increased in relation to the almost zero figure which was evident 20 years ago. Nevertheless they still only represent 8 per cent of the 'Liceu' population and 15 per cent of the overall secondary education in Mozambique (which is low, considering that in Mozambique, Africans represent 98 per cent of the total population). The number of graduates available for the maintenance of 'Liceu' education is very low. According to estimates made, Mozambique would require about 40,000 people holding university degrees, but in 1950 there were only 5,373. Although this figure has increased steadily, it still has not yet reached the required 40,000. The Group concerned with Social Improvement proposed, as a means to accelerate the expansion of secondary education,

[64] F. M., 'Uma planificacao do ensino de acordo com a realidade', in *Voz de Moçambique*, No. 172, April 11, 1965.
[65] *Ibid.*

that the government should allow some sort of economic assistance to private education. If, as stated, a pupil who obtains a pass in official secondary education, costs the state Esc. 8,775, it seemed a good way to encourage education if private schools were to receive a subsidy of Esc. 4,000 per pupil in the provision of secondary education.

As for university education, the creation of universities in Angola and Mozambique came about after serious consideration of many aspects. The advantages of university establishments in relation to investment made will remain in doubt for some years to come. This is a characteristic very common to all African universities in which the cost per student is three to five times higher than in European universities. It should be pointed out here that in Angola, where the number of students was 590 in 1966–7, the number of teachers was 77, i.e., approximately 8 students per teacher – a very low ratio, which results in a very high cost per student.

As to the quality of the education itself, it must be stated that primary as well as secondary education show faults mainly due to the excessive passiveness of the pupil. Often he makes no real effort. To add to this there are no practical language lessons (with recording machines for instance). There are no history or geography rooms. Education is not audio-visual. There are almost no film sessions. It should be noted, however, that mainly in secondary education there has in many instances been a remarkable improvement in quality of textbooks.

Experience seems to indicate that the classical form of tuition on the basis of reading, writing and arithmetic is of little profit in rural areas. To cite the wording of a recommendation made to the government by the above mentioned Social Development Group of Field Workers: Experience has shown that tuition administered on a merely intellectual basis is of no value. To try and impose ways of life at variance with the ancestral ones normally gives rise to conflict between the school and the environment, causing serious emotional confusion. The European methods of teaching represent a complete revolution for native societies resulting in weak and even adverse results, in relation to the efforts made. Besides, without adequate intercultural contact, it is impossible to bring about the necessary transition from one culture to another only by teaching reading, writing and arithmetic. It has been found that the efficiency of schooling is very much reduced in areas far from civilized centres where there is a complete lack of the conditions necessary for the intensive use of reading and writing the Portuguese language. May we add in parenthesis here that the problem of using the Portuguese language as a means of instruction, together with the necessary attention which must simultaneously be given to native idioms, is one major area liable to cause repercussions, since emotional, and quite often, political aspects, override a purely objective analysis of facts.

Dr Manuel Saraiva Barreto, in his previously mentioned work *O Ensino do Portugues como Lingua Segunda em Africa* (*The Teaching of Portuguese as a Second Language in Africa*), presented at the First Portuguese/ Brazilian Symposium on the Portuguese language, succinctly described the official attitude in relation to the usage of the Portuguese and native languages in schools: 'It would prove tiresome to describe the various attitudes which have been taken, depending on the varied political concepts which have periodically defined the part played by the Overseas Provinces in the nation as a whole. Decree No. 5,239 of March 8, 1919 established 'the teaching in the native or Portuguese languages'. Decree No. 6,322 considered 'The teaching of the Portuguese language and history of Portugal as compulsory and the use of any other European language (apart) from Portuguese, as strictly forbidden' . . . It should be underlined that the *strict* prohibition fell on 'another *European* language' and that the obligation to use the national language alone as a means of instruction promoted the neglect of the native languages. The 1941 Missionary Statutes confirm this situation but allow Christians to resort to African languages for catechism. 'In schools the teaching in the Portuguese language is compulsory. Outside schools, missionaries and assistants shall also make use of the Portuguese language. In the teaching of religion, however, the native language may be freely used'.[66]

In this same work, Dr Manuel Barreto, with exemplary calmness and objectiveness not often found, points out that 'in circles with political ideas different from ours, even among the leading groups more imbued with "negritudinist" ideologies such as the leaders of the "Presence Africaine", the necessity of adopting a free foreign language, French or English, according to the country upon which their relative nations had depended, was considered necessary, both in view of the multilinguism of Africa and the requirement of contact with the technical and cultural outside world'. In his work he also adds, in conclusion, the following point of utmost importance:[67] 'There will be no diffusion of our language overseas just because we want to diffuse it; the pupil must feel a greater urge, he must feel the *cultural necessity* to speak the language, and not only use it as demanded daily in administrative contact. This influence on the mind and strengthening of the culture

[66] Barreto, Manuel Sariava, *O Ensino do Portugues como Lingua Segunda em Africa*.
[67] *Ibid.*

– of which teaching the alphabet is the first step – is achieved by instruction in the native languages themselves. From this there would result a more open and definite option for Portuguese as a language of culture and internal and external contact.'[68]

The words cited above are written in a tone of clarity and boldness to which we are not accustomed and, therefore, we wish to place them on record in the hope that they will be heeded and come to fruition, as we sincerely think they deserve to be.

Referring to the type of tuition, which is almost merely *informative* – the following statement, made on February 16, 1968, to the newspaper *Diario de Lisboa* by a lady teacher of philosophy and history at the 'Liceu Pedro Nunes' in Lisbon regarding the necessity to reform 'Liceu' education, reads as follows: 'Young people, who are not in a position to foresee clearly that an effective reform would cover multiple aspects of national life do, however, strongly feel the anachronism of an institution which presses upon them the monotony and the weight of uninteresting tasks. They want some life at school, as they are to take away from school the necessary preparation for life. Thus they call various programmes "so much useless matter" and state: "what we are taught is too extensive on the one hand and too incomplete on the other".'[69] It is significant that outdated programmes, their lack of 'relation to life', the almost general lack of preparation of teachers and the very low level of salaries paid to them, were the problems which were considered most important by practically all the teachers requested to make a contribution to the *Diario de Lisboa*. If it is true in Metropolitan Portugal of 'Liceu' education that the school is not 'a part of life', when we look at the Overseas Provinces and the primary education over there, the problem really becomes one of major importance.

It was also pointed out in this connection in 1964 (Mozambique) by the Social Development Group of Field Workers (*agentes rurais*) that:

It happens that the teaching of the alphabet is today a means of evading physical activities particularly of those involved in farming. To know how to read, write and calculate is considered a way of attaining the leisure of bureaucracy. The notion of a merely informative tuition brought about the result that teaching, even rudimentary teaching, was transformed into one of the most powerful factors to displace the African. It has intensified the conviction of the inferiority of farming and, consequently, led to the abandonment of

[68] *Ibid.*
[69] 'O que considera mais importante numa reforma do ensino liceal?', *Diario de Lisboa*, February 16, 1968, p. 23.

the fields and the flight to the urban centres, the development of slums and a state of misery and moral degradation.

We have maintained that only a predominantly agricultural and technical tuition can, in fact, meet the requirements of rural communities and strengthen the links that unite them, integrating them in their traditional habitat and giving them the most valuable assistance to improve the economic and social level of their life without this resulting in any psychological conflict capable of causing individual and social disturbances.

With these thoughts as background, we quote some of the comments hereunder, recommendations and objects proposed by the Technical Committee for Integration and Economic Planning of the Province of Mozambique for the 3rd Development Plan (1968–1973) especially with reference to 'rural environments'.

'The problem of education', it is stated on page 115 of volume II, Part II (Education), 'seems to be very serious and calls for urgent measures to be taken in favour of that overwhelming majority of rural Africans who still live on a subsistence level of economy, complemented here and there by the hard migratory type of work.

It is necessary to tie these people to the land by means that will do away with the migratory current and that will lift the subsistence level of the economy; only in this way will education prove of benefit.

The modernization of farming techniques, and the integration of rural masses into administrative units, which facilitate social contact and mutual participation in various enterprises by means of promoting community work, will allow the school to achieve full benefit through its formative and informative role, especially if, apart from normal teaching, the school were to include the elementary techniques of farming and animal husbandry.

It follows that in more developed population centres where this community activity begins to take place in a positive manner, some native farmers will very quickly feel interested to partake in activities related to other spheres of work. It may then be time for the primary school installations to be used for workshop activities. And so, here and there, according to requirements, the teaching of tailoring, shoemaking, masonry, carpentry etc. etc., will take place. . . . The school must be placed at the service of the common good and simultaneously improve the people and the village, at the risk of at the same time being the most serious destroyer of the gregarious and collective nature of the native. In cultures of an intense collective nature, any progress on the part of the individual, as a result from a European type of schooling, is isolating in that it breaks the bonds of the person with the group, and tears up something inherent in his being, because he does not regard himself as autonomous, but feels and holds himself as part of a joint entity.

In general we conclude from the recommendations made by the above mentioned Technical Committee for the 3rd Development Plan, the following programme to be followed by the Mozambique Government (we hold no data regarding Angola):

Rapid schooling facilities in order that by 1973, an enrolment rate of 44 to 50 per cent will be attained: intensifying the opening of monitorial schools in rural areas, establishing at least one central school in the area of each Catholic mission. (There are at present 218 Missions of which 7 are closed.) In certain instances, the Missions could provide schoolrooms and living quarters for teachers.

Schooling must be aimed mainly to allow the desired rooting to the land to take place and therefore counteract the growing migratory movement;

The monitorial school, with its vegetable garden, must take on the additional new role of teaching adults reading, writing and elementary methods of farming and animal husbandry;

To increase the number of permanent primary school teachers, by means of training at the central schools and others spread throughout the Province. To assure that they will stay in these areas and will support the work of field workers (agentes rurais) and so perform a profitable and stable teaching activity, which cannot be attained by temporary teachers.

As it is being recognized that the major effort of mass education will fall upon schools and missions, it is necessary to bring into operation, by new legislation schools for the training of monitorial teachers so that in each district there may be one school for each sex:

Careful and intensive attention must be paid to the training of monitorial school teachers, offering them conditions in salary and accommodation that will bind them to the rural environment and, therefore, ensure long and constant service;

Progressive courses for the training of monitorial school teachers must be created and intensified;

Stimulate private tuition through adequate government action like granting of subsidies to private schools etc.

The development of the teaching of farming and animal husbandry. Schools for training of technical and secondary farming staff (schools for those majoring in Agriculture and Agricultural Training) are to pay attention to the necessity of the specialized field of animal husbandry, training specialized technicians;

Spreading the teaching staffs of the Province, in order to reduce as much as possible the number of temporary teachers, and the allocation of at least one permanent teacher to each group of teachers in each secondary teaching establishment;

Attention should be drawn to the requirement of school premises and their equipment. The more functional and at the same time, more economic type of building must be borne in mind;

Education of adults be administered so as to extend it to the large mass of the population gathered on the periphery of the most important population centres and to those who, being socially and economically dependent on the westernized population, may wish to learn to read;

Central schools must wherever possible correspond to the requirements created by the improvement in the life of the rural people. They must be transformed for this purpose into elementary schools for the learning of trades;

Teaching at school should be consolidated outside through the Social Centre, and must be supported by audio-visual material and a library for cultural development;

The placing of married couples as teachers in the same locality should be favoured. Accommodation, however modest, should be offered to them so that they will enjoy some comfort and local prestige;

In all rural schools the education programmes for female education and the promotion of the teaching of the Portuguese language amongst the female natives should be stepped up by means of meetings and other possible activities for the village women;

In the cities a welfare campaign amongst the women should take place, by means of courses specially intended for them lasting from four to six months and with a maximum attendance of 40 periods per group or class;

Teacher training should be improved and the same standards that apply in Portugal should be brought into force in Portuguese Africa;

Organization of refresher courses to up-date earlier educational training, and allocation to the schools of essential teaching materials. The use of audio-visual methods and materials to be encouraged.

These are in brief the 'priority recommendations' made for the 3rd Development Plan by the Technical Committee mentioned above. As stated, these are *recommendations* and they do not necessarily represent what will be *done*. Whether it will or not will depend greatly on political, administrative and economic factors, detailed discussion of which does not fall within the scope of this contribution.

Assuming a 50 per cent rate of school attendance aimed at by 1973, in Mozambique, we arrive at the tables on pages 308–9.

The table on page 309 indicates the number of additional teachers required (in comparison to 1965):

These requirements, which relate only to the additional expenses during the period 1968–73, involving construction, equipment, teaching and other additional items, are estimated at 866 million Escudos. Additional expenses to be incurred for the progress of *all* types of education, during the same period 1968–73 comes to Esc. 1,561 million. Primary tuition alone therefore will represent 55 per cent of the additional expenses required by the educational progress.

George Skorov in his excellent study: *Integration of Educational and Economic Planning in Tanzania*, says: 'Whatever may be said of the cultural importance and value of education, it would hardly perform its social function if it did not serve economic development to the fullest possible extent. This means that the skills produced by the educational system must correspond, in timing, numbers and quality, to the requirements of society and, not least, that they must be produced at a minimum cost to society.' And further on, after indicating the four essential means of overcoming the problem of manpower requirements, he says: 'It would be difficult to assess the relative importance of these four complementary ways of meeting manpower requirements. It would seem, however, that in most of Africa south of the Sahara, the lion's share of manpower requirements must be met by formal education and training.'[70] That is the core of the matter, well stated!

Therefore, the final test of the whole educational plan sketched above will finally be the capacity to produce. To implement the total 5-year plan 1968–73, the following additional manpower is required:

(a) *Bachelors of Arts and Sciences*
Primary school teachers 1170
Regentes Agricolas (those who major in agriculture) including field works—animal husbandry 98
Licentiates in Engineering 17
Topographers 29
Other professions (Accountants etc.) 32

(b) *Graduates in various professions*
Doctors—medicine 152
Veterinary Surgeons 27
Agronomists 19
Silviculturists 2
Mining Engineers 11
Geologists 19
Petroleum Engineers 2
Geographers 6
Chemists 8
Geophysicists 2
Civil Engineers 17
Electrical Engineers 3

[70] Skorov, George, *Integration of Educational and Economic Planning in Tanzania*, U.N.E.S.C.O., Intern. Inst. for Educ. Planning, p. 37.

Mechanical Engineers 3
Others to lecture in secondary and medium schools 59

It is accepted that, of the above-mentioned additional people, which according to the 3rd Development Plan forecast would be required for the economy of Mozambique, at least the following would have to be imported from Metropolitan Portugal:

30 medical practitioners
60 degreed people of various qualifications
50 to 60 *Regentes Agricolas* (those who major in Agriculture).

FORECAST OF THE SCHOOL POPULATION IN 1973

Districts	Children between 6 and 12 years —school age (1973)	Number of children actually to be enrolled (50%) (1973)	Difference in relation to 1965			
			Total	Government schools	Missions (officialized)	Private schools
L. Marques and Gaza	302,700	151,350	65,670	11,188	50,291	4,191
Inhambane	143,500	71,750	25,987	2,800	21,355	1,832
Manica e Sofala	168,500	84,250	35,817	3,820	27,559	4,438
Tete	116,400	58,200	49,740	5,293	35,447	0
Zambezia	311,500	155,750	109,799	8,756	93,599	7,444
Mozambique	311,300	155,650	25,443	8,056	9,678	7,709
Cabo Delgado	118,200	59,100	38,582	3,423	35,159	—
Niassa	71,500	35,750	17,528	2,235	13,876	1,417
Total	1,543,600	771,800	359,566	45,571	186,964	27,031

ADDITIONAL REQUIREMENTS IN TEACHERS AND INSTALLATIONS

Districts	No. of Teaching Agents					No. of Classrooms		
	In government schools	In officialized schools (missions)			Total	Government	Missions	Total
		Teachers	Monitors	Total				
L.M. and Gaza	280	160	470	630	910	140	460	600
Inhambane	70	70	200	270	340	40	170	210
Manica e Sofala	100	90	260	350	450	50	230	280
Tete	140	120	330	450	590	70	300	370
Zambezia	220	300	870	1,170	1,390	110	700	810
Mozambique	210	30	90	120	330	110	170	280
Cabo Delgado	90	110	330	440	530	50	270	320
Niassa	60	50	130	180	240	30	120	150
Total	1,170	930	2,680	3,610	4,780	600	2,420	3,020

TABLE I MOZAMBIQUE—PRIMARY SCHOOL
NUMBER OF STUDENTS ENROLLED COMPARED TO ACTUAL
POPULATION AGED BETWEEN 6 AND 12 YEARS—1965/66

Districts	Total population in 1966	Children* aged between 6 and 12 years (school age)	Number of students actually enrolled				
			Official Elementary schools	Officialized schools (missions)	Private schools	Total	% enrolled
Lourenco Marques	569,100	91,056	13,550	28,145	1,773	43,463	47·7%
Gaza	746,900	119,504	4,475	32,921	2,935	40,331	33·7%
Inhambane	658,100	105,296	3,124	40,436	2,702	46,262	43·9%
Manica e Sofala	827,300	132,368	6,337	39,149	1,064	46,550	35·1%
Tete	533,800	85,408	2,826	18,817	56	21,699	25·4%
Zambezia	1,489,100	238,256	4,108	48,529	949	53,586	22·9%
Mozambique	1,527,800	244,448	4,837	130,861	195	135,893	55·6%
Cabo Delgado	580,100	92,816	1,527	27,771	—	29,298	31·5%
Niassa	319,000	51,040	768	18,373	775	19,916	39%
Total	7,251,200	1,160,192	41,552	385,002	10,449	437,003	37·6%

* To calculate the number of children between 6 and 12 we worked on the basis of 16 per cent of the total population. Note that some students aged 11 and 12 are attending already secondary schools, that is to say, the figures shown in the last column should in fact be slightly higher.

TABLE II ANGOLA—PRIMARY EDUCATION

NUMBER OF STUDENTS ENROLLED COMPARED TO ACTUAL

POPULATION AGED BETWEEN 6 AND 12 YEARS 1964-65

Districts	Total population in 1965	Children aged between 6 and 12 years (school age)	Number of students actually enrolled			
			Official Elementary schools	Private schools	Total	% enrolled
Benguela	526,897	84,304	13,735	3,827	17,562	20·8
Bié	488,913	78,226	14,194	10,162	24,356	31·1
Cabinda	63,227	10,012	6,300	—	6,300	62·9
Cuando Cubango	122,074	19,532	1,364	—	1,364	6·9
Cuanza-Norte	284,091	45,455	12,302	147	12,449	27·4
Cuanza-Sul	437,018	69,923	7,922	938	8,860	12·7
Huambo	645,116	103,219	19,256	10,344	29,600	28·7
Huíla	642,177	102,748	18,046	1,762	19,808	19·3
Luanda	374,499	59,920	16,017	7,828	23,845	39·8
Lunda	267,057	42,729	5,430	4,186	9,616	22·5
Malange	487,993	78,079	14,296	3,592	17,888	22·9
Moçâmedes	46,444	7,431	2,117	102	2,219	29·9
Moxico	287,761	46,042	6,544	1,574	8,118	17·6
Uige	431,364	69,018	14,566	217	14,783	21·4
Zaire	112,118	17,939	2,370	169	2,539	14·2
Total	5,216,749	834,567	154,459	44,848	199,307	23·9 %

TABLE III MOZAMBIQUE—1964-65
STUDENTS ENROLLED AND NUMBER APPROVED
ACCORDING TO CLASS AND SEX
PRIMARY EDUCATION SCHOOL-AGE CHILDREN 1964-65

Students	Per Classes								
	Total			Preparatory (pre-primary)			1st		
Enrolled and Approved	MF	M	F	MF	M	F	MF	M	F
1	2	3	4	5	6	7	8	9	10
Students enrolled	358,378	237,277	121,101	241,462	151,908	89,554	66,216	49,443	16,773
In official tuition	35,001	21,029	13,972	—	—	—	12,019	7,058	4,961
In officialized tuition	320,279	214,542	105,737	240,788	151,571	89,217	53,231	41,858	11,373
In private tuition	3,098	1,706	1,392	674	337	337	966	527	439
Students admitted to exam	6,917	4,745	2,172	—	—	—	—	—	—
In official tuition	4,264	2,622	1,642	—	—	—	—	—	—
In officialized tuition*	2,424	1,994	430	—	—	—	—	—	—
In private tuition	229	129	100	—	—	—	—	—	—
Students approved	106,498	74,040	32,458	52,334	34,460	17,874	23,175	17,101	6,074
In official tuition	20,740	12,463	8,277	—	—	—	6,545	3,847	2,698
In officialized tuition*	83,879	60,554	23,325	51,985	34,276	17,709	16,070	12,958	3,112
In private tuition	1,879	1,023	856	349	184	165	560	296	264

Students

Per Classes (Concluded)

Enrolled and Approved	2nd			3rd			4th		
11	MF *12*	M *13*	F *14*	MF *15*	M *16*	F *17*	MF *18*	M *19*	F *20*
Students enrolled	26,824	19,531	7,293	13,994	9,815	4,179	9,882	6,580	3,302
In official tuition	8,770	5,266	3,504	7,780	4,807	2,973	6,432	3,898	2,534
In officialized tuition	17,400	13,894	3,506	5,685	4,698	987	3,175	2,521	654
In private tuition	654	371	283	529	310	219	275	161	114
Students admitted to exam	—	—	—	—	—	—	6,917	4,745	2,172
In official tuition	—	—	—	—	—	—	4,264	2,622	1,642
In officialized tuition*	—	—	—	—	—	—	2,424	1,994	430
In private tuition	—	—	—	—	—	—	229	129	100
Students approved	16,017	11,944	4,073	9,586	6,695	2,891	†5,386	†3,840	†1,546
In official tuition	5,883	3,490	2,393	5,326	3,239	2,087	2,986	1,887	1,099
In officialized tuition*	9,743	8,234	1,509	3,875	3,241	634	2,206	1,845	361
In private tuition	391	220	171	385	215	170	194	108	86

* Due to lack of information the number of students from the officialized schools in the districts of Lourenco Marques and Gaza are not included.

† Not included are the students who were approved in the entrance examination for the secondary schools without having been submitted to the 4th class examination.

TABLE V MOZAMBIQUE—1964-65

STUDENTS ENROLLED AND NUMBER APPROVED

BY CLASSES AND DISTRICTS

PRIMARY EDUCATION SCHOOL-AGE CHILDREN 1964-65

	Total			Pre-Primary			1st		
	Enrolled	Exam passed	%	Enrolled	Exam passed	%	Enrolled	Exam passed	%
Students Districts									
1	2	3	4	5	6	7	8	9	10
Lourenco Marques*	14,032	8,643	61·6	637	319	50·1	4,484	2,695	60·1
Gaza*	3,827	2,194	57·3	—	—	—	1,409	734	52·1
Inhambane	39,129	12,282	31·4	29,305	5,629	19·2	4,207	2,815	66·9
Manica and Sofala	47,768	16,767	35·1	29,745	6,626	22·3	8,234	4,144	50·3
Tete	27,327	5,965	21·8	7,643	1,367	17·9	13,087	2,458	18·8
Zambezia	58,354	35,162	60·3	27,911	27,169	97·3	23,986	3,581	14·9
Mozambique	128,689	15,516	12·1	114,691	6,448	5·6	6,813	4,055	59·5
Cabo Delgado	19,937	5,109	25·6	15,532	2,156	13·9	2,246	1,572	70·0
Niassa	19,315	4,860	25·2	15,998	2,620	16·4	1,750	1,121	64·1
Total	358,378	106,498	29·7	241,462	52,334	21·7	66,216	23,175	35·0

Per Classes

Per Classes (Concluded)

Students	2nd			3rd			4th			
	Enrolled	Exam passed	%	Enrolled	Exam passed	%	Enrolled	Approved to go up for exam	Exam passed†	%
Districts 11	12	13	14	15	16	17	18	19	20	21
Lourenco Marques*	3,417	2,344	68·6	2,987	2,183	73·1	2,507	1,705	1,102	44·0
Gaza*	968	601	62·1	799	536	67·1	651	463	323	49·6
Inhambane	3,083	2,122	68·8	1,458	1,098	75·3	1,076	757	618	57·4
Manica and Sofala	4,935	2,994	60·7	2,969	2,054	69·2	1,885	1,267	949	50·3
Tete	5,057	1,247	24·7	898	567	63·1	642	382	326	50·8
Zambezia	3,047	2,221	72·9	2,060	1,263	61·3	1,350	1,032	928	68·7
Mozambique	4,286	3,051	71·2	1,785	1,203	67·4	1,114	855	759	68·1
Cabo Delgado	1,356	921	67·9	498	285	57·2	305	205	175	57·4
Niassa	675	516	76·4	540	397	73·5	352	251	206	58·5
Total	26,824	16,017	59·7	13,994	9,586	68·5	9,882	6,917	5,386	54·5

* Due to lack of information the number of students from the officialized schools in the districts of Lourenco Marques and Gaza are not included.

† Not included are the students who were approved in the entrance examination for the secondary schools without having been submitted to the 4th class examination.

TABLE IV MOZAMBIQUE—PRIMARY EDUCATION
SCHOOLS, TEACHERS AND STUDENTS PER DISTRICT 1964–65

Districts	*Pupils aged between 6 and 12 years*				
				Pupils	
	Schools	Teachers	Enrolled	Approved (*Preparatory 1st, 2nd and 3rd classes*)	Approved (*4th class*)
1	*2*	*3*	*4*	*5*	*6*
Lourenco Marques	63	397	14,032	7,541	1,102
Gaza	45	112	3,827	1,871	323
Inhambane	390	506	39,129	11,664	618
Manica e Sofala	473	728	47,768	15,818	949
Tete	313	376	27,327	5,639	326
Zambezia	528	729	58,354	34,234	928
Mozambique	909	1,001	128,689	14,757	759
Cabo Delgado	226	264	19,937	4,934	175
Niassa	253	373	19,315	4,654	206
Total	3,200	4,486	358,378	101,112	5,386

Districts	*Adolescents and adults*			
			Students	
	Courses	Teachers	Enrolled	Approved (*3rd and 4th classes*)
7	*8*	*9*	*10*	*11*
Lourenco Marques	90	326	5,185	726
Gaza	4	2	60	49
Inhambane	31	48	1,167	434
Manica e Sofala	40	80	1,098	280
Tete	22	34	479	137
Zambezia	—	—	—	—
Mozambique	38	59	1,126	122
Cabo Delgado	17	31	345	83
Niassa	10	19	291	100
Total	252	599	9,751	1,931

TABLE VI ANGOLA—PRIMARY SCHOOL
SCHOOLS, TEACHERS AND STUDENTS PER DISTRICT—1964-65

Districts	Schools			Teachers			Students Enrolled			Approved		
	Total	Official Elementary	Private	Total	Official Elementary	Private	Total	Official	Private	Total	Official	Private
1	*2*	*3*	*4*	*5*	*6*	*7*	*8*	*9*	*10*	*11*	*12*	*13*
Benguela	193	156	37	371	276	95	17,562	13,735	3,827	11,046	8,325	2,721
Bie	249	189	60	466	229	237	24,356	14,194	10,162	11,374	6,449	4,925
Cabinda	87	87	—	148	148	—	6,300	6,300	—	2,906	2,906	—
Cuando Cubango	33	33	—	41	41	—	1,364	1,364	—	729	729	—
Cuanza-Norte	160	158	2	247	240	7	12,449	12,302	147	6,885	6,794	91
Cuanza-Sul	143	128	15	220	195	25	8,860	7,922	938	5,339	4,647	692
Huambo	414	240	174	708	400	308	29,600	19,256	10,344	17,670	11,876	5,794
Huila	245	220	25	430	377	53	19,808	18,046	1,762	9,911	8,899	1,012
Luanda	150	72	78	625	413	212	23,845	16,017	7,828	15,526	9,892	5,634
Lunda	135	92	43	192	106	86	9,616	5,430	4,186	4,360	2,454	1,906
Malanje	266	209	57	404	312	92	17,888	14,296	3,592	10,261	8,296	1,965
Mocamedes	20	19	1	56	52	4	2,219	2,117	102	1,203	1,129	74
Moxico	137	112	25	184	139	45	8,118	6,544	1,574	4,060	3,159	901
Uige	194	191	3	287	281	6	14,783	14,566	217	8,360	8,172	188
Zaire	39	38	1	55	47	8	2,539	2,370	169	1,511	1,398	113
Total	2,465	1,944	521	4,434	3,256	1,178	199,307	154,459	44,848	111,141	85,125	26,016

Average number of students per teacher — $\dfrac{199,307}{4,434} = 45$

for official schools — $\dfrac{154,459}{3,256} = 47$

for private schools — $\dfrac{44,848}{1,178} = 38$

TABLE VII ANGOLA—PRIMARY EDUCATION
STUDENTS ENROLLED PER CLASSES, SEX AND DISTRICTS 1964–65

Students	Total			Per classes					
				preparatory (Pré-primária)			1st		
Districts	MF	M	F	MF	M	F	MF	M	F
1	2	3	4	5	6	7	8	9	10
Benguela	17,562	11,286	6,276	6,473	4,525	1,948	4,697	3,041	1,656
Bié	24,356	16,311	8,045	11,481	7,490	3,991	6,705	4,553	2,152
Cabinda	6,300	4,408	1,892	2,480	1,611	869	2,197	1,544	653
Cuando Cubango	1,364	907	457	796	532	264	307	193	114
Cuanza-Norte	12,449	9,765	2,684	5,172	4,003	1,169	4,185	3,377	808
Cuanza-Sul	8,860	6,347	2,513	4,081	3,148	933	1,977	1,379	598
Huambo	29,600	20,014	9,586	10,019	6,846	3,173	9,308	6,339	2,969
Huíla	19,808	12,337	7,471	8,095	5,105	2,990	5,930	3,728	2,202
Luanda	23,845	12,985	10,860	2,645	1,558	1,087	7,436	3,862	3,574
Lunda	9,616	7,570	2,046	7,028	5,645	1,383	1,362	1,018	334
Malanje	17,888	12,958	4,930	7,504	5,531	1,973	5,444	3,858	1,586
Moçâmedes	2,219	1,115	1,104	151	69	82	774	372	402
Moxico	8,118	5,565	2,553	3,573	2,402	1,171	2,594	1,784	810
Uíge	14,783	11,646	3,137	5,953	4,583	1,370	5,127	4,046	1,081
Zaire	2,539	1,691	848	1,479	964	515	790	581	209
Total	199,307	134,905	64,402	76,930	54,012	22,918	58,833	39,675	19,158

Students

Per classes (concluded)

Districts	2nd			3rd			4th		
1	*MF* *11*	*M* *12*	*F* *13*	*MF* *14*	*M* *15*	*F* *16*	*MF* *17*	*M* *18*	*F* *19*
Benguela	2,803	1,667	1,136	1,995	1,141	854	1,594	912	682
Bié	3,361	2,264	1,097	1,926	1,402	524	883	602	281
Cabinda	971	744	227	473	383	90	179	126	53
Cuando Cubango	155	110	45	73	50	23	33	22	11
Cuanza-Norte	1,810	1,451	359	829	600	229	453	334	119
Cuanza-Sul	1,331	907	424	872	549	323	599	364	235
Huambo	5,243	3,585	1,658	2,906	1,893	1,013	2,124	1,351	773
Huíla	2,557	1,597	960	1,618	1,025	593	1,608	882	726
Luanda	5,563	3,054	2,509	4,454	2,429	2,025	3,747	2,082	1,665
Lunda	674	513	161	333	242	91	219	152	67
Malanje	2,724	2,044	680	1,388	956	432	828	569	259
Moçâmedes	496	246	250	419	229	190	379	199	180
Moxico	1,036	740	296	524	370	154	391	269	122
Uíge	2,318	1,915	403	901	721	180	484	381	103
Zaire	142	78	64	79	44	35	49	24	25
Total	31,184	20,915	10,269	18,790	12,034	6,756	13,570	8,269	5,301

TABLE VIII STUDENTS ENROLLED ACCORDING TO
RACES AND SEXES AND BY TYPE OF TUITION
PROFESSIONAL TECHNICAL TUITION 1964–65

Types of Tuition	Total			Asiatic		White		Indian		African		Coloured	
	MF	M	F	M	F	M	F	M	F	M	F	M	F
1	2	3	4	5	6	7	8	9	10	11	12	13	14
Commercial and Industrial Schools for Crafts and Trades	11,779	8,222	3,557	186	84	4,276	2,133	815	302	1,808	390	1,137	648
Commercial and Industrial Schools	185	185	—	—	—	2	—	4	—	171	—	8	—
Commercial and Industrial Institutes	11,224	7,745	3,479	181	84	4,040	2,070	789	296	1,630	390	1,105	639
Agricultural Training	370	292	78	5	—	234	63	22	6	7	—	24	9
Schools	61	61	—	—	—	48	—	—	—	13	—	—	—
Teaching Staff for Public Tuition	260	156	104	—	—	33	30	7	7	102	48	14	19
Total	12,100	8,439	3,661	186	84	4,357	2,163	822	309	1,923	438	1,151	667

Somatic Types

TABLE IX   UNIVERSITY EDUCATION ACCORDING TO RACES
STATISTICS FOR MOZAMBIQUE
SCHOOL YEAR 1967/68

Courses	Races				
	White	Coloured	African	Indian	Asiatic
Civil Engineering	67	5	1	9	—
Chemical Engineering	56	2	1	5	1
Mining Engineering	3	1	—	—	—
Electrical Engineering	88	5	—	13	1
Mechanical Engineering	46	3	1	6	1
Veterinary Medicine	39	6	—	9	—
Biology	9	—	—	—	—
Formation of teachers for the 11th group (Technical Education)	25	—	—	3	—
Applied Mathematics	1	—	—	—	—
Pure Mathematics	1	—	—	—	—
Physics	—	—	—	—	—
Chemistry	1	—	—	—	—
Miscellaneous	20	—	—	2	—
Medicine/Surgery	133	11	5	21	3
Agronomy	33	1	—	1	—
Silviculture	2	—	—	—	—
Pedagogical Science	61	2	—	4	—
Formation of teachers for the 8th group (Technical Education)	40	—	—	—	—
Totals	625	36	8	73	6
Grand Total					748

Date Due